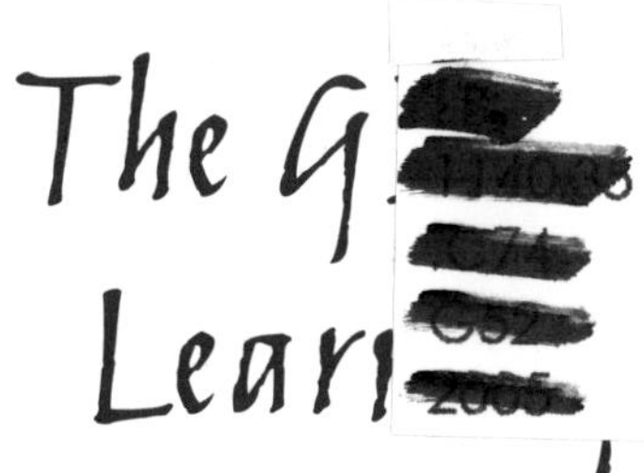

The G[illegible]dia of Lear[illegible]vities

Edited by Kathy Charner, Maureen Murphy, and Jennifer Ford

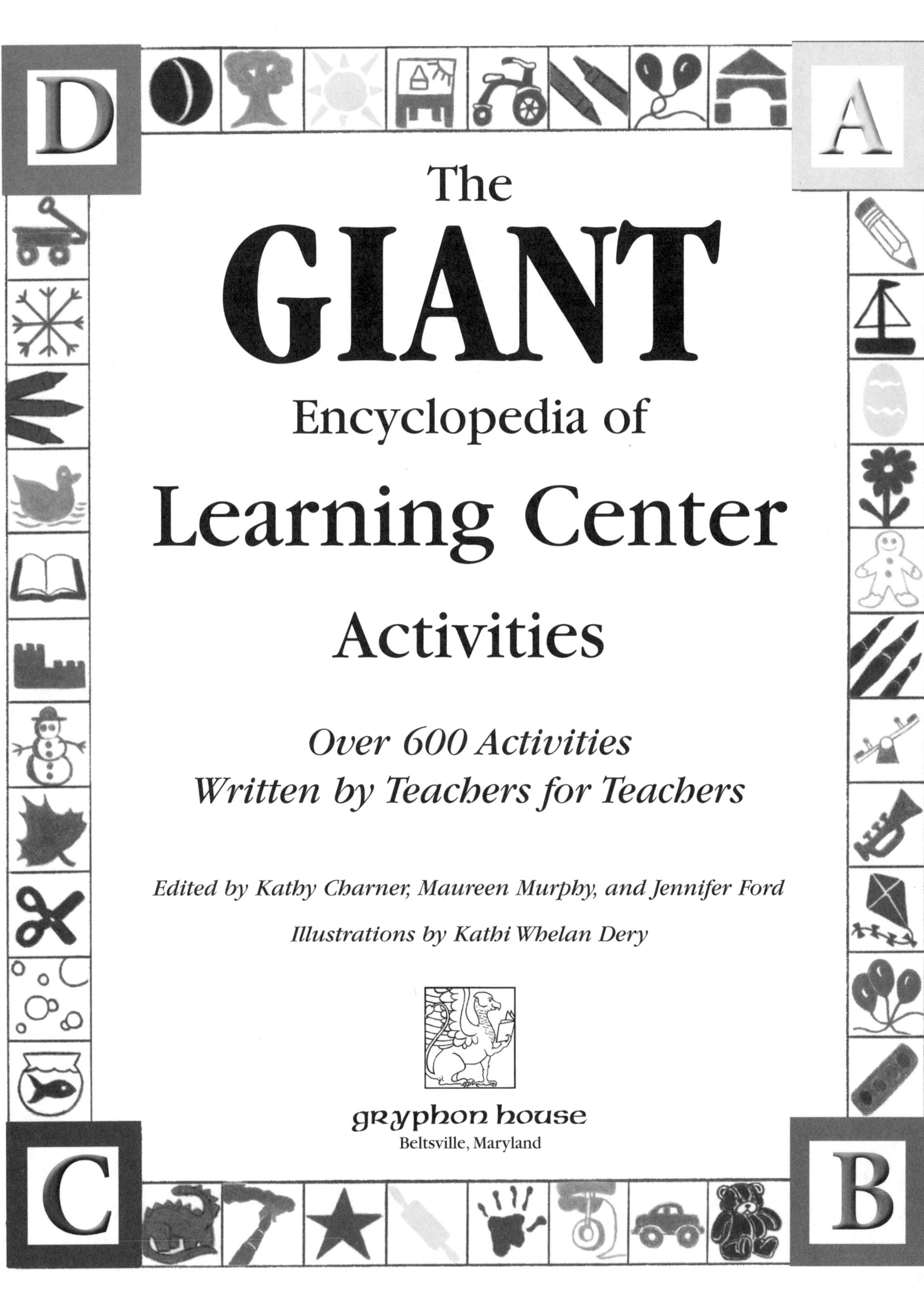

The GIANT Encyclopedia of Learning Center Activities

Over 600 Activities Written by Teachers for Teachers

Edited by Kathy Charner, Maureen Murphy, and Jennifer Ford

Illustrations by Kathi Whelan Dery

gryphon house
Beltsville, Maryland

Published by Gryphon House, Inc.
10726 Tucker Street, Beltsville, MD 20705
800.638.0928; 301.595.9500; 301.595.0051 (fax)

Visit us on the web at www.gryphonhouse.com

Illustrations: Kathi Whelan Dery

Cover Art: Beverly Hightshoe

Library of Congress Cataloging-in-Publication Data

The giant encyclopedia of learning center activities / edited by Kathy Charner, Maureen Murphy, and Jennifer Ford.
p. cm.
Includes bibliographical references and index.
ISBN13: 978-0-87659-001-0
ISBN10: 0-87659-001-6
1. Education, Preschool--Activity programs. 2. Classroom learning centers. I. Charner, Kathy. II. Murphy, Maureen. III. Ford, Jennifer, 1980-
LB1140.35.C74G52 2005
372.21--dc22
2004024037

Bulk purchase Gryphon House books are available for special premiums and sales promotions as well as for fund-raising use. Special editions or book excerpts also can be created to specification. For details, contact the Director of Marketing at Gryphon House.

Disclaimer Gryphon House, Inc. and the authors cannot be held responsible for damage, mishap, or injury incurred during the use of or because of activities in this book. Appropriate and reasonable caution and adult supervision of children involved in activities and corresponding to the age and capability of each child involved, is recommended at all times. Do not leave children unattended at any time.
Observe safety and caution at all times.

Table of Contents

Table of Contents

Table of Contents

Table of Contents

Table of Contents

Table of Contents

Introduction

A teacher is interacting with a group of children who are busy constructing their spelling words, and a visitor walks into the room. The visitor finds the classroom teacher sitting on the floor and, with moves similar to a defensive tackle, makes her way over to the teacher. After finishing the conversation she is having with the group, the teacher stands to converse with her visitor. The guest smiles and says, "Oh, it looks like I caught you at a perfect time. You're having recess." The teacher slowly looks around the room and at the children. She turns back to her guest and says, "It's not recess. It is center time and we are working with money, comparing seasons, practicing our spelling words, creating sentences, and following directions." Her visitor looks again, but only sees young children playing.

Learning is fun. A center-based classroom may look like chaos to adults, but to a young child it is play. It is an opportunity for them to understand classmates, concepts, and how the real world works. A grocery store with priced foods and paper coins makes a great math activity about money. Painting a picture that compares all four seasons is an excellent science center. Using letter cookie cutters with playdough allows students to practice spelling words while engaging their sense of touch. Cutting out magazine pictures serves as a great tool for oral language development as children talk about their pictures. And using an overhead projector to sequence the letters of the alphabet or create pictures of colored transparency shapes lets children not only follow directions but be creative as well. To many who enter a center-based classroom, they only see the playdough, paints, and play food. To an early childhood educator, it is the purest form of learning. It is more than play. It is center time.

By reading this book, you have found a wonderful tool to bring life into your classroom and inspire your three- to six-year-olds to learn more. Teachers, directors, caregivers, and others in the early childhood field have authored this book. They know how important learning centers are and wish to share their ideas with the world. They may not know you, but they do know what you and your children need. Gryphon House has used their unique perspective to create a book for teachers written by teachers. Early childhood educators are professionals who are constantly looking for ways to touch and improve the lives of each child in their care, and this book captures that effort.

About This Book

Many readers who pick up this book may be novices. Others may have been teaching children for years and realize their day needs a jumpstart. For both, a few basics about centers are necessary.

First, what is a learning center? Learning centers are activities that focus on a particular theme, skill, or content area. Many centers are self-managed by children doing independent work. Others may be completed with the help of a partner, a group of friends, or an adult. Learning centers are effective in allowing children to create meaning and understanding about a subject of study. Centers provide cooperative learning and social experiences, which are key elements of the actual working world. It is a time for discovery, child-centered learning, and an extension of concepts. Children can think without adult intervention and teachers can observe children's growth. It also provides a time for teachers to work with small groups to practice a skill while the rest of the class is engaged in their own work. Learning centers are the glue that can connect the class theme and challenge children to look at people and things differently.

Second, centers provide opportunities for play as children learn. Piaget and Vygotsky, early childhood researchers, found play to be one of the most important components to a child's success in school. Through their play, children learn to communicate, negotiate, manage rules, gain knowledge, and stretch their cognitive thinking skills.

Third, centers provide a wonderful means to meet the different ability levels of the children in your class. Each child does things differently from others. One child may cut well, while another is better at retelling a story heard on tape. The children take from centers what they know and what they need. The point is you can help more children by using centers that represent a variety of ways children learn. Careful planning of lesson objectives will provide an environment that embraces the individuality of each child and the skills she needs to improve.

Looking though this book, you will find that there are learning centers for a large assortment of themes. Centers should not be based on one area of interest but should represent a variety. You can plan for each area of study such as math, reading, science, and so on to create centers that are cross-curricular. You can also integrate the many topics of interests your children have, the themes that engage them, and the skills they must acquire. Once again, our focus is on the needs of each child.

Finally, center arrangement must be considered. Whether you have a large room or just a few shelves, centers can be managed in your classroom. Let's examine two plans: temporary centers and permanent centers.

Temporary centers require just a couple of shelves and five medium-sized storage boxes. First, write each child's name on an index card, dividing them into groups or teams of five. (Children can be moved around to work with other groups of children, but this shuffle should occur every one to two months.) Attach the name cards to the lid of each box using sticky tack or tape. Next, put in each box a center (activity) that is developmentally appropriate for the age you teach. Remember to include all the necessary materials needed for completion. Doing this eliminates any confusion during your center time. Following are some examples of temporary center boxes:

Science box: Make colors with paint.
Dramatic Play box: Use puppets to retell the focus story for the week.
Math box: Make noodle sets to match numerals.
Fine Motor box: Use playdough and tools to cut, smash, and form.
Critical Thinking box: Children work puzzles.

In the Science box, for example, put brushes, paper, paint aprons, and covered paint cups. Move the name cards every day to another center box so that children play in all five centers by the end of the week. With temporary centers, it is important to plan an instruction time each Monday to teach the children how to use the center, any rules for use, and what things must be done to complete the center. The benefits of temporary centers are easy management, assurance that each child participates, and adaptability to themes or skills.

Permanent centers stay in place all year long. A particular area of the room is set up to feature that center. For example, you will have an area designated for science, reading, dramatic play, art, math, and so on. Each week you may add different materials to the centers to correspond with the theme. For example, the water center may have floating and non-floating materials one week and the next week measuring tools are added. In permanent centers, children may rotate as a group to centers or have free movement as long as no more than a certain number of children occupy the space. Permanent centers allow children to independently choose which centers are of interest to them. One major drawback is the amount of space that permanent centers require in the classroom.

This book features wonderful ideas that can be adapted for temporary or permanent centers. The book is easily navigable with chapters featuring different categories of centers. Center activities are easy to follow as each one lists the materials, step-by-step directions, additional suggestions, books, and original songs, and even some ideas to expand or extend the center.

The Giant Encyclopedia of Learning Center Activities will soon become your favorite resource for lesson planning. Use it often as a way to provide interesting and appropriate learning for your three to six year olds. When you use learning centers, not only do you help each child develop as an individual, but you also nourish the natural child that is seen when children create their own play and their own learning.

 *Marzee Woodward, Early Childhood Educator*

Setting Up Learning Centers

What to do

1. The day before starting a new learning center or changing an existing one, be sure to plan carefully what the children are expected to do. Brainstorm a set of rules that the children can understand clearly. Before starting, come up with a signal that tells the children to stop their activity and clean up. If the teacher chooses the centers for the children to go to, it helps to have an area where children who don't want to participate can go. Examples of this are the classroom library or a quiet corner where children can rest until they feel confident enough to go to their assigned centers.
2. Put books in each center that relate to the activity. For example, put children's books about houses and architecture in the block center. Choose books that have few words and many pictures.
3. Also put writing materials in each center. For example, children may write "recipes" in the house area, "blueprints" in the block area, and make lists of materials needed at other centers.
4. Following are some suggested materials to put into open-ended centers:
   - **Art center**: easel, paint, brushes, easel paper, a clothesline or drying rack and clothespins to hang wet paintings, a can of water to put dirty brushes in, pencils for names and stories about the paintings, and lids for the paint pots. Old T-shirts in large sizes are great to use as smocks.
   - **Block center**: large set of blocks, play hardhats, plastic tools and tool belts, books about houses and building, and paper to write on.
   - **House center**: empty cans with labels (peas, peaches, and so on), broom and dustpan, small table and chairs, tablecloth, plastic flowers in a plastic vase, plastic tableware, old pots and pans, recipe books with lots of pictures, and paper to write on, and aprons.
   - **Carpentry table** (this needs adult supervision): hardhats, leather gloves, and safety glasses.
   - **Dress-up center**: shoes, hats, costumes, jewelry, crowns, and other accessories; keep the clothes in a closet or drawer.

- **Water table**: plastic boats, funnels, small tubes, straws, corks, measuring spoons, and measuring cups; raincoats or plastic smocks are a necessity here.
- **Puzzles**: Before children put the puzzles together, put a symbol on the back of each puzzle piece for easy sorting. For instance, for a puzzle of a bear, make a star on the back of each piece.

Barbara Saul, Eureka, CA

Learning Center Organization Idea 1

Materials

two pieces of white cardboard
scissors
pen
brad paper fastener
educational materials catalog
glue
thumbtack
camera (optional)

What to do

1. Cut out a large circle from one piece of cardboard. Cut out a smaller circle from the other piece of cardboard. Mark both circles into sections—one section for each learning center. Make sure the smaller circle sections align with the large circle.
2. Connect the small circle on top of the large one by putting a brad in the center of each circle. Make sure that the inside circle can be turned easily.
3. Find a photo to represent each learning center in an educational materials catalog (for example, clay, a painting easel, and crayons could represent the art center). Glue one photo in each section of the large circle and label the center.
4. On the inner circle write children's names.
5. Staple the circle on the bulletin board where the children can see it, making sure that the outer circle does not move, but the inner circle does. Use a thumbtack to keep the center wheel in position.
6. During center time, focus the children's attention on their names on the circle. Show them that the pictures will tell them where they are to go.

7. When it is time to move to a new center, move the inner wheel to align with the next picture. Continue until each child has visited each center.
8. If a camera is available, take pictures of the centers and the children and use them to show the children where to go.

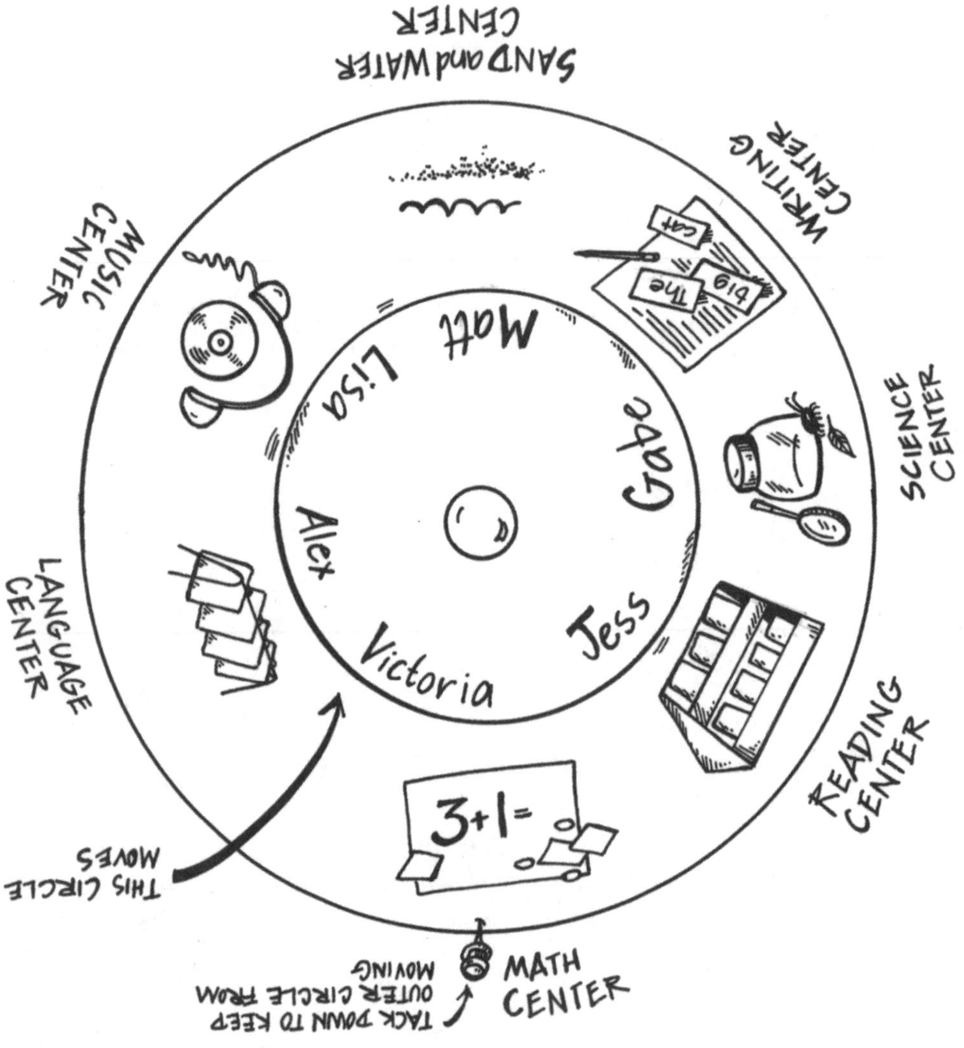

Barbara Saul, Eureka, CA

Learning Center Organization Idea 2

Materials

clipboards (one for each center)
paper and pencils
photos of children (optional)

What to do

1. Place a clipboard with paper in each center. On each clipboard, write the children's names. If possible, put photos of each child next to her name.
2. Assign groups of children to different centers. The children cross off their names on the clipboard to indicate that they have visited the center.
3. Continue in this manner until each child has visited each center.

Barbara Saul, Eureka, CA

Learning Center Organization Idea 3

Materials

educational materials catalog
scissors
pocket chart
sentence strips

What to do

1. Cut out pictures from educational materials catalogs that represent the centers in your room (for example, a toy stove for the housekeeping area). Put a picture in each pocket of the pocket chart. Next to each picture, write the number of children that may go into that center at one time.
2. Print each child's name on a sentence strip.
3. Let the children put their sentence strips next to the picture of the learning center that they want to go to. If the number next to the center is four, for example, only the first four children to put their names in the chart may attend at that time.
4. When the children want to change centers, they move their names to another pocket.

Barbara Saul, Eureka, CA

Learning Center Organization Idea 4

Materials

sentence strips
writing paper attached to clipboards or journals
pencils

What to do

1. Use sentence strips to label each learning center.
2. Put writing and drawing materials at each center.
3. Encourage the children to write and draw about their learning experiences. For example, in the housekeeping center they can write recipes, in the block center they can make blueprints, and so on.

Barbara Saul, Eureka, CA

Learning Center Organization Idea 5

Materials

pen
library pockets
cardstock
scissors

What to do

1. Have one library pocket for each center. Write the names of the activities in each center on the library pockets.
2. Cut cardstock into 2″ x 6″ pieces. Write each child's name on pieces of cardstock so that the name is visible when put into the library pockets.
3. Let the children put their names in the pocket of the activity they wish to do.

Barbara Saul, Eureka, CA

Learning Center Organization Idea 6

Materials

scissors
yarn in different colors, one for each learning center
glue
pen

What to do

1. Cut different colors of yarn into 1″ pieces.
2. Glue the yarn to whichever organizational method you use, such as clipboards or pocket charts (see organization tips 1 through 5 on previous pages). Make sure that each center has a different color of yarn.
3. Cut lengths of yarn and tie together to make necklaces for the children.
4. Give each child a yarn necklace that corresponds to the center they go to.

Barbara Saul, Eureka, CA

Learning Center Organization Idea 7

Materials

1″ dowels cut into 12″ long pieces
clothespins
hot glue gun (adult only)
rubber bands
empty coffee cans
quick-drying plaster of Paris
pictures and names of each center

What to do

1. Glue clothespins to one end of each piece of dowel to make label holders. Put rubber bands around both until the glue dries.
2. Fill each coffee can with plaster of Paris. Insert the opposite end of the dowel in the center of the plaster of Paris and hold until it dries. Make sure that the clothespin is facing up. Continue in this manner until there is one label holder for each center.
3. Make labels for each center by writing the name of the center and adding a picture that represents it.
4. Attach a label to each clothespin and place it in the appropriate center. As the centers change, change the label to correspond. For example, if the housekeeping area becomes a "vet's office," change the label to reflect that.
5. The mobility of these labels allows you to pick them up and take them into another center.

Barbara Saul, Eureka, CA

Learning Center Organization Idea 8

Materials

16-ounce cans
colored contact paper
3″ x 4″ labels
pictures of centers and children
glue
1″ wide craft sticks

What to do

1. Cover the 16-ounce cans with colored contact paper. Attach a label to each can and glue a picture of a center on each can.
2. Glue the pictures of the children on craft sticks and write their names.
3. At center time, the children or teachers put the sticks into the can of the center that they are going to.
4. If needed, designate how many children can go to each center by writing a large number on the labels.

Barbara Saul, Eureka, CA

Learning Center Organization Idea 9

Materials

large piece of colored cardboard
markers
teacher supply catalogs
scissors
glue
clothespins

What to do

1. Divide colored cardboard into sections, one section for each center.
2. Using teacher supply and educational materials catalogs, cut out pictures representing each center. For example, a picture of an easel could represent the art center.
3. Glue each picture to a different section on the cardboard.
4. Write each child's name on a clothespin. Clip the children's names on the cardboard next to the chosen center.

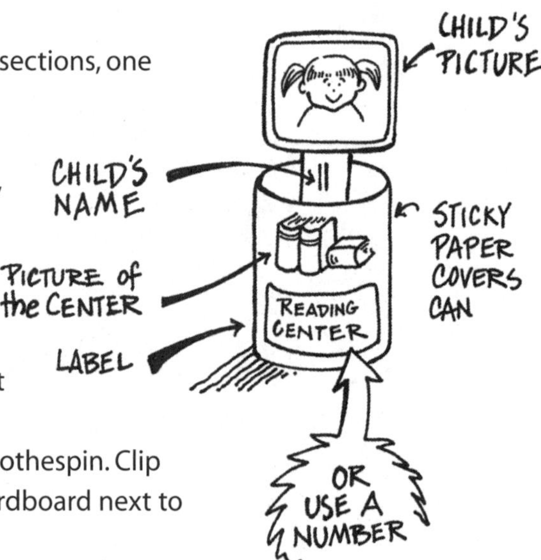

Barbara Saul, Eureka, CA

Snip, Snip, Snip!

Materials

laundry marker
children's scissors
old wallpaper samples
craft paper in a variety of colors
textured papers
old laminating film
aluminum foil (precut into squares)
cardstock paper
cardboard squares
quart-size zipper-closure bags
yardstick, ruler, and/or measuring tape
clear adhesive tape
yarn
bucket

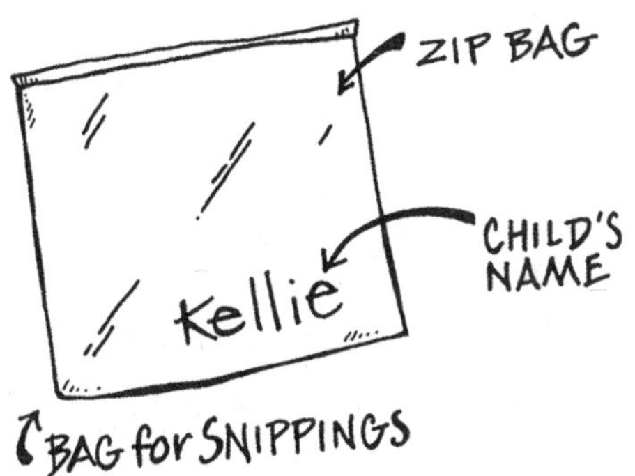

What to do

Free Play

1. Put the materials listed above in the art center.
2. Give one zipper-closure bag to each child. Explain that they will use their bags to collect their snippings.
3. Have the children use a laundry marker to write their names on the bags.
4. Show the children how to use scissors to snip pieces from the various materials.
5. Let the children use the materials freely during center times.

Cut and Stop

1. Draw vertical lines on a large sheet of paper. Tape the paper to a wall at a height that the children can easily reach.
2. Challenge the children to use scissors to cut on the lines and stop at the tape. Vary this activity by drawing curved lines of different lengths.

Cutting Cards

1. Using cardstock paper, make a variety of cutting cards. Draw designs on the paper, such as triangles, squares, zigzags, curlicues, strips, or "cut and stop."
2. Put the cards in the art center and challenge the children to cut the cards by following the designs.
3. Put the cut pieces in your collage tray for later use.

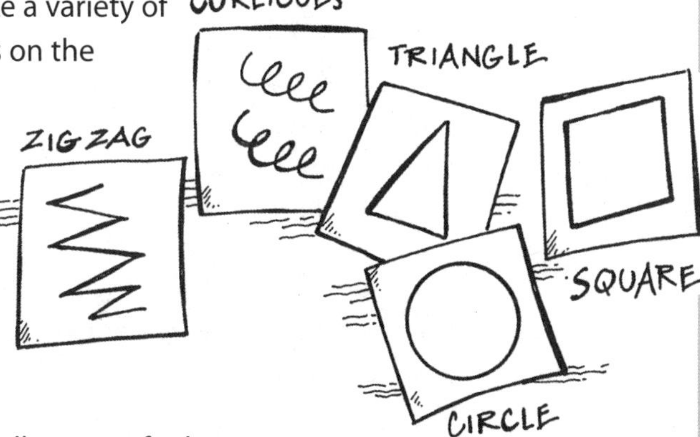

Paper Chains

1. Encourage the children to cut short strips of paper in a variety of colors.
2. Help them loop and tape the strips together to form a colorful class chain.
3. Challenge the children to use the chain to measure things in the classroom. For example, ask, "How many chain links high is the door?" or "Can you guess how many chain links long the room is?"

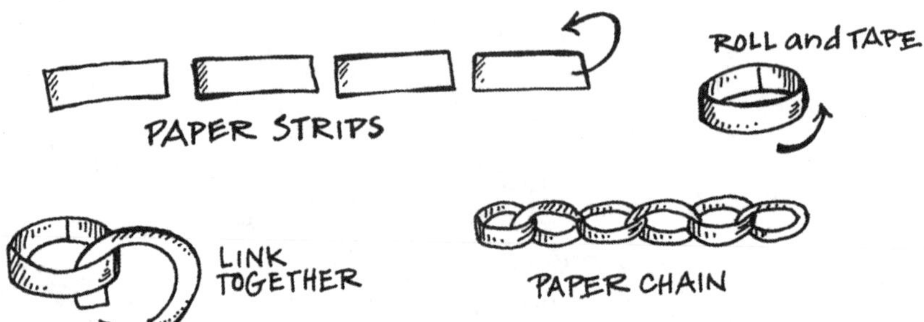

Cut and Sort

1. Place a yardstick or ruler on a table. Ask a child, "I wonder how many of your paper snips are one inch long?" Help the child measure the strips to find out.
2. Encourage the children to continue measuring and sorting their paper snips.

Playground Sculptures

1. Put scissors, yarn, and paper scraps in a bucket and take them outdoors.
2. Challenge the children to use the materials to create playground sculptures. The children can cut yarn into a variety of lengths and tie the strings to the trees, bushes, and fences.
3. Bring out yardsticks, rulers, or tape measures so the children can measure their cuttings.
4. Have the children cut long strips of paper from butcher paper or art paper. Let the children weave these papers through the fence.

Related book *Lucy's Picture* by Nicola Moon

Related chant **Open Them, Shut Them**

Open them, shut them,
Open them, shut them,
Make a little snip.
Open them, shut them,
Open them, shut them,
Snip a little bit.

Open them, shut them,
Open them, shut them,
Cutting is lots of fun!
Open them, shut them,
Open them, shut them,
And then you are done!

* Chant this adapted rhyme to help the children get into the rhythm of cutting as they do the activities listed above.

 *Virginia Jean Herrod, Columbia, SC*

A Rainbow of Hands

Materials

large piece of butcher paper or construction paper
tempera paint (red, orange, yellow, green, blue, and purple)
Styrofoam trays
paintbrush (optional)

What to do

1. Place a large piece of paper on the table or floor.
2. Pour a different color of tempera paint into each Styrofoam tray.
3. Ask children to press their hands on the tray with red paint or brush paint onto their hands with a paintbrush.
4. Ask children to make red handprints near the bottom of the paper, near the center.
5. Have them wash their hands. Ask children to press their hands into the orange paint and make handprints in an arc over the red handprints.
6. Continue with yellow, green, blue, and purple to make a rainbow of handprints.
7. Label hands with names, if desired.

Related song *One Light, One Sun* by Raffi

Related book *Eight Hands Round* by Ann Whitford Paul

Shirley Salach, Northwood, NH

All About Me—Pack of Crayons

Materials

8 ½" x 11" and 12" x 18" construction paper
scissors
markers
magazines
glue
photos of the children (optional)
tape
pipe cleaners

What to do

1. Let each child choose his favorite color of construction paper.
2. Help the child cut out a crayon top shape and a rectangle for the bottom of a crayon.

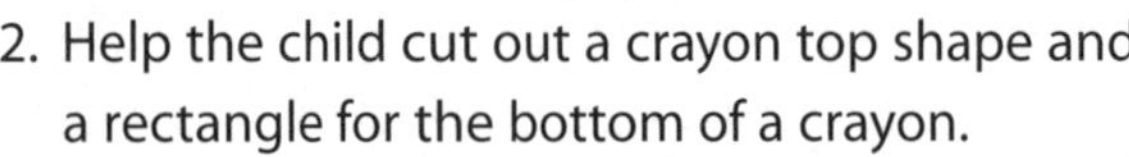

3. Cut a piece of 12" x 18" construction paper in half lengthwise to create a "crayon wrapper."
4. Encourage the children to decorate their "crayon wrappers" with things about themselves (for example, their families and pets, favorite foods and toys, and so on). They can draw pictures or cut out and glue pictures from magazines.
5. When finished, ask the children to glue the crayon top to the top of the wrapper. Let them glue their photos on the crayon top. If photos are not available, children can draw a picture of themselves on the crayon top.
6. Ask the children to glue the base of the crayon at the bottom of the wrapper, and attach pipe cleaners to the back to make arms and legs.

More to do

Home-to-School Connection: At the beginning of the year, this can be a "get to know me" activity. Send the wrappers home for children to decorate with their family members. Explain that the drawings on the crayon should describe the child, such as favorite foods and hobbies, places the child has been, and who lives in the house. When the children bring the wrappers back to school, they can add the top, bottom, arms, and legs. Encourage the children to share what is on their crayons with the class during a show and tell time. Display the finished "crayon people" on a bulletin board for all to see and talk about.

 *Sandra Nagel, White Lake, MI*

Art Show

Materials

white pillowcase for each child
pie tins
paint
paintbrushes and toothbrushes
art smocks
soapy water and towels
paper
crayons
markers
art supplies

What to do

1. Hang pillowcases (one for each child) outside on a nice day. Hang them from a tree branch or in an area where the children can splatter paint on them.
2. Put pie tins full of paint next to the pillowcases. Encourage the children to splatter paint on their pillowcases using their hands, toothbrushes, or paintbrushes.
3. This is a messy activity, so make sure children wear art smocks. Also put out plenty of soapy water and towels for easy cleanup.
4. When the children are finished painting, encourage them to make invitations for an art exhibit for their parents. Provide markers, art supplies, glitter, and feathers.
5. On the day of the art exhibit, hang the pillowcases and place each child's name next to his masterpiece. Set up chairs in the art exhibit area. When parents arrive, encourage the children to stand next to their creations to answer any questions.

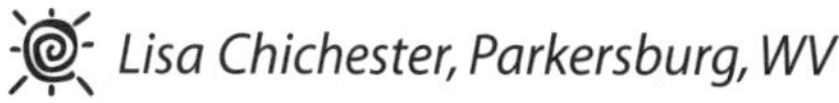
Lisa Chichester, Parkersburg, WV

Blowing Paint

Materials

paint in cups
paper
small spoons
straws

What to do

1. Put out cups of paint and paper. Encourage the children to scoop spoonfuls of paint on their paper.
2. Demonstrate how to hold a straw at one end of the paper near a small puddle of paint and blow into the straw to move the paint around the paper.
3. As the paint spreads, colors may run together.
4. Try using the primary colors: red, yellow, and blue. Let the children experiment to see if the colors change as they run into each other.

More to do

More Art: Provide gray, black, or brown paint for children to blow and spread. Encourage the children to make fingerprints with colorful paints to make spring flowers.

Sandra Nagel, White Lake, MI

Bubble Bear

Materials

white tagboard
scissors
bubble wrap
brown paint
paintbrushes
wiggle eyes
pompoms, buttons, and scraps of material
markers
glue

What to do

1. Cut out teddy bear shapes from tagboard. Give one to each child.
2. Tape bubble wrap to the table.
3. Encourage the children to paint the bubble wrap with brown paint and then press their bear shape on the painted bubble wrap. Remind them to *gently* lift the bear shape when done.
4. When the bears dry, the children can decorate them with faces, buttons, and so on.

Related books

Brown Bear, Brown Bear, What Do You See? by Bill Martin, Jr.
Jamberry by Bruce Degan
A Pocket for Corduroy by Don Freeman
The Three Bears by Paul Galdone

Sandy Scott, Vancouver, WA

Build a Face

Materials

digital or 35mm camera
computer and printer (if using digital camera)
scissors
small plastic containers
glue
paper

What to do

1. Take a photo of each child's face. Make sure the child's face fills the camera frame.
2. If using a printer, make several copies of each child's face on plain paper.
3. If using a 35mm camera, develop the film and then make copies (preferably color) on your photocopier. You will need several photos of each child.
4. Ask the children to cut out the eyes, ears, noses, mouths, and eyebrows from the photos. These are the only parts you will need for the activity.
5. Sort the facial features into separate containers and place in the art center.
6. Encourage the children to use different facial features to make fun and wacky face collages.

More to do

Games: Challenge the children to identify which facial features belong to which classmate. This game is very hard but should lead to a lot of giggles.
Math: If you have color copies, use one of each child's eye cutouts to make an eye color graph.

Related books

Africa Dream by Eloise Greenfield
Grandpa's Face by Eloise Greenfield

 *Virginia Jean Herrod, Columbia, SC*

Central Collage Station

Materials

small- to medium-size machine screw case
variety of small collage materials such as beads, sequins, glitter, fabric scraps, wood scraps, leather scraps, felt pieces, paper scraps, and materials collected from nature
sturdy cardstock paper or cardboard
markers, pencils, and crayons
glue sticks

What to do

1. Ask the children to help you gather all of the loose collage supplies and put them in the middle of a large table.
2. Start a discussion by saying something about the amount of materials on the table. For example, "We sure have a lot of collage supplies. Isn't there a lot of stuff here?" Encourage the children to make comments about the items on the table.
3. Continue the discussion by saying, "I wish there were a way for us to organize the collage supplies so that everything is in the same place."
4. Let the children brainstorm for a while as they try to figure out different ways to organize the materials. Gently lead them to the conclusion that it would be useful to have a case with several drawers for storing the materials.
5. Show the children the machine screw case. Ask them if they think this would solve the collage material storage problem.
6. Help the children figure out which materials should go in which drawer. Let them fill the drawers with the materials.
7. Provide cardstock or cardboard for the children to design and decorate a sign for the new storage cabinet. Attach the sign to the top of the box.
8. You now have a great collage storage unit that the children can use with ease. Place it on top of art shelves.
9. After finishing the Collage Central Station, have a collage fest! Let the children make a few collages and display them around the room.

Author Note: You might be tempted to label the individual drawers to indicate which materials are stored there, but don't! They will inevitably get mixed up and the children may feel a sense of failure that they could not keep them separated.

Hint: Keep a supply of cut cardboard near the collage station. Cardboard is easier for young children to use when creating collages, and it holds up to a large amount of glue!

Related book *Lucy's Picture* by Nicola Moon

Coffee Filters in the Rain

Materials

coffee filters
watercolor markers
rainy day or spray bottle of water
permanent marker

What to do

1. Place filters and markers on a table and encourage children to color on the filters.
2. Write each child's name on his filter using a permanent marker.
3. Place decorated coffee filters out in the rain for a few minutes (misty rain works best) to allow colors to run. To do the activity inside, use a spray bottle of water.
4. If possible, let children watch their filters from a window and decide when they'd like to bring them back in. If they are kept out too long, the color washes away.
5. Hang them in windows, give them as gifts, or display them on a light table, if available.

Related books

Cloudy With a Chance of Meatballs by Judi Barrett
Splash! by Ann Jonas
Thundercake by Patricia Polacco

Related songs

"Clean Rain" by Raffi
"It's Raining, It's Pouring"
"Singin' in the Rain"

 *Shirley Salach, Northwood, NH*

Fall Leaf Rubbings

Materials

fall leaves
thin aluminum foil
erasers
construction paper
glue

What to do

1. Place leaves flat on a table.
2. Cover each leaf with a thin piece of foil.
3. Encourage children to rub an eraser back and forth gently on the foil until it makes an imprint of the leaf.
4. To display, glue each foil leaf print on a piece of construction paper, and glue the leaf next to it.

Related books

Autumn Days by Ann Schweninger
Clifford's First Autumn by Norman Bridwell
Red Leaf, Yellow Leaf by Lois Ehlert
When Autumn Comes by Robert Maass

 *Kaethe Lewandowski, Centreville, VA*

Felt Faces

Materials

felt
scissors
flannel board

What to do

1. Cut out facial features from felt, such as eyes, noses, and mouths (smiling, frowning, open wide, and so on).
2. Encourage the children to create faces with the body parts on a flannel board. Help them to label an appropriate emotion that reflects how the face might "feel," for example, happy, sad, mad, or scared.

Barb Lindsay, Mason City, IA

Fish Prints

Materials

rubber fish
watercolor or tempera paints
paintbrushes
newsprint or thin paper
pictures of fish
magnifying glass

What to do

1. Explain to the children that they will be making fish prints using a technique called *gyotaku* (gyo: fish, taku: rubbing). *Gyotaku* (gee-oh-tah-koo) is the Japanese art of fish printing. This is said to have originated in the early 1800s in Asia by sportsmen to preserve records of their catches. It then developed into an art form.

2. Use rubber fish with detailed fins and scales. The children usually enjoy exploring the fish and its parts.
3. Let each child paint a fish.
4. Demonstrate how to place a piece of paper on top of the fish and then rub the paper to make a fish print. Carefully peel off the paper to reveal the fish print.
5. Supply pictures of different fish for children to view. Provide magnifying glasses for children to get a close look.
6. Send a note home with the fish that explains the art form of *Gyotaku*.

1. PAINT RUBBER FISH
2. PUT PAPER OVER PAINTED FISH and RUB

Tip: These make great gifts as note cards, prints on T-shirts (with fabric paint), and framed pictures.

Related books *Carl Caught a Flying Fish* by Kevin O'Malley
Char Siu Bao Boy by Sandra S. Yamate

Sandra Nagel, White Lake, MI

Hoppy Easter

Materials

long piece of white paper
purple paint
large pie tins
pre-cut construction paper rabbit ears
glue
crayons
bunny pattern
construction paper
purple, pink, and yellow pastel crepe paper strips
string
eggs (one per child)
needle
bowls

toothbrushes
pastel-colored paint
glue gun (adult only)
yarn

What to do

1. Tell the children they will be making a variety of springtime crafts! Start by holding the egg over a bowl and poking a hole in the top and bottom of the egg with a needle. Blow the egg out from the shell into the bowl. Rinse the shells and dry them. This is an adult step, because of food allergy and food poisoning precautions.
2. Place long white paper on the floor for children to make "bunny footprints." Help each child dip one foot into a pan of purple paint and then make a footprint on the paper.
3. Provide construction paper ears for children to glue above the toes of their footprints. Encourage the children to draw eyes, nose, and whiskers on their footprints with crayons.
4. Make a bunny windsock by pre-cutting paper bunnies. Help the children glue colored crepe paper strips to the bottom of the bunny's head as shown. Attach string and hang in the spring wind!
5. Paint the empty, clean eggshells. The children should try their best to be gentle with the shells. Put out paintbrushes and tins of pastel-colored paints and encourage the children to spatter the paint onto the eggs by flicking the toothbrush bristles with their fingers. They can use as many colors as they like!
6. After they have finished, use a glue gun to attach yarn to the eggs as shown (adult only).

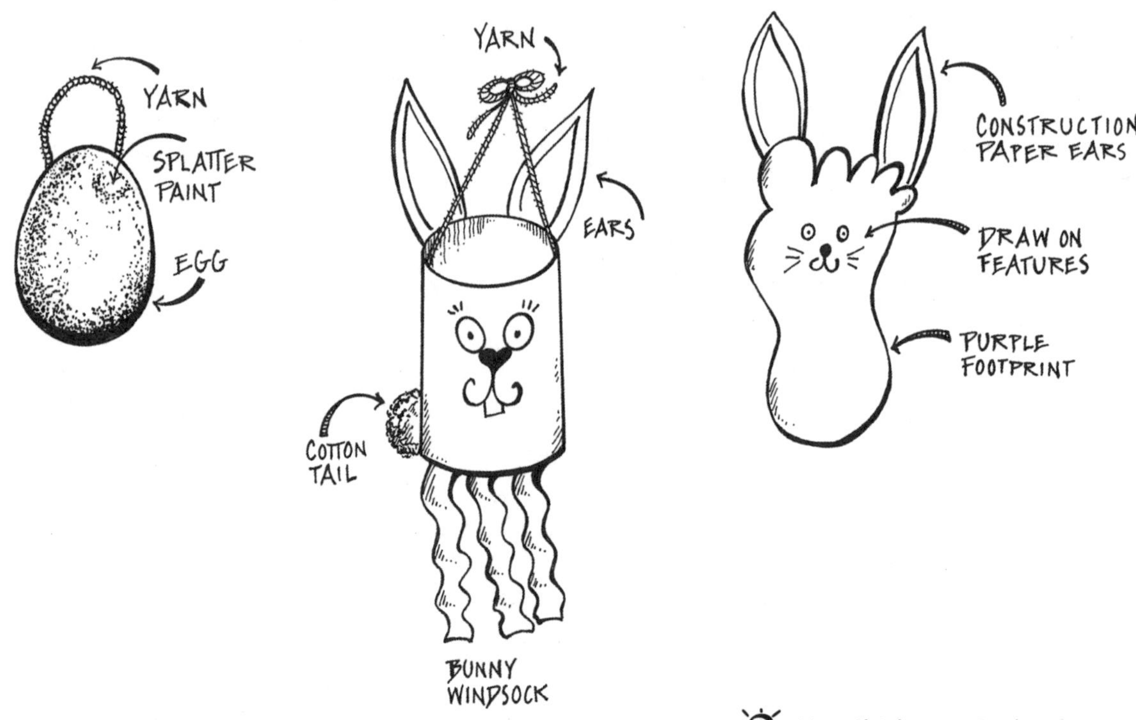

Lisa Chichester, Parkersburg, WV

I've Seen Beautiful Trees

Materials

Have You Seen Trees? by Joanne Oppenheim
cotton swabs
tape
brown, red, yellow, green, and orange tempera paint
thin paintbrushes
meat trays
white construction paper

What to do

1. Read the book *Have You Seen Trees?* by Joanne Oppenheim to the children. Tell them that they will make their own trees.
2. Prepare cotton swabs to act as dot painters by taping five cotton swabs together in the middle.
3. Place each color of paint in a separate meat tray. Put thin paintbrushes next to the tray of brown paint.
4. Give each child a piece of construction paper. Encourage the children to paint a tree trunk with branches with brown paint.
5. Next, encourage the children to dip the cotton swabs into the paints and dot all around their branches to create a beautiful display of fall foliage.
6. Allow the paintings to dry, and display these beautiful trees.

Leaf Splatter

Materials

leaves from outdoors
white construction paper
tape
shallow boxes
small screens
toothbrushes
liquid watercolor paint in fall colors

What to do

1. Provide white paper and fall leaves. Encourage the children to tape several leaves on a sheet of paper.
2. Put the paper with the leaves into a box. Place the screen on top of the box.
3. Ask the child to dip a toothbrush into paint and brush the toothbrush across the screen to create a splatter effect. Encourage the children to use several colors of paint.

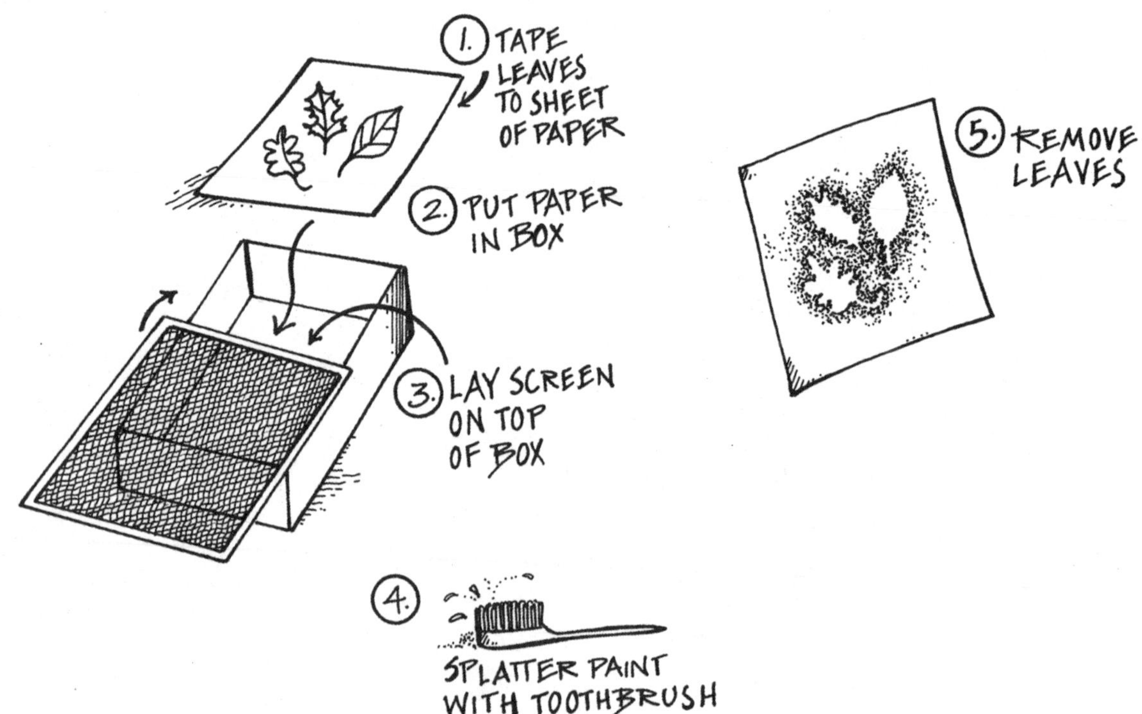

4. Remove the screen and carefully remove the leaves. The print of the leaves should remain on the paper.

Related books *Autumn* by Gerda Muller
Red Leaf, Yellow Leaf by Lois Ehlert

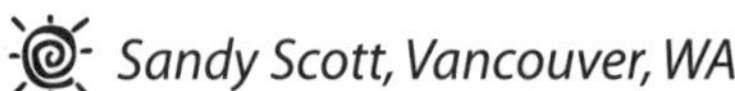
Sandy Scott, Vancouver, WA

Magic Dough

Materials

plain playdough
food coloring
placemat or table covering to protect table, if needed
tray

What to do

1. Beforehand, prepare plain playdough from any recipe.
2. Form playdough into as many balls as you like, about 2" in size.
3. Poke a finger into a ball of dough. Drop in a small dot of food coloring. Close it over with playdough. Poke another hole, and put in another tiny drop of color. Repeat closing. Make a third hole with a third color.
4. Do this for all the balls of dough.
5. Place balls of dough on a tray for the art center.
6. Encourage the children to explore and squeeze the balls of playdough. Encourage them to squeeze, roll, explore, and manipulate. As they play with the dough, the colors will start to mix into rainbow colors, eventually completely changing the color of the ball of dough.

Related books

First Art: Art Experiences for Toddlers and Twos by MaryAnn F. Kohl
Have You Seen Birds? by Joanne Oppenheim

Related song

Squeeze My Dough by MaryAnn F. Kohl
(tune: "Three White Mice")
Squeeze my dough.
Squeeze my dough.
See how it goes.
See how it goes.
I play with dough on my playdough mat.
I roll it up, and I pat it flat,
I make a dog, and I make a cat.
Squeeze my dough.

 *MaryAnn F. Kohl, Bellingham, WA*

Making Fingerpaint

Materials

newspaper
paint shirts
liquid dish soap
tempera paint
bowls and spoons
paper
cooking extracts or gelatin mixes (optional)

What to do

1. Cover the work table with newspaper and put paint shirts on the children.
2. Let children help make fingerpaint. Add 1 teaspoon of liquid dish soap, 1 teaspoon of liquid starch, and ½ cup of tempera paint to each bowl. Mix a different color in each bowl.
3. Stir the ingredients to mix.
4. Encourage the children to paint pictures with the paint they helped mix. Ask them to mix two primary colors to see what happens.
5. If desired, add fragrance to the fingerpaint, such as banana to the yellow, mint to the green, and berry to the red. Use a cooking extract or gelatin mix for this.

Sandra Nagel, White Lake, MI

Me, Myself, and I

Materials

large paper (big enough for child's outline)
crayons
scissors
felt and old fabric
yarn
glue
photos of children
oak tag or heavy paper
plastic baggies
pie tins with paint
colored paper

What to do

1. Talk about self-concept and how it is nice to feel good about oneself.
2. Put the children into pairs and have each pair take turns tracing his partner on a large piece of paper. Encourage them to color faces on their outlines and cut out material and felt for clothing and yarn for hair.
3. Ask children to bring in a picture of themselves.
4. Glue each child's photo to a piece of oak tag or sturdy paper.
5. Help the children cut the photo into a few large shapes to make a personal puzzle. Place puzzle pieces in a plastic baggie and let the children solve their puzzles.
6. Copy the poem "Baby Feet" by Edgar Guest on a sheet of paper. This poem can easily be found in compilations or on the Internet.
7. Help each child dip a foot into paint and make a footprint next to the poem. This can be framed with a photo of the child.

Lisa Chichester, Parkersburg, WV

Melted Crayon Art

Materials

old crayons
egg carton or sectioned container
small food processor, coffee bean grinder, or cheese grater
wax paper
cup warmer or hot plate

What to do

1. Ask children to assist in peeling paper off crayons (preferably old scraps of crayons).
2. Sort the colors into a sectioned container or egg carton sections.
3. Grind colors up separately and dump shavings back into the sections.
4. Place wax paper on a cup warmer or hot plate (or an iron, if necessary). Let children place a pinch at a time of shavings on the wax paper.
5. When finished, cover their design with another piece of wax paper, turn on cup warmer or hot plate, and watch the beautiful designs created as the crayon melts!

Tip: If using a cup warmer, small wax paper about the same size as the warming section works best.

6. Hang them in windows, give them as gifts, or display them on a light table, if available.

Related books

Color Dance by Ann Jonas
The Color Wizard by Barbara Brenner
Color Zoo by Lois Ehlert
Growing Colors by Bruce McMillan
Harold and the Purple Crayon by Crockett Johnson
Wax to Crayons (Welcome Books: How Things Are Made) by Inez Snyder

Mirror Butterfly Handprints

Materials

black and white construction paper
markers (including black)
scissors
glue
tempera paint
meat trays

What to do

1. Beforehand, trace the body (thorax) of a butterfly on black construction paper. Make one for each child.
2. Give each child a piece of white construction paper and a piece of black paper with the butterfly's body traced on it.
3. Encourage the children to cut out the butterfly's body and glue it to the middle of the white construction paper.
4. Pour tempera paint into meat trays. Encourage the children to dip both hands into the paint.
5. Demonstrate how to place each hand on the opposite side of the body. Encourage the children to spread their fingers out to make a handprint.
6. Turn the paper upside down and have children repeat the handprints, mirroring the other print and creating the butterfly's other wings.
7. Encourage the children to complete the butterfly by drawing legs and antennae with markers.
8. After the butterflies dry, encourage the children to cut around the shapes and then hang them for display.

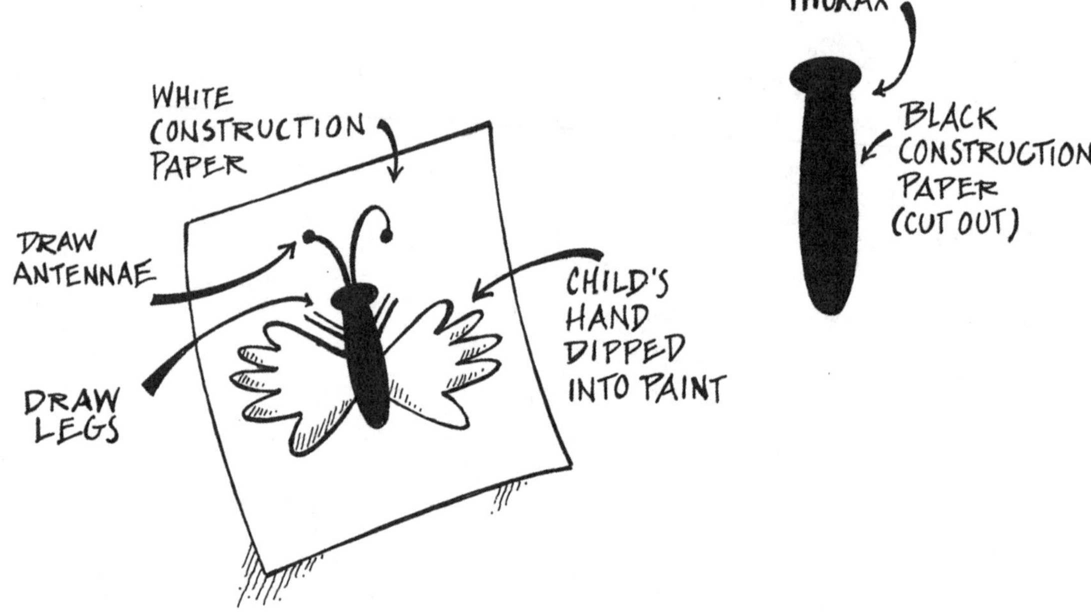

Quazonia J. Quarles, Newark, DE

Multicultural Puzzle Piece Art

Materials construction paper in different colors
scissors
markers

What to do

1. Cut different colors of construction paper into the shape of a large puzzle piece (at least floor puzzle size).
2. Ask the children to decorate the puzzle pieces with information about themselves, such as their favorite foods or colors.
3. Collect all the puzzle pieces and make a bulletin board display that reads, "We are all pieces of the same puzzle!" Puzzle pieces do not need to connect for display. They can be scattered all over the bulletin board.

My Name Looks Like This

Materials paper
art supplies

What to do

1. This activity works well with children who are beginning to label the sounds that the letters in their names make.
2. Give each child enough paper so that he has one piece for each letter in his name. Write one letter of the child's name on each piece of paper.
3. Assist the children in identifying something that begins with each of the letters in their names. For example, a child named Tom could have "twig" (T), "orange" (O), and "mom" (M).
4. Write the words they choose, one on each piece of paper. Encourage the children to use art supplies to create an artistic representation of each word.
5. Share the pictures at group time.

Related books *Baby Einstein: the ABCs of Art* by Julie Aigner-Clark
Baby Einstein: Van Gogh's World of Color by Julie Aigner-Clark

Pottery Studio

Materials

clay (earth clay works well, purchase at craft shops, art supply, or school supply stores) or any recipe for basic art dough
turntable (such as a plastic one used on shelves)
craft sticks or tongue depressors
sculpting tools
play oven
cooking sheet
paint
paintbrushes

What to do

1. Turn your art center into a pottery studio. Encourage the children to make colorful signs for the area. Display pictures of pottery items, such as bowls, cups, and jewelry.
2. Prepare a small table where the children can work on the clay. Let them take turns being the "potter." Encourage the children to shape the clay any way they please using whatever sculpting tools are available. Some playdough tools will work, but don't use cookie cutters. The process should be free form.
3. Put the finished sculptures on a tray and place it in an "oven." Explain that pottery is put in an oven called a kiln. Older preschoolers can use clay that can be baked in a real oven. If the sculptures are not baked, allow them to dry so that they are firm enough to paint.
4. After the clay is dry, invite the children to paint the pottery and display it in the "studio." Place it on shelves as in a museum or a pottery store. If desired, set up a cash register, pretend money, shopping bags, and gift wrap in the center. The "shoppers" will enjoy seeing each other's work!

More to do

Blocks: When setting up the pottery studio, the children can incorporate blocks from the block center as a way of displaying the pottery.

Maxine Della-Fave, Raleigh, NC

Rain Splatter Painting

Materials

drawing paper or construction paper
tempera paint
paintbrushes
rainy day

What to do

1. Provide paper and encourage children to paint on it. They can use wet or dry tempera paint. If children paint both ways, they can compare the results at the end.
2. When it is raining, put the paintings outside for a few moments. Count to five with the children. Children can experiment with how long they leave the paintings in the rain, and compare differences. When time is up, bring the paintings inside to dry.
3. Allow the paintings to dry on a flat surface so the spatter spots remain and run together.
4. Encourage the children to examine and compare the resulting patterns.

More to do

More Art: This activity can also be done when talking about snow. The children can place snow or ice chunks on their paintings and watch as they melt.

Sandra Nagel, White Lake, MI

Rainbow of Colors

Materials

camera
large white paper
paint in many colors
paintbrushes
easel paper
plastic sippy cups in different colors
different colors of candy
old board books or heavy paper
glue
feathers, pompoms, and scraps of material

What to do

This is a week-long project. Children will work with one color per day.

1. Send home a note explaining to parents that for one week, the class will be focusing on one color each day. Ask parents to dress their children in the color you specify each day.
2. Tape a large piece of white paper on a wall to make a photo background. Each day of the "color week," take a picture of each child wearing the color of the day.
3. Read or tell them a story containing the color of the day.
4. Encourage children to paint on the easel with whatever color is assigned for the day.
5. Play "I Spy" by looking for items in the room that are the same color as the color of the day.

6. Let children make their favorite color sippy cup. Purchase different colored sippy cups with lids (in most craft stores) and candy in the same colors as the cups. Ask the children to pick their favorite color cup and candies in the same color. Let them take their treats home.
7. At the end of the week, help the children make personal color books. Glue colored paper to old board books or staple heavy paper together. Give the children their photographs of them wearing different colored clothing to glue on each page of the book. The children can add feathers, pompoms, or scraps of material for added fun.

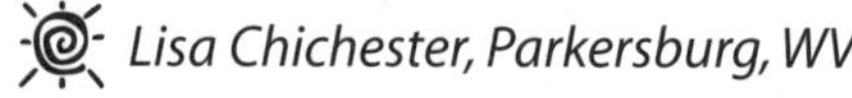
Lisa Chichester, Parkersburg, WV

Silhouettes and Shadows

Materials

overhead projector, slide projector, or lamp
assortment of materials from home or classroom
white paper
pencils
tape
white pencil or chalk
black paper

What to do

1. Encourage the children to experiment by placing various items from the classroom on a table in front of a slide projector or overhead projector in order to see the shadows they make on the wall.
2. Suggest they make a design they like, and then copy the shadow by tracing it on paper taped to the wall.
3. Ask the children if they would like to sit still so you can trace their shadows on the wall, using white pencil on black paper. It helps if someone sits behind the child to help hold his head still. Tell them this is called a "silhouette." Let them trace your silhouette, too!
4. Cut out silhouettes and glue them on a different color of paper. Show the silhouettes to the children during group time and challenge them to recognize their friends.
5. Keep the slide or overhead projector in the classroom for several days, moving it to any area where children can create things that might be fun to "shadow" on the wall. For example, bring it to the block area to make a shadow of an interesting tall structure, bring it to the playdough table and let children make shadows by placing their creations on a table, and put it near the sand and water so children can see the shadows from pouring water or drops of water.

Related books *Moonbear's Shadow* by Frank Asch
My Shadow by Robert Louis Stevenson
Shadows by Marcia Brown
Shadows: Here, There, and Everywhere by Ron and Nancy Goor
What Makes a Shadow? by Clyde Robert Bulla

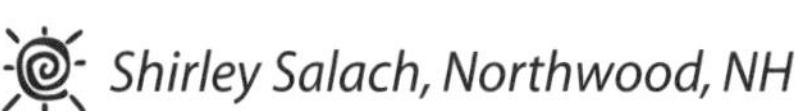
Shirley Salach, Northwood, NH

Snowflakes Dancing

Materials
white paper
scissors
glitter
glue
wagon wheel pasta
white tempera paint
yarn
Popsicle sticks
strips of white crepe paper
tape

What to do

1. Create different types of snowflakes with the children.
2. Help the children fold white paper and cut out snowflakes. Then provide silver glitter to add sparkle.
3. Help the children paint wagon wheel-shaped pasta noodles white and let dry. Then demonstrate how to string the pasta on yarn and tie to make a "snowflake" necklace.
4. Tell the children they are going to act like snowflakes. First, help them make white "snowflake sticks" by taping one strip of white crepe paper to the end of a Popsicle stick. Then show them how to wrap the white crepe paper around the stick. Encourage them to wave their crepe paper sticks and move like snowflakes.

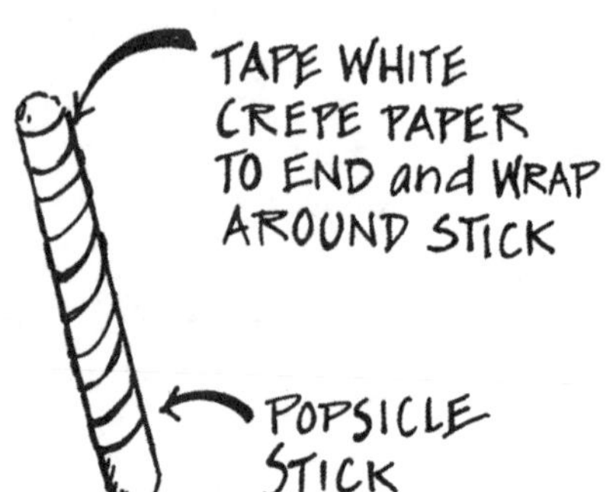

Lisa Chichester, Parkersburg, WV

Texture Kites

Materials

large sheet of white construction paper or watercolor paper
clear-drying glue
watercolor paints
paintbrushes
cups
water
kite pattern (diamond-shaped pattern about 10" long by 7" wide)
bow pattern (about 1 ½" long by 3" wide)
pencils
string

What to do

1. Explain to the children that they are going to do an activity that focuses on texture, color blending, and kites and that it will take two days to complete.
2. Discuss the different types of kites that children are familiar with and tell them they are going to make a kite with their very own color design and texture.
3. Give one large sheet of watercolor paper or construction paper to each child. Make sure the kite and bow pattern fits on one sheet of paper.
4. Provide glue and demonstrate how to make a "texture design." Do this by holding the glue bottle about 12-15 inches above the paper and squeezing. As the glue starts to come out in a stream, move the bottle around in a twirling motion. Point out that even though the glue comes out in a stream, sometimes it forms a small round ball when it hits the paper.

5. Let the children continue this until they have created a glue design they are happy with. However, caution the children not to put too much glue on the paper because it will be difficult to cut and the paint will not stick to the glue. Wherever there is glue, there will be white space on the painted paper. Also, you may want to point out to the children that they are going to be cutting their design apart, so they may not have the entire design on the finished kite.
6. Once the children have completed their designs, let the papers dry for at least 24 hours. The glue must be completely dry and hard before you continue.
7. The next day, give the children their dried glue paper and have them paint the entire paper with watercolors. You might want to talk about mixing colors and choosing colors that go well together, or how colors combine to make new colors.
8. Once the children have painted their kites and cleaned their brushes in the cups of water, refill the cups with clean water and show the children how to use water to "blend" the colors and create a soft, flowing look. To do this, children wet the brush with clear water and drag it back and forth over the painted paper. If they do this before the paint is completely dry, they will get a much nicer blended look.
9. Set the papers out to dry. This time, drying should only require about an hour.
10. Next, redistribute the painted papers and the kite and bow patterns. Encourage the children to trace the kite pattern over their favorite part of their design. Then ask them to trace the bow pattern at least five times. They can make more bows if they have space on their papers. If the children have extra scraps, you might want to save them for use on another project.

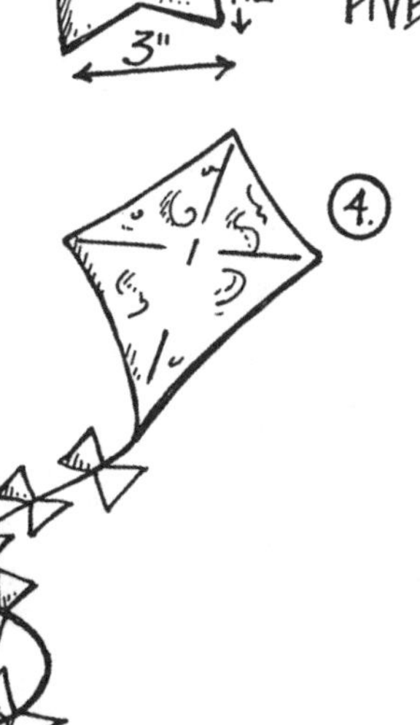

11. Ask the children to cut out their patterns. If they traced over an area with a large amount of glue on it, you may need to help them cut it because the glue is difficult to cut through when dry.
12. Once the cutting is complete, distribute string and glue and ask the children to glue the string onto the back of the bows and the bottom of the kite to make a tail for the kite.
13. When these have dried, the children will enjoy touching the finished product and feeling the texture.

 *Mike Krestar, Latrobe, PA*

The Wreath

Materials

poster board or heavy paper
paint (tempera paint or fingerpaint with liquid soap added)
sponge shapes (optional)
glue
ribbons
cupcake liners
scrap items
scissors

What to do

1. Cut out a large circle from poster board or heavy paper, and then cut out a smaller circle from the middle. It should have a donut or bagel shape to it.
2. Talk to the children about the symbol of a wreath. Explain that it is a welcome sign that people put on their front doors.
3. Use wreaths to learn about the seasons. Let each child make his own wreath for spring, summer, fall, and winter near the beginning of each new season. A fall wreath could include leaves, and cutouts or stamps of pumpkins and apples. Winter wreaths could include snowflakes, snowmen, mittens, and the colors white, blue, and purple. In the spring, the children can look outside for spring colors, such as yellow, purple, green, and pink for leaves and flowers. Children may want to include familiar animals of the season as well. The same can be done for summer.

4. The wreath becomes a concrete symbol of when the seasons change. It provides an opportunity for families to talk with the child about the changes of the seasons and the special aspects of each one. When the wreath is displayed each year, the parent and child can discuss what to expect during that new season.

 *Sandra Nagel, White Lake, MI*

For all cooking activities, take special precautions when working with young children.

1. First, check for food allergies.
2. Make sure children wash their hands before handling the ingredients, and before eating their creations.
3. While you are cooking with the children, supervise at ALL times, and especially the use of any sharp utensils, as well as appliances. If children will be using sharp utensils, try practicing this exercise with safe materials first, and explain to the children how to use the utensil correctly.
4. Certain appliances should always be used by an adult only, such as ovens, hot plates, and toaster ovens. Be sure that children are far enough from these appliances that they do not run the risk of being burned. When you cook in a pot on the stove, keep pot handle turned away from children so that the pot is not bumped.
5. Try to involve children as much as possible. You may even want to go shopping with them. Involve them in cleanup as well, and thank them for their efforts.

Shaping Up

Materials

cookie cutters of different shapes, such as triangle, square, circle, and star
refrigerated cookie dough
oven (adult only)
icing
sprinkles
sponges
scissors
pie tins
paint
paper

What to do

1. Explore shapes with the children by making shape cookies. Help the children use cookie cutters of different shapes to cut out shapes from cookie dough.
2. Place the cookies on a tray and put in an oven to bake according to package directions.
3. After the cookies have cooled, let the children use plastic knives to ice the cookies. Sprinkles are fun to put on top!
4. For more shape fun, cut sponges into different shapes, such as a square and circle. Give each child a shape sponge to dip into paint and make sponge paintings.

Lisa Chichester, Parkersburg, WV

Cinnamon Dough Bears

Materials

1 cup flour
2 cups sugar
¼ cup cinnamon
1 packet yeast
mixing bowl
oven (adult only)
baking sheet
white felt
letter stickers
camera (optional)
scissors
raisins

What to do

1. With the children, mix together flour, sugar, cinnamon, and one packet of yeast in a bowl.
2. Show them how to roll balls of dough and make a teddy bear as shown. Let each child make three or four bears. Place the teddy bears on a baking sheet.
3. Put the baking sheet in an oven and bake at 350° for 30 to 35 minutes.
4. Use white felt and letter stickers to make nametags for the bears. If desired, take a photo of each child to glue on the nametag later.
5. As the bears bake, read *Teddy Bear's Picnic* by Mark Burgess to the children.
6. Remove the bears from the oven when they are done. Help children spread butter on the bears' bellies, and then sprinkle with cinnamon.
7. Have a class teddy bear picnic with teddy bear bread as the treat!

Related book *Teddy Bear's Picnic* by Mark Burgess

Lisa Chichester, Parkersburg, WV

Coconut Boom Boom Tree

Materials

Chicka Chicka Boom Boom by Bill Martin, Jr. and John Archambault
paper plates
plastic knives
plastic serving cups
pretzel logs
chocolate cake icing
spearmint leaf gummy candy (or other leaf-shape candy)
small round chocolate candy, such as Almond Joy bites or malted milk balls
assorted cake-decorating icing (in tubes)

What to do

1. Beforehand, prepare portions of chocolate icing in individual serving cups. Put a plastic knife next to each cup. Also put out four spearmint leaves and two round chocolate candies per child. Put pretzel logs in an open container for easy access.
2. Also, in advance, prepare rebus instruction cards for making the treat.
3. Read *Chicka Chicka Boom Boom*. Then model how to make this yummy coconut tree treat.
4. Place one pretzel log on a paper plate.
5. Spread chocolate icing over the entire pretzel log.
6. Place four spearmint green leaves around the top sides and tip of the pretzel log.
7. Place the two chocolate candies at the top of the pretzel log, underneath the spearmint leaves. These represent coconuts.
8. Let everyone enjoy the coconut trees during snack.

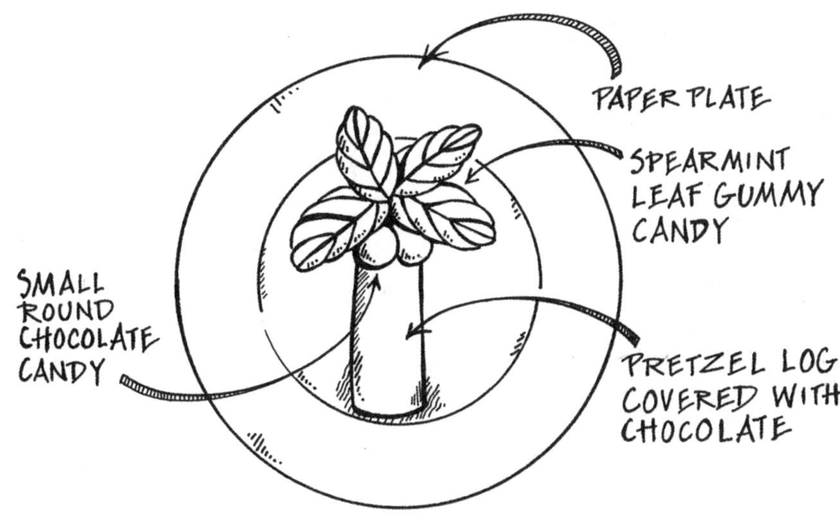

 *Quazonia J. Quarles, Newark, DE*

Colored Applesauce

Materials

applesauce
¼ teaspoon measuring spoon
gelatin mix
paper cups
plastic spoons
serving spoon

What to do

1. Ask children to wash their hands.
2. Arrange the ingredients and utensils on a table.
3. Invite the children, in turn, to create their own snack. Each child puts applesauce in her cup, adds ¼ teaspoon of gelatin mix, and stirs with a plastic spoon.
4. This makes a colorful snack time treat. For holiday fun, use cherry gelatin for Valentine's Day or lime gelatin for St. Patrick's Day.

Related book *Color Dance* by Ann Jonas

Jackie Wright, Enid, OK

Cook-A-Doodle-Doo!

Materials

Cook-A-Doodle-Doo by Susan Stevens Crummel and Janet Stevens
paper and markers
strawberries
plastic knives
all-purpose baking mix (such as Bisquick)
butter
milk
sugar
whipping cream
vanilla
measuring cups and spoons
mixing bowl and mixing spoon
oven (adult only)

What to do

1. Before reading *Cook-A-Doodle-Doo* to the children, show them the front cover and ask them individually how they think strawberry shortcake is made. Write down what each child tells you (in her own words) on a piece of paper. Ask the children to draw a picture of the strawberry shortcake on the paper.
2. After the children are finished, read the book. It is a wonderful and humorous book about teamwork and cooperation that will help children learn about the cooking process and cooking terms.
3. After reading the story, make strawberry shortcake with the children. Make sure to break up the recipe depending on how many children are in the class so that each child has a job. If desired, take a picture of each child doing each step in the recipe.
4. Remove stems from strawberries and cut into thin slices using plastic knives. Put the slices in a large bowl, mix in 1 tablespoon of sugar, and set aside.
5. Make biscuits according to the directions on the package of all-purpose baking mix. Add butter, milk, and sugar. Bake according to package directions.
6. Mash strawberries lightly.
7. Add a couple of drops of vanilla and one teaspoon of sugar to whipping cream and beat together.
8. When the biscuits have cooled, break up the biscuits into pieces in a bowl. Add strawberries and whipped cream. Enjoy!
9. Make a great bulletin board display for this activity by including the pictures of the children cooking, along with their own illustrated pictures and words on how to make strawberry shortcake. Make sure to include a group picture with the book and the finished cake.

Gail Morris, Kemah, TX

Cookie Craze

Materials

ingredients for three favorite cookie recipes
cookie cutters
flour
rolling pins
sprinkles
baking sheets
oven
large poster board
markers

What to do

1. Gather ingredients for three different cookie recipes.
2. Help the children make cookies by measuring the ingredients and mixing. Make three different types of cookies (or more if you like).
3. Let children roll out the dough, cut different shapes with cookie cutters, and sprinkle with decorative sprinkles.
4. Put the cookies in the oven to bake (adult only).
5. After the children have tasted the different cookies, make a graph of their favorites using a large piece of poster board.

Lisa Chichester, Parkersburg, WV

Cookie Cutter Puzzles

Materials

variety of sets of cookie cutters (transportation, fruits, animals, shapes, numbers, letters, and so on)
markers
black construction paper
scissors
file folders
glue
clear contact paper
zipper-closure plastic bags
stapler

What to do

1. Trace the cookie cutters on black construction paper and cut them out.
2. Glue each set of black cutouts to the inside of separate file folders.
3. Cover the inside of the folders with clear contact paper.
4. Place the matching cookie cutters in zipper-closure bags and staple each bag to the matching folder.
5. Label the front of each folder with the name of the set.
6. Put the folders in the bakery center and have the children match the cookie cutters to the cutout shapes.
7. If the sets of cookie cutters become mixed up, turn cleanup into a sorting activity as the children find all the transportation, fruit, or animal cutters.

Related books

At the Bakery by Carol Greene
Cookie Count by Robert Sabuda
The Doorbell Rang by Pat Hutchins
Emeril's There's a Chef in My Soup by Emeril Lagasse
If You Give a Mouse a Cookie by Laura Joffe Numeroff
Walter the Baker by Eric Carle

Ann Kelly, Johnstown, PA

Counting Cookies

Materials

brown construction paper
scissors
marker
clear contact paper or laminate
cookie sheet
large plate
pancake turner

What to do

1. Cut out cookie-size circles from brown construction paper.
2. Write the numerals 1 to 10 on 10 of the brown circles (one number per circle). On the other 10 circles, put a different number of dots on each one (1 dot on the first, 2 on the second, and so on to 10) to look like chocolate chips. Laminate or cover with clear contact paper.
3. Place the "cookies" with the "chips" on a cookie sheet with the dots facing down so the children cannot see the chips. Place the other 10 "cookies" on a plate with the numbers facing up. Put the cookie sheet and plate in the bakery center.
4. Let the children take turns turning over one of the cookies on the cookie sheet using the pancake turner. The child counts the number of chips and looks for the matching number from the cookies on the plate.

Related books

The Doorbell Rang by Pat Hutchins
If You Give a Mouse a Cookie by Laura Joffe Numeroff

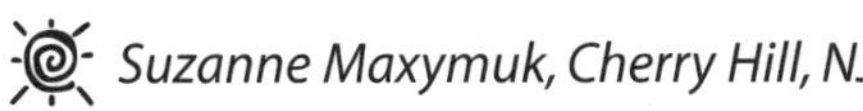
Suzanne Maxymuk, Cherry Hill, NJ

Deviled Eggs in a Bag

Materials

one egg for each child
large pot
stove
mayonnaise
yellow mustard
sugar
three small containers
quart-size zipper-closure bags, one for each child
small plastic spoons and knives

What to do

Note: Before doing this activity, check for egg allergies.

1. Boil one egg for each child. If you have access to a stove, you can do this step with the children. If not, do this before the activity. Try to involve the children as much as possible.
2. After the eggs have cooled, have the children wash their hands and take one egg. Show the children how to peel the eggs and let them peel their own. This may take time, but is well worth the wait.
3. As children peel the eggs, put mayonnaise, sugar, and mustard into separate small containers and put them on the workspace within easy reach.
4. Give each child a plastic knife to cut the egg in half. Don't worry about which way the children cut the eggs—any way is fine as long as they end up with two halves.
5. Give each child a zipper-closure plastic bag and a plastic spoon. Ask them to scoop the yolks into the bags.
6. Let the children spoon some of each of the three ingredients on the table into the bag.
7. Ask them to securely seal the bags. Make sure that there is not so much air in the bag that it will burst when the child squeezes it. To do this, show them how to lay the bag on the table to seal it.
8. Encourage the children to use their hands to squish the mixture in their bag until all of the ingredients are combined. After a sufficient amount of squishing, have the children spoon the mixture from the bag to fill the egg halves.
9. Enjoy your deviled eggs!

More to do

Circle Time: Say the "Humpty Dumpty" rhyme together.

Games: Have an egg race using plastic eggs. Use masking tape to mark a start and finish line anywhere in the room. Place two plastic eggs at the start line. Encourage two children to use their noses to push the eggs across the floor to the finish line. Don't make a competition of it, just have fun!

Related books

The Chicken Sisters by Laura Joffe Numeroff
Cook-a-Doodle-Doo! by Susan Stevens Crummel and Janet Stevens
Pigs in the Pantry: Fun With Math and Cooking by Amy Axelrod

Virginia Jean Herrod, Columbia, SC

Dough Tools

Materials

playdough
cheese grater
egg slicer
sieve
tomato slicer
French fry cutter
apple corer
garlic press
plastic knives and forks
plastic cups
tweezers

What to do

1. Provide real cooking tools for children to slice, press, roll, cut, and imprint playdough. Be sure to closely supervise this activity if using any sharp utensils. Explain to the children how to handle these items correctly. To make this activity more interesting, do not provide cookie cutters.
2. Encourage exploration and experimentation to create different effects. Explain that many tools can be used to cut as well as make prints by varying the pressure. Children can use tweezers to pick up small pieces, a plastic fork to make lines or holes, and cups to roll playdough or cut out circles.

More to do

Use tools of other trades such as bolts, pliers, or plumbing parts.
Art: Use cooking tools to dip in paint and make prints.

Related books

A Day in the Life of a Chef by Liza N. Burby
The Little Red Hen (Makes a Pizza) by Philemon Sturges
Pancakes, Pancakes! by Eric Carle
Stone Soup (a folk tale available in many versions)

Sandra Gratias, Perkasie, PA

Edible Art

Materials

confectioner's sugar and four cans of frosting, or homemade frosting
food coloring
six cloth or plastic pastry bags
rubber bands
un-iced cupcakes or large cookies, one per child
plastic knives
camera

What to do

1. Prepare homemade frosting or thicken canned frosting with a bit of confectioner's sugar. Divide the frosting into seven portions. Color each one a different color: pink, blue, green, yellow, purple, and orange. Keep one portion white.
2. Place a decorator tip into each pastry bag. Put one color of icing into each bag. Twist the top shut and secure with a rubber band.
3. Let each child take a cupcake or cookie and spread a thin layer of white frosting on the top.
4. Using the pastry bags, the children squeeze out icing to decorate their cupcake or cookie. A squeeze and release motion works best to get different shapes.
5. Demonstrate how to twist the bag and move the rubber band down as the icing is used.
6. Take a picture of each masterpiece, and then eat this artwork for snack!

Related books

Eight Animals Bake a Cake by Susan Middleton Elya
Froggy Bakes a Cake by Jonathan London
If You Give a Mouse a Cookie by Laura Joffe Numeroff
Who Took the Cookies From the Cookie Jar? by Rozanne Lanczak Williams
Yummy Yummy by Judith Grey

Sandra Gratias, Perkasie, PA

Hum Hum Hummus

Materials

3 oz. chickpeas
1/8 cup lemon juice
2 tablespoons tahini
1 clove garlic
2 tablespoons olive oil
1 teaspoon parsley
pita bread
mortar and pestle
wax paper
hammer
scissors (sanitized for cooking)
wooden spoons or rubber spatula
mixing bowl

What to do

1. Add chickpeas in the mortar until it is half full. Let the children take turns using the pestle to mash the chickpeas, and then place them into a bowl. Continue until all are mashed.
2. Add the tahini and lemon juice, and stir with a spatula or wooden spoon.
3. Cut two pieces of wax paper. Place garlic between the papers. Let the children use the hammer to smash the garlic. Add the garlic to the bowl.
4. Ask the children to cut the parsley with scissors, and then add it to the bowl.
5. Sprinkle olive oil on top, and let the children take turns stirring the mixture.
6. Give each child a small bowl of hummus and a piece of pita bread. Show them how to tear the bread and dip it into the hummus.

More to do

Make sun tea to go with the hummus. Measure 4 cups of cold water into a large jar. Add two tea bags and 1 tablespoon of honey. Place the jar in a sunny spot for three to six hours. The tea is done when it is a nice, hearty, brown color. Remove the tea bags and let the jar sit at room temperature for an hour, then refrigerate.

Related books

In My Momma's Kitchen by Jerdine Nolen
Pigs in the Pantry: Fun With Math and Cooking by Amy Axelrod

Virginia Jean Herrod, Columbia, SC

Ladybug, Ladybug, Fly Away Home

Materials

book about ladybugs
red and black construction paper
black fingerpaint
wiggle eyes
glue
refrigerated cookie dough
confectioner's sugar
red food coloring
butter knives or plastic knives
black gel icing

What to do

1. Read a story about ladybugs to the children. If possible, show them a real ladybug. Make ladybug headbands by cutting out circles from red construction paper and having the children finger paint dots on them with black fingerpaint. Add wiggle eyes. Attach to strips of construction paper and fit to each child's head.
2. Make ladybug cookies using store-bought, refrigerated cookie dough. Bake the cookies as directed.
3. Mix confectioner's sugar with water until it is a smooth consistency and thick enough to spread on cookies. Tint a large portion of the icing red.
4. Let the children use butter or plastic knives to ice the ladybug cookies, using white for a head and red for the wings. The children use black gel icing to draw eyes and spots.
5. Have a ladybug cookie snack wearing your ladybug headbands.

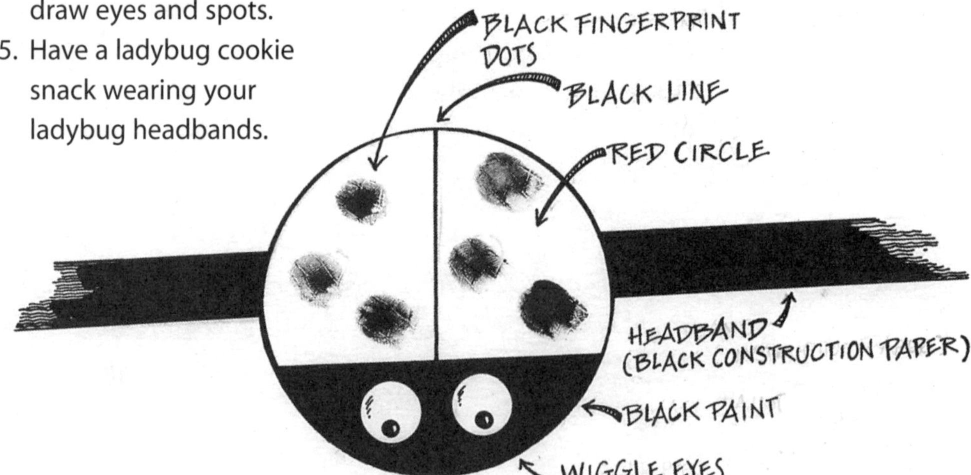

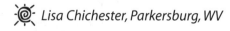

Lisa Chichester, Parkersburg, WV

Making Applesauce

Materials

7 apples
½ cup sugar
½ cup water
cinnamon
vegetable peeler
sharp knife (adult only)
large saucepan
stove

What to do

1. Let children help peel the apples. Remove the core from each one (adult only).
2. Cook the apples in boiling water until tender.

Note: Supervise closely, and do not let children near the boiling water.

3. Drain the apples and let cool. Ask children to mash them with a fork.
4. Add sugar and a bit of cinnamon and mix. The applesauce is ready to eat!

Rhonda Murphy, Los Angeles, CA

Nutty Numbers

Materials

store-bought cookie dough
number cookie cutters
small candies (such as mini M&M's)
baking sheet
oven
clay dough

What to do

1. Help the children roll out the cookie dough and cut out number-shaped cookies.
2. Help them add the number of candies to the cookie that corresponds to the number they cut out. Bake according to package directions.
3. Using different colors of clay, roll out "snakes" to make numbers or roll out a flat "pancake" and cut out numbers with the cookie cutters. Encourage children to make and re-make numbers.

More to do **Art:** Purchase wooden numbers from a craft store. Let the children use craft paint to decorate the numbers. After the numbers are dry, children can glue on the appropriate amount of buttons or pompoms.

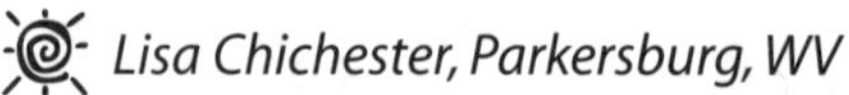

Pastry Painting

Materials

construction paper
scissors
easels
paint cups and paint
pastry brushes
sequins
small squares of tissue paper
glitter
glue

What to do

1. Cut out shapes of different baked goodies (such as cake, cookies, crescent rolls, cupcakes, and so on) from construction paper.
2. Set up the easels, paint, and pastry brushes next to a place where the paper cutouts can be displayed.
3. Ask each child to choose a baked goodie that she wants to decorate and place it on the easel.
4. Let children paint their cutouts. When they are finished, remove the paper and let them dry.
5. When dry, encourage the children to further decorate their cutouts by gluing sequins, glitter, and/or balls of tissue paper to their treat.
6. When dry, assist the children in hanging their work in a place they choose.

Related books

At the Bakery by Carol Greene
Emeril's There's a Chef in My Soup by Emeril Lagasse
Walter the Baker by Eric Carle

Pigs in a Blanket

Materials

oven
hot dogs
refrigerated biscuit dough
butter knife
cookie sheet

What to do

1. Preheat oven to 350°.
2. Cut hot dogs in half lengthwise to avoid choking hazard, and in half widthwise to fit into the biscuits.
3. Separate the flaky biscuit layers (uncooked). Encourage the children to use their fine motor skills to roll a layer of biscuit around their hot dog.
4. Place the rolled hot dogs on the cookie sheet. Place in the oven for approximately 15 minutes.
5. Let cool and enjoy "pigs in a blanket" for snack.

More to do

Gross Motor: As a gross motor activity, let each child have a turn rolling up in a blanket (like the hot dog), and then unroll. This is a good motor and sensory activity.

Sandra Nagel, White Lake, MI

Pizza Pie Match

Materials

colored felt pieces: cream, brown, red, pink, yellow, green, and black
scissors
large index cards
markers in colors to match the felt
laminator

What to do

1. This activity gives children practice reading numbers and counting sets to match the numerals. The children practice one-to-one correspondence by matching the pizza ingredients to the pictures on the recipe cards.

2. Prior to presenting the center, cut out the felt to resemble toppings on a pizza. Cut a medium brown circle for the crust, a smaller red circle for the sauce, green heart shapes for the peppers, black ovals for the black olives, small pink circles for the pepperoni, yellow rectangles for the cheese, and brown peg shapes for the mushrooms.
3. Create recipe cards using index cards and markers. On each card, draw a picture of an ingredient and the number children should add to the pizza. For example, for one pizza crust, draw one brown circle and write "1 pizza crust" underneath. For eight peppers, draw eight green heart shapes and write "8 peppers" underneath. Make at least 9 to 10 different cards. Laminate for durability.
4. Ask each child to select a recipe card.
5. Encourage them to count out the number of each pizza topping they need. Explain that they can double check by matching their felt shapes to the drawn shapes on the card (one-to-one correspondence).

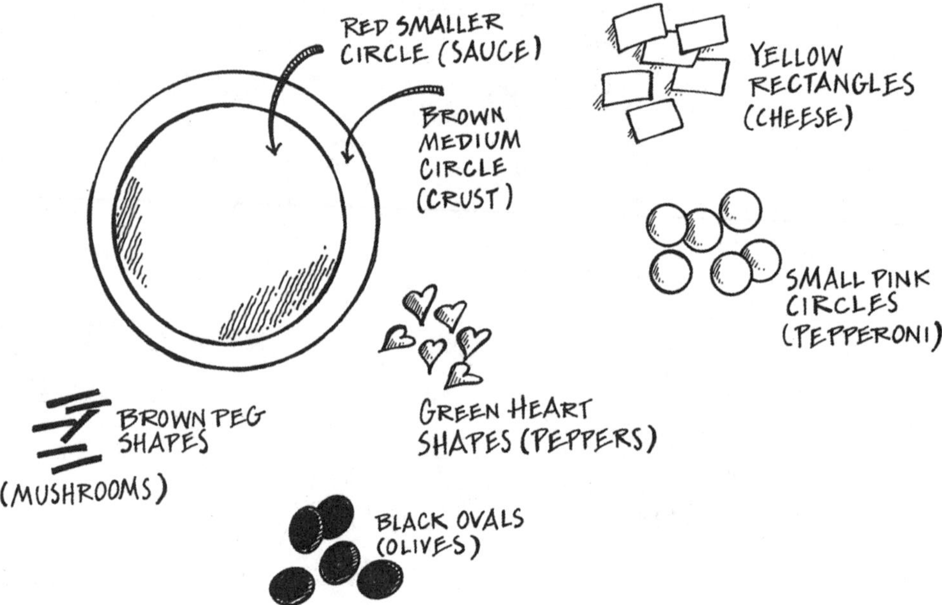

More to do

Art: Provide paper plates and markers. Let children use markers to create their own pizza drawing. Provide yellow yarn for them to glue on top.

Snack: Provide round crackers and pizza sauce. Let children add sauce on top of their crackers and top with different ingredients, including cheese, pepperoni, mushrooms, and so on.

Marzee Woodward, Murfreesboro, TN

Pretend Cooking

Materials

large non-breakable bowls
large spoons
small pitchers filled with water
measuring spoons and cups
various dry food substances such as salt, flour, sugar, cornmeal, oatmeal, cornstarch, and so on
chef hats and aprons (optional)

What to do

1. Set up materials as desired. This is a good indoor or outdoor experience. Let the children explore freely through mixing and measuring.
2. Guide the process by asking questions such as "how many?", "how much?", "what happens if…?" and "what is the difference between…?"
3. As pretend cooking dwindles, extend the exploration by having the children wash and dry the utensils.
4. Afterward, use the same materials to bake cookies.

Jean Lortz, Sequim, WA

Playdough Pumpkin Pies

Materials

1 cup flour
½ cup salt
1 cup water
1 tablespoon vegetable oil
1 teaspoon cream of tartar
saucepan
stove
heavy large spoon
orange food coloring
pumpkin pie spice
small pie plates
rolling pins

What to do

1. Add flour, salt, water, vegetable oil, and cream of tartar into the saucepan and mix over medium heat until it thickens. Children can help measure and add the ingredients, but an adult should do the stirring over heat.
2. Remove from heat and while still warm, mix in orange food coloring.
3. Add pumpkin pie spice.
4. Encourage the children to explore with the pumpkin playdough using pie pans and rolling pins.
5. The children will enjoy creating mini pumpkin pies.

Note: Remind the children that the dough is for playing, not eating.

6. This can be done with a variety of colors and scents.

Related books

It's Pumpkin Time! by Zoe Hall
Pumpkin Pumpkin by Jeanne Titherington

Sandy Scott, Vancouver, WA

Stoplight Snack

Materials

rectangle crackers
butter
plastic knives
pickle slices
pepperoni slices
cheddar cheese

What to do

1. Give each child a rectangle cracker. Let them spread butter on the crackers.
2. Give each child a pickle slice, a slice of pepperoni, and a slice of cheddar cheese. Encourage them to add the circular slices to look like a stoplight.
3. Talk with the children about traffic safety as they eat their delicious snack.

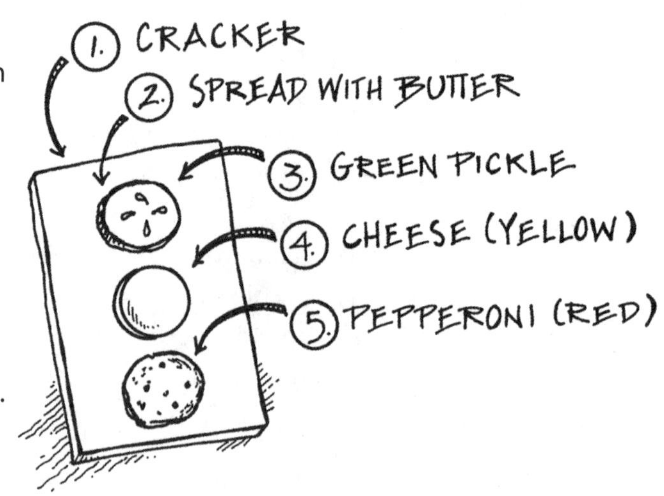

Related books *The Adventures of Taxi Dog* by Debra and Sal Barracca
Caboose Who Got Loose by Bill Peet
Go, Dog, Go! by P.D. Eastman
Things That Go by Anne Rockwell

Related songs "The Wheels on the Bus"
"The Ants Go Marching"

Sandy Scott, Vancouver, WA

Sweets for the Sweet

Materials

three small tables and four small chairs
cash register and pretend money
paper cups and plates
biscuit cutters
loaf pans, muffin cups, and muffin tins
playdough
rolling pins
serving trays
powdered sweetened drink mix
small pitchers
baker's hat or headband
hairnets
several small aprons
small clipboards and notepads
pencils

What to do

1. Take the children on a field trip to a local bakery or donut shop. Watch as the bakers make donuts and bake and decorate cakes. If possible, invite a local baker to visit the classroom and show the tools of the trade to the children.
2. Encourage the children to help set up a bakery in the classroom.
3. On one table, place tools for making baked goods (biscuit cutters, loaf pans, muffin cups, muffin tins, and rolling pins), serving trays, and playdough.
4. On another table place the cash register and pretend money.
5. Place one or two tables with two chairs each in another area to make a dining area.
6. Add hats, hairnets, and aprons to the dress-up clothes.
7. Show the children how to mix juice from the powdered drink mix.

8. Encourage the children to use the materials freely during center time. This activity offers many things for everyone to do. Two children can be bakers as they use the playdough and baking tools to make donuts, muffins, and cakes. One child can be the cashier, and two others can seat the customers and take orders using clipboards, notebooks, and pencils.
9. Supervise this activity closely so that the children do not reuse the paper cups. Make sure they throw away used cups in the trash can.
10. Occasionally put more powdered drink mix in the area. It is sure to go fast!

More to do Make real cupcakes with the children. Purchase cupcake mix or use a favorite recipe. Make sure the children do all the measuring and mixing of ingredients. Let children eat the cupcakes for snack, or they can sell them in their "bakery." Give the parents pretend money as they arrive to pick up children, and they can buy cupcakes from the bakery.

Related books
Arthur's Christmas Cookies by Lillian Hoban
A Cake for Herbie by Petra Mathers
Cherry Pies and Lullabies by Lynn Reiser
Cook-a-Doodle-Doo! by Susan Stevens Crummel and Janet Stevens
Pigs in the Pantry: Fun with Math and Cooking by Amy Axelrod
The Unbeatable Bread by Lyn Littlefield Hoopes

 *Virginia Jean Herrod, Columbia, SC*

The Edible Spaceship

Materials
2 egg whites
1 ¼ cups sugar
pinch of cream of tartar
cookie sheets
cake cones and sugar cones
ice cream, any flavor
marshmallows
honey
chocolate "silver dollars"
white frosting

What to do
1. Make meringues by whipping together egg whites, sugar, and cream of tartar until fluffy. Form one six-inch round disc for each child on cookie sheets.

2. Bake the meringues at 350° for 15 minutes. Give each child a disc. This is the "launch pad" for the "rocket."
3. Give each child one cake cone and one sugar ice cream cone. Let each child scoop one scoop of ice cream into the cake cone. This is the "fuel" for their spaceship.
4. Give each child two marshmallows to press into the ice cream, flat side up. These are the "rockets."
5. Show them how to make a base for their spaceships by putting honey on a chocolate disc and sticking it to the marshmallows. Put another drop of honey on top of the disc.
6. Ask the children to turn their creations upside down and place them chocolate side down on the meringue. Encourage them to gently press the cone down into the meringue so that it is steady, and then place the sugar cone upside down on top of the cake cone.
7. Children can use frosting to decorate the outside of their rockets.
8. Have a spaceship party and enjoy your spaceship snacks!

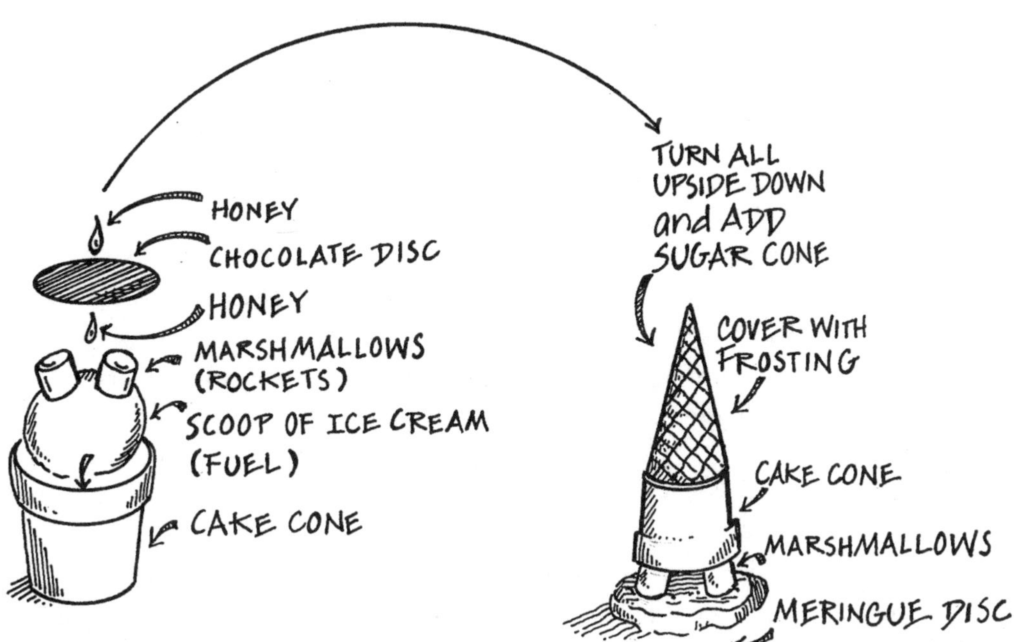

Barbara Cocores, Duarte, CA

Children's Central Bank

Materials

two refrigerator boxes
box cutter (adult only)
real paper money in denominations of $100, $50, $20, $10, $5, and $1
one dollar worth of each coin (4 quarters, 10 dimes, 20 nickels, 100 pennies)
two money drawers from old cash register, or make your own from two shoeboxes
photocopier
chart paper
markers
two small tables
dress-up clothes such as dresses, suits, and vests
two old large buttons with the pin removed
craft paper
markers
scissors
tape
yarn

What to do

1. Use a box cutter to cut a teller window in each refrigerator box (adult only). Cut a door in the back of each box. Make a "Teller" sign to put above each teller window.
2. At large group time, ask the children if they have ever been in a bank. Show the children real money, and let them touch and examine the bills. Talk about each type of denomination. Have the children help you count each type of coin. Ask the children what they think they could buy with that amount of money.
3. Tell the children that they will be playing "bank." Explain that they cannot use real money in their play, so they will use photocopies of the bills instead. Cut apart the photocopied bills and place them in the cash register drawers. Divide the coins between the two drawers.
4. Ask the children if they know the name of the bank their parents use. Help them think of a name for their bank. Write the name on a large piece of craft paper and post it in a prominent spot.
5. Place a small table inside each refrigerator box and place one cash drawer on each table. Put the dress-up clothes in an easily accessible area.
6. Using the buttons as a template, trace a circle on craft paper for each button. Print the bank's name on the circles. Cut out the circles and tape them to the buttons. Loop some yarn and tape it to the back of the buttons, making two necklaces. Tell the children that if they want to "work" in the bank, they must wear one of the bank necklaces. This will help control the flow of children in

the bank. The children wearing necklaces are tellers, and the rest are customers.

7. Put the two teller windows in an easily accessible area of the room. There should be plenty of room for the children to enter and exit the teller window from the rear and room for the customers to line up at each window.
8. The customers can approach the windows and withdraw money. Then they can use the money in other interest areas before returning to make a deposit.
9. If you notice a child making a lot of withdrawals and stockpiling money, suggest that he return to the bank to make a deposit. This will help keep the money flowing.
10. For added fun, distribute large denominations of play money to children and staff from other classrooms. Ask teachers to bring their children to your bank. The children can ask for change for their large bills, and make deposits or withdrawals.

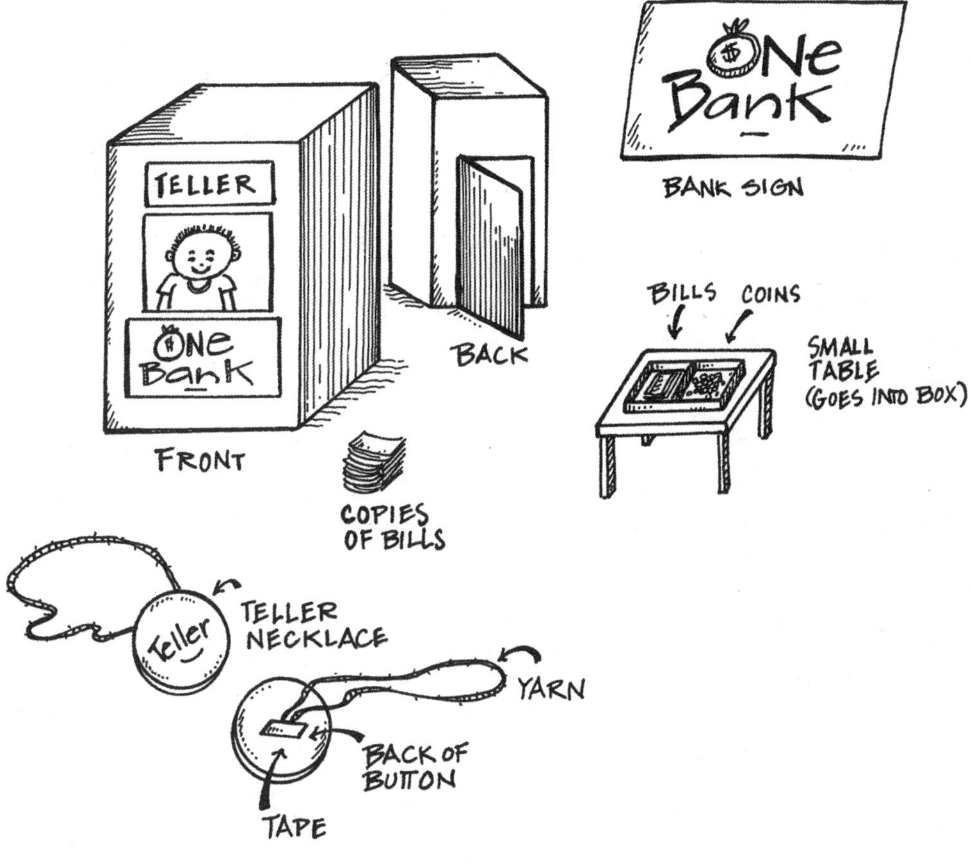

Related books *26 Letters and 99 Cents* by Tana Hoban
Arthur's Funny Money by Lillian Hoban
Bunny Money by Rosemary Wells
Four Dollars and Fifty Cents by Eric Kimmel
Max Makes a Million by Maira Kalman
My Rows and Piles of Coins by Tololwa M. Mollel

Related song **A-Banking We Will Go** by Virginia Jean Herrod
(tune: "The Farmer in the Dell")

A-banking we will go,
A-banking we will go,
Heigh-ho the derry-o,
A-banking we will go.

I have a hundred dollars,
I have a hundred dollars,
Heigh-ho the derry-o,
I have a hundred dollars.

I'll go make a deposit,
I'll go make a deposit,
Heigh-ho the derry-o,
I'll go make a deposit.
(Have fun and make up more verses.)

 *Virginia Jean Herrod, Columbia, SC*

Coin Sorting Center

Materials

pennies
nickels
dimes
quarters
clear, wide book tape
four bowls
file folders
markers
variety of coin sorting machines (these are great to borrow from parents)

What to do

1. Tape one of each coin to the bowls.
2. Make a variety of coin-counting folders. For example, write "pennies" on the outside of a folder and tape a penny under the word. On the inside of the folder, trace five pennies, write an equal sign, the numeral 5, and "nickel" after. Repeat this for ten pennies=10 (dime), and 25 pennies=25 (quarter). Make another folder for nickels, one for dimes, and one for quarters. Have enough coins for children to match to the traced circles.
3. Place the coins and the sorting materials on a table.

4. Introduce the materials to the children at small or large group time.
5. Encourage the children to sort the coins in a variety of ways, into the bowls or using the machines.
6. The coin-counting folders are best used in a small group of children who are ready to understand the more difficult concept of value. Or, they can simply be used with children who need practice counting, and the value aspect can be disregarded.

Related book *My Piggy Bank* by Thomas Lewis

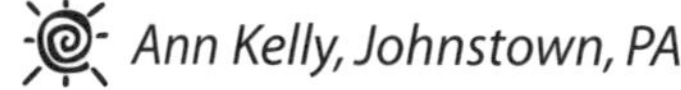

Drive-Up Banking

Materials

access to a large outdoor play area
tricycles, scooters, and wagons
two or three refrigerator boxes
box cutter (adult only)
tempera paint
two or three empty tissue boxes
masking tape
small heavy-duty sandwich bags
two or three pieces of black felt
fake paper money
colorful markers
3″ x 5″ heavy stock index cards (one for each child)

What to do

1. Ask the children if they have ever been in the car when their parents went to a drive-up ATM. Tell them that they will be making a drive-up ATM to play with on the playground.
2. Ask the children to help you paint the refrigerator boxes. Be creative! Details will be added later. Let the boxes thoroughly dry.
3. Away from the children, use a box cutter to cut a small slot in each box. This will be where the children insert their ATM cards. Also, cut a rectangle the size of the tissue box next to and a little bit below the card slot. Make sure to cut these areas so a child seated on a tricycle can reach them.
4. Tape a heavy-duty sandwich bag to each card slot so that when the children insert their ATM cards in the slots, the cards won't fall inside. Make sure to

tape the bags close enough to the boxes so the pretend ATM cards won't go all the way in. They should stick out a bit so the children can retrieve their ATM card without trouble.

5. Cut the tops off the tissue boxes and tape them to the inside of the boxes where you cut the rectangles. These will be the money drawers. Cover the openings with black felt.
6. Above the money drawers, draw a number pad using colorful markers. Make the number buttons oversized to make it easier for children to see and read.
7. Encourage the children to add finishing touches to the boxes.
8. Give each child a 3" x 5" heavy stock index card. Let them use the markers to create their own ATM cards. Help the children print their names on the cards. If desired, add each child's photo to his ATM card.
9. Set up the ATMs on the playground. Put fake money in the "money drawers."
10. Encourage the children to use tricycles, scooters, and wagons to "drive up" and use the ATM machines.

Tip: To make a more durable, longer-lasting ATM card, cover a wood-panel sample tile with paper and let each child create his ATM card on it. You can get wood panel sample tiles from your local home decorating store.

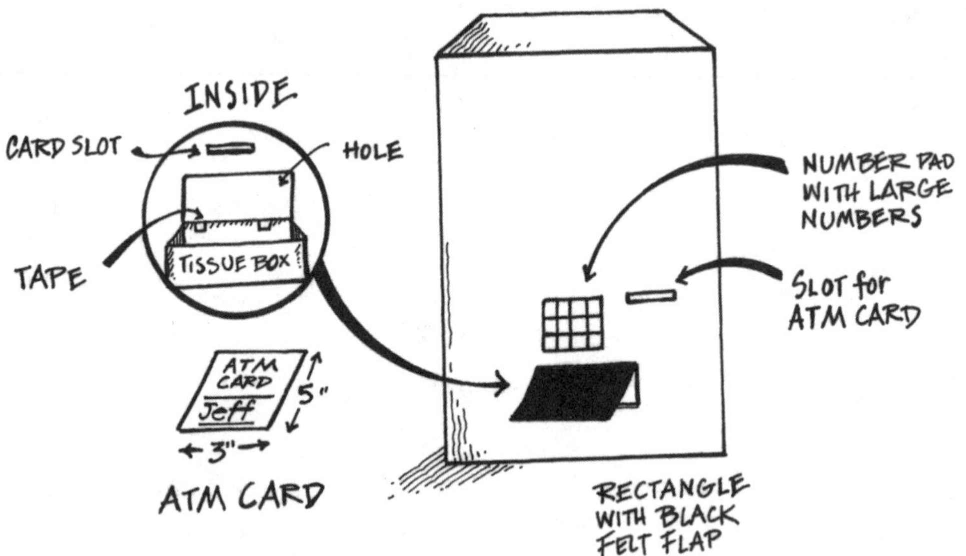

More to do Create a few "shops" around the playground. Make one that that sells dolls, for example, or one that sells toy trucks and cars. Simply set up some small tables with the items for sale on them and let some of the children pretend to be storekeepers. Encourage the children to go to the ATM, and then head to a store to spend their money. The storekeepers can go to the ATM to make a deposit!

Related song **We're Going to the Bank** by Virginia Jean Herrod
(tune:"The Farmer in the Dell")
We're going to the bank
We're going to the bank
Heigh-ho the money-o,
We're going to the bank.
We're going to get some money
We're going to get some money
Heigh-ho the money-o,
We're going to get some money.

 *Virginia Jean Herrod, Columbia, SC*

Egg Carton Money Match

Materials
egg carton
number stickers or blank labels
marker
assortment of coins

What to do

1. Label each section of an egg carton with a monetary value. You may want to begin with the face value of coins, and progressively make the amount more challenging.
2. Provide an assortment of coins and invite children to fill each section with the corresponding amount of money. To make the activity self-correcting, provide only the amount of money to fill the carton correctly. If all the coins aren't used or not enough coins are available, the child knows he needs to make a change.
3. Let children make their own cartons for friends to fill.

Related book *Alexander, Who Used to Be Rich Last Sunday* by Judith Viorst

Related song "Piggy Bank" by Greg and Steve, *We All Live Together, Vol. 3*

 *Shirley Salach, Northwood, NH*

Loan Officer

Materials

table and chairs
phone
message pad
appointment book
paper
pens
calculator

What to do

1. During circle time, discuss where people get money to buy houses and cars or other expensive things that they do not have cash for.
2. Talk briefly about loans (borrowing money) and add the word to your word wall if you have one in your classroom.
3. Ask the children to help you set up a station for a loan officer inside the dramatic play area that is already set up for bank play.
4. Encourage math/number talk and writing during children's play.

Ann Kelly, Johnstown, PA

Money Bingo

Materials

photocopied images of coins
scissors
glue
½ sheets oak tag or cardboard
markers
bingo markers (beans, teddy bear counters)
piggy bank or box
real coins

What to do

1. Provide children with various sheets of photocopied coins that they can cut out.
2. Depending on the age of the children, decide upon the number of "coins" to be glued onto each "bingo" board (9, 12, or 15). Mark the rows on oak tag or cardboard (three, four, or five). Give one to each child.

3. Encourage the children to glue the pictures of coins on their board in rows of three, four, or five. All of the boards must have the same number of coins and rows.
4. Gather the bingo boards and distribute one to each child. Encourage the children to take turns removing a real coin from a piggy bank or box and calling out that coin to the children. When a child's row or column is filled, the player can call out "BINGO!"
5. You may want to vary the game by having one child be the "banker" who selects and calls out the coins until a winner takes the position next.

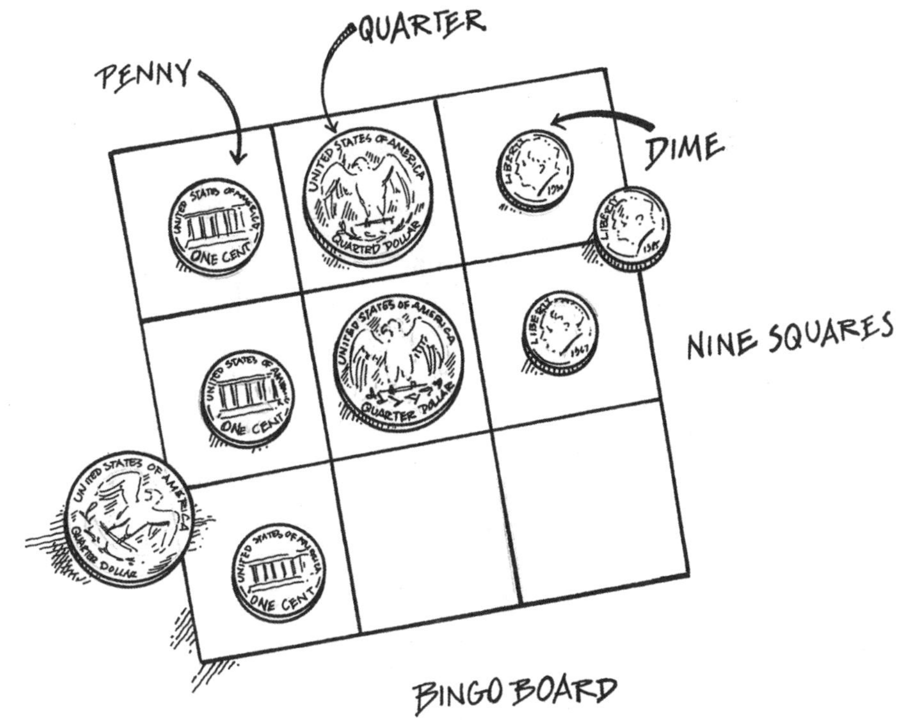

Related book *Alexander, Who Used to Be Rich Last Sunday* by Judith Viorst

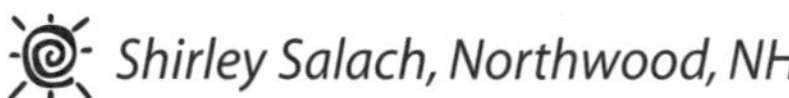
Shirley Salach, Northwood, NH

Pennies for a Popcorn Party

Materials

pennies
clear plastic jar
large piece of heavy white paper taped to a wall or table near the jar
crayon or other marking utensil

What to do

1. Put a clear, plastic jar in a prominent spot in the classroom. Explain to the children that when they arrive each day, they may put pennies into the jar in order to save for a classroom celebration activity.
2. Each time a child adds a penny, draw a line on a piece of paper. This helps them learn to count using one-to-one correspondence.
3. The children will observe the quantity increasing over time, both in the jar and on the paper.
4. At the end of the month, count the pennies (and the marks on the paper) together. Use the pennies to have a special popcorn party!

Milk Carton Piggy Banks

Materials

milk cartons
glue
tissue paper, construction paper, or wallpaper
other collage materials (optional)
knife or scissors (adult only)

What to do

1. Give each child a milk carton to decorate with glue and tissue paper, construction paper, or wallpaper. If desired, they also may glue a few collage materials on their cartons, such as buttons or pompoms.
2. When the children have finished decorating their cartons, make a slit on one top side of the carton (adult only). Make sure the slit is wide enough so that coins will slide through easily.
3. Children can use these as piggy banks. Demonstrate how to put coins into the slit and how to open the carton to empty the piggy bank.

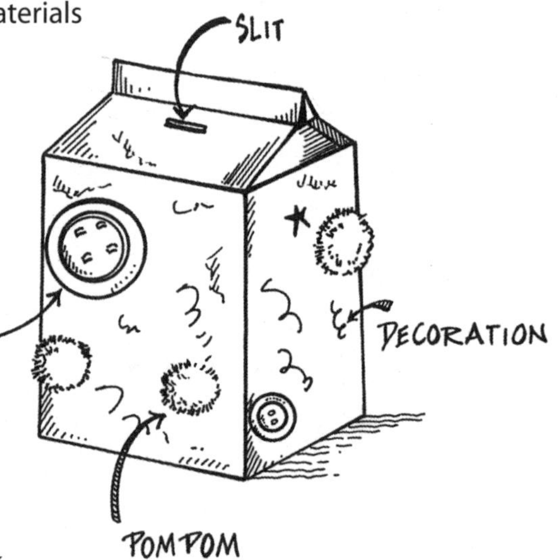

The Bank

Materials

play money
cash registers
calculators
office equipment (file folders, pads of paper, pens/pencils, telephone, and envelopes)

What to do

1. Set up the designated area to resemble an office or bank. Include books about money and coin collecting, and bank brochures.
2. Encourage the children to explore with the money and cash register.
3. Join the children and model how to properly use the money, cash register, and office equipment.
4. On a large piece of paper, write some bank-related vocabulary such as *money, deposit, teller, cash register*, and *withdraw*. Hang it in the bank center and use the words while playing in the bank.

Sue Myhre, Bremerton, WA

The Piggy Bank

Materials

cardboard box
white paper
glue
markers
knife (adult only)
real, plastic, or cardboard pennies
piggy bank that can be opened

What to do

1. Turn the cardboard box upside down. Cover it with white paper and decorate it to look like a bank. Cut a two-inch slit in the bottom of the box (adult only), big enough for the coins to slip through easily.
2. One child puts any number of pennies in the "bank" while the other children count how many the child put in. After everyone has predicted how many pennies are in the bank, lift the bank and count to see who has the right number.

3. Repeat so that each child gets at least one turn.
4. If the children are familiar with nickels, dimes, and quarters, use them as well.

Related book *One Gorilla* by Atsuko Morozumi

Barbara Saul, Eureka, CA

The Safe

Materials

boxes with lids
tape
markers
brads
small round pieces of cardboard
paper
pictures of safes
art supplies

What to do

1. Have a discussion about how banks keep money safe. If possible, visit a local bank with the children and ask to see the outside of the safe.
2. Provide materials from the list above and encourage the children to create their own safes to hold their money.
3. Talk about combinations and let each child designate one for his safe.
4. Write the combination down somewhere, such as on the bottom of the box, so that it is not forgotten.

Ann Kelly, Johnstown, PA

Work Station

Materials

paper
pencils
calculators
money
bank brochures

What to do

1. During large group time, discuss what children know about banks and what they want to know about banks. Visit a local bank, if possible.
2. Ask the children to help set up a work station like those in the center of banks. As a group or a few small groups, make a list of materials needed.
3. Make deposit slips. Leave a space for the child's name, account number, deposit amount, withdrawal amount, and total.
4. Assemble the materials and set up the work station for free play time.
5. Work with the children during their play to help them understand the purposes of the supplies. Extend their learning of math concepts through questioning and suggestions while they play.

Ann Kelly, Johnstown, PA

At the Barber Shop

Materials

plastic or fabric haircutter's cape (a wrap-around skirt with Velcro closures works great)
one small plastic comb for each child
one large chair
several small chairs
two or three small square tables
old magazines or comic books
cardboard or cardstock paper
markers
pretend cash register
pretend money
old (non-functioning) hair clippers
old posters and hairstyle books from barber shops

What to do

1. Rearrange the housekeeping center to create a barber shop. If possible, remove the stove and refrigerator from the center. If you can't remove them, turn them to the wall. You can use the backs to post photos of hairstyles.
2. Place the large chair in the middle of the room. If you have a large group, then set up two or three barber chairs.
3. Put the smaller chairs around the edge of the area to create a waiting area, and place small tables between the small chairs.
4. Put old magazines and hairstyle books on the tables.
5. Place the cash register and pretend money on a small table at the entrance to the barber shop.
6. Use cardboard or cardstock paper and markers to create a sign for your barber shop. Hang the sign over the entrance to the "barber shop."
7. Give each child her own small plastic comb. (It's a good idea to print each child's name on her comb.) Remind the children to take their own comb to the barber shop with them. Remind the children who are playing barber that if they comb a friend's hair, they must use their friend's comb.
8. Let the children pretend to wash and cut each other's hair. Encourage them to use all the materials available as they pretend to cut and trim.
9. Encourage the other children to make use of the "waiting area." They can read magazines or browse through old hairstyle books.

More to do

Books: Ask the children to describe a time when they got their hair cut. Let them draw a simple picture to illustrate this event. Print their story next to their picture and bind the pages together into a book. Create a cover with a catchy title, such as "Cutting Up!" Let the children take turns taking the book home to share with their families.

Related books *Erandi's Braids* by Antonio Hernandez Madrigan
Happy to Be Nappy by Bell Hooks
I Love My Hair! by Natasha Anastasia Tarpley
Mop Top by Don Freeman
Nappy Hair by Carolivia Herron
Sit Still! by Nancy Carlson
Stephanie's Ponytail by Robert Munsch
There's a Bird in Your Hair! by Harriet Lerner and Susan Goldhor
Tim to the Rescue by Edward Ardizzone

Virginia Jean Herrod, Columbia, SC

The Barber Shop

Materials

several empty paper towel or wrapping paper rolls
tape
red and white paint
paintbrushes
stuffed animals or dolls with smooth heads
scissors
hair dryers (plugs removed)
empty, clean shampoo bottles
razors without blades or shavers (plugs removed if using old electric shavers)
empty, clean shaving cream and after-shave bottles
magazines and chairs for waiting area

What to do

1. Tape empty paper towel or wrapping paper rolls together and paint red and white stripes on them to make a barber pole.
2. Talk about barbers and their equipment. With children's help, demonstrate and discuss the shave and haircut process.
3. Encourage children to visit the center and give doll or animal "clients" shaves and haircuts.
4. Follow up with discussion about the barber service they performed.

Margery Kranyik Fermino, Hyde Park, MA

Dolls' Day Out

Materials

several chairs
small desk or table
books and magazines
appointment book or calendar
keyboard
telephone
dolls with various types of hair
small combs and brushes
rollers, clips, and barrettes
tiered racks
baskets or trays
small pieces of tarp or thick plastic to use as drapes
hairdryers (with cords removed)
small and large unbreakable mirrors

What to do

1. Choose an area for a beauty salon. Decorate with posters, photos, or pictures of various types of hairstyles and old magazines and books from beauty salons.
2. Set up a reception area in front of the hairdressing area. Arrange several chairs and put out books and magazines. Place an appointment book or calendar, pencil, keyboard, and telephone on a small desk or table to make a reception desk.
3. Arrange chairs in the hairdressing area. Put out baskets or trays of small combs and brushes, rollers, and barrettes. Add haircutter's drapes, hair dryers (with cords removed), and small and large unbreakable mirrors. Choose a variety of dolls with different types of hair for children to play with.
4. If desired, fill tubs with water for children to shampoo and rinse dolls' hair.
5. Explain to the children about the area. The dolls "wait" in the reception area, the receptionist calls out names and makes appointments, and the hairdressers pick up the dolls and style their hair.
6. Children may also escort and wait for dolls in the waiting area as though they are the parents. If bringing in dolls from home, this will be more important to children and they may want to be hairdresser as well.

Hairstyles Galore

Materials magazine or catalog pictures of a variety of different hairstyles
playdough or modeling clay
small balls (Ping-Pong balls)

What to do

1. Put pictures of different hairstyles, playdough or modeling clay, and small balls in the barber shop/beauty salon learning center.
2. Gather a small group of four to six children in the barber shop/beauty salon.
3. Ask each child to select a picture and a small blob of playdough or modeling clay and a ball.
4. Ask the children to first describe the hairstyle, prompting for words such as *curly, wavy, straight, braided, long, short*, and so on. Color words are acceptable.
5. Encourage the children to mold the playdough onto the ball so that it looks like the hairstyle in the picture.
6. Ask the children to find something in the room that looks similar to the hairstyle (wavy, curly, etc.). For example, a toy snake may represent long hair and a ruler may represent straight hair.
7. After they have gathered matching items in the room, ask them to return to the learning center. Display the picture with its matching item and the playdough representation.
8. Have the children compare their own creations with others in the group.

Related books *Cornrows* by Camille Yarbrough
I Love My Hair! by Natasha Anastasia Tarplay
Wild, Wild Hair by Nikki Grimes

Kate Ross, Middlesex, VT

Manicure

Materials

small chairs and table
trays
cotton swabs
baby oil
plastic condiment cups
tissues

What to do

1. Talk about personal grooming with the children. Ask them if they know what a manicure is. Describe proper nail care.
2. Set up a manicure area. Arrange chairs around a table and put manicure materials on trays. Pour a small amount of baby oil into plastic condiment cups. Put one on each tray.
3. Make sure the children wash and dry their hands before working in the center.
4. Let children take turns being the "manicurist" and the customer.
5. The manicurist uses a cotton swab to apply oil to the cuticle of each of the customer's fingernails. Then she uses the swab to rub and buff the nails.
6. The child uses a tissue to remove excess oil from fingers before discarding it.

Mary Jo Shannon, Roanoke, VA

Tiny Trims

Materials

scissors
yarn or ½"-wide strips of paper
rubber or Styrofoam balls
bowls (strong enough and big enough to hold the ball)
tape
dustpan
paper and pencil

What to do

1. Cut strips of yarn or paper into equal length long enough to reach from the top of the ball to the table. Tape a row of "hair" (yarn or paper strips) across the top of each ball. Place each ball in a bowl to hold it steady, and place the bowl on a table.

2. Make a sign-up sheet by writing "Needs a turn to give hair a trim" at the top of a piece of paper. Place the paper and a pencil on the table and let children sign up to "cut hair." Call the children for a turn in the order that they sign up.
3. Show the children how much hair a person might get trimmed.
4. Let the children trim a short length of hair. Make sure they use the dustpan to clean up the hair they cut off before the next person comes to work.

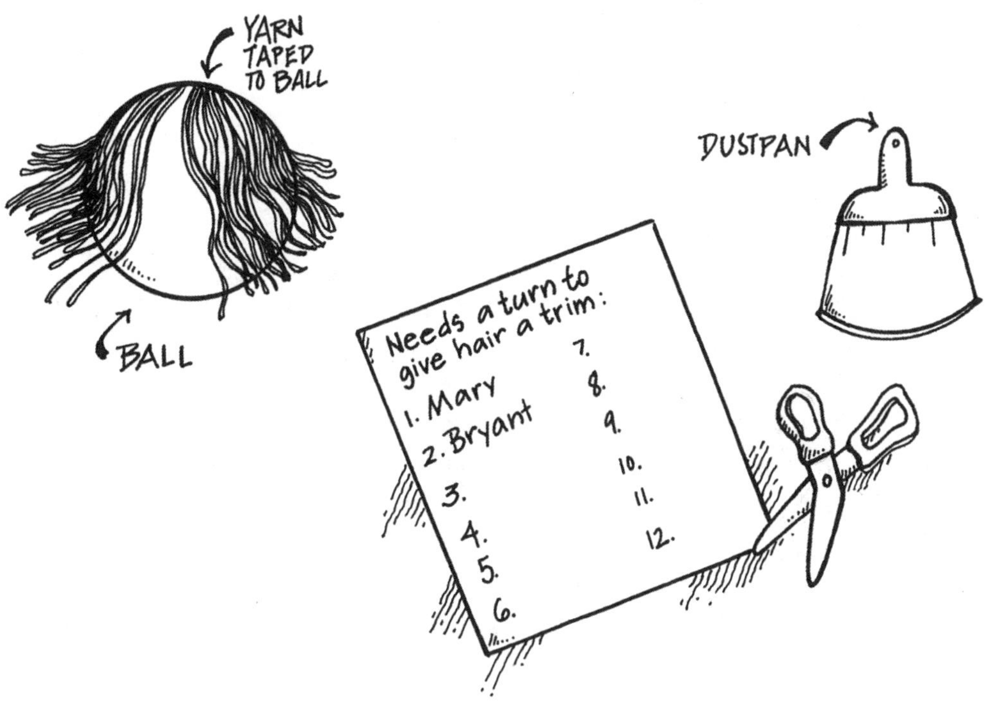

Related books *Getting a Haircut* by Melinda Beth Radabaugh
Saturday at the New You by Barbara Barber

Ann Kelly, Johnstown, PA

Beach Vacation

Materials

yellow and white craft paper
scissors
newspaper
dental floss or white string
medium-size wading pool
two or three low beach chairs
one child-size folding chair
life preservers
beach clothes (swimsuits, sunglasses, visors)
beach props (picnic basket, blanket, plastic plates, empty sunscreen bottles)
beach towels

What to do

1. Ask the children to help you make a sun and some fluffy white clouds out of craft paper. Make clouds extra puffy by stapling two cloud shapes together and stuffing with batting or newspaper.
2. Hang the sun and clouds from the ceiling with floss or string.
3. Put the wading pool underneath the sun. Make a sign that reads "Swimming Area" and place it by the pool.
4. Set up the folding chair next to the pool and label it with a sign that reads "Lifeguard."
5. Put beach chairs in the area along with beach toys, life preservers, beach clothes, props, towels, and so on. Make sure swimsuits are larger than the children's size so they may be worn over clothes. Let the children use all these props freely during center time.
6. Talk to the children as they play. Ask them to tell you about their own beach experiences. Ask them about times they have gone on picnics. Enjoy your beach vacation as long as you like!
7. If possible, ask a lifeguard to come visit your classroom to talk about beach safety. He or she can bring rescue equipment and explain its use.

More to do

Field Trip: Take a field trip to the beach, if you live near one, or to a local lake with a beach area.

Related books

Lottie's New Beach Towel by Petra Mathers
Nate the Great and the Boring Beach Bag by Marjorie Weinman Sharmat
Tar Beach by Faith Ringgold

 *Virginia Jean Herrod, Columbia, SC*

Beach Day

Materials

two wading pools or sensory tables
water
sand
stuffed animals or dolls
several beach towels
sunglasses
sand buckets
shovels
paintbrushes
shells

What to do

1. Bring the wading pools or sensory tables outdoors and fill one with water and one with sand.
2. Let the children pick an animal or doll to bring to the "beach."
3. Ask the children to help pack the beach supplies including towels and sunglasses. If desired, also pack a snack and water to drink.
4. Bury shells in the sand table for the children to discover. If desired, add water to the sand table so children can build sandcastles.
5. Children can paint on the sidewalk with the water.

Related book *Ocean Alphabet Book* by Jerry Pallotta

 *Sandy Scott, Vancouver, WA*

Beach Time

Materials

book about the beach
blue construction paper
shells
sand
pre-cut sunbathers
glue
fingerpaint
sheet

What to do

1. Read a book about the beach to the children.
2. Provide blue construction paper, shells, real sand, and pre-cut sunbathers for children to make a beach scene collage. The children can use fingerpaint to make the sea and the sky.
3. Play "Shells and Waves." Give each child a small shell. Write his initials on it with permanent marker. Place their shells in the middle of a sheet. Each child holds a corner of the sheet, and when you say, "Go," children shake the sheet, making "waves." The child whose shell stays on the sheet longest wins!

Lisa Chichester, Parkersburg, WV

Beach Weight

Materials

two-bucket scale
shells
pencils
journal

What to do

1. Place the materials in the beach area.
2. Encourage the children to manipulate the shells, the scale, and other items of their choice in the classroom.
3. Ask them to predict how many shells it will take to make the shell side of the bucket go down (weigh more). Let them choose items from the classroom to weigh against the shells and use in their predictions (blocks, books, stapler, etc.).
4. Assist the children in documenting their predictions and findings in the journal.

Ann Kelly, Johnstown, PA

Beach in a Bottle

Materials sand
water
Mason jars with lids (one per child)
small seashells
small shark teeth
hot glue gun (adult only)

What to do

1. Tell the children they will be making their own "beach in a bottle." These are similar to snow globes.
2. Children put about one inch of sand in the bottom of their jars.
3. Then they put in a few seashells and shark teeth.
4. Next, they fill the jar about $3/4$ full with water.
5. Use a hot glue gun (adult only) to place a bead of glue around the inside edge of the lid so that when the lid is screwed onto the jar, it touches the lip of the jar.
6. Let the glue dry and the water settle.

Related books *All You Need for a Beach* by Alice Schertle
At the Beach by Anne F. Rockwell
At the Beach by Eugene Booth
Beach Day by Mercer Mayer
Beach Day! By Patricia Lakin
Come Away From the Water, Shirley by John Burningham
Going to the Beach by Joe S. Kittinger
Grandma's Beach by Rosalind Beardshaw
Let's Go to the Beach by Mary Hill
On My Beach There Are Many Pebbles by Leo Lionni

Don't Be Crabby

Materials

seashells
glue
pens, markers, and paint
cardstock paper

1. Provide a variety of seashells for the children to explore.
2. Ask them to sort the shells in any manner they want. Encourage the children to discuss their groups.
3. Encourage children to glue shells on a piece of cardstock to make a design. Let them use pens, markers, and paint to decorate their design.

More to do

Large motor: Do the "crab" walk! Children lie down on their backs and use their arms and legs to walk sideways like a crab.

Related book

Is This a House for a Hermit Crab? by Megan McDonald

Barbara Saul Eureka, CA

Exploration Bottles

Materials

1-liter plastic soda bottles
water
food coloring
clear shampoo
small toys that fit in bottles such as fish and seashells
glitter or sand
marbles
baby oil
blue food coloring

What to do

1. Make an assortment of exploration bottles for children to explore.
2. Fill a bottle with clear, thick shampoo and add a few marbles. Seal the lid. Encourage children to turn the bottles over and watch the marbles slowly move through the shampoo. Ask why the marbles are moving so slowly.

3. Make an "ocean" bottle. Put glitter (or sand), water, and blue food coloring in a bottle. Add small plastic fish and small seashells. Children love to explore what's in the ocean.
4. Make a "wave" bottle. Fill a bottle halfway with baby oil, and add water to fill the bottle. Add blue food coloring. Ask children why they think the water and oil don't mix.

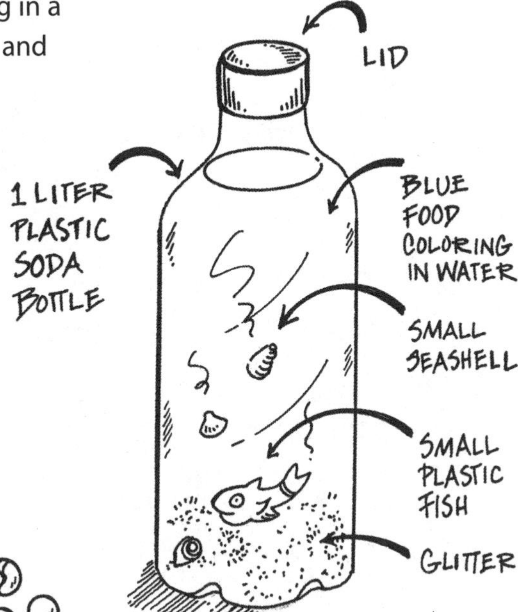

More to do Other ideas include color bottles (water with food coloring and objects that match the color, for example, green food coloring, a plastic green frog and turtle, tree, plastic grapes, and a plastic string bean) and letter bottles (fill a bottle with water and plastic letters).

Audrey Kanoff, Allentown, PA

Fish in the Sea

Materials

white construction paper
glue diluted with water
paintbrush
several fish shapes cut from white paper and neon-colored paper
blue tissue paper

What to do

1. Encourage children to color white fish cutouts and glue them to their paper. Provide neon-colored fish cutouts for them to add, too.
2. After the glue has dried, demonstrate how to glue several pieces of torn blue tissue paper on top of the fish.
3. Ask children to add a layer of glue on top of the tissue paper.
4. Allow to dry overnight and the fish will appear to be swimming in the blue ocean.

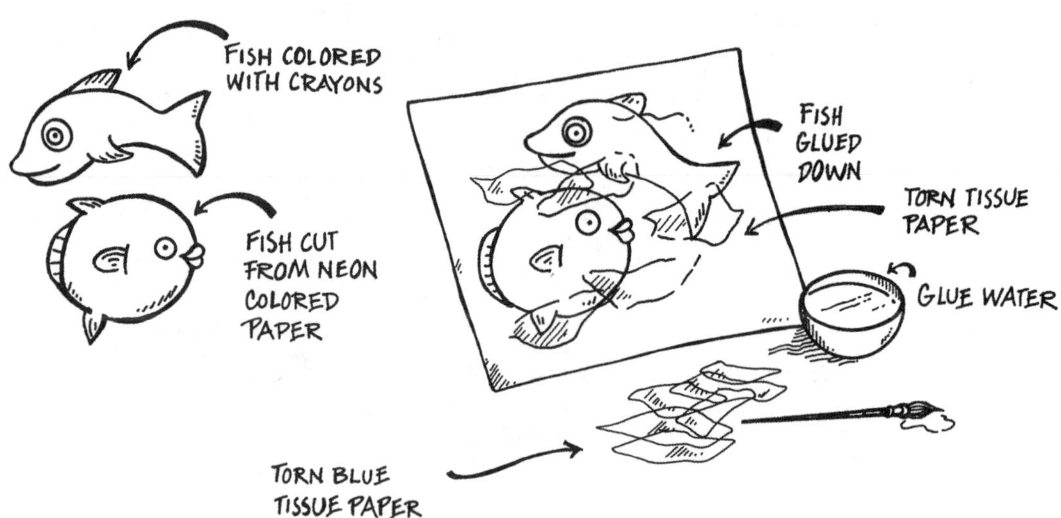

Related books *Fish Is Fish* by Leo Lionni
Fish Who Could Wish by John Bush
Ocean Alphabet Book by Jerry Pallotta
One Fish, Two Fish, Red Fish, Blue Fish by Dr. Seuss

Sandy Scott, Vancouver, WA

Beach Fun

Materials

beanbags
Frisbees
tumbling mat

What to do

1. In separate areas of the playground, set up beanbags, Frisbees, and a tumbling mat.
2. Divide the large group into smaller groups and send each to a different center. An adult should be at each center. Suggested activities are as follows.
   - **Large play area**: Play Follow the Leader.
   - **Beanbags**: Children put the beanbags on their feet, head, and backs of their hands. Let them take turns choosing which part of their bodies to balance the beanbags on.

- **Frisbees**: Children throw Frisbees to each other.
- **Tumbling mat**: Encourage children to practice somersaults and different modes of movement such as crawling and the crab walk. Let the children make up their own movements.

Related book *The Very Hungry Caterpillar* by Eric Carle

Barbara Saul, Eureka, CA

Neon Fish

Materials

black construction paper
scissors
bright neon colored paint
combs
white dot stickers for eyes

What to do

1. Cut out a basic fish shape from the black construction paper. Give one to each child.
2. Demonstrate how to paint the fish using combs.
3. Ask them to add a white dot to make the eye.
4. These make a great decoration for the classroom.

Related books

Fish Is Fish by Leo Lionni
Fish Who Could Wish by John Bush
One Fish, Two Fish, Red Fish, Blue Fish by Dr. Seuss
Swimmy by Leo Lionni

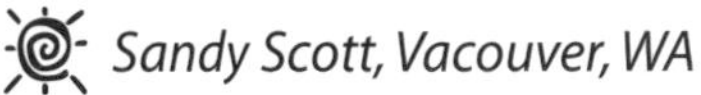
Sandy Scott, Vacouver, WA

Sand Search Bottles—Visual

Materials

plastic bottles, such as Gatorade bottles
sand
items that will fit in the bottles (straws, small plastic animals, marbles, rocks)
pictures of items and index cards (optional)

What to do

1. Put two to three items in each bottle and fill the bottle two-thirds with sand. If desired, choose items that relate to the weekly theme.
2. Encourage the children to tilt the bottles to discover the hidden treasures.
3. With older children, write on the bottle: "Can you find ____?" Glue pictures of the hidden items on index cards so children will know what to search for.

Related books

Brown Bear, Brown Bear, What Do You See? by Eric Carle
I Spy by Jean Marzollo and Walter Wick

Sandy L. Scott, Vancouver, WA

Sewing Beach Cards

Materials

scissors
poster board
yarn
hole punch

What to do

1. To prepare, cut out patterns of beach items (such as shells, fish, starfish, shovels, and so on) from poster board.
2. Use a hold punch to punch evenly spaced holes around the edge of each cutout. Attach a piece of yarn to one hole of each pattern.
3. Let children practice sewing on the cards of their choice.

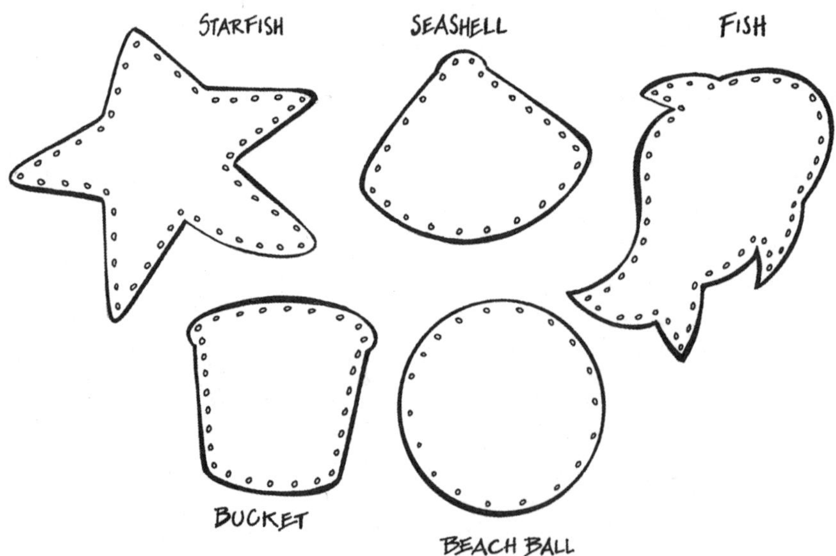

Vicki Whitehead, Satsuma, AL

Shell Games

Materials large pages from a book about shells or a placemat featuring shells
assorted shells
baskets
sentence strips
marker
laminate
box with lid

What to do

1. Look at the pictures of shells and match actual shells to them by placing them on the pictures.
2. Encourage the children to sort the shells into baskets by characteristics such as shape (pointed, round, flat), color (pink, purple, black, brown, gray, white), or pattern (solid, striped, or dotted).
3. Make counting strips by printing a numeral at the left side of each sentence strip. Make an appropriate number of marks along the strip (for example, if the number is three, make three marks). Cut off the strip at the end of the marks. Laminate. Let the children place shells on the marks and count.
4. Place distinctly different shells (scallop, mussel, oyster, and conch) into a box. Make a hole in the lid that is large enough to fit a hand through. Provide pictures of each shell that is in the box. Encourage the children to reach into the box, pick up a shell, feel it, and try to decide which shell it is by looking at the pictures. Then let them remove the shell to see if it matches the picture they chose.

Related books *At the Beach* by Anne Rockwell
The Ocean Alphabet Book by Jerry Pallotta
Rainbow Fish: Hidden Treasures by Gail Donovan
What Do You See Under the Sea? by Bobbie Kalman
The Undersea Search by Kate Needham

Sandra Gratias, Perkasie, PA

Sun Tag

Materials

two yellow soft foam discs or two pieces of yellow paper
sheet
two folding chairs

What to do

1. This game can be played outdoors or in a large play area inside.
2. Select two children to represent "sunrays." Give a yellow foam disc or piece of paper to both of them. (For larger groups, more sunrays can be used.)
3. Ask the other children to pretend to be enjoying a day at the "beach."
4. On the teacher's signal, the children move through the play area.
5. If a child is tagged by a "sunray," that child must remain still and say, "I'm melting." The child then acts as if he is melting.
6. Another child at the beach uses an imaginary hose to spray down the melting child to cool him off, and then escorts him to a shaded area for a drink of water, an application of sunscreen, and a pair of sunglasses and a hat. Then he can rejoin the play. To make a shaded area indoors, place two chairs side by side and spread a sheet over the top of the chairs. Outdoors, a designated tree can represent the shaded area.
7. If children are tagged a second time, the process is repeated. This is a great way to reinforce the need to reapply suntan lotion and drink plenty of fluids while outside.
8. This game may be played in rounds by designating approximately two minutes per round. Between each round, have children sit while new sunrays are selected. Make sure the children all know who the sunrays are.
9. Safety issues to consider:
   - Make sure all obstacles are removed from the area.
   - Check to see that all shoes are tied.
   - Have boundaries clearly marked.
   - If playing in a small space, emphasize the word "WALK" or other slow-moving pattern.
   - Emphasize to the "sunrays" to use GENTLE touches using foam or paper only in contact.

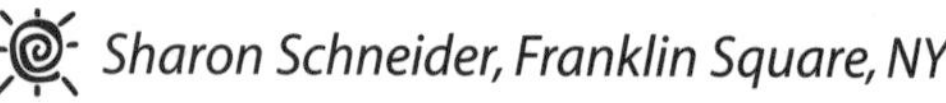
Sharon Schneider, Franklin Square, NY

Walking on the Beach

Materials

chart paper
flannel board
felt
scissors

What to do

1. Sing the following song to the tune of "Farmer in the Dell."

Walking on the Beach
Walking on the beach,
Walking on the beach,
When you're walking on the beach
You might find a shell.

2. Encourage the children to contribute other ideas for what they might find on the beach (for example, a crab, rock, or seaweed) and substitute these in the song.
3. Write the words to the song on chart paper and place it on flannel board.
4. Create flannel pieces of items children might find on the beach.
5. Encourage them to sing the song while playing with the flannel board.

Related books

At the Beach by Anne Rockwell
Beach Day by Karen Roosa

 *Kaethe Lewandowski, Centreville, VA*

Blockheads

Materials small Legos® or blocks that connect

What to do

1. Beforehand, make some models of varying degrees of difficulty out of Legos or connecting blocks and display them.
2. Let children choose a model and try to construct a replica with the remaining blocks.
3. Children can build their own model and let their friends try to replicate it.

Vicki Whitehead, Satsuma, AL

Blocks Galore!

Materials

blocks of various shapes and colors
baskets or bins in the same colors as the blocks
construction paper
markers
scissors

What to do

1. Draw each shape of block on construction paper, cut out, and use them as labels for each bin. Help the children sort blocks by shape and put them into the correct bin.
2. Encourage the children to sort the blocks by color and place them into different-colored buckets or bins that match the blocks.
3. Ask the children to count all of the blocks.
4. After all of the children have done these steps, gather them together to build a class fort out of blocks.
5. Take a photo of the children posing by their block fort creation and hang it in the classroom.

Lisa Chichester, Parkersburg, WV

Blueprint Books

Materials

blocks
construction paper the same color as the blocks
markers
scissors
stapler
glue

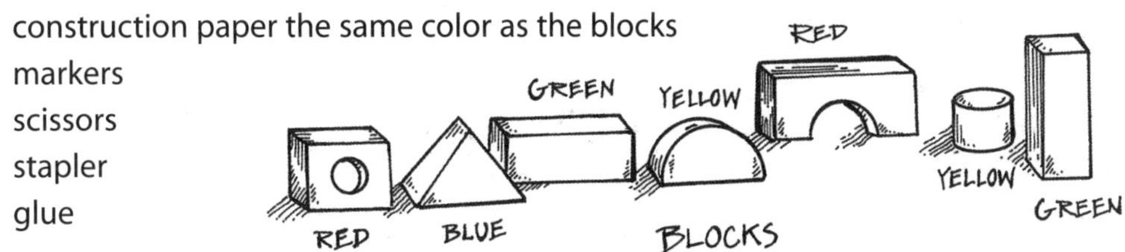

What to do

1. Trace the different shapes of the blocks onto matching construction paper. Cut them out. Make sure that there is plenty of each shape available.
2. Sit with a child in the block center and ask if you may make a "blueprint" of her block creation. Proceed if given permission.
3. Recreate the child's work by gluing cutouts of the blocks that match the first layer of the child's building on a piece of paper.
4. Repeat this process on a new piece of paper for the second layer of blocks. Continue with a new sheet of paper for each layer of the child's building. Number the pages as you go.
5. Let the child name her creation and make a cover for the blueprint book. Staple all the pages together.
6. If there are enough blocks, recreate the building using the blueprint book. Encourage the child or children to compare the buildings as they build the second one.
7. Leave the materials in the block area for the children to make their own blueprint books. (Some children may need more assistance than others.) Leave the blueprint books in the block area for other children to follow.

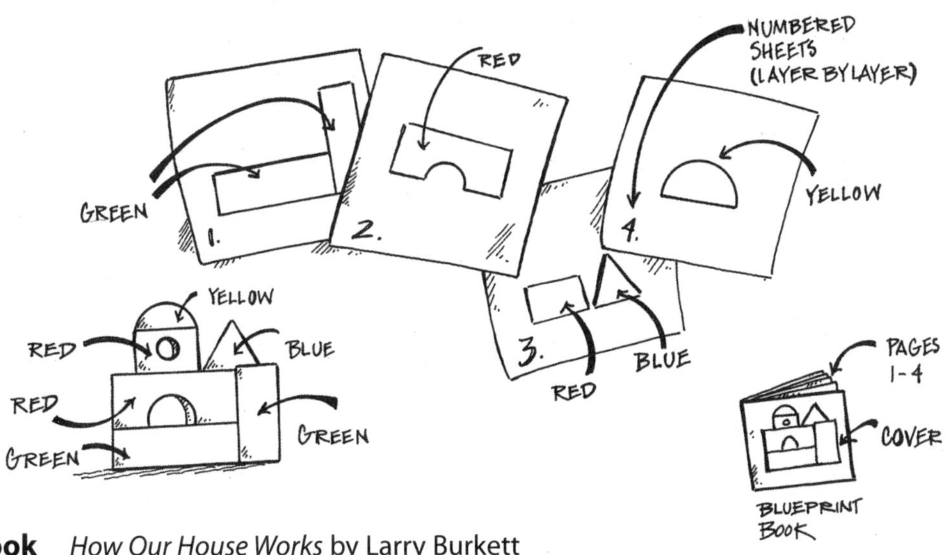

Related book *How Our House Works* by Larry Burkett

 *Ann Kelly, Johnstown, PA*

Food Pyramids With Blocks

Materials

wooden blocks
toy food or magazine pictures of food from all six food groups
picture or poster of the food pyramid

What to do

1. Using a picture of the food pyramid as a guide, ask the children to help you build a large food pyramid on the floor out of blocks. Lay the blocks flat against the floor (for a picture of the food pyramid, go to http://www.pueblo.gsa.gov/cic_text/food/food-pyramid/main.htm).
2. Gather toy food or pictures of food from all six food groups and place them next to the food pyramid.
3. Encourage the children to look at the food and decide where each food should be placed on the food pyramid. Talk about the different food groups and good nutrition.
4. Continue the discussion by asking the children what they like to buy at the grocery store and have them guess which food group the item belongs in.

More to do

Math: Encourage children to count the number of food items in each section of the food pyramid. Subtract or add food and count again.
Field Trip: Visit your local grocery store.

Related books

Gregory, the Terrible Eater by Mitchell Sharmat
Growing Vegetable Soup by Lois Ehlert

 *Deborah Roud and Diana Reed, New Wilmington, PA*

Hand-Made Blocks

Materials

sturdy shoeboxes
newspaper
masking tape or clear packing tape
stickers or markers (optional)

What to do

1. Show the children how to stuff shoeboxes with newspaper.
2. Help the children use masking or clear packing tape to tape the lids securely on the boxes.
3. Add these hand-made blocks to the block area. They are great for building walls and tall structures.
4. If desired, children may decorate the blocks with stickers or color them with markers.

More to do

Math: Use the new blocks to measure the children. Make a graph that shows how many blocks tall each child is.
More Math: Line up the blocks end-to-end and measure how long the line is. Stack the blocks as high and possible and count now many blocks there are.

Related book

Changes, Changes by Pat Hutchins

Virginia Jean Herrod, Columbia, SC

Making Shape Patterns

Materials

sentence strips
blocks in a variety of shapes
pens
glue
laminate or clear contact paper

What to do

1. To prepare, trace the different shapes of blocks on one half of each sentence strip to make a pattern, such as square/circle/square/circle and so on.
2. Color the outlines the same color as the real blocks and laminate them.
3. Place the shape patterns and shape blocks in a container in the block center. The children pick a pattern and replicate it by putting real blocks across the sentence strip.

Barbara Saul, Eureka, CA

Masterpieces in the Community and on the Road

Materials

reproductions of artwork depicting houses, roads, places in the community, and other places of interest
clear contact paper

What to do

1. Cut out reproductions of artwork from calendars, old books, and so on. Cover each picture with clear contact paper to preserve it.
2. Attach the pictures to a backdrop suitable to your space, for example, a wall, poster board, or back of a shelving unit. Place it in the block area.
3. Show the children the pictures and discuss the similarities and differences in the buildings, vehicles, clothing, and so on. Note the various artistic styles.
4. Use this discussion to introduce new vocabulary, such as "levels," "arch," "clapboard," "fire escape," and "skyscrapers."
5. Encourage the children to build a road or structure with blocks using the art reproductions as inspiration.

Our Town in the Block Area

Materials

blocks
camera and film or existing pictures of town
clear contact paper
toy cars

What to do

1. Take photos of various buildings, structures, or landmarks in your town. Examples include a hospital, grocery store, bank, post office, police station, statues, fountains, and so on. You may want to take (or obtain) photos of the children's houses and street name signs for them to practice addresses.
2. Use clear contact paper to attach photos on standard wooden building blocks. If you have old blocks that are no longer safe for play due to splintering, this is a great way to make use of them. You can use tape or glue, but contact paper protects photos best.

3. Encourage the children to use the blocks to construct roads and buildings. They can drive toy cars through town.

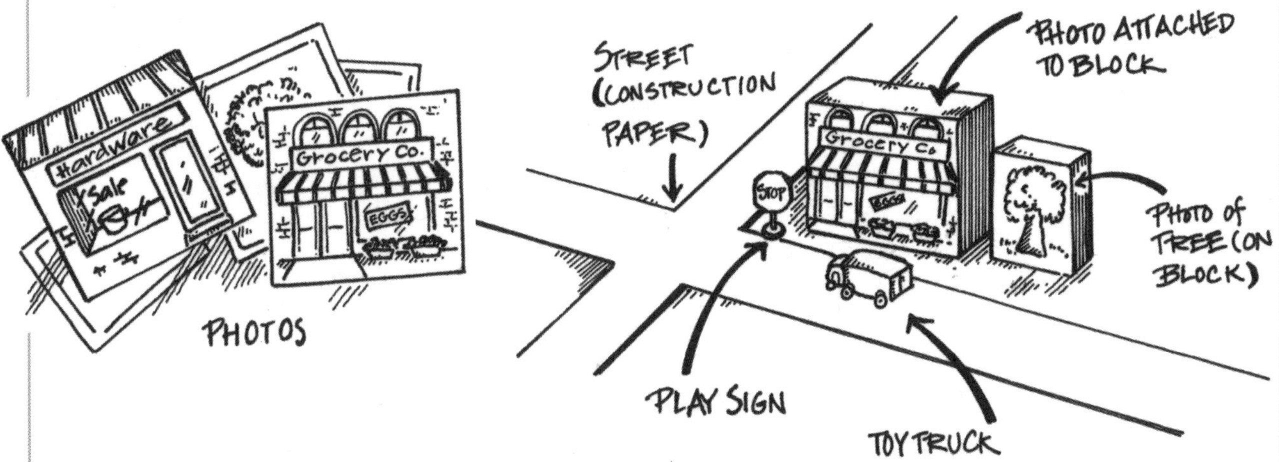

Related books *The Fire Station* by Robert Munsch
I Read Signs by Tana Hoban
I Read Symbols by Tana Hoban
The Little House by Virginia Lee Burton
Mommies at Work by Eve Merriman

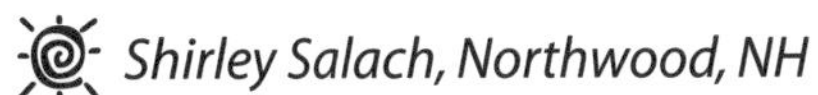
Shirley Salach, Northwood, NH

The Amazing Balancing Blocks

Materials

balance scale
assorted sizes of unit blocks
toys or household objects of various weights

What to do

1. Show the children the balance scale and explain how it works. Demonstrate how two objects of equal weight can be balanced if the balancing point is in the center. Also show how several small blocks can balance a large block with the point in the center, and then, show how a single small block can balance a large block if the balancing point is moved closer to the big block.
2. After several demonstrations (testing the children's suggestions), place the scale, blocks, and household objects in the block center for independent exploration.

More to do **Gross Motor:** Attach a length of yarn to the floor (or use a balance beam, if available) and encourage children to balance on the line and walk along from one end to the other. Challenge them to try different poses and styles of walking.

Related books *The Fabulous Flying Fandinis* by Ingrid Slyder
Harold's Circus by Crockett Johnson
Paddington Bear at the Circus by Michael Bond

Sandra Gratias, Perkasie, PA

A-Camping We Will Go!

Materials

large index cards
markers
laminate or clear contact paper
small tent or blanket to use as a tent
sleeping bags
play dishes and silverware
tablecloth
sticks
logs or empty paper towel and toilet paper rolls
newspaper
yellow, orange, and red tissue paper
pre-made books on tape about camping
tape recorder

What to do

1. Beforehand, make instruction cards by drawing symbols of activities on index cards (see steps below). Laminate them for durability.
2. Encourage the children to do a variety of camping activities by following the steps on the instruction cards.
3. Draw a tent on the first card, signaling that the children should put up a tent or drape blankets over a table. Assist them in putting up the tent. If using a tent, keep the zipper open.
4. Draw a sleeping bag on the second card. Children should put the sleeping bag neatly inside the tent.
5. Draw a picnic tablecloth on the third card, and help the children set up a picnic table with a tablecloth and dishes.
6. The fourth card is a campfire, so children may set up sticks or cardboard tubes and tissue paper to look like a campfire. Demonstrate how to crumple newspaper to look like rocks to make a fire ring around the campfire.
7. Draw a pot or pan on the fifth card. Children can pretend to cook dinner over the fire, and serve it to their friends.
8. On the last card, draw a tape recorder. Encourage children to choose a book and a tape from pre-recorded camping books, and listen to it while lying on the sleeping bag.

Related book *Just Me and My Dad* by Mercer Mayer

Vicki Whitehead, Satsuma, AL

Camp-In

Materials

several small pop-up tents
several sleeping bags
masking tape
four to six small fishing poles with no hooks
magnets
several small- to medium-size plastic fish
small twigs and branches
several small- to medium-size stones
red, yellow, and orange tissue paper (optional)
one or two camp skillets
camp dishes (optional)
disposable silverware
small pitchers of apple or white grape juice
healthy snack foods such as grapes, dried fruit, and pretzels

What to do

1. Remove most of the materials from your housekeeping area. Set up one or two tents with sleeping bags in the housekeeping, block, and reading areas.
2. Use masking tape to mark off a "river" in the block area.
3. Attach a small magnet to the end of each fishing line, and attach a small magnet to the mouth of each plastic fish.
4. Put the fish in the "river" and place one or two fishing poles by each tent.
5. Place snack foods in an easily accessible place by the housekeeping area.
6. Demonstrate how to use small stones to make a fire ring. Arrange small sticks in the ring to simulate a campfire. If desired, make a flame for the campfire using yellow, orange, and red tissue paper. Tuck the paper in and around the twigs in the campfire.
7. At large group time, explain the concept of camping to the children. Tell the children that campers catch fish and cook them over a campfire, sleep in sleeping bags in tents, swim in lakes and rivers, and explore the natural world around them.
8. Lead the children around the room and explore the camping area. Point out the "river" and fish and the "campfire."
9. Let the children help themselves to the juice and snacks, but remind them that they must eat while seated around the campfire. Watch this area to prevent children from eating too much, and to emphasize sharing.
10. Encourage the children to use the materials freely during center time. They will have a great time building with blocks and reading books inside a cozy tent! The children can catch fish in the river and use the camp skillet to cook their fish over the campfire. Sing songs around the campfire!

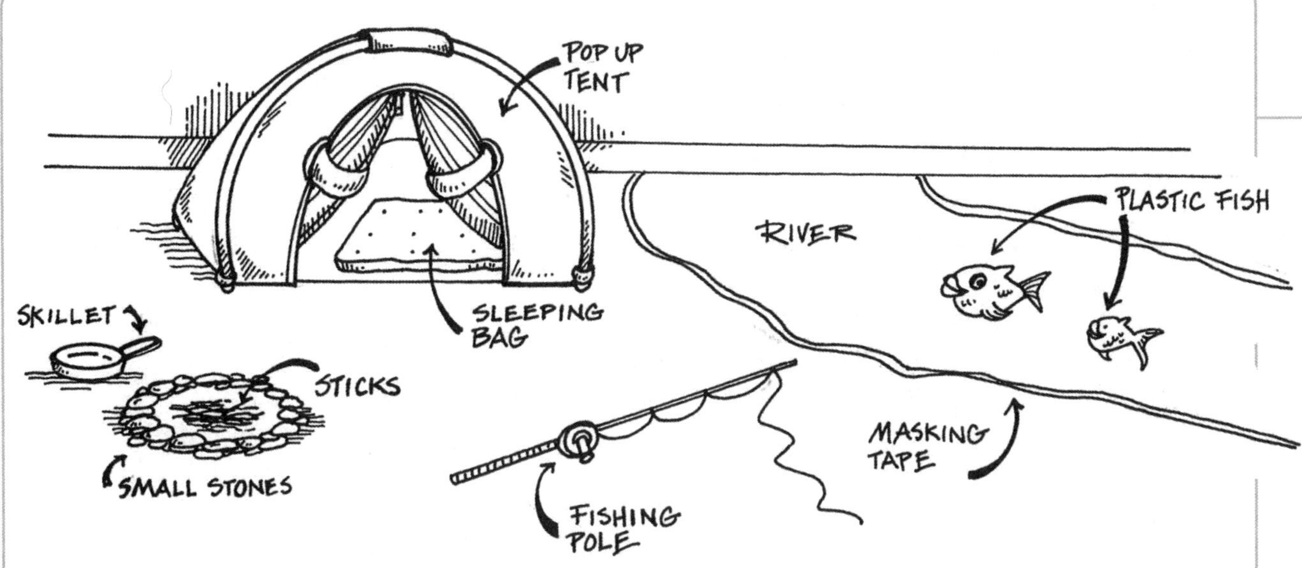

More to do **Literacy:** Enhance the fishing experience by affixing a letter of the alphabet, a color swatch, or a shape to the fish. As the children catch fish they can identify what they have caught.

Outdoors: Set up some tents outdoors on a nice day.

Related books *Amelia Bedelia Goes Camping* by Peggy Parish
Arthur's First Sleepover by Marc Brown
The Big Alfie Out of Doors Storybook by Shirley Hughes
Grandma's at the Lake by Emily Arnold McCully
Where the River Begins by Thomas Locker

Virginia Jean Herrod, Columbia, SC

Camping Fun!

Materials

children's camping books
pop-up tent
sleeping bag
folding camp chair
twigs, logs, and branches
camping gear
graham crackers
marshmallows
chocolate squares (one for each child)
EASY-BAKE Oven

What to do

1. Read a camping book to the children.
2. Help the children set up a pop-up tent complete with a sleeping bag and folding chair.
3. Make a campfire (without the fire!) using small twigs, logs, and branches.
4. Make s'mores for snack. Put a large marshmallow on a stick, toast it in an EASY-BAKE Oven, and place the marshmallow and a chocolate square between two graham crackers. Adults should closely supervise this step.
5. Have a class "camp-out party." Ask each child to bring in a sleeping bag (or a blanket if a sleeping bag is not available), a pillow, and a stuffed toy. The children can pretend to camp out during naptime.

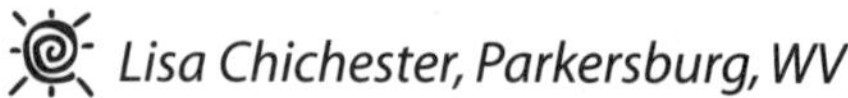

Sample Camping Center Letter

Materials none

What to do

1. Before setting up a camping center in your classroom, send home the following letter to parents:

Dear families,

The dramatic play area is one of the busiest learning centers in our classroom. We like to keep it this way by changing the themes periodically and transforming it into a new and exciting place for children to role play, discover new ideas, use their imaginations, use real-life tools of the trade, and continue practicing the everyday social skill of getting along with one another.

We are getting ready to change the dramatic play area into a camping theme and would like to invite you to help by donating any of the following items to help make this area a fun and exciting place for children. These items are things you may find in your closets or garages. It is a great way to get rid of a few things you no longer have a use for! Here are some items we could use:

- *child-size sleeping bag*
- *child-size tent*
- *camping utensils*
- *pretend lanterns*
- *clean frying pan*
- *toy camping stove*
- *metal coffee cans*
- *children's books about camping*
- *branches from trees*

- *flashlights*
- *picnic baskets*

Thank you all for your donations. We appreciate your help in making this new change to the dramatic play area happen. The children will love it!

Sue Myhre, Bremerton, WA

Fishing Hole

Materials

construction paper in a variety of colors
scissors
tape
paper clips
wooden stick or bamboo pole
string or twine
small horseshoe magnet
small plastic wading pool or blue blanket

What to do

1. Cut out a variety of fish shapes from construction paper. If desired, you can cut out pictures of real fish to use. Attach a paper clip on the back of each fish with tape.
2. Tie string or twine to one end of a stick and tie the other end of the string to a magnet to make a fishing pole. Make enough for the children to share.
3. Place the fish in an empty wading pool or on a blue blanket.
4. Let children take turns lowering the magnet on the fishing pole into the pool to "catch" fish.
5. Use this activity as a counting activity, or if using pictures of real fish, an identification activity.

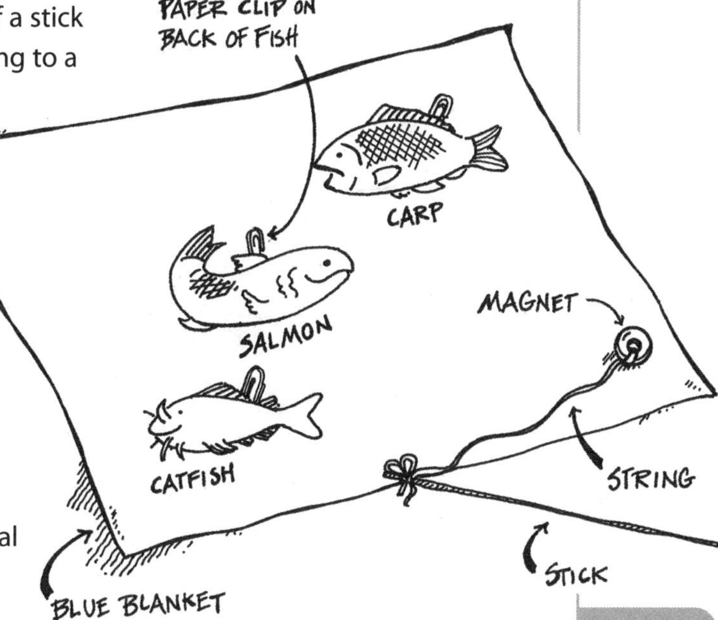

Kathleen Wallace, Columbia, MO

Nighttime Magic

Materials

camping tent and/or blanket
sleeping bag
large pillows
children's books about nighttime and nocturnal animals
three flashlights
shoebox
transparency sheets of various colors
stuffed nocturnal animals (optional)

What to do

1. Set up a tent. If the inside of the tent is not dark enough, place a blanket over the top. If a tent is not available, a blanket over the top of a table will work just as well.
2. Open the sleeping bag to cover the bottom of the tent. Add pillows to make a snug place. A quilt or blanket will work, but not as well.
3. Place three flashlights in a shoebox. Place the flashlights and nighttime books inside the tent.
4. Children enter the tent, zip up the opening, and enjoy their "nighttime retreat." It is important that only three children enter at one time. Any more than this will be too crowded.
5. At first the children will enjoy the novelty of playing with flashlights. After the novelty has worn off, cut out circles from colored transparencies to fit inside the lens of the flashlight to make different colors.
6. If desired, introduce stuffed nocturnal animals for dramatic play.

 *Susan R. Forbes, Daytona Beach, FL*

Star Viewing

Materials

empty paper towel rolls
black paper
scissors
tape
pencil

What to do

1. Give each child a piece of black paper and an empty paper towel roll.
2. Ask children to tape black paper over one open end of the paper towel tube.
3. Demonstrate how to use a pencil to poke holes in the black paper on the end of the paper towel roll.
4. Encourage the children to look into the other end of the roll as if using a telescope, while angling it toward a light. The children will see "stars!"

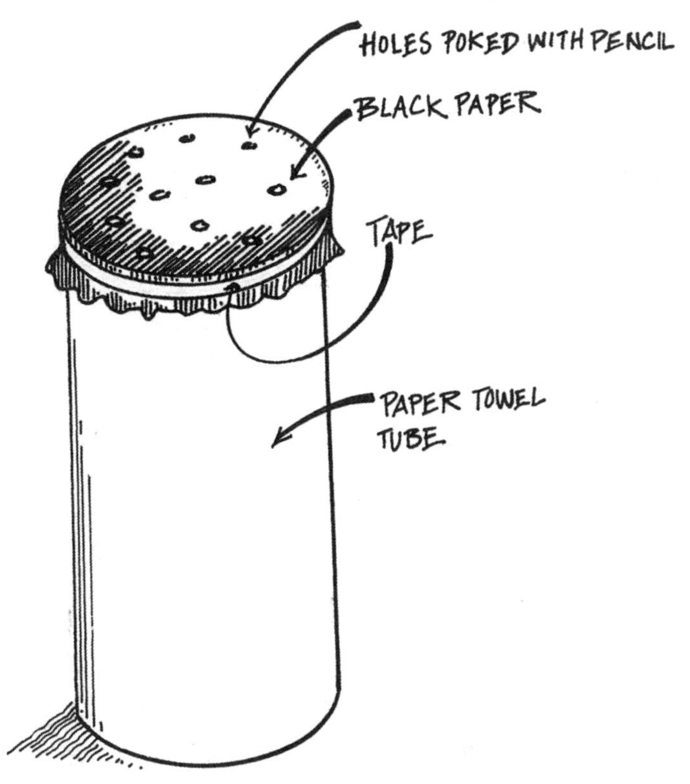

Liz Thomas, Hobart, IN

Stringing S'mores

Materials

corrugated cardboard
brown poster board
scissors
large cotton balls
white poster board
markers
glue
¼" dowel rods
red and yellow tissue paper

What to do

1. Make "graham crackers" by cutting corrugated cardboard into 2" x 2" squares and poking small holes through the center. Make "chocolate" by cutting dark brown poster board into 1" x 2" rectangles.

2. Using white poster board, draw a pattern of a s'more for children to copy. Draw a straight brown line to represent the toasting stick, and then glue a cotton ball (marshmallow), two brown corrugated cardboard squares (graham crackers), and one brown poster board square (chocolate piece) to the line in a pattern. Cut out each item, so that there is only one pattern on a piece.
3. Place the dowels (toasting sticks), "marshmallows," "graham crackers," "chocolate," and patterns in the dramatic play area. Add a fake fire (cut from red and yellow tissue paper) for toasting.

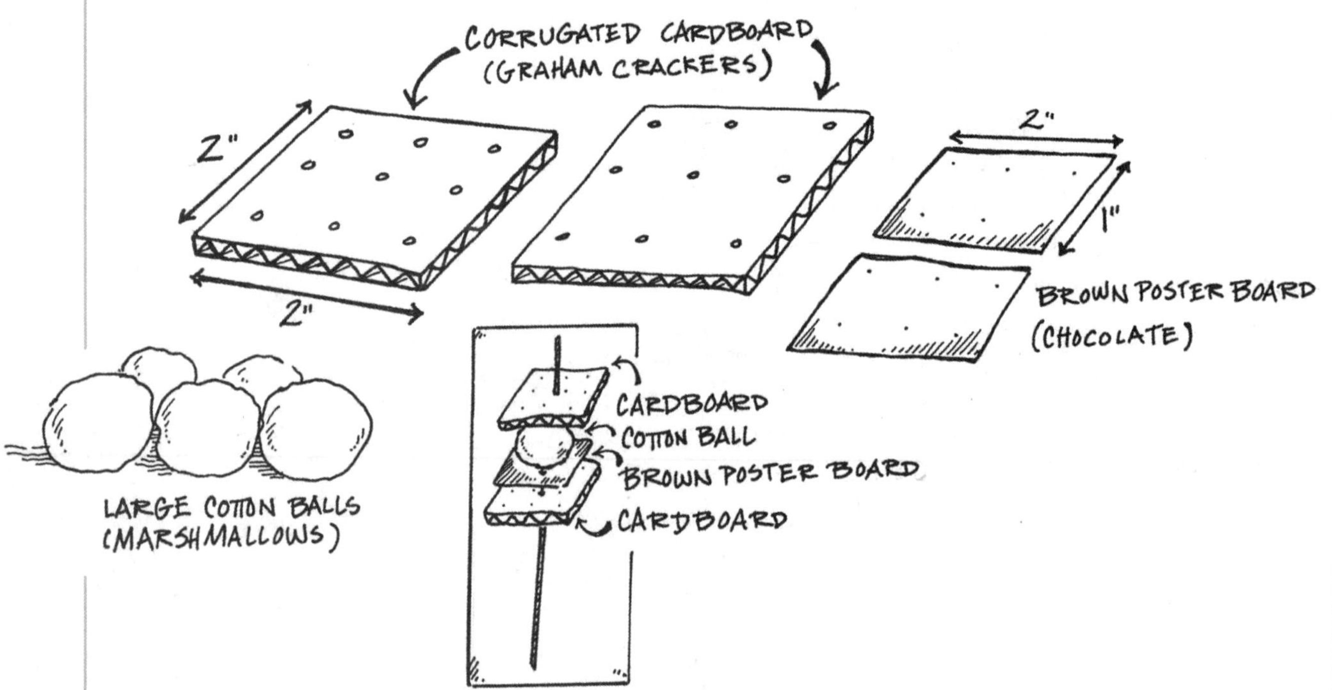

Related books *Bailey Goes Camping* by Kevin Henkes
The Kids Campfire Book by Jane Drake

Ann Kelly, Johnstown, PA

The Great Outdoors

Materials

tape recorder and tape of animal sounds (see #1 below)
pictures of animals (heard on tape)
large index cards or cardstock
laminate
backpack or pillowcase
lantern
nature items (pinecones, sticks, leaves, rocks, logs, feathers, nuts, and so on)
marshmallows
graham crackers
goldfish crackers
different "camping smell" items (marshmallows, peanut butter, cocoa powder, hickory chips, sunscreen or pine-scented air freshener)
cotton balls and film canisters
chart paper and marker
basket
zipper-closure bags

What to do

1. Make a tape of night sounds and find a picture of each animal making the sound (frog, cricket, owl, wolf, raccoon, and so on). Put one picture on each index card and laminate. Place the cards in a backpack along with an answer key (pictures in the order they are heard on the tape).
2. Play the tape of night sounds. Challenge the children to try to find the picture of what is making the sound. Ask them to place the cards in the order they hear the sounds. They can use the answer key to check their answers. This can be an individual activity if you give children headphones to wear while listening to the tape.
3. Fill a backpack or pillowcase with nature items typically seen on a camping trip. Ask the children to reach in and try to identify an item by feeling it.
4. Gather items with different "camping smells" and place on cotton balls (liquid items) or inside film canisters (solid items). Challenge the children to identify the different smells.
5. Draw a picture of each item on a piece of chart paper. When a child smells an item, he places the film canister or cotton ball on the picture.
6. Put nature items in a big basket and encourage the children to sort them into zipper-closure bags. Challenge them to guess how many items are in the bags when they are finished. They may then count the items in the bags, and order the bags from fewest items to most.

Vicki Whitehead, Satsuma, AL

Woodland Animals Bulletin Board

Materials

brown, black, and white construction paper
scissors
glue
photos of each child
pictures of woodland animals and their footprints
green leaves
green and brown bulletin board paper
stapler

What to do

1. Cut brown construction paper into pieces approximately 8″ x 16″. Fold each one in half.
2. Help each child trace his hand on white construction paper that is cut slightly smaller than the front of the folded brown construction paper (about 7″ square).
3. Glue each handprint to the front flap of the folded brown construction paper.
4. Open the flap and glue the picture and write the name of the child whose handprint is on the front inside. Repeat for each child.
5. Do the same steps with the pictures of animal footprints. Glue footprints to white construction paper, glue to the front of the folded brown paper, and glue a picture of the animal and its name inside.
6. Staple green bulletin board paper to the bulletin board. Cut brown paper into a trail and staple it onto the bulletin board, covering some of the green paper.
7. Cut out a large tree from the brown bulletin board paper and add it to the bulletin board. Attach green leaves at the top.

8. Staple a large black circle on the tree to make a hole. Add the handprints and animal footprints at the bottom of the bulletin board trail at the children's eye level. Add the words "Whose handprints are these?" Glue animal pictures to the background to make it more creative.

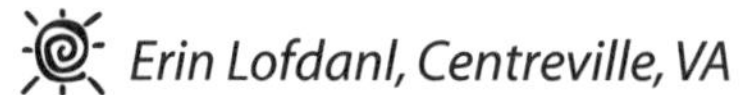
Erin Lofdanl, Centreville, VA

Castle

Materials

large cardboard boxes
wooden planks, about 3′ long
pictures and posters of castles
basket of books about castles
camera

What to do

1. Let the children's imagination run wild with this learning center! Encourage them to design their own castle, and build and rebuild it however they want using boxes and planks.
2. Hang castle pictures and put out books about castles in the area for inspiration.
3. Take photos of the children next to their finished product and display them on the wall in this area.

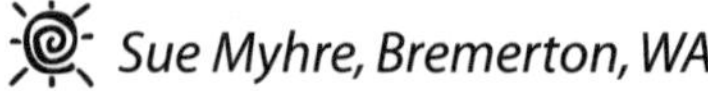

Sue Myhre, Bremerton, WA

Castle Mania

Materials

Magic Sand or Squand Sand (or very fine sand and silicone spray)
aquarium
squeeze bottles
water
plastic tableware

What to do

1. Magic Sand and Squand Sand is sand that when submerged in water, is easily sculpted. If you don't have access to it, make your own by spraying very fine sand with silicone spray.
2. Set up this learning center in an area that can be easily cleaned up.
3. Fill squeeze bottles ¾ of the way with the colored sand.
4. Fill the aquarium half full with water.
5. Encourage the children to create their own underwater castles by submersing the squeeze bottles in the water and squeezing the sand out to make colorful castles.
6. Children may want to use plastic tableware to sculpt the sand.
7. To clean up, place a coffee filter in a large funnel and pour the mixture through the funnel. The Magic Sand will remain in the coffee filter and can be reused.

Related books *Castle* by David MacAulay
Castles, Caves, and Honeycombs by Linda Ashman
Castles: Towers, Dungeons, Moats, and More by Matt White

Mike Krestar, Latrobe, PA

Creative Castle

Materials

several large packing boxes
paint and brushes
two refrigerator boxes
two large, round ice cream containers (bins used in ice cream shops)
masking tape
poster board
scissors
felt
sequins and glitter
glue
dowel rods
markers
cardstock paper
ropes (optional)

What to do

1. Turn your art area into a creative castle!
2. Create a "wall" around the area using large packing boxes. Let the children paint the wall, if desired (this takes a lot of paint).
3. Place the refrigerator boxes on each side of the front of the area. Tape a round ice cream container on top of each box.
4. Roll a piece of poster board into a cone shape and tape it to the top of the ice cream container. Do the same for the other side. You now have two very nice turrets for your castle entry.

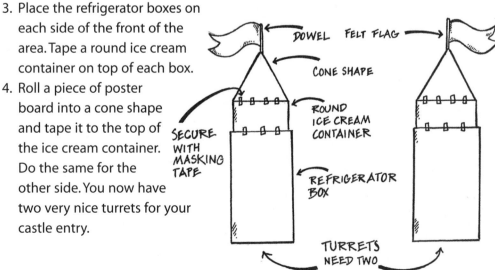

5. Cut two large pieces of felt into pennant shapes. Let the children decorate them as desired. Attach them to dowel rods and slide the dowel rods into the opening of each cone at the top of the turrets. These make great castle flags!
6. If desired, make a drawbridge for your entryway. Flatten a large box and draw boards on it with markers or paints. Tape one end of the box to the floor near the turrets. Attach two lengths of rope to the other end of the box. Poke a hole in each refrigerator box and thread the rope through. Tie a knot in the ends of the rope to keep it from coming back through the holes. The children can raise the drawbridge by pulling on the ropes.
7. Stock the art area with of felt, cardstock, sequins, buttons, and yarn. Encourage the children to use the materials to make castle flags, princess hats, and crowns. They

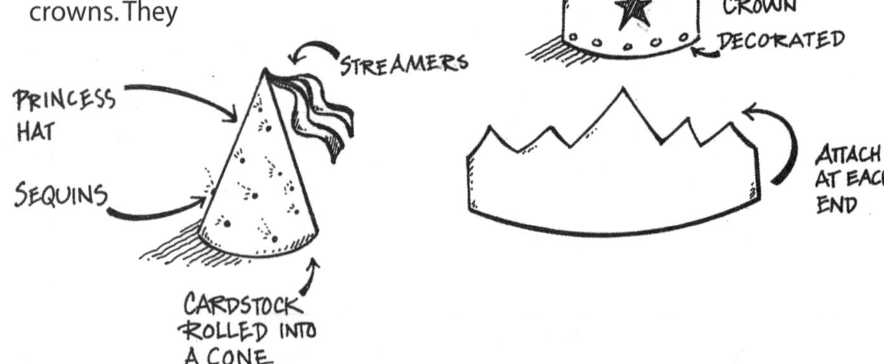

can draw pictures and paintings of castle life to hang on the castle walls.

8. Encourage the children to think of a name for their castle. Write the name on a large cardstock banner and hang it over the entryway.

More to do

Home-to-School Connection: Encourage children to create a coat of arms. Send home a shield-shaped piece of cardstock with each child. Ask the parents to work together as a family to create a family coat of arms. Explain that a coat of arms bears images that say something about the family, the family history, or the type of work the family members do. Ask parents to bring the coat of arms back when finished. Display them all together.

Related books

Castles, Caves, and Honeycombs by Linda Ashman
Lottie's Princess Dress by Doris Dorrie
The Paper Bag Princess by Robert Munsch

Virginia Jean Herrod, Columbia, SC

Once Upon a Time

Materials

purple and yellow construction paper
scissors
glue
tape or stapler
purple crepe paper strips
aluminum foil
white paper
crayons
green fingerpaint
red glitter
battery-operated lollipop spinners (parents may purchase and send in with child)
dowel rods
gold or silver paint
gold glitter
camera
books about princes, princesses, and castles

What to do

1. Make princess hats by rolling purple or yellow construction paper into cone shapes and gluing or stapling together. Add crepe paper strips to the tip.
2. Make prince crowns by cutting construction paper into a crown shape as shown. Cover with aluminum foil.

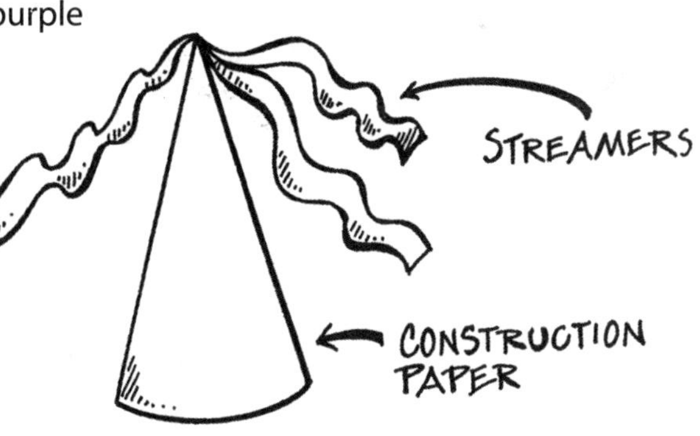

3. Make fire-breathing dragons with the children. Cut out dragons from white paper using the pattern below. Encourage the children to use fingerpaint to paint their dragons green. When dry, children glue their dragons to white paper. Show them how to draw fire coming from the dragon's mouth, and provide red glitter for them to add to it.

4. Let children make magic wands using battery-operated lollipop spinners. Remove the lollipop and replace it with a dowel of the same diameter. Make sure the dowels are at a safe length. Encourage the children to paint a paper star, sprinkle glitter on it, and glue it to the dowel.
5. Start a block castle in the block area. When children finish their wands, they can come to the block area and help finish building a class castle. Take pictures of the children next to the castle, wearing their crowns and holding their wands.
6. Close the day by reading a fairy tale complete with prince, princess, dragons, and castles.

Lisa Chichester, Parkersburg, WV

Out of Place at the Castle

Materials

books with pictures of castles
contemporary household items made of plastic, wood, stone, or clay (a clock, wooden spoon, toy airplane and car, and so on)
"medieval" items (such as pestle and mortar, stone paperweight, pretend sword, clay mug, sundial, cannonball, toy horse, and so on)
plastic bins or dollhouse and castle

What to do

1. Gather the children in a circle. Share the books about castles. Discuss the pictures showing specific items found in castles. Discuss the differences in functional items used during medieval times to household items used today. For example, people in medieval times used a mortar and pestle to grind food; modern people use food processors.
2. Place four pre-assembled items in the center of the circle. Choose three items that would be appropriate for use in medieval times (for example, a horse, ox, and cart) and one contemporary item (a car). Or, choose three contemporary items and one medieval item.
3. Ask the children to identify what doesn't belong in the group and why. Show the children enough sets of items so that they understand the objective.
4. Place the materials in a learning center for exploration. Children may sort the items into appropriate bins (put a picture of a contemporary house on one bin and a castle on the other) or in an actual dollhouse and castle.
5. If desired, change the groups of items on a daily basis. Discuss the children's findings at closing circle or as the children leave every day.

Related books *The Castle on Hester Street* by Linda Heller
Gray Rabbit's Odd One Out by Alan Baker

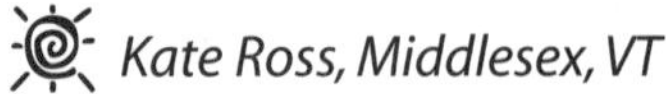
Kate Ross, Middlesex, VT

Picture This!

Materials

poster board
markers
scissors
oak tag
white glue
sand (in various colors, if possible)
pretend jewels
construction paper

What to do

1. Make a castle pattern on poster board and cut it out. Make several patterns for children to share.
2. Ask the children to draw an outline of a castle on oak tag using the castle pattern and cut it out.
3. Provide glue for children to spread all over one side of their castle outlines.
4. Encourage children to sprinkle various colors of sand all over their castle outlines. They may want to add pretend jewels, too.
5. When complete, set them aside to dry.
6. Encourage the children to use markers and scissors to make people cutouts for their castles.
7. Children can glue their castles and people to another piece of construction paper to give it support. If desired, they may want to make a frame out of construction paper to frame their work.
8. Hang them to display.

Related books *Castle* by David MacAulay
Castles, Caves, and Honeycombs by Linda Ashman
Castles: Towers, Dungeons, Moats, and More by Matt White

Mike Krestar, Latrobe, PA

Royal Costumes

Materials

books and pictures with royal characters depicted
cardboard
markers
scissors
fabric scraps, beads, ribbons, and yarn
glue, staplers, and tape
paint and brushes

What to do

1. Through books and pictures, give the children background information about people who lived in castles, including how they lived and dressed, and what they were called, (princess, duke, king, and so on).
2. Pre-cut cardboard into 2′ x 3′ pieces. Turn the cardboard sideways and cut out holes for a face and hands to stick through. Make one for each child.
3. Put the pre-cut cardboard and art materials in the art center.
4. Let the children put their face and hands through the cardboard and stand in front of a mirror. Talk to them about how they want their character to dress. Encourage their creativity by showing them pictures in books.
5. When children are finished, encourage them to use their royal costumes in dramatic play or to act out a story at group time.

Related books

DK Pocket's: Castles by Philip Wilkinson
Ms. Frizzle's Adventures: Medieval Castle by Joanna Cole

Ann Kelly, Johnstown, PA

Sandcastles

Materials

pictures and books about sandcastles
blocks
wet sand and sand toys
construction paper
thin glue in bowls
paintbrushes
dry, fine-grained sand

Castle

What to do

1. Read books about and show pictures of sandcastles. Discuss the children's experience with building sandcastles. Explore sandcastles in a variety of classroom centers!
2. Supply foam, wooden, or cardboard blocks in the block center for children to make castles.
3. Place wet sand and molds in a sandbox outdoors or sand table indoors. Encourage children to manipulate and explore the sand. Challenge them to build castles with the wet sand.
4. In the art center, demonstrate how to paint glue on paper, smooth it with the paintbrush, and sprinkle sand on top to make a castle.
5. Finish this theme by having a classroom "beach party" with beach balls and water play!

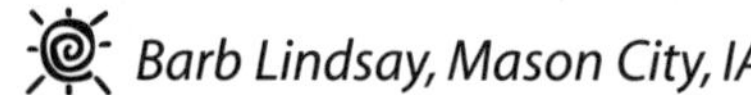
Barb Lindsay, Mason City, IA

Circus Train

Materials

construction paper
magazines
scissors
decorative-edging scissors
glue

What to do

1. Cut out a picture of an animal from a magazine that will fit onto a piece of 9" x 12" construction paper.
2. Turn the paper horizontally and glue the picture on the paper.
3. Cut out two small circles from black construction paper and glue one to the bottom left of the paper and one to the bottom right to make wheels.
4. Cut ½" to 1" strips of paper from any color of construction paper using decorative-edging scissors, and glue across the top and/or bottom edge of the paper (this will look somewhat like curtains).
5. Let each child make a "box car" and attach them together to make a circus train around the classroom.

Andrea Hungerford, Plainville, CT

Circus

Materials

small stage or platforms (a step bench used for fitness works great for this)
various costumes (clown clothes, ballet leotards, suit jackets, top hats, white gloves)
wigs and hairpieces
hula hoops
circus posters
tickets
play money and cash register
crepe paper streamers
balloons
extra chairs for audience

What to do

1. Welcome to the Big Top! Set up your room to look like a circus by hanging balloons and crepe paper streamers around the room. Encourage children to dress up and pretend to be different circus acts.
2. Set up a row of chairs and encourage the children to hand in their tickets to see the circus acts.

Sue Myhre, Bremerton, WA

Circus Play

Materials

beach umbrella or gazebo on poles
buckets with sand
circus story books
purchased animal face paper plates
hole punch
rhythm instruments
tape or CD with marching music
hula hoops
masking or duct tape
assorted large embroidery hoops
parasol or child-size umbrella
large soft material or beach balls or pompoms
beanbags
softballs

What to do

1. Set up poles for a gazebo or a beach umbrella in buckets with sand or in the ground if outdoors.
2. Select animal paper plates that represent circus animals (elephant, tiger, lion, seal, horse, and bear). Punch a hole into each side of the paper plate and attach yarn or string to make a "necklace" to go around a child's neck.
3. After reading a story and having a discussion about a circus, introduce the circus props and encourage children to have a circus.
4. Invite the children to select animal necklaces and rhythm instruments and have a circus parade. Play marching music and encourage children to march around the room or outdoor play area.
5. Encourage children to pretend to be different circus animals. Another child can be an "animal trainer" who has the "animals" do tricks, such as moving on all fours, standing, rolling over, hopping, dancing, trotting, and jumping through a hoop.

6. Place a strip of duct or masking tape on the floor for "tightrope walkers" to balance on as they walk with a parasol or umbrella. Challenge them to walk forward, backward, and sideways.
7. Invite the children to "juggle" large embroidery hoops, twirling them around their wrists, ankles, or hands.
8. Challenge the children to try to balance beanbags by placing beanbags on various body parts while twirling, gliding, and galloping. "Seals" can balance softballs on their noses.
9. Follow up with a group discussion about favorite circus acts.

Margery Kranyik Fermino, Hyde Park, MA

Circus Fun!

Materials

construction paper
scissors
markers and paint
yarn
white paper lunch bag for each child
red crayons
unpopped popcorn and popcorn popper
oak tag
bright-colored streamers and balloons
plate for each child

What to do

1. Make hats and masks using the patterns below. Trace the patterns onto construction paper and cut out. Color or paint details, cut out eye holes, and attach yarn to go around a child's head.
2. Show children how to make popcorn bags by coloring red stripes on white lunch bags.
3. Help the children pop popcorn and put some in each bag.
4. Cut oak tag into ticket-size pieces. Make circus tickets that read, "Admit One to the Circus!"
5. Help the children hang streamers and balloons. Invite parents in for "circus day."
6. Children can play different roles, such as lions, tigers, acrobats, tightrope walkers, ringmasters, and so on.

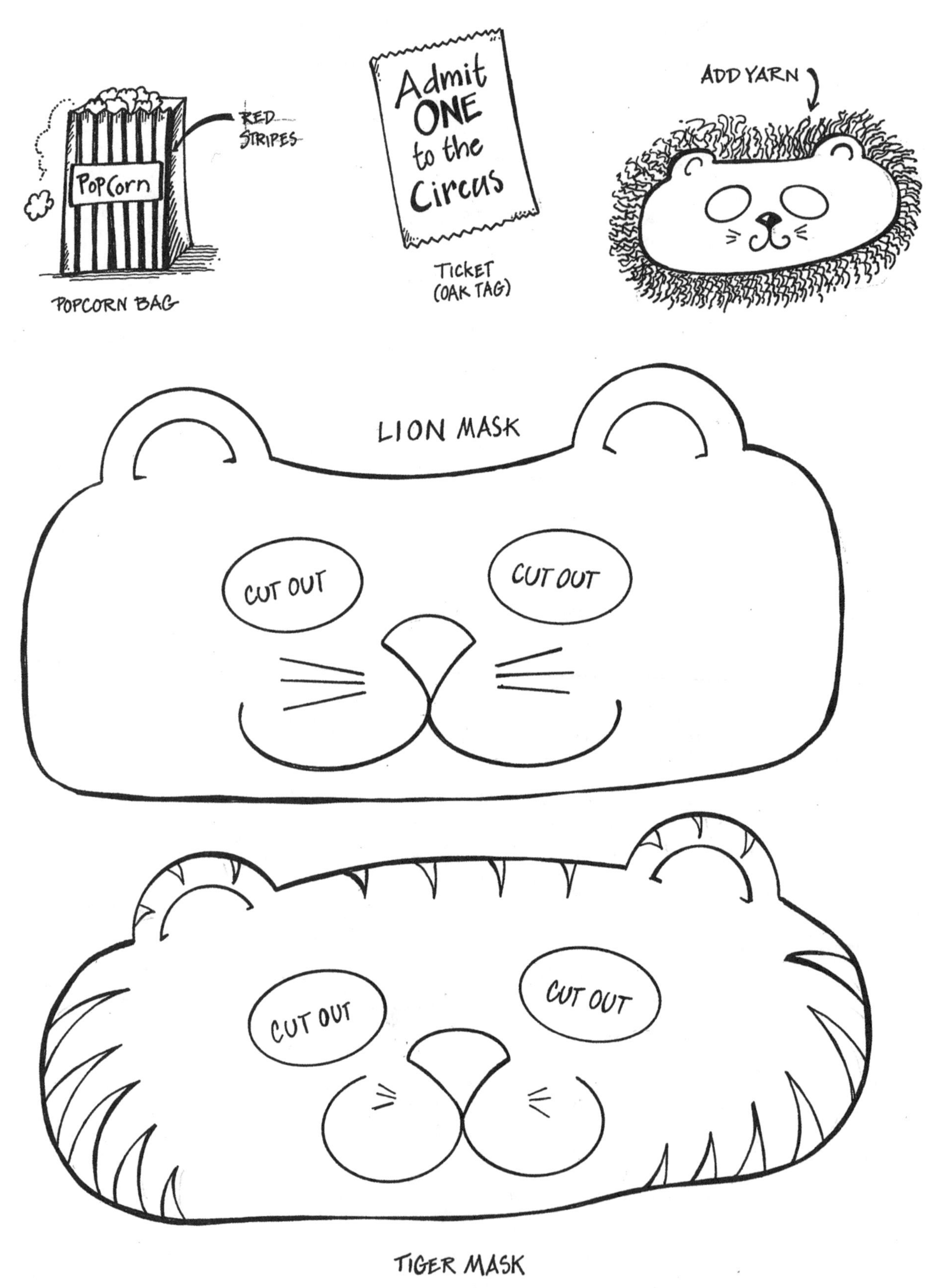

Lisa Chichester, Parkersburg, WV

Clown Face and Silly Day

Materials

paper plates
scissors
large pompoms for the tip of the hat
glue
bright-colored construction paper
foam piece shapes for the eyes and nose
colorful yarn

What to do

1. Give each child a paper plate for to make a clown face mask.
2. Cut out triangle "hats" from bright colored construction paper. Children glue the triangle hats to their plates and attach a pompom to the tip.
3. Encourage children to glue foam shape pieces to their plates to make eyes and a nose.
4. Help children cut out construction paper "smiles." Children can glue on smiles and add yarn hair to complete their clown faces.
5. Encourage them to name their clown faces.
6. This is a great day for the class to dress silly. Encourage them to wear an interesting combination of clothes, wear their clothes backwards, or put on a funny hat.

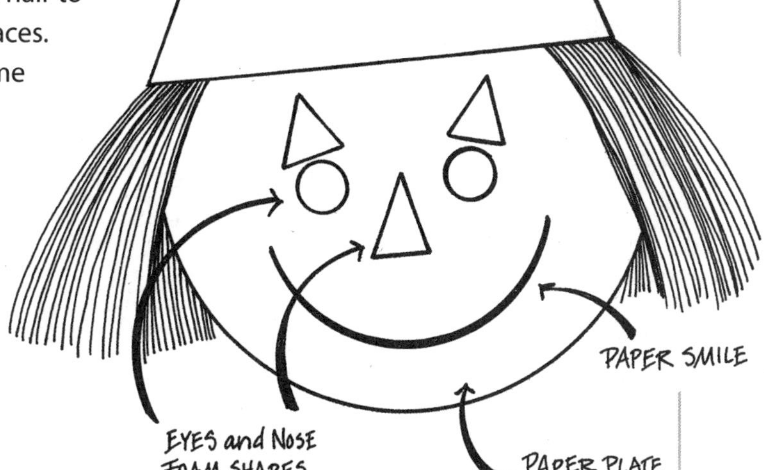

Related books

Circus by Lois Ehlert
Mirette on the High Wire by Emily McCully
Paddington Bear at the Circus by Michael Bond

 *Sandy Scott, Vancouver, WA*

Clown Faces

Materials

face paint
brushes
pictures of clown faces
mirrors

What to do

1. During a circus theme, set up a face-painting station in the art area. Provide face paint, brushes, mirrors, and clown pictures (for inspiration).
2. Make sure an adult (volunteer) supervises this area. He or she does not need to do all the painting, but can ensure that the children are being safe as they paint the faces of their friends.

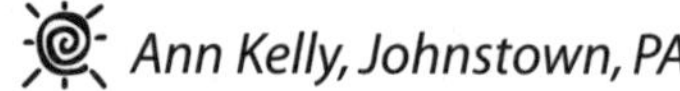

Ann Kelly, Johnstown, PA

Clowning Around an Obstacle Course

Materials

gross motor equipment
chalk or masking tape
tape
paper and markers
red sponge or paper
scissors

What to do

1. Place the gross motor equipment around the room or playground to form an obstacle course that the children will have to follow.
2. Draw a trail using chalk or masking tape to connect the equipment, indicating the path to take.
3. Label the equipment with circus names. For example, a balance beam could be a "tightrope," hula hoops could be "lion-taming rings," a swing could be a "trapeze," and balls and beanbags can be the "juggling area."
4. Cut out red clown noses from a red sponge or paper. Place the clown noses at the beginning of the course and encourage each child to wear one (attached using tape) as they traverse the course.

Related books *Harold's Circus* by Crockett Johnson
Olivia Saves the Circus by Ian Falconer

Ann Kelly, Johnstown, PA

Cotton Candy Fun

Materials
white tempera paint
paintbrushes
empty paper towel rolls
fluffy pink pompoms
craft glue

What to do

1. Ask the children to paint the paper towel rolls white and set aside to dry.
2. Glue fluffy pink pompoms into a big ball and allow to dry.
3. Let children glue the big ball of fluffy pink pompoms onto the painted paper towel roll.
4. When dry, it will look like freshly made cotton candy from the circus (minus the calories and sugar!).

Related books *Circus Fun* by Margaret Hillert
The Circus Surprise by Ralph Fletcher
If I Ran The Circus by Dr. Seuss
Sara Joins The Circus by Thera S. Callahan

Mike Krestar, Latrobe, PA

Just Clowning Around

Materials

clown clothes (baggy pants, suspenders, brightly colored oversized shirts and suit jackets, hats, large gloves, big funny shoes, and so on)
hoops
stuffed animals
full-length mirror
batons
balance beam
tumbling mats
colorful streamers
clown makeup (see recipe below)
circus music
camera

What to do

1. Invite a clown to visit the classroom. Ask him or her to come dressed but without makeup. Ask the clown to apply makeup in front of the children, and talk with the children about what it means to be a clown.
2. Put the clown clothes, hoops, stuffed animals, and a full-length mirror in the housekeeping area, and the batons, balance beam, and tumbling mats in the block area.
3. Decorate the room with colorful streamers.
4. Let the children experiment freely with the materials during center time.
5. If the children wish to wear clown makeup, and if you have parents' permission, use the recipe below to make clown makeup and help the children apply it.
6. Encourage the children to dress like clowns and perform tricks with the hoops and stuffed animals. Other children can line up chairs and sit in the audience.
7. Create a flyer for a clown show and distribute it to other classrooms. Invite the other children to come see the show.
8. Take a photo of each child dressed as a clown and display the photos in the room.
9. Let the children dance freely to circus music, and have fun!

Clown Makeup Recipe

4 tablespoons shortening
10 tablespoons cornstarch
1 tablespoon flour
¼ tablespoons glycerin
food coloring

Use a rubber spatula to blend the first three ingredients into a smooth paste. Add glycerin and blend again. Divide into smaller portions. Mix each portion with a few drops of food coloring for a variety of colors. Use fingers to apply the makeup sparingly to children's faces. Remove the makeup with cold cream, shortening, or baby oil.

Note: Get parental permission before applying the clown makeup to any child!

Related books

Clown by Quentin Blake
The Clown of God: An Old Story by Tomie dePaola
Morris and Boris at the Circus by B. Weisman
Jingle the Christmas Clown by Tomie dePaola

Virginia Jean Herrod, Columbia, SC

Parade of Clowns

Materials

poster board (two per child)
hole punch
scissors
yarn
paper plates
markers
glue
pompoms
construction paper

What to do

1. Punch two holes at the top of each piece of construction paper. Tie yarn through the holes to attach two pieces together. Children will slip these over their heads, one poster board in the front and one in the back. Make one for each child.
2. Create clown faces using paper plates. Add yarn for hair and a small red pompom for a nose.
3. Help children attach their paper plate faces to the top of the poster board.
4. Encourage children to decorate their poster board with markers and a variety of shapes cut from construction paper.
5. Finish with a clown parade.

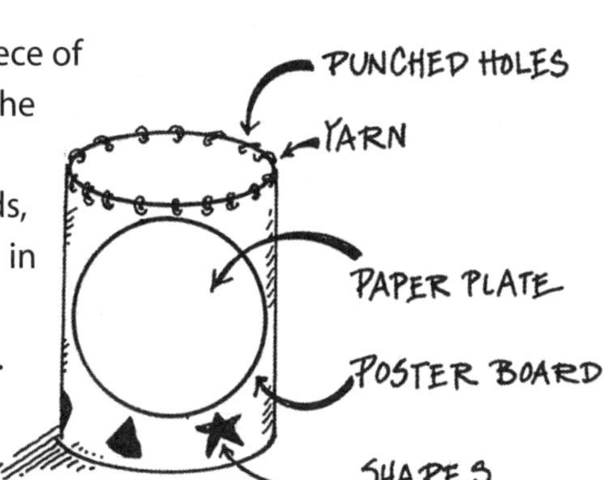

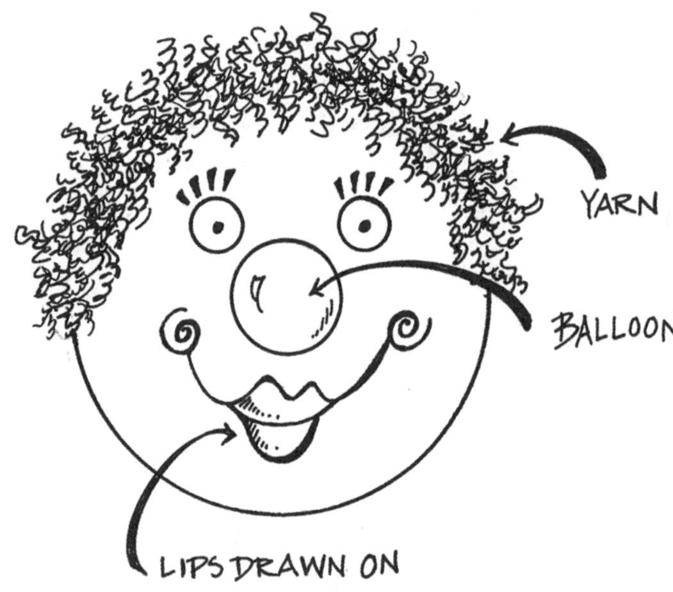

Related books *Circus* by Lois Ehlert
Mirette on the High Wire by Emily McCully
Paddington Bear at the Circus by Michael Bond

 *Sandy Scott, Vancouver, WA*

Peanuts and Popcorn

Materials

pretend peanuts (packing peanuts) and popcorn (cotton balls)
small paper bags
flat boxes
ribbon
apron with pockets
pretend money

What to do

1. Put "peanuts" and "popcorn" into small paper bags. Make serving boxes by attaching ribbon on each side of a flat box so that a child can wear it around his neck while holding the box in front of him. Put the full bags into the flat box.
2. Children can put on an apron with pockets (money belt) and carry the popcorn serving boxes.
3. Encourage the children to develop chants to promote their product.
4. Introduce math concepts by having children collect money and helping them make change and count how much money they made.

 *Ann Kelly, Johnstown, PA*

Silly Potato Clowns

Materials

Mr. Potato Head® kit
potatoes
material scraps (pipe cleaners, toothpicks, small sticks, Styrofoam pieces, yarn, cut-up pictures of body parts from catalogs, and so on)
construction paper
markers

What to do

1. Place all the materials on a small table. Show the children the different parts from the Mr. Potato Head kit and discuss what they are.
2. Make a character from the kit with the help of the children.
3. Show them a potato and briefly discuss what it is. Ask questions such as, "What is it?" "Where does it come from?" "What does it look like?"
4. Explain that the children will be creating their own "silly potato clown" by adding material scraps to the potato. Provide sufficient time for them to make their creations.
5. When they are finished, gather them around in a circle. Ask the children to describe their own creations. You may wish to point out any similarities and differences. Make a chart for similarities and differences.
6. If desired, use the silly clowns in a puppet show, encouraging the children to create their own dialogue.

Related books

Circus by Peter Spier
Harold's Circus by Crockett Johnson
If I Ran the Circus by Dr. Seuss
Olivia Saves the Circus by Ian Falconer
Spot Goes to the Circus by Eric Hill

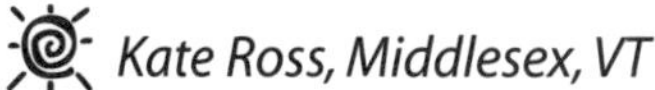

Three Ring Circus Match

Materials

several sets of items varying in size from small to medium to large (such as a small, medium, and large plastic dog)

three rings varying in size from small to medium to large

What to do

1. Ask the children to join you in a circle. Place the three rings on the floor in the middle of the circle.
2. Explain that you will be setting up a learning center like a three-ring circus. There will be a large ring for large objects, a medium ring for medium-sized objects, and a small ring for small objects.
3. Practice at the circle first by giving each child an object. Encourage the children to make comparisons among themselves to see which items are small, large, and medium sized.
4. Ask them to place their items, one at a time, in the appropriate rings in the center of the circle.
5. Briefly discuss and compare the sets of objects as they are placed. Use comparison words, such as "bigger," "smaller," and "medium" to foster understanding of this basic concept. You may wish to physically compare the like items by placing them in order from smallest to largest for the children to see.
6. Once all children have taken turns matching the object to the ring, set up the activity at a learning center for children to experiment with.

Related book *The Grouchy Ladybug* by Eric Carle

Kate Ross, Middlesex, VT

Build a House

Materials

foam pieces in a variety of shapes
empty paper towel tubes
boxes
masking tape

What to do

1. Since children love playhouses, provide materials for them to build their own area. Encourage their creativity.
2. Add stuffed animals, cars, and so on to the area.

Related books

Building a House by Byron Barton
How a House Is Built by Gail Gibbons

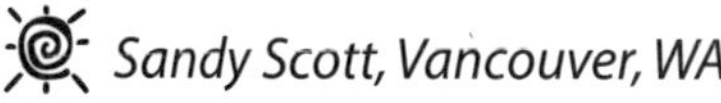
Sandy Scott, Vancouver, WA

Building Center

Materials

woodworking table
scraps of wood
hammers
nails
wood glue
paint and brushes
pencils and paper

What to do

1. Set up an old woodworking table and put out scraps of wood, hammers, nails, and wood glue.

Note: Supervise this area closely.

2. Encourage the children at this center use the materials to make creations.
3. When the glue is dry, the children can paint their creations.
4. Help the children draw blueprints and write instructions for making their creations.

Related books

Building by Elisha Cooper
Mike Mulligan and His Steam Shovel by Virginia Lee Burton

Barbara Saul, Eureka, CA

Carpenter's Toolbox

Materials

12″ x 18″ tan construction paper
markers
scissors
cardboard
white glue
oak tag
pinking shears
paper fasteners
small squares of sandpaper and tape measure (optional)

What to do

1. Cut a strip of tan paper 2″ wide and 12″ long to make a handle.
2. Make a toolbox pattern as shown on cardboard (see illustration). Trace it on tan paper and cut out.
3. Fold on the dashed lines. Glue the ends of the handle piece to the inside of the end flaps, and glue the side flaps to the end flaps to form a rectangular box.
4. Use cardboard to make patterns for tools (see illustration). Trace the patterns on oak tag.
5. Color the tools' handles with markers and cut out the tools. Use pinking shears to cut the sharp side of the saw.
6. Cut two sides of pliers, and connect them with a paper fastener.
7. Put the tools, tape measure, and sandpaper into the toolbox.

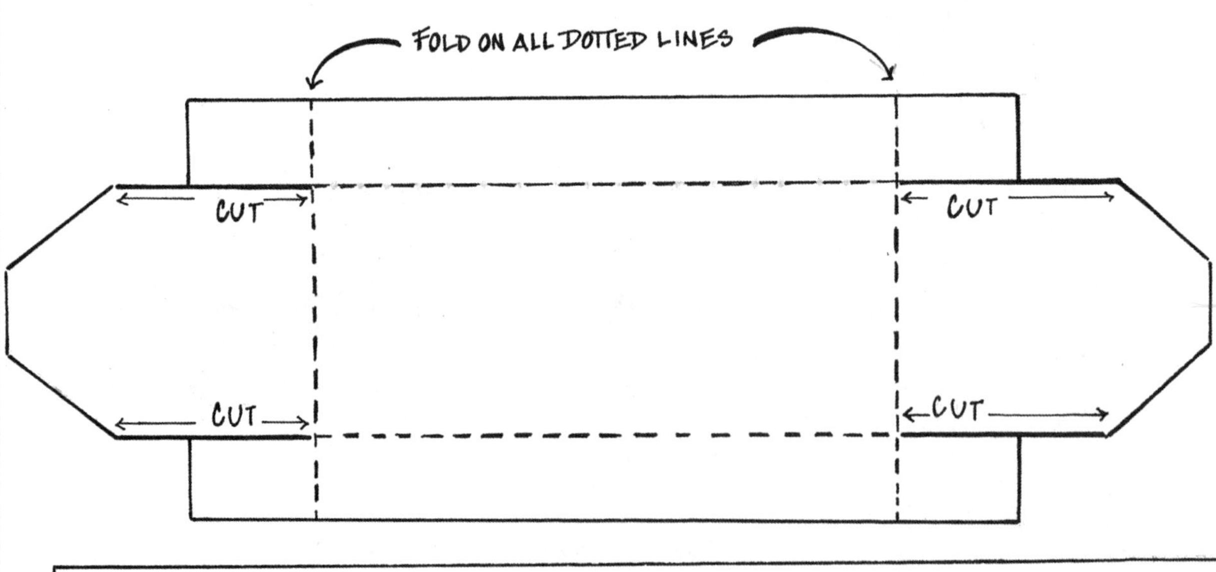

PLIERS

CUT OUT

HAMMER

SCREWDRIVER

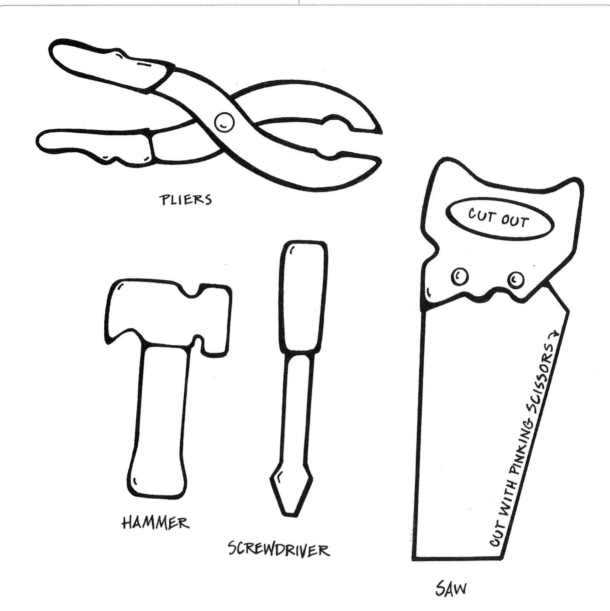

CUT WITH PINKING SCISSORS

SAW

Related song **The Carpenter Builds a House** by Mary Brehm
(tune: "The Farmer in the Dell")

The carpenter builds a house,
The carpenter builds a house,
Heigh, ho, the sawdust, oh,
The carpenter builds a house.

The carpenter pounds the nails…
The carpenter measures the wood...
The carpenter saws the boards...
The carpenter drills a hole...
The carpenter planes a plank...
The carpenter sands the wood...

Mary Brehm, Aurora, OH

Construction Time

Materials

children's books on construction
children's tools (such as a hammer, saw, and screwdriver)
large Styrofoam balls (one for each child)
craft knife or scissors (adult only)
yellow paint and paintbrushes
oak tag cut into small squares
permanent marker
Legos® or blocks

What to do

1. Read books about construction to the children. Talk to the children about construction and show them children's tools such as a hammer, saw, and so on.
2. Cut out the middle of each Styrofoam ball so that it fits on a child's head. Give one to each child.
3. The children use paint and paintbrushes to paint their hats yellow. Help them write their names on oak tag and attach the tag to the front of their "hard hats."
4. Encourage the children to wear their hard hats as they make towers out of Legos® or blocks.

Lisa Chichester, Parkersburg, WV

Creative Construction

Materials

Styrofoam in a variety of shapes and sizes
golf tees
plastic hammers
safety glasses
paper and pencils
hard hats (optional)
camera

What to do

1. If possible, visit a construction site or a woodworking shop with the children. Back in the classroom, ask the children the following question of the day: "If you were a builder, what would you build?" Write down the children's answers and post the list in the woodworking/construction area.

2. Supply the woodworking area with Styrofoam, golf tees, hammers, and safety glasses. Some children may also want to wear hard hats, especially if they choose to build a large structure.
3. Encourage the children to build the item they stated when they answered the question of the day. If they want to make something different than what they mentioned, accept their wish. Show them that print has meaning by adding the child's new idea next to her old one on the list.
4. Because there may not be enough supplies for the children to keep their creations, take a picture of the completed projects and post them on the "question of the day" list.

Related books *Alphabet Under Construction* by Denise Fleming
B Is for Bulldozer by June Sobel
Construction Zone by Tana Hoban
The New Way Things Work by David MacAulay

Encouraging Choices

Materials

toy construction vehicles
sandbox or material to dig in (such as clean dirt in a box)
construction toy people

What to do

The goal of this activity is to help children learn to make choices and to communicate by answering with a word, phrase, or simple sentence.

1. Place construction toys in the sandbox ahead of time.
2. Join a small group of children at the sandbox.
3. Carefully enter into their play scenario by picking up a vehicle and moving it around in the sand, mimicking some of the activity already present.
4. Observe the children for a short time, and then ask a child if she would like the backhoe or the digger to help with her construction project.
5. Wait for an answer and then provide the needed piece of equipment upon request.
6. Observe for a short time again. Approach another child in the same manner.
7. Again provide a choice of equipment. The children will need to provide an answer before getting the toy.
8. Continue playing with the children, following their lead and engaging in their play. Expand upon what they are doing and offer them choices.

Related books *Katy and the Big Snow* by Virginia Lee Burton
Machines at Work by Byron Barton

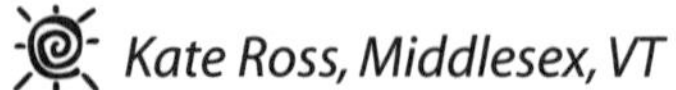

Kate Ross, Middlesex, VT

Here's Tool You

Materials

holed masonite board with fitted pegs (optional)
permanent marker
simple tools (such as garlic presses, potato mashers, egg beaters, cookie cutters, pizza wheels, nesting funnels, rolling pins, clothespins, scissors, and zippers)
rulers
large stamp pads
paper
playdough

What to do

1. If desired, trace the outline of some hanging items (see materials) with permanent marker on masonite board and hang it at child's height on the wall (optional). Put a worktable next to the tools.

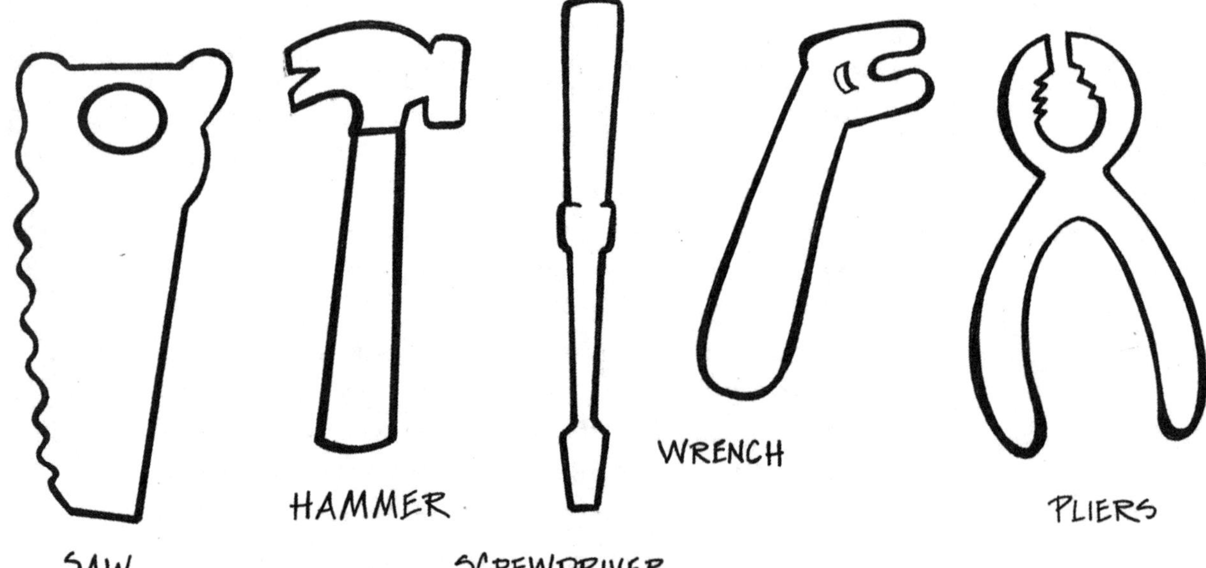

2. Choose a variety of simple tools to promote discovery, problem solving, and creative thinking. Arrange the tools and other props on the table. Hang any hanging tools on the masonite board, if available.

3. Encourage children to be creative with the materials. Following are some ideas for using the materials. Children can:
    - use a garlic press, cookie cutters, a pizza wheel, and rolling pins with playdough.
    - use potato mashers or cookie cutters on stamp pads and stamp shapes onto paper.
    - cut paper and playdough with scissors.
    - manipulate egg beaters and clothespins.
    - nest the funnels like a puzzle.

More to do

Snack: Use simple tools to make a snack. Use a simple manual citrus squeezer/juicer to make orange juice or lemonade. Grate cheese with a plastic grater.

Related books

Tool Book by Gail Gibbons
Tools by Ann Morris
Who Uses This? by Margaret Miller

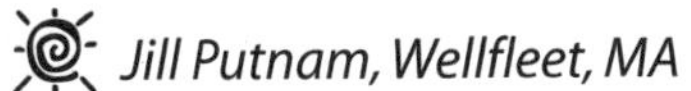
Jill Putnam, Wellfleet, MA

Home Building

Materials

wooden shapes
watercolor markers
5″ x 8″ tagboard sheets
glue

What to do

1. Ask the children to color the wooden shapes with watercolor markers.
2. Encourage them to glue the wooden shapes to tagboard sheets.
3. Watch the wonderful creations that the children make, from homes to fantastic designs.

Related books

The Biggest House in the World by Leo Lionni
Houses and Homes by Ann Morris

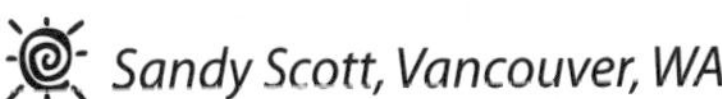
Sandy Scott, Vancouver, WA

Building Center

Materials

various pieces of wood, pipe cleaners, and tongue depressors
glue
paint and brushes
buttons, rocks, and pompoms

What to do

1. Place all the materials in the art area and encourage children to create their own sculptures or creations.
2. Provide paint for children to paint their creations.
3. Children may add decorative items to their creations after they paint them, such as pompoms and buttons.

Melissa Browning, Milwaukee, WI

Match That Tool

Materials

children's gift wrap with a variety of tools printed on it
scissors
laminating machine

What to do

1. Ahead of time, cut out a square of gift wrap large enough so that a picture of each tool fits on it. Laminate for durability.
2. Cut out pictures of individual tools from the leftover paper and laminate.
3. Encourage the children to match the individual tools to the same tool on the large square.

Tip: This activity can be adapted to almost any subject, such as dinosaurs, holidays, sports, jungle, and water animals, by using different types of wrapping paper.

Vicki Whitehead, Satsuma, AL

Nuts and Bolts

Materials variety of nuts, bolts, and washers
paper and pencils

What to do

1. Provide a variety of nuts, bolts, and washers in the construction area. Encourage the children to explore these items and how they can be screwed together.
2. Children can sort them and count how many of each type there are.
3. Trace around a nut, a bolt, and a washer on a piece of paper, and chart how many of each there are.

Barbara Saul, Eureka, CA

Sandpaper to Sand and Back

Materials sandpaper
rocks (small enough to be held in a child's palm, but larger than a pebble)
small container or box
glue
paper

What to do

1. Assemble all the materials on a table. Gather the children around the table and display the materials.
2. Ask the children to examine the sandpaper. Discuss how it feels. Ask questions such as, "What does it look like?" "What do you think it is used for?" "Where did it come from or how do you think it was made?"
3. Next, examine the rocks. Ask the children to describe the rocks.
4. Give each child a rock, a small piece of sandpaper, and a container.
5. Ask them to rub their rock with the sandpaper over the container. Give the children ample time to obtain some rubbed-off material.
6. When the children are done, ask them to describe what happened. "What is now inside of the container?" Examine the pieces carefully. "Are there differences?" "Did anything happen to the rock?"
7. Let children use a small amount of glue to glue the loosened material onto the piece of sandpaper. It has now become like sandpaper again!

Related book *Stone Soup* by Ann McGovern

 *Kate Ross, Middlesex, VT*

Tool Board

Materials

yellow and white poster board or tagboard
black marker
plastic or real tools
scissors
laminate or clear contact paper
self-adhesive Velcro

What to do

1. Using a black marker, trace the outline several tools on yellow poster board or tagboard.
2. Outline the same tools on white poster board and cut out the shapes.
3. Laminate the poster board and tools for durability.
4. Attach Velcro to the back of the tools and to the board so that the Velcro will stick when the tool is lined up with its outline.
5. Mount the board on the wall and explain to the children that tools are sometimes kept on "pegboards" so they can be found easily. Encourage children to hang the tool shapes in their designated places on the board.

Related book *The Toolbox* by Anne and Harlow Rockwell

Jackie Wright, Enid, OK

Accordion Print Clues

Materials several large, colorful photos from any magazine

What to do

1. Carefully tear out pages from a magazine and trim edges. Choose pages with large, colorful photos on them.
2. Fold each picture accordion-style fashion.
3. Present a folded picture to a child and expose one flap of the picture at a time. Ask the child to be a "detective" and guess what will be represented in the entire picture.
4. Continue exposing one flap at a time until the child has guessed the picture.

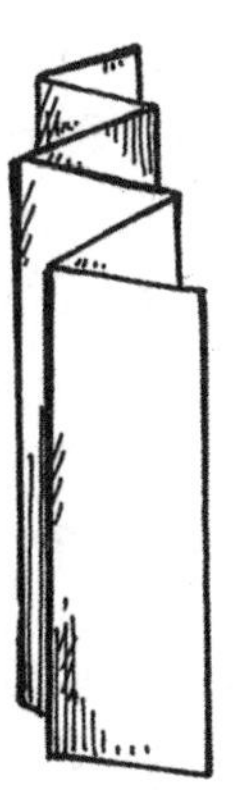

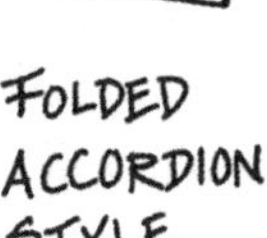

More to do Remove all of the pieces from a puzzle. Show a child only one or two pieces of the puzzle and challenge him to guess what makes up the whole puzzle.

Related books *Alphabet Adventure* by Audrey Wood
I Spy Mystery: A Book of Picture Riddles by Jean Marzollo and Walter Wick

Deborah Roud and Diana Reed, New Wilmington, PA

Dandy Detectives

Materials

two small tables and four small chairs
two small lamps with the cords and bulbs removed
two old phones with cords removed
four clipboards
four pencils
four old trench coats
four detective-style hats
poster board
four magnifying glasses
four old cameras

What to do

1. While learning about community helpers, invite a detective from your local police force to visit the classroom. Ask him or her to explain what a detective is and how detectives do their job. Remember to keep information developmentally appropriate for your age group. If you cannot get a real detective to visit, ask someone you know to pretend to be one.
2. Turn your housekeeping area into a "detective agency." Add two small tables, chairs, and other props.
3. Put four trench coats and hats in the dress-up area.
4. Make an "open/closed" sign by writing OPEN on the front of a piece of poster board and CLOSED on the back. Hang it at the entrance of the area.
5. Open the agency by flipping the sign to the OPEN side. Let four children be detectives at a time. Encourage the other children to visit or call the detective agency for help finding things.
6. Hide something in the room, such as a teddy bear. Ask the detectives to find your lost bear. Encourage the "detectives" to ask the other children if they have any information on the lost bear. Remind them to use cameras to take pictures of the clues, and the clipboards and pencils to take notes.
7. For added fun, ask the center director or another classroom teacher to hide something in the center. Have him or her come to the room and "hire" the detectives to find the "lost" item. Remind the children to ask for details about what was lost and to take notes on the clipboard. Supervise the group as they look for the lost item in the center. Provide enough clues so they find the item (but not too easily).

Related books *The Case of the Cat's Meow* by Crosby Bonsall
I Lost My Bear by Jules P. Feiffer
The Mystery of King Karfu by Doug Cushman
Nate the Great by Marjorie Weinman Sharmat
Sheep in Wolves' Clothing by Satoshi Kitamura
Where Does the Teacher Live? by Paula Kurzband Feder

Virginia Jean Herrod, Columbia, SC

Detective Hunt

Materials
roll of wide masking tape
magnifying glasses

What to do

1. Divide the children into small groups of two or three and explain that they are going on a detective hunt.
2. Give each "detective" a piece of masking tape about 5" in length.
3. Ask them to collect "evidence" by going around the classroom and pressing their masking tape to flooring, tables, toys, clothing…anything!
4. After they have collected their evidence, encourage them to use magnifying glasses to investigate what stuck to their piece of masking tape.

More to do

Games: Have the children form a circle. Select one child to stand in the center of the circle. Ask the other children to look closely at the child standing in the center. Choose one child ("detective") to turn around and close his eyes while you change some detail on the child in the center (for example, untie a shoe, place a sticker on the child's shirt, or push up one pant leg). Ask the detective child to turn around and figure out what is different on the child in the center.

Related books *The Bear Detectives: The Case of the Missing Pumpkin* by Jan Berenstain and Stan Berenstain
The Missing Mitten Mystery by Steven Kellogg

Deborah Roud and Diana Reed, New Wilmington, PA

I'm Thinking of a Clue

Materials

large sheet of paper
marker
tape recorder and tape
book

What to do

1. Use this activity when something new is added to the classroom, a special activity is going to take place, or to make a connection to a story that you are about to read to the class.
2. Develop some clues about the activity you want the children to try and guess. For example, if a special guest is coming to speak to the class about detective work, you could give clues about this visitor.
3. Label a large sheet of paper "The Visitor."
4. One by one, write the clues for the children underneath the label. After you read each clue, ask the group if they have a guess about whom the visitor may be. Write each child's name and guess after each clue. Continue writing clues and guesses until the class knows who is coming to visit. You can choose to give all the clues in one sitting (as an introduction for the visitor) or you can spread them out over the day or even a week depending on your group's interest in the activity.
5. Before the children guess who the visitor is, tape record the clues and place the tape in the listening area so that the children can listen to the clues over and over again. This works especially well when the clues are about a story you are going to read. Place the book and tape in the listening center.

Related books

Figure Out Blues Clues by Jennifer Twomey Perello
The Shape Detective (Blues Clues) by Angela Santomero

Ann Kelly, Johnstown, PA

Mystery Sound Boxes

Materials

shoeboxes

several items all beginning with the same sound (such as a toy car, stuffed cat, empty can, miniature kite, and a carrot for the /k/ sound)

What to do

1. Fill several shoeboxes with a few items all beginning with the same sound. For example, place a bug, stuffed bear, small bag, banana, and a ball in a box for the /b/ sound; put a toy fish, the number four, a fan, and stuffed fox in a box for the /f/ sound.
2. Gather the children in a circle and place a box of items in the center.
3. Tell the children they are going to play a game to find out what sound all of the objects in the box have in common. Explain that they will work together as a detective team.
4. Ask a child to take an item out of the box and name it out loud.
5. Ask the children to think about the sound at the beginning of the word. You may wish to repeat the word, emphasizing the beginning sound.
6. After three children have presented clues, all can offer guesses. If more clues are needed, continue letting children remove objects and guessing after each choice.
7. The game continues until the sound is discovered or all items are displayed.

Note: A variation is to find final sounds or medial sounds within words. An extra challenge might be to insert one odd object having a different target sound and have the children investigate the difference.

Related books

Have You Seen My Duckling? by Nancy Tafuri

Look-Alikes Jr. by Joan Steiner

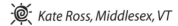

Kate Ross, Middlesex, VT

The Mystery of the Disappearing Pictures

Materials

old white candles
watercolor paints and brushes
light-colored construction paper

What to do

1. Invite the children to draw a picture on construction paper using an old white candle. Remind them to press firmly.
2. Tell them a detective's job is to look for clues to solve mysteries or problems. Ask them if they can see the picture they have drawn on their paper.
3. Encourage the children to paint over their candle picture with watercolor paint.
4. As their pictures emerge, praise the children's detective skills. The mystery of the disappearing picture is solved!

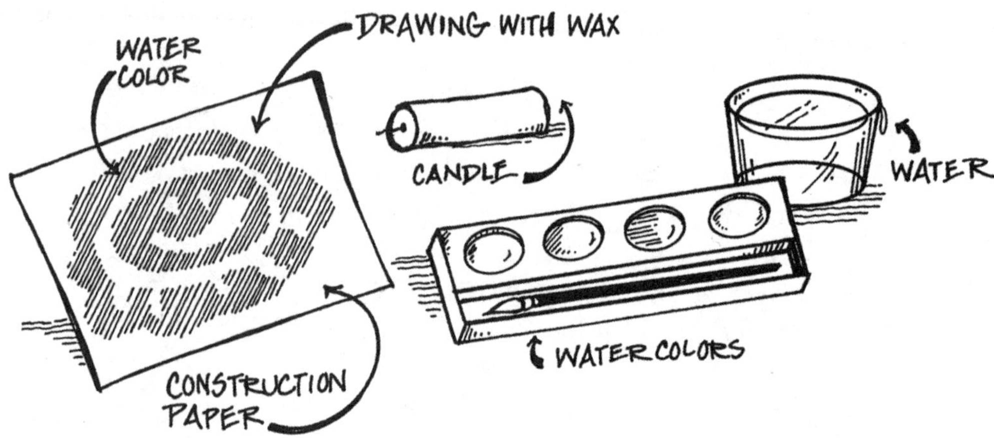

Related books *The Bear Detectives: The Case of the Missing Pumpkin* by Jan Berenstain and Stan Berenstain
The Mysterious Tadpole by Steven Kellogg

Deborah Roud and Diana Reed, New Wilmington, PA

Picture Concentration

Materials

sets of pictures for each thematic unit
scissors
glue stick
3″ x 5″ index cards
tagboard
laminate or clear contact paper
rubber bands
box or container to hold the cards

What to do

1. Since a picture concentration game can reinforce ideas covered in every unit of study, collect a supply of pictures that relate to each of your thematic units. You will need two copies of each picture.
2. Cut out 18 pictures (nine matching pairs) for each thematic unit.
3. Glue each picture to a 3″ x 5″ index card.
4. Cut a large piece of tagboard into a 17″ x 22″ piece and divide it into a grid of 18 spaces (three rows of six spaces).
5. Laminate the cards and the tagboard for durability and cut them out.
6. Put a rubber band around each set of 18 and store them in the detective learning area until you are working on that theme.
7. To use, randomly spread one set of cards facedown on the grid. Arrange them into three rows of six cards.
8. The players take turns turning over two cards. If they match, the child keeps the cards and may have another turn. If the cards do not match, the child returns the cards to their original place and waits for another turn. By memorizing where certain pictures are located (initially as a result of trial and error), players have a chance at clearing the playing area.
9. Continue play with the next child until all the matches have been found. The child with the most cards is the winner.
10. Once children understand how to play, make the cards available for pairs or small groups during center time.

Rhyme Spy

Materials none

What to do

1. Gather the children in a circle and explain that they are going to play a spy game. Talk about the word "spy."
2. Explain that they are going to find something that rhymes with a particular item. For example, if the chosen item is "rug," say, "I spy something that rhymes with "rug." Without telling the children, pick something that rhymes with "rug" (such as "mug").
3. The children take turns trying to find the targeted item that rhyme with rug. Examples might be "rug/bug," "rug/Doug," "rug/shrug," and "rug/hug."
4. After each guess, encourage the children to repeat the two rhyming words for clarity.
5. Once the targeted item is guessed, choose a child to find an item to rhyme. Again the rest of the children attempt to guess the targeted item.

Note: It is fine for the children to create nonsense words while rhyming, as this is part of the learning process.

Related books *The Awful Aardvarks Go to School* by Reeve Lindbergh and Tracey Campbell Pearson

Over in the Meadow by Ezra Jack Keats

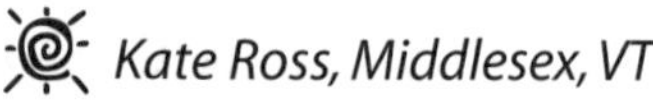

Kate Ross, Middlesex, VT

Searching for Rhyming Pairs

Materials

8 ½" x 11" tagboard or medium cardstock
picture of a detective
glue
scissors
20 colored pictures of rhyming objects
scissors or paper cutter
pocket charts
laminator

What to do

1. Send children on a hunt for rhyming words with this center.
2. Write the activity title on a piece of 8 ½" x 11" tagboard paper (for example, "Searching for Rhyming Pairs"). Write the directions underneath: "Place cards on the word wall to make rhyming pairs." Glue a detective picture to it.
3. Find 20 pictures of rhyming objects. Enlarge, if necessary, so that they are about 3" in size.
4. Use scissors or a paper cutter to cut the objects to fit into the pocket charts.
5. Laminate the title card and picture cards for durability and cut them out.
6. Hang the pocket charts at children's eye level and gather the children around the charts.
7. Insert the title card into the top pocket of the chart. Put half of the cards in the chart, leaving empty pockets for their mates. Pass out the remaining cards and discuss the pictures in the chart. Ask the children if anyone has found a rhyming pair.
8. Continue until all pairs have been made.
9. For added fun, make a file jacket with an answer key (colored picture or scan of completed pocket chart) on the back. Use it to store the activity and for children to self-check their work in this center.

Sherlock's Clues

Materials

candy coins or other small treats (one for each child)
construction paper
crayons
scissors

What to do

1. Ahead of time, hide candy coins (or small treat items). Hide one for each child.
2. Cut out footprints from construction paper. Place the paper footprints so they lead to the candy.
3. Write a clue on each small slip of paper. For example, "I'm where the books are," or "Look for me in the housekeeping area."
4. Gather the children in a group and give each child a clue to follow to find the hidden treasure. Guide the children in following the steps or clues to the candy.

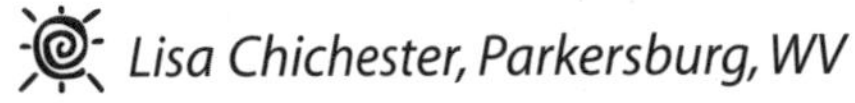

Treasure Hunt

Materials

new classroom item
paper and marker
map of the classroom

What to do

1. Choose a new classroom item that the children will enjoy, such as a new animal, book, or other item.
2. Before children arrive, hide the new item somewhere in the classroom. Write clues on pieces of paper and place them in each area of the classroom. The first clue should lead children to the second clue, which leads to the third clue, and so on, until the children find the hidden item.
3. Show the children a map of the classroom and explain that they will be going on a treasure hunt to find a new classroom "treasure."
4. Begin the treasure hunt by reading the first clue, such as, "Look at the bulletin board and what do you see? A message written all in green!"
5. The children go to the message on the bulletin board, which may read, "Look, look, what do you know? Five little BLOCKS all in a row!"
6. Children go to the block center and see five blocks lined up. On the blocks could be another note that says, "Wash a dish, one, two, three. Find the surprise for you and me!" The children go to the housekeeping area and look in the sink for the next clue.
7. Continue with as many clues as desired, until children find the new treasure.

Related books *We're Going on a Bear Hunt* by Michael Rosen
We're Going on a Lion Hunt by David Axtell

 *Kaethe Lewandowski, Centreville, VA*

We Spy Books

Materials

I Spy books by Wick and Marzollo (optional)
miscellaneous materials from home or classroom
paper
stapler or hole punch and yarn
markers
camera and film
glue

What to do

1. Read *I Spy* books, if available, to the children.
2. Invite the children to bring in an assortment of small items from home to make a classroom "We Spy" book. It is helpful to provide a list of items the children could bring.
3. Staple a few blank pages together, or punch holes in paper and attach with yarn.
4. Ask children to sort all the contributed items and decide on names for different pages of their "We Spy" book, such as vehicles, ocean creatures, animals, and so on.
5. Let children arrange or display items in any fashion. You may with to assign two or three children to each page to avoid crowding and confusion. Blocks, shelving, or knick-knack shelves are great for displaying the items.
6. When children have finished organizing items for a specific page, photograph the display.
7. Let children create as many displays for as many pages as time, film, or funds allow! Arranging items and photographing takes much longer than you may anticipate, so you may want to allow an entire week for this project.
8. Develop film, and if funds allow, make enlarged color copies for your book.
9. Glue all the photos into the book on the appropriate pages. Ask children to examine the pages and name a few things they spy. Keep a list of page numbers and items children name on each page.
10. Be sure there are at least one or two entries for each child, and print the text on the page.
11. Make a cover for the book using children's illustrations or a group creation. Title it "We Spy…"

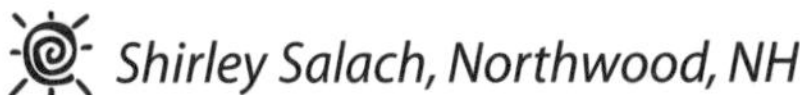

Lotto for Little Learners

Materials

dinosaur pictures, two identical picture sets for each player
8″ x 8″ squares of oak tag or poster board
2 ½″ squares of oak tag or poster board
scissors
glue stick
laminator

What to do

1. Cut out pictures of dinosaurs from books, the Internet, magazines, and so on. Make copies of each picture so that there is a set of pictures for game cards and an identical set of pictures for the lotto boards. Each picture should fit within a 2 ½″ square.
2. To make the lotto boards, create a grid of nine squares (three down and three across) on each 8″ x 8″ square of oak tag. Make each square 2 ½″.
3. Glue one of each picture pair to a square on the board.
4. Glue the matching pictures to 2 ½″ oak tag squares. These will be the cover cards.
5. Make a variety of lotto boards and cover cards, making sure that there are enough for each child to have one.
6. Laminate the lotto boards and cards and cut out.
7. To use, invite the children to place the lotto boards and cards on a table or floor. Place the cards in a pile, face down.
8. Let the children take turns drawing a card from the pile and placing it over the matching picture on their board. If the picture does not match any on the grid, the child puts the card at the bottom of the pile and the next child has a turn.
9. The goal is to cover all pictures on the grid.

Colorful Dinosaurs

Materials

computer and color printer (optional) or colored construction paper
colored pictures of dinosaurs
8 ½ x 11″ tagboard or medium card stock
paper cutter or scissors
laminate
pocket chart

What to do

1. If you have a computer, customize your own collection of dinosaurs in a variety of colors. Use a color ink cartridge when printing to save time. Otherwise, use colored construction paper.
2. Print the title "Colorful Dinosaurs" on a piece of tagboard.
3. Cut tagboard into 7" x 11" pieces. Using large type, print the color words that match the colors of the dinosaurs.
4. Use a paper cutter or scissors to cut around the color words and dinosaurs so that they are all the same size and fit nicely into the pocket chart pockets. Laminate all for durability, and cut out.
5. Hang the pocket chart at children's eye level, and gather the children in a circle around it. Insert the title card in the top pocket of the chart, and distribute the colored dinosaurs to each child.
6. Place the color words in the pocket chart, leaving room for their matching dinosaurs. Invite each child to put a dinosaur in the pocket chart next to the correct color word.

Dino Bones: Measure Up

Materials

clean chicken and turkey bones
bones from pork or beef ribs that have been boiled, bleached, and dried
permanent markers
tape measures and rulers
pencils
paper

What to do

1. Mark each bone with a letter code such as A1 or C3 to identify it. If desired, let the children help label the bones and develop their own system of labeling.
2. Put out the bones and encourage children to use the measuring tools to measure each bone. Children may work individually, in pairs, or in groups.
3. Ask children to write the code of each bone and its length on a piece of paper.
4. Children can trace the bones on their paper and write descriptions for them.
5. Encourage children to compare their results.

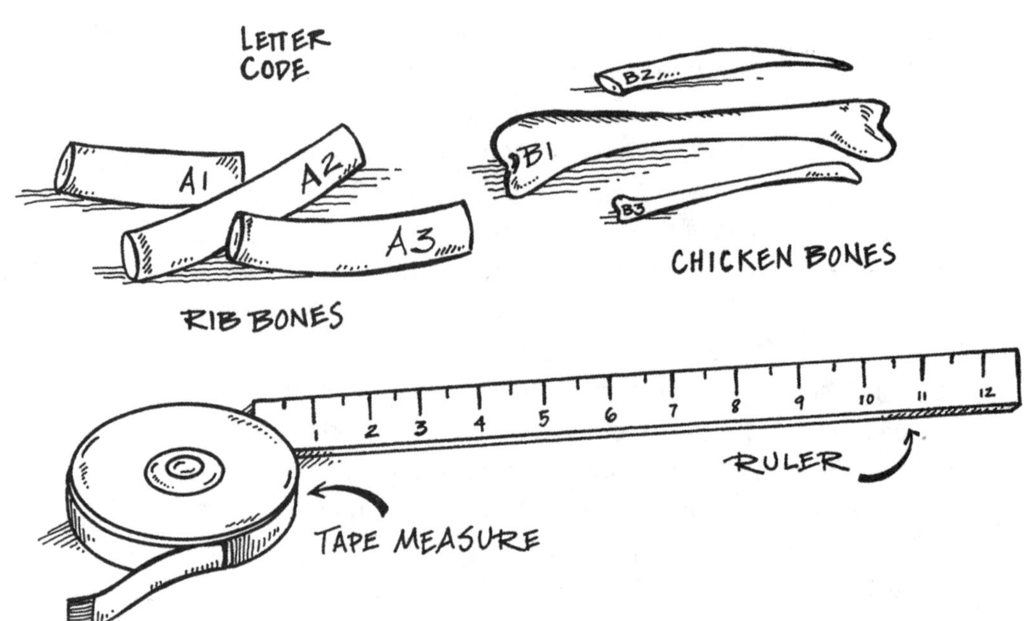

More to do **Sand Table:** Hide the bones in a sandbox or the sand table. The children can hunt for the bones as if they were paleontologists.
Math: Use the bones for sorting activities.

Related books *Digging up Dinosaurs* by Aliki
Finders Keepers by William Lipkind
The Magic School Bus in the Time of the Dinosaurs by Joanna Cole

Sandra Nagel, White Lake, MI

Dinomania!

Materials

book about dinosaurs
dinosaur outlines on butcher paper
crayons
dinosaur-shaped sponges
pie tins
bright-colored tempera paint
paper cups
clay

What to do

1. Draw dinosaur outlines on butcher paper.
2. Read a book about different types of dinosaurs while the children color in the outlines of the dinosaurs.
3. Provide dinosaur-shaped sponges and pie tins full of bright-colored tempera paint. Help the children make prints of different dinosaurs and label them with their species name.
4. Give each child a cup and enough clay to fill half of the cup. Ask the children to push the clay down into the bottom of the cup. Talk to the children about fossils. Encourage the children to make their own fossils by putting their fist into the cup and making an imprint.

Lisa Chichester, Parkersburg, WV

Dinosaur Cakes

Materials

rice cakes
peanut butter
small plastic knives
dinosaur fruit snacks
paper plate or paper towel

What to do

1. Give each child a rice cake. Encourage them to spread peanut butter on their rice cakes, noticing the pits, mountains, and valleys.

Note: Be aware of any peanut allergies. If a child is allergic to peanut butter, choose a different spread such as cream cheese.

2. Children place three to five dinosaur fruit snacks on the peanut butter.
3. As children eat their dinosaur creations, practice math skills by creating story problems. For example, "There were five dinosaurs in the tar pits, and one was eaten. How many were left?"

Related books

How Big Were the Dinosaurs? by Bernard Most
Oh My Oh My Oh Dinosaurs! by Sandra Boynton

Sandra Nagel, White Lake, MI

Dinosaur Dig

Materials

Styrofoam trays
dinosaur pictures
dull pencil
colored permanent markers
large tub, water table, or small plastic pool
Styrofoam packing pieces

What to do

1. To prepare, cut dinosaur-shape pictures so that they fit onto Styrofoam trays.
2. Using a dull pencil, trace the picture over the tray, pressing to make an indentation. Remove the picture.
3. Trace the indented outline on the tray with a permanent marker. Use a different color for each dinosaur you make.
4. Cut the tray pictures into puzzles using different shaped cuts for each puzzle.
5. Fill a tub, table, or pool with Styrofoam packing pieces and bury the puzzle pieces among them.
6. Encourage the children to discover the "fossils" and assemble the pieces to create dinosaurs. Encourage cooperation and remind children to trade pieces to match up colors correctly and complete all the puzzles.

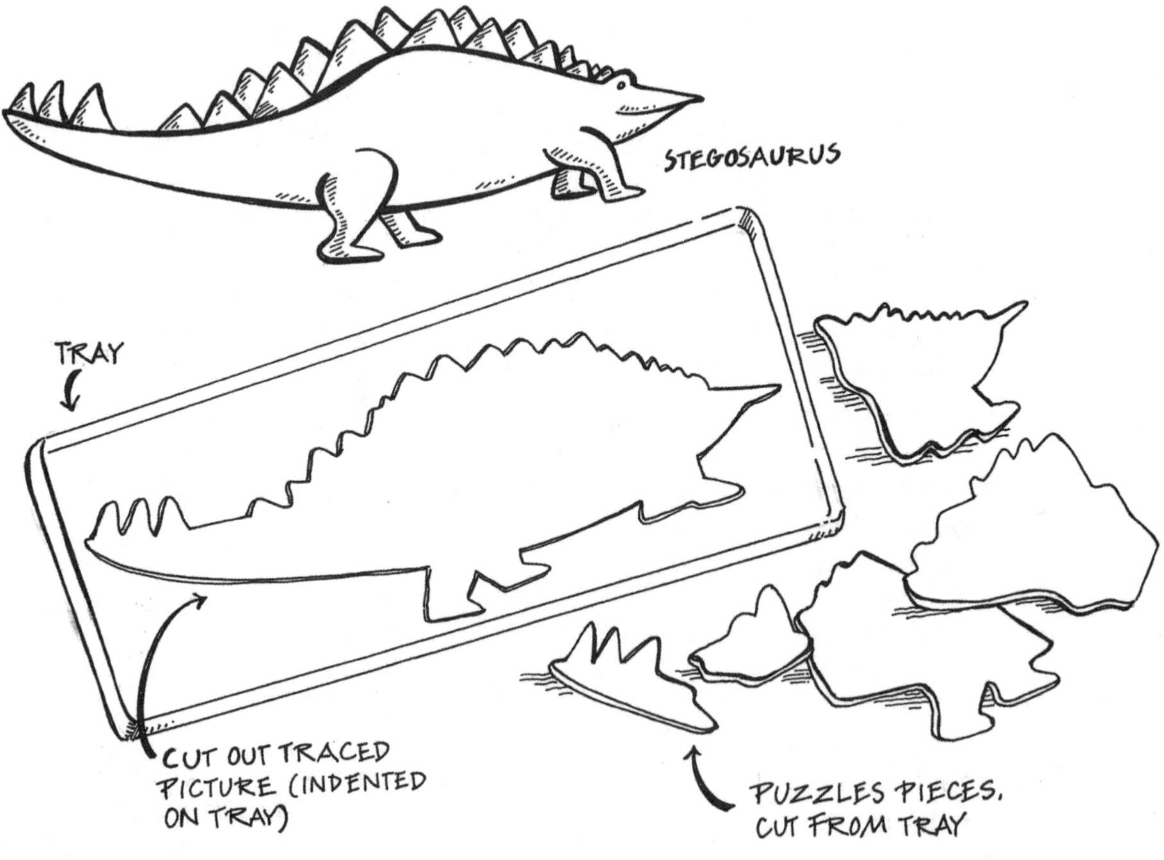

Related books *Digging Up Dinosaurs* by Aliki
Dinosaurs by Peter Zallinger
Dinosaurs, Strange and Wonderful by Laurence Pringle

 *Sandra Gratias, Perkasie, PA*

Dinosaur Parachute Play

Materials small parachute

What to do

1. Move the parachute to imitate the movement of different dinosaurs. Following are some examples:
   - Pterodactyl: Raise the parachute up and down like flapping wings.
   - Brontosaurus: Raise the parachute as high as you can.
   - Stegosaurus: Shake the parachute rapidly like the stegosaurus' tail, which it swishes back and forth at its enemies.
   - Tyrannosaurus Rex: Raise the parachute up slowly, then pull down slowly, resembling big footsteps.

Andrea Hungerford, Plainville, CT

Dinosaur Soap Egg Surprise

Materials

Ivory® soap bars
cheese grater
water
paper lunch bags
shredded green construction paper
small plastic dinosaurs

What to do

1. Grate the bars of soap using a cheese grater. If the children in your class are older and developmentally ready, let them help with this step.
2. Add a little water to the grated soap to make a paste-like consistency.
3. Give each child a paper lunch bag. Demonstrate how to roll down the lunch bags to form a nest.

4. The children add some shredded green paper to resemble grass.
5. Give each child a large handful of soapy paste.
6. Let each child pick out one of the plastic dinosaurs. Ask them to place their dinosaur in the middle of the soap mixture and begin to form an egg shape around it. When the children are through, the dinosaur should be hidden.
7. Allow the soap "egg" to dry for several hours or overnight.
8. Children place their egg in their nest to take home. Encourage them to bathe with the "egg" soap until their "dinosaur" is born.

Wanda Guidroz and Stacie Bemis, Santa Fe, TX

Dinosaur Song

Materials

large paper
scissors
markers
newspaper
paint and brushes
stapler

What to do

1. Draw a large outline of a dinosaur on paper. Cut out two matching dinosaurs for each child.
2. Staple them together, leaving an opening to stuff newspaper.
3. Encourage the children to paint their dinosaur (both sides), stuff with newspaper, and staple closed.
4. Sing the following song to the tune of "Twinkle, Twinkle, Little Star" with the children. Encourage them to "dance" around with their stuffed dinosaurs!

Many, Many Years Ago by Kaethe Lewandowski
Many, many years ago,
Lived the great big dinosaurs.
Some ate plants,
Some ate meat,
They traveled by air or on feet.
Then the earth turned very cold,
And they died, or so I'm told.

More to do

Transitions: During transition times, call children by their names and add "-osaurus" at the end, for example, "Amberosaurus."

Related books *Dazzle the Dinosaur* by Marcus Pfister
Digging Up Dinosaurs by Aliki
Dinosaurs by Gail Gibbons
Dinosaurs, Dinosaurs by Byron Barton
My Visit to the Dinosaurs by Aliki

Kaethe Lewandowski, Centreville, VA

Footprint Match

Materials
playdough or clay
assorted sizes and shapes of toy dinosaurs
oven (optional)
sealant (optional)

What to do
1. Divide the playdough into portions. Roll each into a ball and flatten to a smooth circle about ½" thick.
2. Press a dinosaur's feet into a circle to make footprints. Leave the dough or clay out to harden, or bake it. Coat the fossils with sealant afterward, if desired.
3. Encourage the children to match the fossil footprints to the correct dinosaur. After making a guess, they can test it by fitting the feet into the print.
4. Provide dinosaurs and natural objects at the playdough table to for children to create prints.

More to do Make fossils of children's handprints in Plaster of Paris.

Related book *A Look Around Dinosaurs* by Dan Duffee

Sandra Gratias, Perkasie, PA

Hatching Dinosaur Eggs

Materials

hard-boiled eggs
vinegar
food coloring
paint in different colors
small bowls
small spoons

What to do

1. Explain to the children that they are going to color "dinosaur eggs."
2. Pour just enough vinegar into each bowl to cover the egg.
3. Add three to four drops of food coloring to each bowl of vinegar and stir.
4. Ask children to place the hard-boiled eggs into the colored vinegar and let them soak. Use a spoon to pick up the egg and check its color. The longer the egg stays in the bowl, the darker the color will be.
5. When satisfied with the color, take the egg out to dry.
6. Display the eggs in the room once daily for a few weeks. Let children handle the eggs. During handling, the eggs may become cracked. If not, make a few cracks yourself. Younger children will believe that a dinosaur is hatching!
7. When each egg is about to open up, paint dinosaur footprints the color of the eggs. The children can celebrate the hatching of their dinosaur eggs!

More to do

A great follow-up to this activity is to have a scavenger hunt for dinosaur toys, so that children may find their "hatched dinosaurs!"

Andrea Hungerford, Plainville, CT

Individual Erupting Volcanoes

Materials

different colored homemade playdough (it's more pliable) or modeling clay
empty film canisters
heavy disposable plates or clean Styrofoam trays
plastic dinosaurs and trees
two small disposable cups
baking soda
vinegar
food coloring

What to do

1. Let each child choose some playdough and a film canister. Ask them to place their canisters on a heavy paper plate and begin forming the shape of the volcano. Be sure to tell them not to cover the opening.
2. After the volcano is formed, the children may choose a few dinosaurs and trees to make a scene that resembles what they imagine that time would have looked like. When everyone has finished their models, sit down at the tables together.
3. Give each child two plastic cups. Fill one with a small amount of baking soda.
4. Pour a small amount of vinegar into the other cup. Each child chooses what color they want for the "lava," and then add food coloring to their cup of vinegar.
5. Talk about the components. Use terms such as "eruption" and "chemical reaction."
6. Together as a class, each child pours the baking soda into her film canister. Then each child begins pouring the colored vinegar into her "volcano."
7. Watch the volcanoes erupt!
8. This is a great idea for the science center, too.

Author Note: Most teachers have made a classroom volcano, but I have found that the preschoolers want more hands-on activities, but they also need something simple so that they are not overwhelmed. These individual volcanoes are perfect for preschoolers.

Wanda Guidroz, Santa Fe, TX

It's a Dino World

Materials

large white paper
variety of stuffed and plastic toy dinosaurs of different sizes
large piece of blue plastic
scissors
two large Styrofoam blocks
inexpensive dinosaur Halloween outfits
one set of plastic dinosaurs that are scaled down accurately
balance scale
small plastic palm trees
small rocks
craft paper
dinosaur books and pictures
glue
black marker
dinosaur shaped sponges
tree-shaped sponges

What to do

1. Create a dinosaur web. Print and circle the word "dinosaurs" in the middle of a large piece of paper.
2. Ask the children to tell you everything they know about dinosaurs. Print their responses around the word in the middle. Don't correct the children's responses. The goal is to find out what their knowledge base is already. Simply record their responses.
3. Draw lines from the word "dinosaurs" to the children's responses to create a web. Date the web and post it in an easily seen place.
4. After a couple of weeks of learning about dinosaurs, create another dinosaur web. Follow the same steps as before. You will notice that the children's knowledge base has greatly increased and now is more fact-based than fantasy-based. Post the new web near the old one. Make sure both are accurately dated.
5. Ask the children to help you create a dinosaur world in the classroom. Arrange the interest centers as follows:

Block Area

1. Add plastic dinosaurs to the block area.
2. Draw a rough circle on a piece of blue plastic. Cut out the circle and place it on the floor to create a large pond.
3. Encourage the children to role play with the dinosaurs. You may have to remind them that dinosaurs did more than just fight. They searched for food and often lived in peaceful community groups.

Housekeeping Area

1. Add the stuffed dinosaurs to the housekeeping area.
2. Encourage the children to role play and care for the dinosaurs.
3. Ask questions such as, "Where are you and your baby dinosaur headed today?" or "What are you feeding your dinosaur?"
4. Create a set of dinosaur feet from Styrofoam. Attach an elastic band to the top of the feet so the children can slip them on. Let the children stomp around the room! Encourage them to wear dinosaur Halloween outfits.

Science Area

1. Add a set of dinosaurs that are accurately scaled to size.
2. Challenge the children to sort the dinosaurs according to size or by the type of food they ate.
3. Encourage them to use a balance scale to compare the weight of the dinosaurs.
4. Encourage the children to use the materials in the science area (such as magnifying lenses) to explore the dinosaurs.

Sensory Table

1. Put the small set of dinosaurs and sand in the sensory table. Add the plastic palm trees and small rocks.
2. Encourage the children to role play with the dinosaurs. They can create scenarios for the dinosaurs using the palm trees and rocks.

Library Area

1. Make a dinosaur book. Choose five or six familiar dinosaurs to be in the book. Paste a picture of each one on the top third of a piece of craft paper. Under the picture print several facts about the dinosaur that the children are learning or already know. Read the book together.
2. Read factual books about dinosaurs to make sure the children learn accurate facts about how the dinosaurs lived.

Art Area

1. Add the dinosaur and tree shaped sponge to the art area. Let the children create dinosaur scenes with them.
2. Add sand to the tempera paint at the art easel for an interesting dinosaur texture.

Related books *Bones, Bones, Dinosaur Bones* by Byron Barton
If the Dinosaurs Came Back by Bernard Most
What Happened to Patrick's Dinosaurs? by Carol Carrick

Virginia Jean Herrod, Columbia, SC

Rub-a-Dub Dinosaurs

Materials

books with pictures of dinosaurs
coloring pages featuring large simple outlines of dinosaurs
textured items (plastic berry basket, corrugated cardboard, sandpaper with assorted grades, cheese greater, colander, piece of screen, piece of bark)
crayons

What to do

1. Ask the children what dinosaurs looked like. Talk about fossils and how scientists use them to gain information about dinosaurs. Explain that skin does not usually become petrified; fossils are most commonly the hard parts of dinosaur bodies (claws, teeth, plates, shells, and bones). Therefore, scientists do not know the actual colors or skin textures of most dinosaurs. Artists use their own ideas when they illustrate them. Show the children some examples from books.
2. Encourage children to use textured objects and crayons to make rubbings on coloring pages of dinosaurs to create skin textures and colors. Demonstrate how to make different rubbings on different body parts or how to layer colors on one dinosaur.

Related books

Dinosaur Days by Joyce Milton
Dinosaur Roar by Paul and Henrietta Strickland
I Can Read About Dinosaurs by John Howard
Saturday Night at the Dinosaur Stomp by Carol Diggory Shields
Ten Terrible Dinosaurs by Paul Strickland

Sandra Gratias, Perkasie, PA

Ten Little Dinosaurs

Materials

none

What to do

1. Sing the following dinosaur song with the children in the dinosaur center.
2. If desired, have ten children line up and pretend to be the dinosaurs in the song. They stand as the numbers are counted, jump together, and then sit as the numbers are counted down.

Ten Little Dinosaurs by Diane Weiss
(tune: "Little Red Wagon")
One little, two little, three little dinosaurs,
Four little, five little, six little dinosaurs,
Seven little, eight little, nine little dinosaurs,
Ten dinosaurs came out to play.
(As you count out dinosaurs, lift one finger for each.)

Jumping up and down went ten little dinosaurs,
Jumping up and down went ten little dinosaurs,
Jumping up and down went ten little dinosaurs,
Making the earth go bump!
(Jump on the word "jump" and clap hands on the word "bump.")

Ten little, nine little, eight little dinosaurs,
Seven little, six little, five little dinosaurs,
Four little, three, little, two little dinosaurs,
One sad dinosaur left all alone.
(Put fingers down as song directs.)

Diane Weiss, Fairfax, VA

To Eat or Not to Eat Meat, That Is the Question

Materials

books about dinosaurs
pictures of different dinosaurs
chart paper
markers
glue or tape

What to do

1. Make several three-column charts with two or more rows than the number of children and adults in the classroom. (For example, if there are 18 children and three adults in the class, make at least 23 rows.) Some groups of children may want to chart only one dinosaur, and others may be interested in charting more. Choose the number of dinosaurs that is appropriate for your group of children.

2. Label each chart "Do I eat meat or plants?" and write the name of one dinosaur on each chart. Attach a picture of each dinosaur next to its name. Label the first column "meat," the second column "plants," and the third with "I'm not sure."
3. After introducing the different types of dinosaurs and reading books about them, ask the children what each may eat. Show them the charts and explain the columns. Put out the charts during free play and if children want to answer the question, they can sign their name in the appropriate column on each chart. Make sure an adult stays at this station to assist the children.
4. To help explain the charts to the group, use one as a transition. Ask the children to sign their name in the column that represents their answer before going to free play.
5. Tally the responses and discuss the results and the correct answers at group time later in the day.

Related books *Dinos to Go* by Sandra Boynton
Dinosaur Stomp by Paul Strickland
Touch and Feel: Dinosaur by Dave King

Ann Kelly, Johnstown, PA

Band-Aid® Pictures

Materials

large, red construction paper
scissors
Band-Aids
markers, crayons, and colored pencils

What to do

1. Cut out large red crosses from red construction paper.
2. Give each child a red cross and four to six band-aids.
3. Encourage them to draw on the cross, attach band-aids, and dictate a story about when they needed a Band-Aid.

Jeanette Denning, Tinley Park, IL

Brush Your Teeth

Materials

small dressing table with mirror (optional) or stand-up mirrors
toothbrushes (one for each child)
plastic cups (one for each child)
small plastic tray
toothpaste
small basins (if possible, use crescent-shaped basins used in hospitals)
tissue

What to do

1. A dental center helps children develop awareness of proper grooming. If available, a small dressing table with a mirror is great to use in this center. If a dressing table is not available, use small stand-up mirrors on a table.
Author's Note: I cut the legs off my table so it would be the proper height for small chairs.
2. Write each child's name on a toothbrush and a plastic cup. Keep these on a shelf out of reach of the children. A teacher or other adult can get them as needed.
3. When children are ready to brush their teeth, give each child his own toothbrush, cup, and basin on a small plastic tray. The children can fill their cups with water and go to the center.

4. When a child enters the center, a teacher or aide places a small amount of toothpaste on the child's toothbrush.
5. Encourage children to brush their teeth using a circular motion. They can watch themselves in the mirror as they brush.
6. The children use the basin to spit out the toothpaste, rinse, and spit again. Provide tissue for them to wipe their lips.
7. When finished, ask children to dip their toothbrush into the remaining water in the cup and stir to rinse well. They can empty the water into the basin.
8. Each child carries his basin to the sink and empties it. Demonstrate how to rinse the basin with clear water, return it to the tray, and wipe it with tissue.
9. The children give their trays to a teacher or other adult to put away. (You need to rinse the toothbrush more thoroughly before returning it to the shelf.)
10. This activity creates interest in caring for the teeth and an opportunity to practice the proper way to brush.

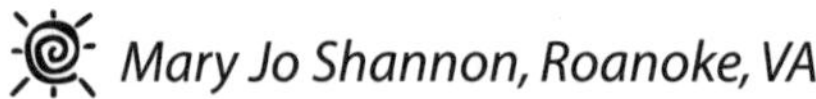

Doctor! Doctor!

Materials

small tables and chairs
appointment book
old telephone
magazines
clean white sheets
tray with medical supplies (stethoscope, pretend plastic syringes, blood pressure cuff, ear thermometer, plastic straws to use as disposable thermometers, tongue depressors, and so on)
large piece of white fabric cut into triangles for a sling
strips of cotton bandages
cardstock paper
markers
disposable hospital hats and gowns
white shirts
plastic gloves
old x-ray film
wastebasket
dolls

What to do

1. If possible, take a field trip to a local hospital or doctor's office or invite a healthcare professional to visit your classroom. Ask him or her to bring along healthcare props for children to touch and explore.
2. Ask the children to help set up a hospital or doctor's office in the housekeeping area. Place the reception area (one table and chair for the receptionist, and two or three chairs and a small table for the patients who are waiting) near the entrance of the center.
3. Put an old telephone, appointment book, and pencil on the receptionist desk. Put magazines on the table in the waiting area.
4. In another area of the center, put two or three small tables. Cover each with a white sheet for "doctors" to use as exam tables. Add another small table and place all the doctor's tools on it. Name the office and create a sign using cardstock and markers. Hang the sign over the entrance.
5. Add doctors' clothes to the dress-up clothes (disposable hats and gowns, white shirts, plastic gloves, and so on).
6. Tape old x-ray films to a window in the area so that the light shines through them.
7. Place a wastebasket near the exam tables. Make sure the children throw away the straw thermometers and tongue depressors after one use.
8. Declare the doctor's office/hospital open for business! Encourage children to take turns playing the receptionist, doctors, and patients.
9. If desired, ask children to bring in their favorite dolls to use as hospital patients.

More to do

Make an ambulance out of a large box. Paint the box so it resembles an ambulance. Cut two handholds in each side of the box. The children can use the ambulance to transport each other to the hospital. Two children can step inside the box at once, and then they can grip the handles and lift the box as they pretend to drive.

Related books

Dr. Duck by H.M. Ehrlich
My Doctor by Harlow Rockwell
Rita Goes to the Hospital by Martine Davison

Doctor's Bag

Materials

oak tag
scissors
markers
12″ x 18″ black construction paper
red construction paper
white Styrofoam tray
white glue
black yarn
adhesive bandages
cotton swabs
cotton balls
craft sticks

What to do

1. Make patterns for a doctor's bag and tools by enlarging the following illustrations, cutting them out, and tracing them on oak tag.
2. Trace the doctor's bag and handle on 12″ x 18″ black paper and cut out. Trace two crosses on red paper and cut out.
3. Trace the pill bottle and syringe on oak tag and cut out.
4. Trace the circle for a stethoscope on oak tag or a Styrofoam tray and cut out. Trace the earpieces of the stethoscope on oak tag and cut out. Connect the earpieces and the circle with black yarn using white glue.
5. Use a marker to draw pills in the bottle and medicine in the syringe.
6. Fold the bag on the fold lines, and glue the sides to form a box. Glue points underneath to secure the bottom.
7. Glue a red cross on each side and put the equipment in the bag. Slide the handle through the slot to close.
8. Add adhesive bandages, cotton swabs and balls, and craft sticks ("tongue depressors") to the bag.

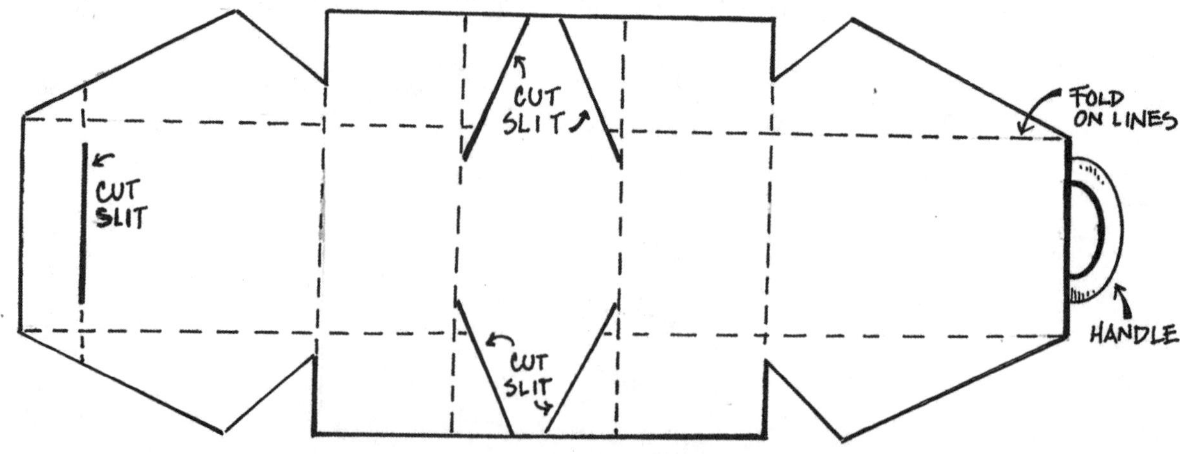

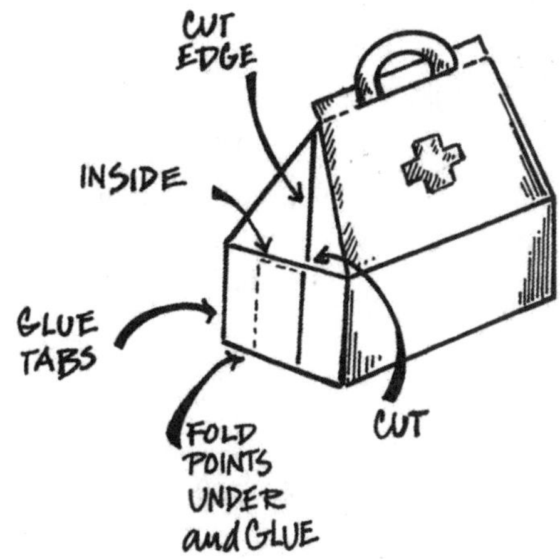

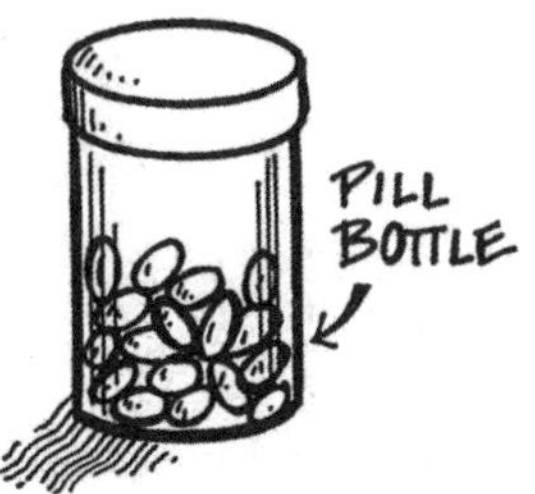

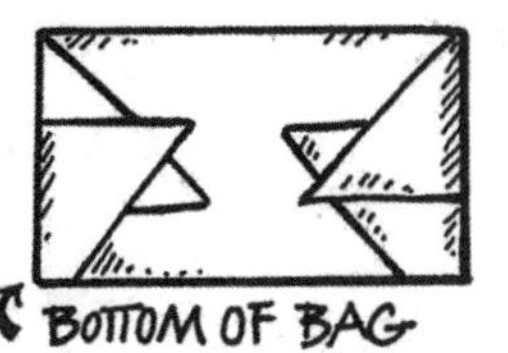

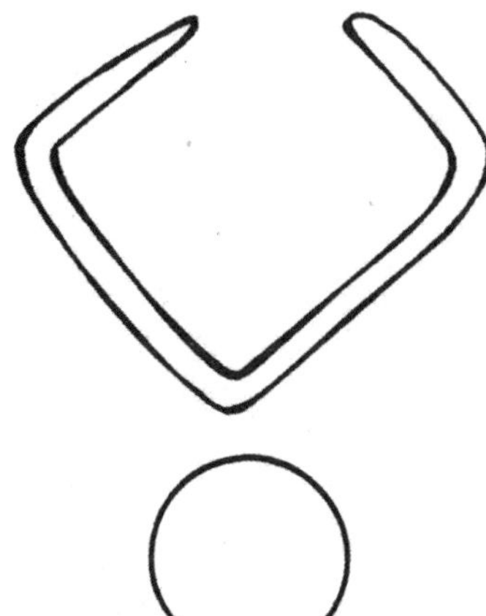

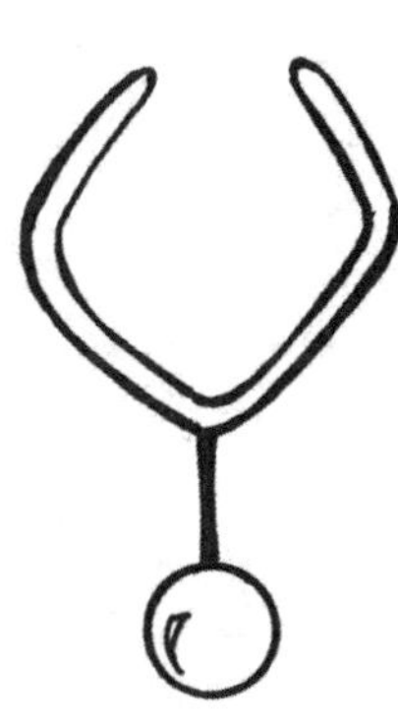

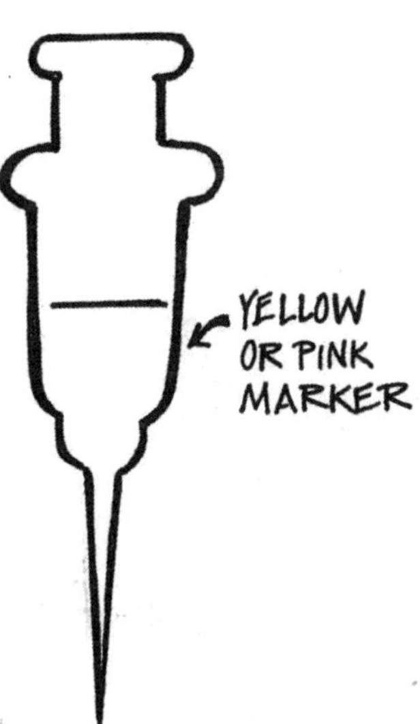

Mary Brehm, Aurora, OH

Doctor's Office

Materials

black bags
stethoscopes
pads of paper and pencils
adhesive bandages
stretch bandages
x-ray films
clipboards
hospital clothing and masks
small flashlights

What to do

1. Set up an area of the classroom to resemble a hospital. Put the above materials in the area.
2. Encourage the children to pretend to be doctors, nurses, and patients. Be sure to mention that boys and girls can grow up to be either doctors or nurses.
3. Read books about visiting a hospital.
4. Include a list of vocabulary words in this center, such as *doctor, nurse, sick, healthy, stethoscope, bandage, x-ray,* and *bones.*

Sue Myhre, Bremerton, WA

Finger Cast Puppets

Materials

cotton roll or gauze
casting plaster (available at medical supply stores or donated by a local hospital)
water
shallow bowls or cups
colored markers
small medicine cups, felt or fabric scraps, buttons, and so on

What to do

1. Children are often fascinated by casts. With this activity they can create their own cast and turn it into something fun to play with.
2. To prepare, cut casting plaster into approximately 2" x 3" strips. Divide cotton or gauze into square pieces large enough to be wrapped around each child's finger. Pour water into shallow bowls or cups.

3. Ask the children to discuss any experiences they may have had with casts. Explain how doctors use casts to set broken bones. If available, show the children an x-ray of a broken bone.
4. Give each child a piece of cotton or gauze and three or four strips of casting plaster. Help each child wrap the cotton or gauze around one of his fingers and hold it in place.
5. Ask the children to take a strip of plaster and soak it in water for a few seconds, and then remove it from the water and wrap it around the cotton or gauze on their finger. This step may be difficult for children to do by themselves; therefore, an adult may want to assist or children might work in pairs.
6. Repeat until the child has covered his entire finger (three strips should be sufficient).
7. As the children work, discuss the differences in the textures of the materials (rough versus smooth, dry versus wet, soft versus hard, and so on).
8. Have the children wet another finger with water and smooth out the small holes in the plaster to create a solid surface.
9. Allow three to five minutes for the cast to dry and then slide it off the child's finger.
10. Let the children decorate their "finger cast puppets" with markers. If desired, provide small medicine cups, felt, or other materials for children to make hats and clothing.

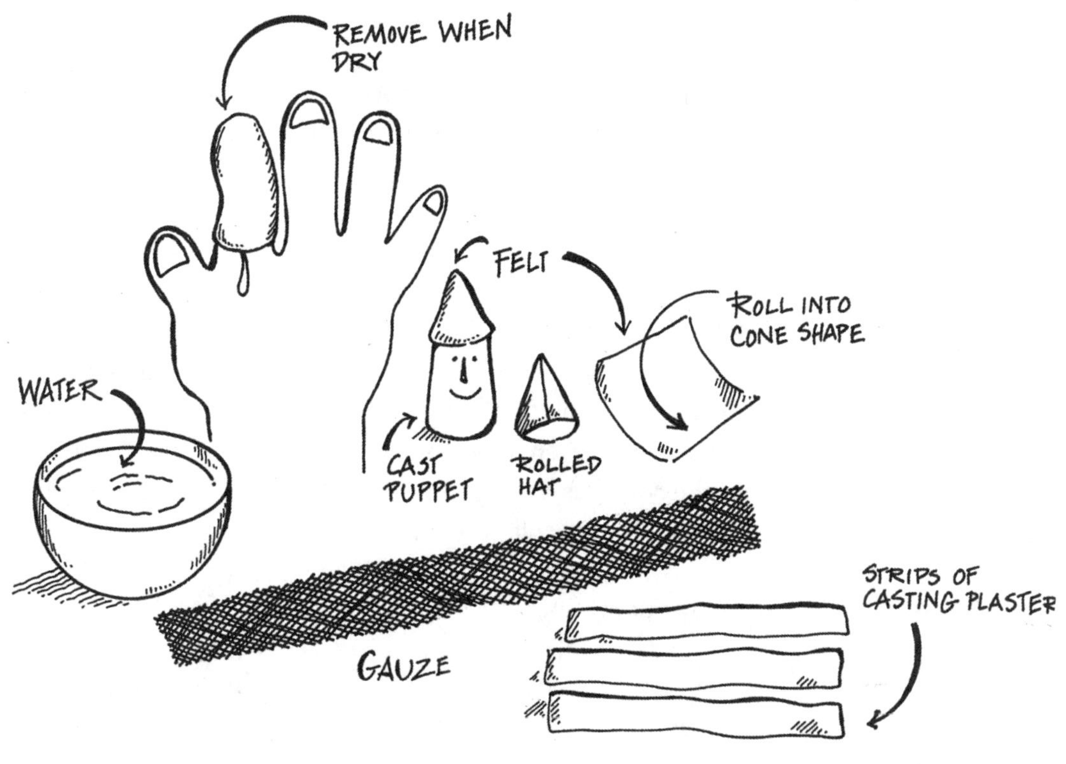

Michelle Barnea, Millburn, NJ

Ice Pack Teddy Bear

Materials

small teddy bear
Velcro
glue or needle and thread
ice pack

What to do

1. Buy a small teddy bear, open up a seam on one side, and remove the stuffing.
2. Glue or sew Velcro to the opening.
3. When a child needs ice for a bump or bruise, put an ice pack inside teddy bear, close the Velcro, and let the child hold the bear where the ice is needed.

Cherra June Wilson, Norman, OK

Medical Collage

Materials

medical supplies (such as medicine cups, surgical masks, adhesive bandages, tongue depressors, plastic gloves, gauze, and so on)
large piece of cardboard or heavy paper
glue
crayons or markers

What to do

1. Show the various medical supplies to the children and discuss their uses. Encourage the children to share their own medical experiences. Let the children examine objects they might see in a doctor's office or hospital.
2. Encourage the children to create a class collage using the medical supplies.
3. Display the collage in the "doctor's office" learning center. Add dictated experiences that the children describe.

Related book *My Doctor* by Harlow Rockwell

Michelle Barnea, Millburn, NJ

Stethoscope

Materials

scissors
oak tag
aluminum foil
hole punch
pipe cleaners
masking tape

What to do

1. Cut a small circle out of oak tag.
2. Cover the circle with aluminum foil.
3. Punch a hole at the top of the circle.
4. Weave a long pipe cleaner through the hole and bend the ends slightly, to go over ears.
5. Tape the ends of the pipe cleaner to cover any sharp edges.

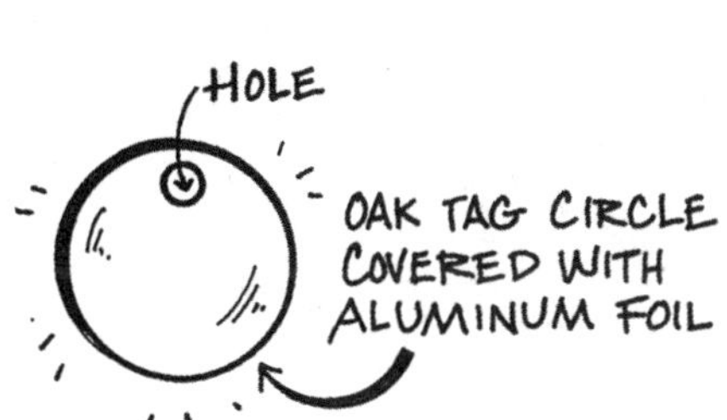

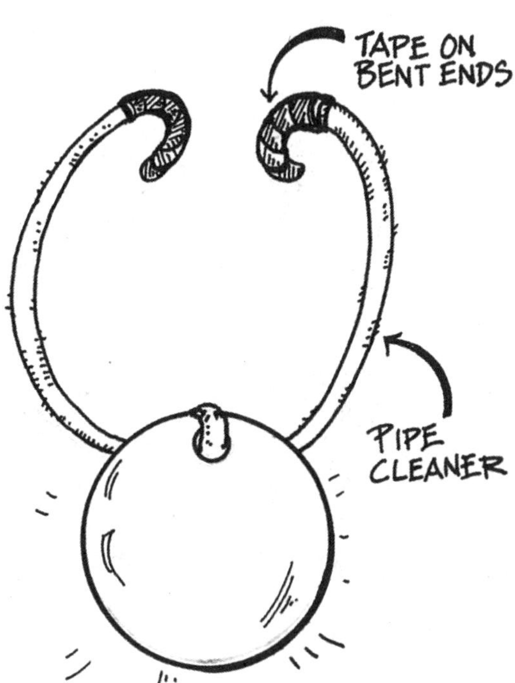

Andrea Hungerford, Plainville, CT

Syringe Painting

Materials

paint
cups or paint containers
paper
syringes without needles (eyedroppers may be substituted)

What to do

1. This project is a great way to introduce a syringe to children in a non-threatening way. Discuss how a syringe works and encourage the children to share their experiences of receiving shots.
2. Pour paint into cups or containers. Place one syringe (with needle removed) in each paint container, or give each child his own syringe.
3. Encourage the children to use the syringes to paint a design on their paper

Related books

Going to the Doctor by Fred Rogers
My Doctor by Harlow Rockwell

Michelle Barnea, Millburn, NJ

Vet's Office

Materials

cardboard
magazines
small boxes or plastic milk crates
small blankets
stuffed animals of various kinds of pets (dogs, cats, guinea pigs, bunnies)
child's doctor kit or small traveling case filled with child-size doctor tools
pet supplies (such as small bowls, leash, empty boxes of dog biscuits, clean pet food containers, and so on)

What to do

1. Set up a veterinarian office in the housekeeping area. Write "Vet's Office" on a piece of cardboard to make a sign for the area. Let children decorate the area with pictures of animals from magazines.
2. Put out several boxes or crates as beds for the sick or injured animals. Use a small table for the examining table.
3. Ask the children to bring in their "sick or injured pets" (stuffed animals) from home or use stuffed animals in the classroom.
4. Encourage the children to pretend to be vets and check the animals using tools such as stethoscopes and tongue depressors. Provide bandages for them to wrap "injured" legs, tails, paws, and so on.

5. Children can let their pets rest on the beds or in the crates.
6. Encourage children to care for the pets by "feeding" them and "walking" them. The children love this center activity as they get a chance to cuddle and care for their pets and others.

More to do **Blocks:** Encourage children to build homes for the animals, such as a doghouse.

Maxine Della Fave, Raleigh, NC

Visit to the Dentist

Materials

cardboard
bottom half of plastic bottles (such as Gatorade)
glue
floss or yarn
toothbrush and toothpaste
dentures

What to do

1. Make large "dinosaur teeth" by attaching four to eight bottoms from plastic bottles to a piece of cardboard. The bottom of the bottle resembles molar teeth.
2. Encourage the children to floss the dinosaur teeth using dental floss or yarn.
3. Provide dentures and encourage children to use real toothbrushes and toothpaste to brush the teeth.

Related books *Brush Your Teeth Please* by Leslie McGuire
I Know Why I Brush My Teeth by Kate Rowan

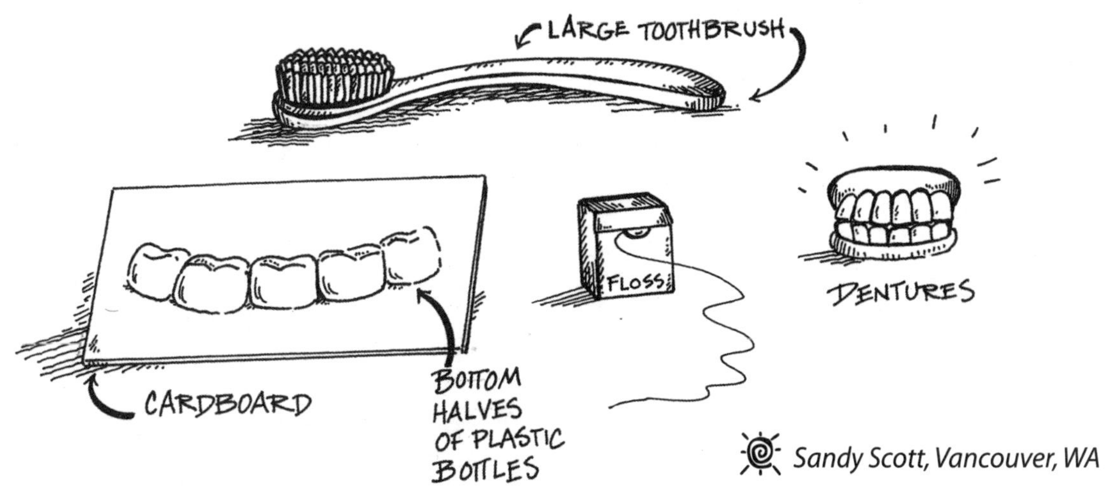

Sandy Scott, Vancouver, WA

Waiting Room

Materials

chairs
coffee table (a box with a piece of fabric or tablecloth covering it works well)
magazines
desk, chair, phone and broken or homemade keyboard
notepad and pencil (for the receptionist)
clipboard, pen and paper numbered down the left side with enough space for the children to sign their name when they come in

What to do

1. After setting up a dramatic play area as a doctor's examination room, arrange furniture in an area next to it to resemble a waiting room. Set up a receptionist area using a desk, chair, phone, keyboard, notepad, and clipboard.
2. Have a group discussion with the children about going to the doctor. Ask them what happens before they can see the doctor. Talk about signing in, parents giving the receptionist an insurance card, reading magazines, and so on.
3. Encourage the children to sign in when they come for an appointment with the doctor.
4. Facilitate dramatic play in this area.

Related books

Blue's Check-Up Sarah Albee
Corduroy goes to the Doctor by Don Freeman
Next Please by Ernst Jandl

Wash Your Hands

Materials

table with chairs and mirror
large tray
plastic dishpan or large bowl
bar of soap in soap dish or small bottle of liquid soap
small plastic pitcher marked to show 1 cup
paper towels

What to do

1. Set up a small table with chairs and mirrors. Place a plastic dishpan, small bottle of soap or bar of soap, and small water pitcher on a large tray. Put the tray on the table.
2. Ask the child to pour water into the pan. The child can dip the soap into the water, or wet his hands, hold one hand under the spout of the dispenser, and press with the other hand to get some soap.
3. Encourage the child to wash his hands, circling each finger. When finished, he can spread his fingers apart and place his hands in the water.
4. The child picks up a paper towel and carefully dries each finger, palms, and backs of hands. Let the child carry the pan to the sink and pour out the water.
5. This activity provides an opportunity to teach vocabulary, such as *thumb, finger, wrist, knuckle, germs* and so on. It also encourages children to wash carefully.

Mary Jo Shannon, Roanoke, VA

Germs, Go Away!

Materials none

What to do

1. Explain that is important to wash your hands to keep the germs away.
2. Teach the children the following poem:

Wash your hands after you play
To make the germs go away,
Germs can make you feel really bad.

Wash your hand before you eat
To make the germs go away,
Germs can make you feel really bad.

Wash your fruits and veggies, too.
To make the germs go away,
Germs can make you feel really bad.

Wash your hands after you potty,
To make the germs go away,
Germs can make you feel really bad.
Germs can be everywhere.

 *Cherra June Wilson, Oklahoma City, OK*

Barn Dance

Materials

country music (CD or tape)
CD or tape player

What to do

1. At group time, ask a child to choose a farm animal and keep it secret.
2. Play country music and encourage the rest of the children to dance the way they think the animal might dance.
3. The child can decide which of the children is dancing like her animal (if at all).
4. Give several children an opportunity to choose a type of animal and repeat the dancing.

Related book *Barnyard Dance* by Sandra Boynton

Ann Kelly, Johnstown, PA

Barnyard Bingo

Materials

cardstock or heavy paper
markers
pictures of farm animals
bingo chips or other markers
tape recorder
cassette tape

What to do

1. Make blank bingo grids on cardstock or heavy paper.
2. Choose several farm animals to use for the game and cut out or draw pictures of each. Make bingo boards by gluing a different picture into each square, randomly, so that all the boards are different from each other. Make enough bingo cards so that each child will get one plus one extra.
3. Show the children the pictures of each animal that will be used in the game. Tape record the children making animal noises of each animal on the bingo cards. To make it is easy to locate the beginning of a game, take note of where each new game starts using the tape counter on the tape recorder.
4. Prior to playing, prepare the children by practicing matching the sounds to animal pictures and naming the animals.
5. Let each child choose a bingo card. Having one extra card gives even the last child to get a card a choice.
6. Play like a regular bingo game.

Related books *Animal Sounds* by Aurellius Battaglia
Down by the Cool of the Pool by Tony Mitton
Touch and Feel Farm by Dorling Kindersley Publishing

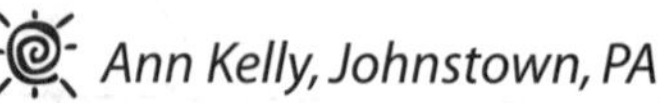
Ann Kelly, Johnstown, PA

Cowboy Bandanas

Materials

plain bandana or white linen napkins
fabric paint
sponges
scissors

What to do

1. Pre-wash the bandanas or napkins.
2. Fold each bandana at the corners so that it resembles a bandana worn at the neck.
3. Make western-themed sponges by cutting sponges into a variety of shapes, such as a horse, cowboy hat, cowboy and lasso, and so on.
4. Provide sponges and fabric paint for children to create designs on the fabric.
4. Children can complete their western outfit with cowboy hats, if available.

Related books *The Big Red Barn* by Margaret Wise Brown
Matthew the Cowboy by Ruth Hooker

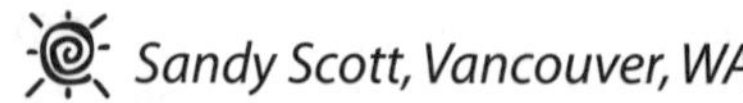
Sandy Scott, Vancouver, WA

Down on the Farm

Materials

farm-related books
farm clothes, such as overalls, boots, straw hats, and gloves
play barn
plastic farm animals
magazines with pictures of farm animals
mural paper
glue

What to do

1. Read farm-related books with the children. Talk about the clothes that farmers wear to protect themselves during the day and why these clothes are needed for the jobs a farmer does.
2. Show the children farm clothes such as straw hats. Encourage them to try on various farm clothes.
3. Talk about farm animals and how a farmer takes care of each. Use a play barn and plastic animals and sing "Old MacDonald" with the children.
4. Encourage children to glue pre-cut pictures of farm animals to mural paper taped to the wall.

Lisa Chichester, Parkersburg, WV

Egg Counting and Sorting

Materials

small bucket
wooden and plastic eggs
baby wipes
empty egg cartons

What to do

1. Put two dozen or more eggs in one or two small buckets.
2. Explain that farmers clean and sort each egg for size before selling them. Provide wipes for cleaning.
3. Provide several types of egg cartons for children to use to count and sort eggs. Also use half-dozen cartons for variety.

Related song **Have You Seen the Mother Hen?**

(tune:"The Muffin Man")

Oh, have you seen a mother hen,
A mother hen, a mother hen?
Oh, have you seen a mother hen?
She lives down on the farm.

Oh, have you seen her baby chicks,
Her baby chicks, her baby chicks?
have you seen her baby chicks?
They hatch from the eggs.

Oh, have you ever gathered eggs,
Gathered eggs, gathered eggs?
Oh, have you ever gathered eggs
From the hen house nests?

Oh, have you ever cracked an egg,
Cracked an egg, cracked an egg?
Oh, have you ever cracked an egg
When helping someone bake?

Oh, have you ever eaten eggs,
Eaten eggs, eaten eggs?
Oh, have you ever eaten eggs,
For breakfast in the morning?

Mary Brehm, Aurora, OH

Farm Animal Patterning

Materials

construction paper (one color)
scissors
long strips of construction paper
glue

What to do

1. Cut out several animal shapes from one color of construction paper.
2. Place the cutouts on long strips of construction paper to make patterns. Make several patterns of varying difficulty, such as AB-AB-… (horse, cow, horse, cow, …) and ABA-ABA-…(duck, lamb, duck,…).

3. Encourage the children to copy the patterns and attempt to continue them on their long sheet of paper.

 *Vicki Whitehead, Satsuma, AL*

Giddy-Up Go!

Materials

plastic horses in a variety of sizes and colors
plastic people
plastic fence pieces
yellow and tan craft paper
scissors
two old coffee cans
plaster of Paris
two dowel rods
craft paper in various colors

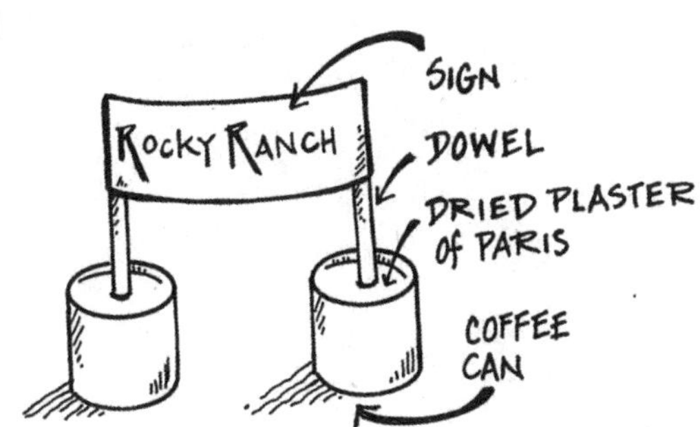

What to do

1. Put the toy horses, people, and fences in the block area. Explain that horses live in barns or stables. Challenge the children to build a place for the horses to live, eat, and sleep.
2. Ask the children to cut tan and yellow craft paper into thin strips to represent hay for feeding the horses.
3. Create an entrance for the "horse farm." Fill two coffee cans with plaster of Paris and put one dowel rod into each can. Let the plaster dry. Encourage the children to choose a name for the horse farm. Write this name on craft paper and attach it a string hung between the two coffee cans.
4. Create three corrals for the horses. Ask children to sort horses by color or size.
5. Create a graph with headings that indicate color or size of the horses. Place a horse sticker on the graph for each type. Ask the children to count the different types of horses and graph the results.

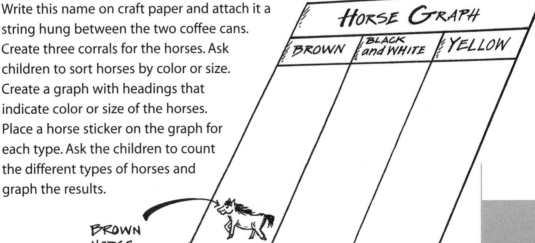

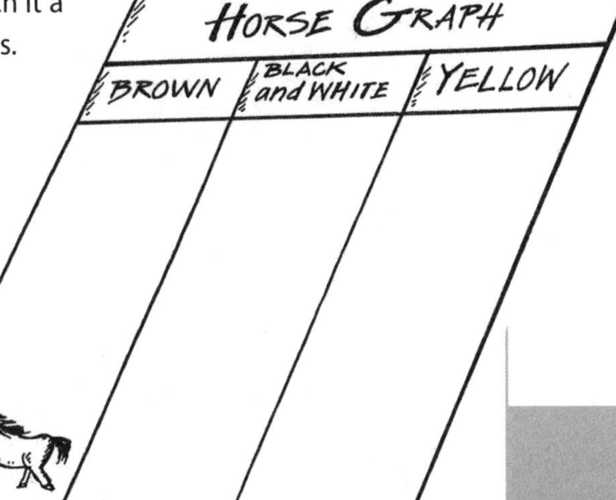

More to Do

Dramatic Play: Extend the horse farm to the house area by adding cowboy clothes. Plaid shirts, denim skirts, overalls, boots, straw hats and riding gloves will surely spark any child's imagination!

More Dramatic Play: Let children make their own hobby horses. Purchase a dowel rod for each child. Fill a white tube sock with batting and let the children create a horse's face with collage materials. Add a mane by gluing on yarn. Slide the tube sock over one end of the dowel rod and tie securely with strong string. Attach a length of heavy yarn to use as a rein. Children can ride their horses!

Sensory Table: Add sand and miniature horses to the sensory table.

Related books

Big Red Barn by Margaret Wise Brown
Billy and the Blaze by C.W. Anderson
Black Cowboy, Wild Horses: A True Story by Julius Lester
Cowboy Dreams by Dayal Kaur Khalsa
The Horse in Harry's Room by Syd Hoff
A Ride on the Red Mare's Back by Ursula K. Le Guin

Related song

Giddy Up Go!
(tune: "Twinkle, Twinkle, Little Star")
Giddy, giddy, giddy up go!
On our horses, off we go!
Riding here and riding there,
We are riding everywhere
Giddy, giddy, giddy up go!
On our horses, off we go!

 *Virginia Jean Herrod, Columbia, SC*

Give 'Em the Boot!

Materials

two posters or pictures of a variety of cowboy boots
scissors
glue stick
tagboard or cardstock
laminator

What to do

1. Make a matching activity with cowboy boots. Use a poster with a variety of boots on them. For a history of boots and photos to share with the children, go to www.traveltex.com.
2. Cut out matching pairs of boots. Glue each boot to a small piece of cardstock and laminate for durability.
3. To play the game, place the cards face down. Let children take turns turning over the cards to find pairs. If a child gets a pair, she keeps the cards and continues her turn. If not, she turns both cards back over.
4. While engaged in this hands-on activity, the children will be honing their visual discrimination skills.

Related book *The Bootmaker and the Elves* by Susan Lowell

Jackie Wright, Enid, OK

Goat Mask

Materials

paper cutter
white construction paper
brown or tan construction paper
cardboard
scissors
crayons
oak tag
stapler
glue

What to do

1. Beforehand, use a paper cutter to cut 2" x 18" paper strips for the headband.
2. Use the illustration below to make a pattern for the goat head and the goat beard out of cardboard. Trace the head pattern on white paper and cut out.
3. Lightly color the goat face brown except for the bridge of the nose, horns, and ears.
4. Draw brown lines as ridges on the horns. Draw a black nose and mouth, and add eyelashes to the eyes.
5. Trace the beard pattern on brown paper. Cut it into fringes and glue it on the goat chin.
6. Cut slits at the eyes so the children can cut out the circles.
7. Staple the headband strip to the mask behind the crown of the goat's head, and measure the headband to the child's head and staple again.

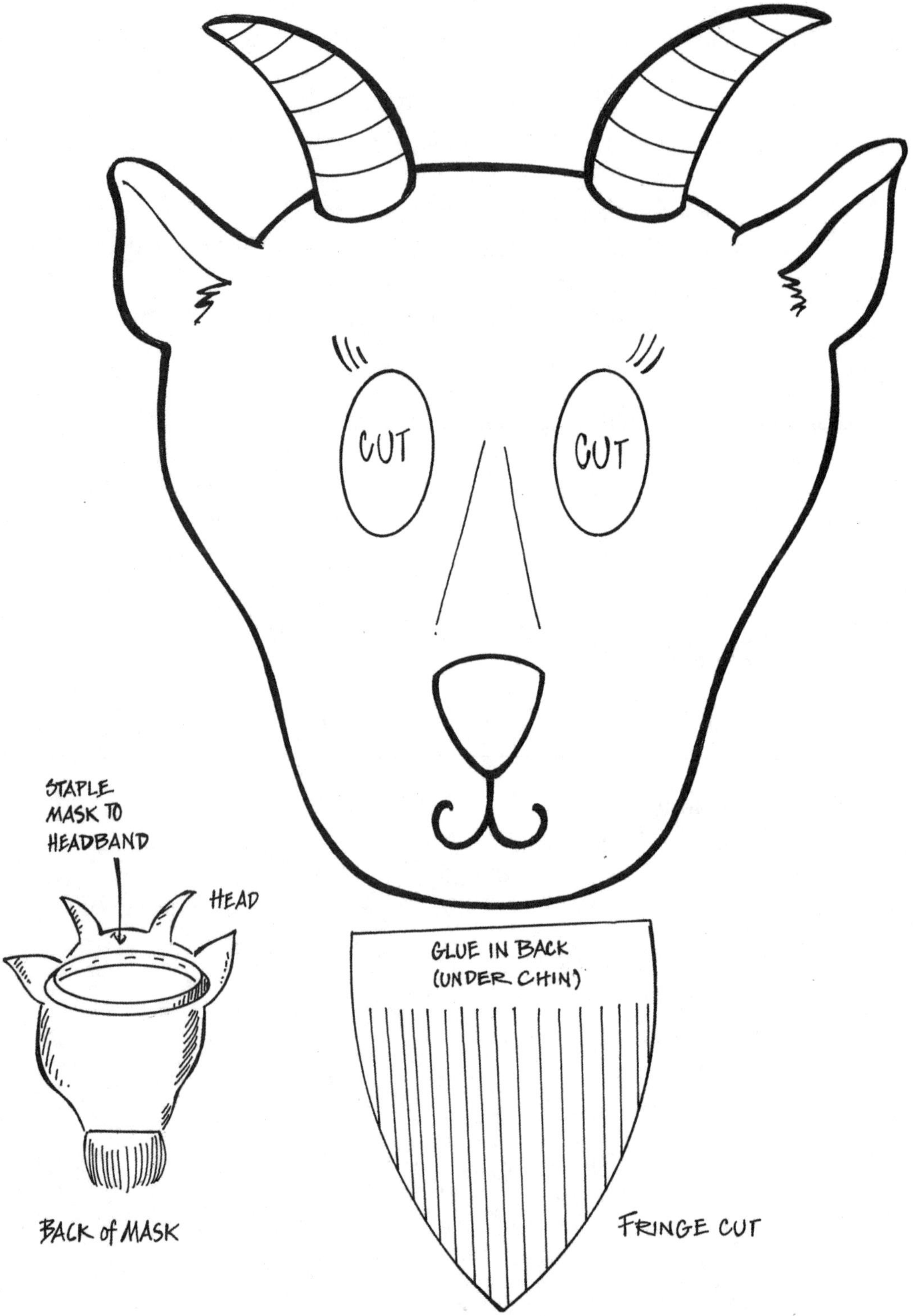

More to do **Stories**: Cut out felt figures of the characters from the "Three Billy Goats Gruff." Have a felt board available for children to retell the story.

Related books *The Little Goat*, a Random House Picture Book
The Three Billy Goats Gruff illustrated by Marcia Brown

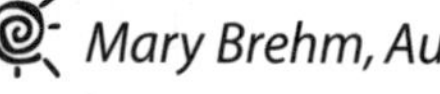 *Mary Brehm, Aurora, OH*

In a Garden

Materials

In a Garden by Ann Kirn
two or three medium-sized cardboard boxes
shredded brown paper
variety of plastic fruits and vegetables (life-sized)
plastic gardening tools (trowel, spade, shovel, rake, watering can, and short length of hose with a nozzle on the end)
fake tree (or make your own)
gardening clothes (apron, hats, gloves, knee pads, flannel shirt, and so on)

What to do

1. Read *In a Garden* to the children. Set up a garden in your house area.
2. Fill two cardboard boxes with brown shredded paper to represent dirt. Put plastic vegetables in the shredded paper according to how they grow naturally. For example, carrots and turnips should go under the "dirt" with only their tops showing, potatoes go all the way under the dirt, and lettuce sits on top. Continue until you have planted all the vegetables. Split them equally between the boxes.
3. Attach a short length of string to each fruit. Tie all the fruit to a fake tree. To save space, tell the children that this is a magical tree in the garden upon which all sorts of fruit grows!
4. Put plastic gardening tools and gardening clothes in the house area. Let the children freely explore the "garden" during center time. Encourage them to dig up the vegetables and pick the fruit from the tree.
5. As the children play, talk to them about what they are doing. Encourage them to work together in the garden and to prepare meals for each other with the foods they have harvested.
6. Occasionally, gather the vegetables and re-plant them and re-hang the fruit so other children can enjoy the activity.

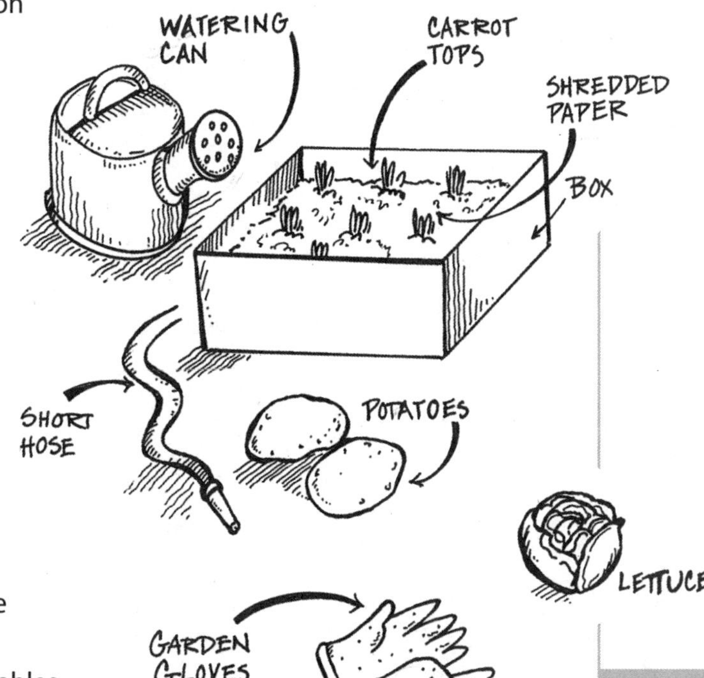

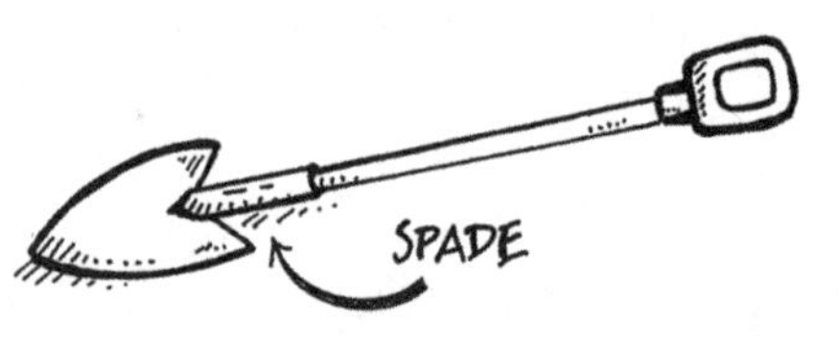

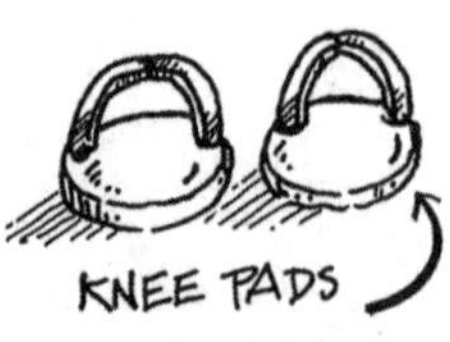

More to do

Math: Ask the children to sort the veggies by how they grow: above ground or below. Create a graph with two headings "Above ground" and "Below ground."
Snack: Make vegetable soup. Enlist a parent to provide a recipe for homemade vegetable soup. Ask each child to bring in an ingredient for the soup. Let the children work together to prepare the veggies for cooking. (Make sure everyone has clean hands!) Add the ingredients to a crock pot and set it to simmer for the day. Enjoy your veggie soup!
More Snack: Make fruit salad. Ask each child to bring in piece of fruit. Give the children plastic knives and let them help prepare the fruit. Mix all the fruit together and enjoy!

Related books

Amelia's Road by Linda Jacobs Altman
How a Seed Grows by Helene Jordan
Stone Soup by Ann McGovern
The Two of Them by Aliki
Vegetable Garden by Douglas Florian

 *Virginia Jean Herrod, Columbia, SC*

Pigs, Pigs, Pigs!

Materials

tempera paint in tray
corncobs with "handles" (short pencils work well)
paper
pink paper
markers
scissors
pipe cleaners (tape optional)
something to curl pipe cleaners on, such as a pencil, dowel, paintbrush handle, or cylinder block
clean dirt in plastic cups
water
paintbrush
heavy paper

What to do

1. Encourage children to explore the farm and appreciate the world of pigs through three easy, fun art activities for the art center.

Corncob Painting

1. Pour tempera paint into a flat tray. Use yellow paint, or any colors children enjoy.
2. Encourage the children to roll corncobs by the handles through the paint, and then roll them onto paper. The corncob makes a polka-dot, bumpy print.
3. Allow prints to dry.

Curly Tail Art

1. Curl a pipe cleaner around a cylinder, and slide off. Make one or make many!
2. Attach the curly tail to pink paper by poking a little hole with the pipe cleaner, or by taping in place. Some children will want to draw a pig and then attach a tail. Others may simply enjoy making curly tails and attaching them randomly to paper. Provide scissors for those who wish to cut out their pig shapes.

Mud Painting

1. Dig up a little clean dirt (no sticks, leaves, or gravel) from a softened soil area of a garden or yard. Fill a plastic cup half full with the dirt and add a little water.
2. Stir with the paintbrush until the dirt becomes smooth mud that is the consistency of tempera paint.
3. Let children paint with mud on heavy paper. Mud makes a surprisingly nice paint (and also works well on fabric stretched over a piece of cardboard or an embroidery hoop). Allow it to dry completely.

Related books

I Love You All Day Long by Francesca Rusackas
If You Give a Pig a Pancake by Laura Joffe Numeroff
Mary Had a Little Ham written and illustrated by Margie Palatini
Olivia Saves the Circus written and illustrated by Ian Falconer
Olivia written and illustrated by Ian Falconer
The Pig in the Pond by Martin Waddell
Pigs From A to Z written and illustrated by Arthur Geisert
Pigs Will Be Pigs by Amy Axelrod
The Three Little Pigs retold and illustrated by Jan Brett
Toot & Puddle: Top of the World by Holly Hobbie

Related song

Do You Love Little Pigs? by MaryAnn F. Kohl
(tune: "Little Surfer Girl" by the Beach Boys)
* Add enjoyable, natural hand motions throughout. Make them up, or use the suggestions throughout the lyrics below:

I have watched pigs on a farm
In the mud all safe and warm.
Do you love them?
Do you love little pigs, little pigs, (hold your hands to your heart)
Those cute little pigs?(make a rocking motion, like rocking a baby in your arms)

Little pigs can squeal and squeak
They are brown or lovely pink.
Do you love them?
Do you love little pigs, little pigs, (repeat motions throughout)
Those cute little pigs? (repeat motions throughout)

When their mommy says, "Snort, snort" (oink twice)
They come running with a "snort" (oink)
Do you love them?
Do you love little pigs, little pigs
Those cute little pigs?

Pigs eat corn and pigs eat spuds, (pretend to eat)
Pigs love sleeping in the mud. (pretend to sleep)
(*Do you love them?*
Do you love little pigs, little pigs
Those cute little pigs?

Pigs have names like Peter and Sue,
Barney, Joe, and Mary Lou. (count on fingers, like counting names)
Do you love them?
Do you love little pigs, little pigs
Those cute little pigs?

Pigs have snouts and pigs have feet,(point to nose and then feet)
Pigs have tails that curl sweet,(make a curly tail with fingers, or point to backside)
Do you love them?
Do you love little pigs, little pigs
Those cute little pigs?

Now our song is at an end,
I hope pigs can be my friends! (make a dreamy face)
How I love them, how I love
Little pigs, little pigs, (make motion of hands over heart)
All the cute little pigs.

MaryAnn F. Kohl, Bellingham, WA

Seed Catalog Games

Materials

poster board
scissors
markers

seed packets
seed catalogs
rubber cement
clear contact paper or laminating film
magnifying classes

What to do

1. Make the following two games using seed packets and catalogs.

Lotto/Bingo

1. Cut poster board into 9″ x 9″ squares.
2. Draw a grid with three rows across and three columns down. Cut out enough 3″ x 3″ squares to cover the boards.
3. Cut out matching pairs of pictures of vegetables, fruits, flowers, and other plants from seed catalogs.
4. Glue one picture on each 3″ x 3″ square. Laminate all and cut out.
5. Use the boards to play Lotto and Bingo the usual way.

Memory/Old Maid Game

1. Cut poster board into an odd number of 2″ x 3″ cards.
2. Cut out matching pairs of pictures (same as Lotto above).
3. Glue the pictures onto the cards with rubber cement.
4. Cut out a picture of a garden and glue it to the last, odd card. Laminate the cards and cut out.
5. Use the cards to play a memory game (without the garden card) or Old Maid, using the garden card as the "old maid card."

Related books

Inch by Inch, the Garden Song by David Mallett
The Surprise Garden by Zoe Hall

Sandra Gratias, Perkasie, PA

Sprouts!

Materials

alfalfa seeds (1 tablespoon)
sentence strips
32 oz. jar
water
cheesecloth
rubber band

What to do

1. Show the children the alfalfa seeds. Ask them what they think the seeds will grow into. Give them time to answer and record their answers on sentence strips.
2. Ask the children to place the seeds in the jar. Help the children pour warm water in the jar until the seeds are covered.
3. Place the seeds in a warm dark place and let them soak for 24 hours.
4. Cover the top of the jar with cheesecloth. Secure with the rubber band.
5. Have a child pour out the water out then rinse and drain the seeds twice. (The cheesecloth will prevent the seeds from falling out.)
6. Repeat steps 3-5 for five days. Make sure all the children get a turn rinsing and draining the seeds.
7. On the last day, place the sprouts in a window to turn green.
8. Bring out the sentence strips from step 1 and compare the children's thoughts about the alfalfa seeds with the actual outcome.
9. Store the sprouts in a refrigerator. Enjoy the sprouts alone, on a salad, or make a sprout and peanut butter sandwich.

More to do

Books: Take photographs of each step of the activity. Paste the photos at the top of a piece of craft paper and make a book about the alfalfa-sprouting experience. Let the children dictate the text for each photo.
Snack: Make your own peanut butter to go with the sprouts! Secure a hand grinder to a sturdy table. Fashion a cone from cardstock paper and attach it to the top of the grinder. This will keep little fingers safely away from danger. Help the children shell some peanuts and add them one handful at a time to the grinder. Add a little oil so the grinder turns smoothly and let children take turns grinding away! Grind about 1 pound of peanuts, adding oil as needed. Stir the peanut butter thoroughly with a spoon. Enjoy!
(**Note:** Be aware of any peanut allergies and plan accordingly.)

Tending the Garden

Materials

assorted artificial flowers and greenery
scissors
sensory table or small tubs
bag of potting soil
gardening gloves
tools such as trowels, rakes
small watering can

What to do

1. Cut artificial flowers and greenery into individual flowers with stems and leaves (scaled appropriately to the size of the table or tub). Place soil in the tub or table. Add flowers, bits of greenery, and small twigs as "weeds."
2. Introduce the activity to the children as practice for caring for a real garden. Describe planting and weeding.
3. Encourage children to care for the "garden" using gardening tools and a watering can. Limit the number of children tending the garden at one time by putting out a certain number of tools.
4. This activity works well as an indoor or outdoor activity.
5. If possible, follow this with planting natural plants and/or caring for a real classroom garden.

Dalmatian Dog Hat

Materials
red and white construction paper
scissors
glue
black inkpad

What to do

1. Cut out large oval shapes from 11" x 18" sheets of red paper.
2. Halve an oval in the center toward the front so that when this is placed on top of the child's head, it will resemble a fire hat.
3. Cut out small oval shapes from white construction paper to resemble Dalmatian ears. Glue the ears to the hats.
4. Let children add black fingerprint spots using inkpads.
5. These are great to wear on a field trip to the fire station!

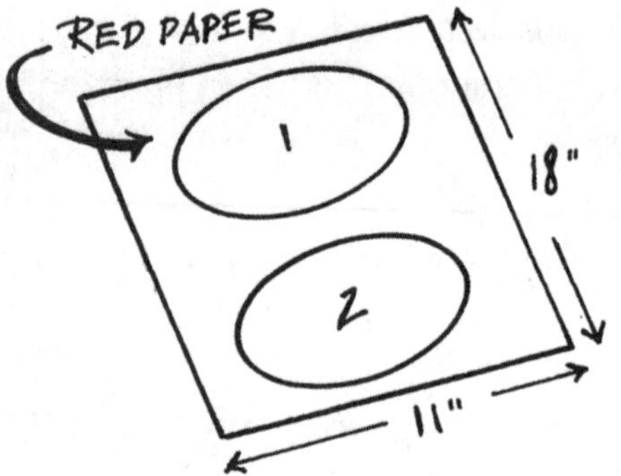

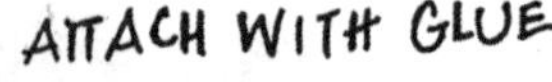

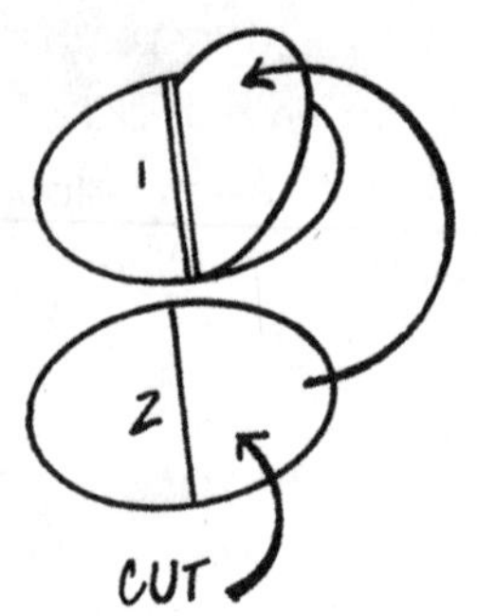

Related books *Clifford the Firehouse Dog* by Norman Bridwell

Sandy Scott, Vancouver, WA

Fire Station

Materials
long hoses
plastic firefighter hats
donated firefighter overalls and boots
suspenders
walkie-talkies
steering wheel and chairs
shiny badges
short stepstool

What to do

1. Set up your area as a fire station. Include firefighter clothing, such as plastic hats, overalls, boots, suspenders, and badges. Let children set up chairs, stools, blocks, and a steering wheel to make a fire truck or fire station.
2. Hang posters of firefighters in action. Include a basket of books about firefighters and emergency volunteers.
3. Model the correct way to hold a fire hose. Let children put out fires!
4. Introduce the children to firefighter vocabulary, such as *rescue, radio, fire truck, and alarm*. Be sure to mention that both boys and girls can grow up to be firefighters.

Fire Station City

Materials

variety of small boxes or milk cartons
white vinyl contact paper
permanent markers
tray
toy fire trucks and cars

What to do

1. Cover the boxes with contact paper.
2. Let children use permanent markers to draw windows and doors on the boxes.
3. Place the box "buildings" on a large tray, and place cars among the buildings. Encourage the children to use the fire trucks to navigate to fires.

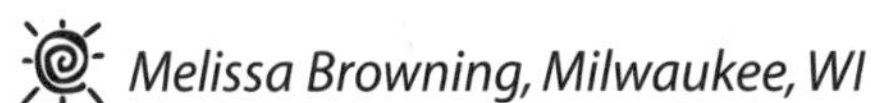

Fire Trucks

Materials

colored poster board
pencil
scissors
hole punch
yarn
tape

What to do

1. Trace the fire truck pattern (see illustration) onto poster board and cut out. Make one for each child in the class.
2. Punch holes around the edges of the trucks.
3. Wrap tape around one end of yarn to make a "needle." Encourage the children to lace through the holes with the taped end of the yarn.

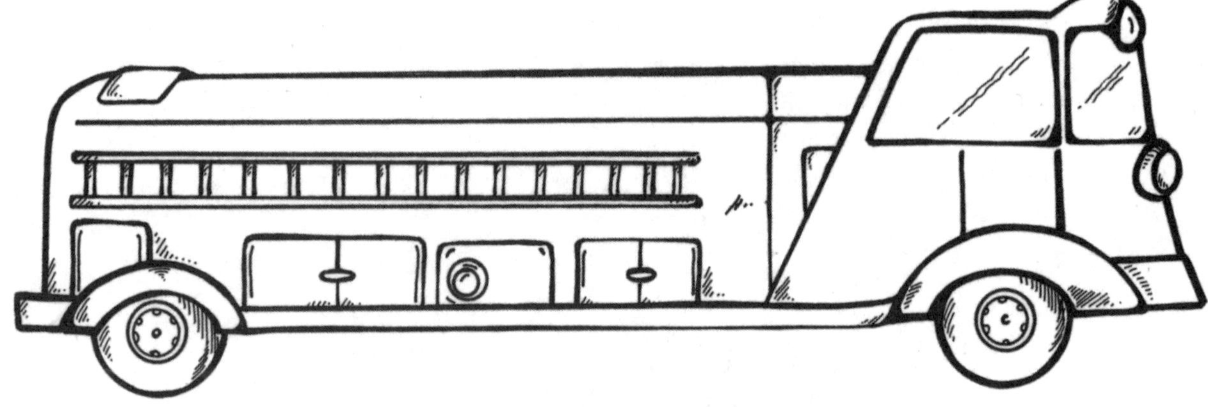

Related books

Fire Truck by Peter Sis
Fire Trucks by Darlene Stille

Related song

There's a Fire by Liz Thomas
(tune: "Frère Jacques")

There's a fire!
There's a fire!
9-1-1!
9-1-1!
Call the fire department!
Call the fire department!
9-1-1!
9-1-1!

Liz Thomas, Hobart, IN

Fire Hose Brigade

Materials

heavy cardboard
scissors
toilet paper tubes
rope or thick yarn, 6′ to 8′ long
glue
round plastic pail
pictures of flames
firefighters' hats and heavy gloves (optional)

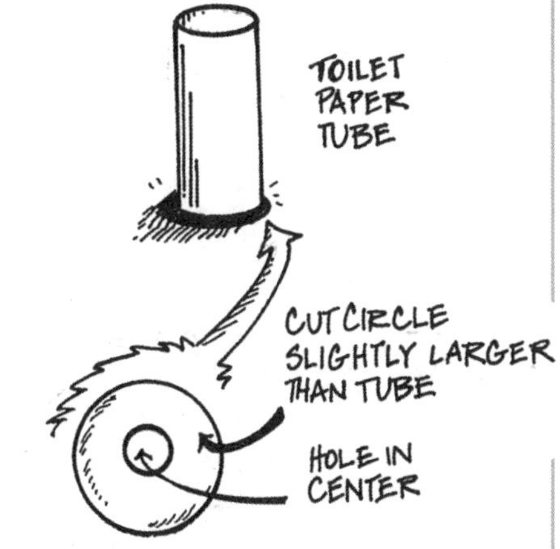

What to do

1. Cut out a cardboard circle slightly larger than the end of a toilet paper tube.
2. Make a hole in the center of the circle and thread the yarn or rope through. Knot or tie the yarn or rope to secure it. Also glue the knot to strengthen the hole and further secure the rope. Let dry.

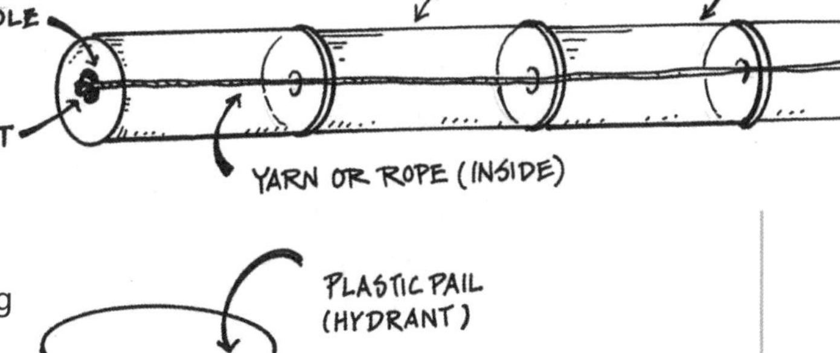

3. Thread empty toilet paper tubes onto the rope, making sure none of the tubes is narrow enough to slip into the one next to it. Keep adding tubes to make a long, flexible hose.
4. Secure another cardboard circle at the other end of the tube to close it.
5. Cut a circle into one side of a plastic pail so that the hose end will fit into it. This will be the hydrant.
6. Cut out pictures of flames from magazines or color some and cut them out. Laminate for durability.
7. Ask the children to place the flames on objects in the room.

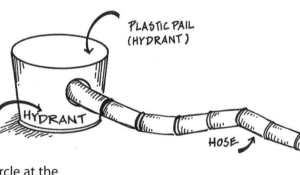

8. Encourage children to work together as a fire fighting team to insert the hose into the hydrant, turn on the water, and carry the hose, support it, aim, and put out the fires. If possible, provide hats and gloves to add realism. Stress the importance of teamwork in fire fighting.

Sandra Gratias, Perkasie, PA

Hurry, Hurry Firefighter

Materials

masking tape or chalk
large bell
two sets of fireman's clothes (two helmets, two pairs of boots, two overalls, two jackets)
four empty 2-liter soda bottles
ribbon
tape
hose

What to do

1. Beforehand, make "air tanks" by taping two 2-liter empty soda bottles together and two large loops of ribbon to the bottles so they can be placed around a child's arms.
2. This activity involves two children racing to get dressed before the other.
3. Set up two stations with equal sets of firefighter clothing.
4. Mark a starting line a few feet away from the clothes stations using masking tape on the floor, or chalk on the ground if outside.
5. Ask two children to line up at the starting line. Encourage the other children to be cheerleaders. If desired, choose a couple of children to be helpers at the clothes stations to assist with the dressing.
6. Have a child ring the bell and the children yell, "Hurry, hurry firefighters!" This signals the start of the race and the two players run to the clothes stations and begin dressing.
7. When both are dressed they run back to the group of children and "put out the fire."

Related book *Fire Fighters* by Norma Simon

Ann Kelly, Johnstown, PA

Learn Not to Burn

Materials picture of a firefighter

What to do

1. Show the children a picture of a firefighter and talk about how this person might save them if they were ever in a fire. Talk about what firefighters do.
2. Play the following game with the children. Explain that smoke rises in a fire. Tell the children that if they ever smell or see smoke, they should get down on the floor below the smoke so they can breathe fresh air. Pick half of the children to play "smoke" while the remaining children try to get away from the smoke. The "smoke" children stand in a line with their legs shoulder-width apart. The other children crawl on their hands and knees and go under the "smoke" (crawl through the children's open legs). Let the children take turns playing smoke and crawlers.
3. Encourage the children to sing the following song as they play.

Related song (tune: "Twinkle, Twinkle, Little Star")

Smoke is bad it hurts our eyes,
And it makes us want to cough.
When we smell it we get low,
And we crawl and crawl some more.
When you smell the smoke and fire,
Don't forget to crawl real low.

Lisa Chichester, Parkersburg, WV

Stop, Drop, and Roll

Materials none

What to do

1. Talk about fire safety with the children. Explain where the emergency exits are in case of a fire at school and talk about having emergency exits at home.
2. Teach the children how to "stop, drop, and roll." Explain that if they are in a fire and a piece of their clothing or hair catches on fire, they should drop to the ground and roll around to extinguish the fire.
3. Encourage the children to practice this while singing the following song.

Related song (tune: "The Mulberry Bush")
Do you know how to stop, drop, and roll?
In a fire it's our goal,
When smoke is thick and a fire is near,
Stop, drop, and roll!

Lisa Chichester, Parkersburg, WV

Paper Plate Football

Materials

paper plates
stapler
brown paint
black marker

What to do

1. Make paper plate footballs with the children. Give each child a paper plate.
2. Children fold their paper plate in half and staple shut.
3. Let children paint the paper plate brown on both sides.
4. When it is dry, use a black marker to draw laces.

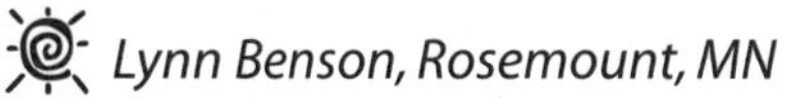
Lynn Benson, Rosemount, MN

At the Gym

Materials

bench
full-length mirror
small table
small pitchers and paper cups
exercise Cds
CD player
wrist weights
basket
gym clothes (belts, headbands, leotards, shorts, t-shirts, wristbands)
small towels
two dowel rods
plastic donuts (like the ones on stacking rings)

What to do

1. Take a field trip to a local gym. Have an instructor talk to the children about health and fitness. If a field trip is not possible, invite an exercise instructor to come to the classroom to talk to the children. Ask him or her to bring along some exercise equipment for the children to explore.
2. Help the children set up a gym in the house area. Include a bench and full-length mirror, and a small table with pitchers of water and paper cups on it. Set up the CD player and exercise CDs where the children can easily reach them.

3. Put small wrist weights on an accessible shelf.
4. Put gym clothes and towels in a basket. Place the basket where the children can easily reach it.
5. Show the children how to slide the plastic donuts over the ends of the dowel rods to simulate weights. The children can lie on the bench and lift the weights. If the plastic donuts fall off too often, simply wrap a piece of masking tape around the ends of the dowel rods to hold them on.
6. Encourage the children to name the gym and create a sign for it. Hang the sign over the classroom door or over the entrance to the house area.
7. Make exercise charts. Take sequential photos of a few children as they do some simple exercises such as push ups, jumping jacks, or sit ups. Use the photos to create a chart that shows how to do each exercise. Post the charts in the fitness area.
8. Let the children use the materials during center time. Remind them to drink lots of water when exercising. Encourage the children to use the exercise CDs.
9. If desired, keep track of the exercises each child does. Create a chart with a variety of exercises listed on it. Let the children place a star or other sticker (use a different color for each child) on the chart when they do each exercise.

More to do

More Fitness: Make a punching bag. Firmly stuff a large plastic grocery store sack with newspaper. Close the bag and secure it with rubber bands. Attach a length of rope to the bag and hang it from the ceiling in the corner of the fitness area. Show the children how to punch the bag. Remind them to not hit so hard that they knock it down.

Blocks: Incorporate the block area by turning it into a tumbling area. Place two or three tumbling mats on the floor. Encourage the children to use the area to safely tumble. Make sure the children know how to tumble safely. Remind them that while cartwheels are fun, they are not for indoor activities!

Related books

2 Is for Dancing: A 1 2 3 of Actions by Woodleigh Hubbard
Here Are My Hands by John Archambault and Bill Martin, Jr.
Tickel Wilby's Fitness Book by Toni Branner
A Yoga Parade of Animals by Pauline Mainland
Your Body From Head to Toe by Nuria Roca

 *Virginia Jean Herrod, Columbia, SC*

Exercise Center

Materials

flip chart or poster
paper
marker
carpeted floor
tape player and audio tapes
full-length mirror

What to do

1. Make a flip chart or poster of stick figures doing the following exercises: jumping jacks, windmills, walking in place, jogging, stepping side to side, and crab walking.
2. Demonstrate the activities for the children.
3. Present choices according to your objectives.
4. Make a check-off list of children's names. Ask the children to check off their names according to what activities they did.

Tip: To avoid overwhelming children with too many activities, "close" some areas according to your plans.

 *Margery Kranyik Fermino, Hyde Park, MA*

Feed Me

Materials

number strip about 1′ x 10′
nine blank index cards
one index card with a picture of a complete meal on it

What to do

1. Ask children to name some things we can do to help keep our bodies healthy, such as eating healthy foods, getting enough sleep, exercising, washing hands before eating, keeping our bodies clean, brushing teeth, and so on.
2. Briefly review the food groups with the children. Ask them to name some examples of foods from each group. Explain that *nutritionists* help us to know how much of which foods we need to eat to stay as healthy as possible.
3. Show the children the blank cards and the one with the complete meal and describe the game they will play. You may want to be the "hungry" person first to demonstrate.

4. Place the nine blank cards and the card with the meal picture on it face down on the floor. Make sure the children do not know which card has the meal on it. Spread the number strip above the row of facedown index cards. The "hungry" child stands on "start" at the beginning of the number strip, while the other children tell her to move forward or backward a number of steps. At each number, the child stops and picks up the card to see if the meal is on it. Continue this way until the child gets her meal.
5. Give each child a turn to be the hungry child.
6. Depending on the children's developmental level, you may want to ask them to put the blank cards down after looking at them to encourage them to remember which ones were blank, or you could collect the blank cards from the hungry child as she picks them up.
7. Review by asking children to name a few of the foods on the meal card and identify which food groups they belong to.

Note: You can vary this game to accommodate any theme, such as children's names, colors, addresses, vehicles, shapes, and so on.

Related books *Bread and Jam for Frances* by Russell Hoban

Shirley Salach, Northwood, NH

Homemade Skis

Materials

cardboard
duct tape
shoelaces or thick string

What to do

1. Cut two ski shapes out of cardboard, about 1 ½' long and 5" wide. Cover both skis completely with duct tape.
2. Place a shoelace across the width of each ski, about one quarter of the way from the tip of the ski. Tape it to the ski to make a loop for the child's shoe.
3. The children may slide across the floor and pretend they are cross-country skiing.

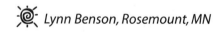

 *Lynn Benson, Rosemount, MN*

How Long/Many Can I...?

Materials

blank cards
pictures from magazines depicting gross motor actions or markers
large sheet of paper
marker

What to do

1. Make a set of cards depicting gross motor action on them (such as hopping, running in place, jumping rope, walking a line, and so on). Find pictures in magazines or draw your own.
2. Place the cards face down in the middle of your circle area.
3. Call one child up at a time to pick a card. The child then guesses how long or how many times she can do the gross motor activity depicted on the card.
4. Write the child's name, the activity, and the child's goal on a piece of paper. The rest of the children count as the child attempts her goal. Write the actual number next to the child's guess.
5. This is a great way to transition to free play. Each child gets a turn before going to free play. To speed things up, several children can go at once and you can write a number for the group.
6. Discuss the results on the chart at a later circle. Who had the most hops? How many children picked the "running in place" card? Who walked the longest line?
7. This activity can be repeated several times to see if children can improve their numbers.

Related books

From Head to Toe by Eric Carle
My Amazing Body: A First Look at Health and Fitness by Pat Thomas

Ann Kelly, Johnstown, PA

Indoor Ice Skating

Materials

pictures of ice skaters
long rope
wax paper
scissors

What to do

1. Talk about winter activities with the children. Ask the children if they have ever seen figure skating or ice hockey on television or if they have ever been ice skating. If possible, show pictures of ice skating.
2. Cut wax paper into rectangles.
3. Demonstrate how to place each foot on piece of wax paper and slide your feet as if skating on ice. The wax and floor become slippery so be careful!
4. Place a rope in a large circle to mark the edges of the "skating rink."
5. This is a great winter activity to do without bundling up. A wooden or tile floor can be more slippery than a commercial-grade carpet. Adult supervision is necessary.

Sandra Nagel, White Lake, MI

Let's Get Fit

Materials

jump rope for each child
plastic water bottle for each child
craft paint
stickers
permanent marker

What to do

1. Talk about how important exercise is to our bodies to keep us healthy. Ask the children if they exercise.
2. Give each child a jump rope and play music while children jump. Talk about how jumping rope is a great way to keep their hearts in good shape.
3. Let children make special water bottles to keep hydrated during workouts. Give each child an inexpensive plastic water bottle.
4. Encourage them to decorate their bottles by finger painting polka dots or putting stickers on their bottles. Help them write their names on the bottles with a permanent marker. Explain how it is important to stay hydrated when they exercise.

Lisa Chichester, Parkersburg, WV

Yoga Studio

Materials

yoga mats or beach towels
soft light lamp (with pink or blue light bulb)
wind chime
portable tape or CD player
relaxing music
indoor fountain with running water (optional)
eye pillows
small blankets
smooth river stones

What to do

1. The first step in creating a yoga studio in the classroom is removing clutter. An uncluttered area leads to better concentration and peace. Cover any distracting objects with sheets or fabric.
2. Use a soft light bulb in this area with a small lamp. To add soft color, use a blue or rose bulb.
3. Play appropriate relaxing music, if desired.
4. Hang a crystal or wind chime and other works of art to promote serenity. You may also post photos of people practicing yoga.
5. Since children should be barefooted while doing yoga, place yoga mats or beach towels on the floor to guard against slipping.
6. If available, include an indoor fountain to add ambience to the yoga center.
7. Provide eye pillows (made from dry rice and fabric) and small blankets for meditation and rest times. Also, smooth stones work well as "worry stones." Tell the children they can rub the stones with their fingers to aid in relaxation.
8. If you are not experienced in yoga, there are many great videos and books for learning. Try a few, and then introduce the children to the joy of yoga. Practice together, working out the poses. When the children are ready, they can try the poses on their own.

Related books

Babar's Yoga for Elephants by Laurent de Brunhoff
Children's Book of Yoga: Games and Exercises by Thia Luby
Fly Like a Butterfly: Yoga for Children by Shatka Kaur Khalsa
Imagine That: A Child's Guide to Yoga by Kenneth Cohen

Related songs

Ocean Moods by Natural Wonders
Raffi Let's Play by Raffi
The Lion King by Walt Disney Records
Yoga Zone: Music for Meditation by Windham Hill Records

 *Sherry Harper, Coventry, RI*

Colors of the Garden

Materials

9″ x 12″ construction paper in various colors found in a garden
scissors
stapler
white craft glue
seed catalogs and magazines
markers

What to do

1. Cut each piece of 9″ x 12″ paper into four sections (each section will be a page). Make booklets by stapling together one of each color of construction paper so that all the pages are a different color. Make one for each child.
2. For very young children, pre-cut pictures of flowers, vegetables, fruits, and trees in all of the different colors. For older children, provide magazines, seed catalogs, and scissors for them to cut out their own pictures.
3. Help young children look through the precut pictures and match the items' colors to a page in their booklets. Let them glue the pictures to the matching color pages.
4. Older children can look through the magazines for pictures of items that match the colors of the pages. They can cut out the pictures and glue them to the pages of the booklets. Ask them to label their pages with the first letter of the picture or color words.

Related books

Let's Make a Garden by Tamara Awad Lobe
The Surprise Garden by Zoe Hall
Planting a Rainbow by Lois Ehlert
Round the Garden by Omri Glaser

Sandra Gratias, Perkasie, PA

Daffodils

Materials

white and yellow cupcake liners
Popsicle sticks
glue

What to do

1. Give each child one white and one yellow cupcake liner. Show them how to flatten one of the cupcake liners.
2. Ask the children to spread glue on the center of the flattened cupcake liner, and stick the bottom of the other liner to the glue to make a daffodil.
3. Provide Popsicle sticks for them to glue to the back of the daffodil to make a stem.

Related books

The Flower Alphabet Book by Jerry Pallotta
Fran's Flower by Lisa Bruce
A Reason for a Flower by Ruth Heller

 *Liz Thomas, Hobart, IN*

Floral Arranging 101

Materials

assorted artificial flowers and greens
florist foam
various baskets or tubs (margarine tubs work well)
photos, posters, or pictures of flower arrangements

What to do

1. Cut artificial flowers and greenery into individual flowers with stems and leaves. Cut foam to fit into each basket or tub.
2. Hang photos, posters, or pictures of flower arrangements in the area. Discuss the pictures with the children. Encourage the children to talk about the placement of flowers in each arrangement.
3. Demonstrate how to push stems into the foam.
4. Encourage the children to create their own arrangements.
5. Children may take their creations home, use them to decorate the classroom, or take them apart for use another day.

More to do

Field Trip: Take the children to a flower shop beforehand for helpful inspiration.

 *Jean Lortz, Sequim, WA*

Flower Shop Alphabet

Materials

construction paper
scissors
markers
glue
craft sticks
Styrofoam cups

What to do

1. Cut out flower shapes from construction paper. Write a lowercase letter on each flower shape. Glue each flower to a craft stick.
2. Invert the Styrofoam cups and label the side of each one with uppercase letters that correspond to the letters written on the flowers.
3. Make a small slit in the top of each cup so that a flower (craft stick) will stand in it.
4. Put the cups in the flower shop center. Be sure to invert the cups so the slit is on top.
5. Encourage the children to look for the flowers with letters that match the letters on the cups. Ask the children to put each flower in its correct "pot."

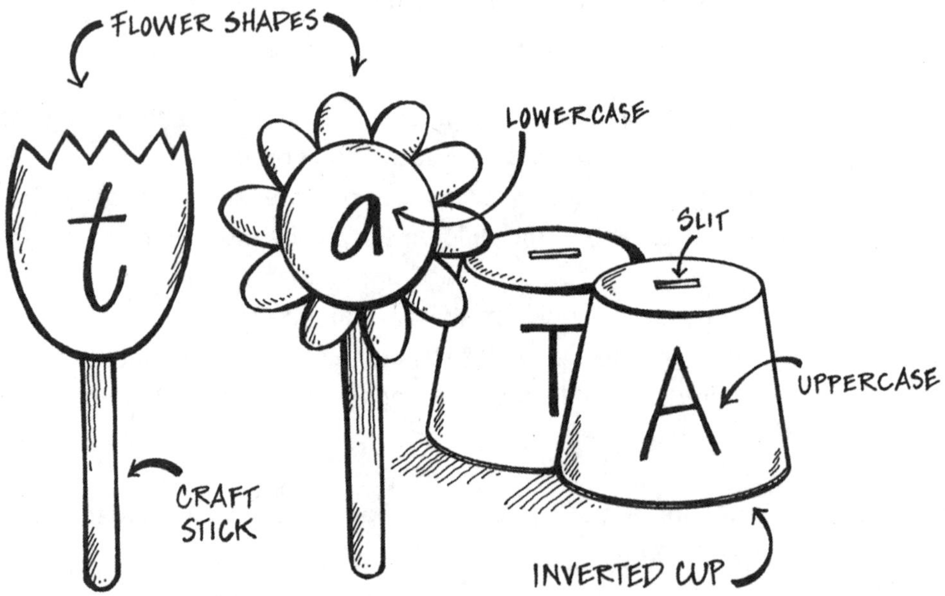

Related books *Flower Garden* by Eve Bunting
Grandma's Purple Flowers by Adjoa Burrowes
The Little Flower Girl by Linda Brandon
The Reason for a Flower by Ruth Heller

 *Suzanne Maxymuk, Cherry Hill, NJ*

Flower Show

Materials

fresh-picked flowers and ferns or other greenery
scissors
unbreakable vases or tall unbreakable glasses
name cards or labels
posters or photos of floral arrangements

What to do

1. Ask parents to help their children gather flowers from their yards or choose an inexpensive bouquet from the supermarket to bring to class. You may also take the children into a field to pick wildflowers.
2. Put all of the flowers and greenery in the flower shop center. Cut stems that are too long, if necessary. Talk about the flowers and floral arrangements with the children.
3. At center time, give each child an unbreakable vase or glass. Ask them to fill their containers ¼ full of water and select flowers and greenery to make arrangements. You may need to limit the amount per child.
4. Place floral arrangements in the hall, entrance, or foyer for everyone to see, or place them in various locations around the classroom. Be sure to include the child's name with the arrangement.
5. Encourage the children to view and smell the flowers. Invite other classes or visitors to do so as well.
6. If desired, have the children deliver the arrangements to a local nursing home. Or use the floral arrangements as centerpieces for a tea, luncheon, or special program for parents.

Painting With Plants

Materials

plant material of different shapes and sizes such as leaves, petals, flowers, stems, roots (rinsed), evergreens, and so on
washable paint
rollers, paintbrushes, and sponges
white construction paper
newspapers

Flower Shop

What to do

1. Show the children the plant material and let them examine it. Encourage them to feel the textures, look for veins, compare shapes, and so on.
2. Let children paint on one side of the plant part with a roller, paintbrush, or sponge.
3. Show children how to place several painted plant parts paint side down onto white construction paper, cover the paper and plants with newspaper, and rub and press down on the objects through the newspaper.
4. Ask them to remove the newspaper and the object to reveal the print.

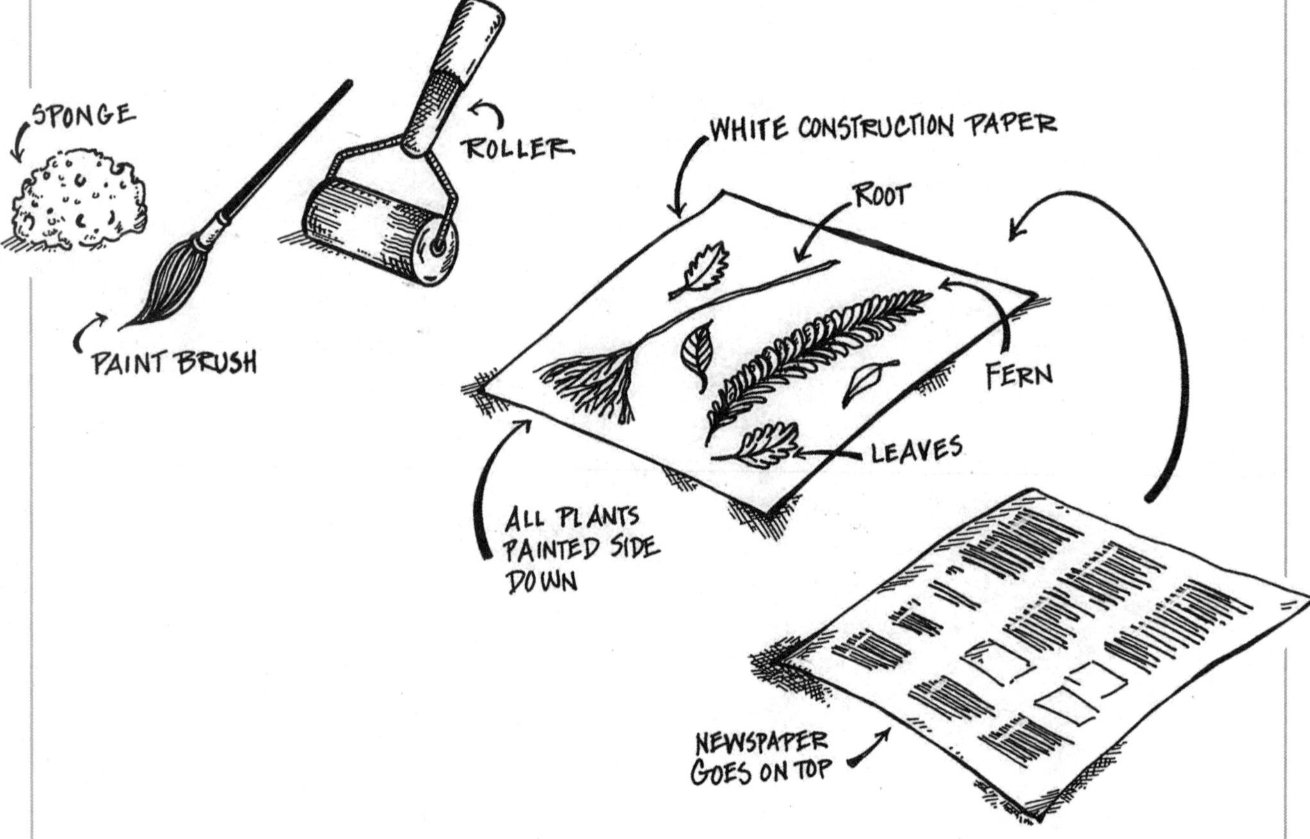

Related books

Fall Leaves by Mary Packard
Fall Leaves Fall by Zoe Hall
From Seed to Dandelion by Jan Kottke
Red Leaf, Yellow Leaf by Lois Ehlert
The Surprise Garden by Zoe Hall

Sandra Gratias, Perkasie, PA

Color Carnations

Materials

white carnations
clear vases
food coloring
water
greenery
several plastic vases

What to do

1. Trim the bottom of each flower at an angle.
2. Fill a few vases with different colors of water.
3. Place the carnations in colored water. It is helpful to keep one white carnation for comparison.
4. The carnations will "drink" the colored water and the petals will turn the same color as the food coloring in the water. Discuss the results with the children.
5. Help the children set up a flower arrangement area. Encourage them to use the carnations and greenery to make arrangements in plastic vases.

Related books

The Flower Garden by Eve Bunting
Growing Colors by Bruce McMillan
The Reason for a Flower by Ruth Heller

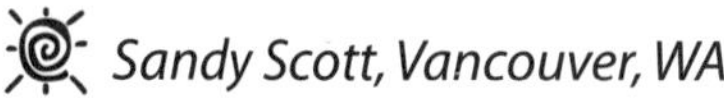
Sandy Scott, Vancouver, WA

Flower Power

Materials

book on flowers and plants and how they grow
old flower pots
toy potting tools
silk or plastic plants or flowers
watering can
price tags
markers
paper money
play cash register
large paper grocery bags, one for each child
paint
precut construction paper flowers
scissors

Flower Shop

What to do

1. Take the children on a field trip to a flower shop. Back in the classroom, show them a book on flowers and plants and discuss.
2. Brainstorm with the children how they could set up a flower store in the housekeeping area. They might suggest using old pots, toy potting tools, silk flowers and plastic plants, a watering can, blank price tags, and so on.
3. After setting up the shop, encourage the children to pretend to be customers, cashiers, and flower arrangers in the "flower shop."
4. Give each child a large paper bag. Cut a hole in the bottom of each bag (big enough for a child's head to fit through) and a hole on each side to make armholes.
5. Encourage the children to paint their bags using bright colors of paint. Provide paper flowers for them to glue all over their bags.
6. The children can wear their flower bags and can pretend to be flowers growing in the sun, rain, wind, and being watered.

Flower Surprise

Materials

various cut flowers and greens
water
scissors
spray glue (found at craft stores)
glitter
camera

What to do

1. Let children pick fresh flowers and greens outside, or get them beforehand from a grocery store. Many stores give old flowers to teachers for free.
2. Demonstrate to the children how to make a simple flower arrangement using the flowers and a vase.
3. Next, demonstrate how to lightly spray the arrangement with spray glue.
4. The final step is the big surprise! Sprinkle the arrangement with glitter. It will stick to the glue.
5. Encourage the children to make their own arrangements. Make sure they don't sprinkle too much glitter on the arrangement or the petals and leaves may collapse.
6. When the arrangements are dry, take a picture of each child with his arrangement. The flowers can be taken home and given to a loved one, as a gift, while each child will still have a picture to brighten a dreary day.

Related books *The Birthday Flowers* by Larry Dane Brimner
Buds and Blossoms: A Book About Flowers by Susan Blackaby
Flowers by Gail Saunders-Smith
Flowers by Jackie Dwyer
Grandma's Purple Flowers by Adjoa J. Burrowes
Plants and Flowers by Sally Hewitt

Mike Krestar, Latrobe, PA

Flowers for Sale

Materials

green pipe cleaners
coffee filters
Liquid Watercolors
paintbrushes
colored construction paper
seed catalogs
plastic flowers
cash register
play money

What to do

1. Show the children how to make flowers from coffee filters and pipe cleaners. Form a flower shape by making a "tent" with one or two coffee filters, and then grab the pointed part and twist it tightly to form the beginning of a stem.
2. Twist the end of a green pipe cleaner around the twisted end of the coffee filter to form the stem.
3. Help the children make their own coffee filter flowers.
4. Encourage them to paint their flowers using Liquid Watercolors.
5. Help the children tape a piece of construction paper into a

cone shape to act as the wrapping for a bouquet of flowers. They may want to decorate this as well.

6. Set up a table for children to "sell" their flowers. Encourage them to dictate words for flower shop signs and glue on flower pictures cut from seed catalogs. You may want to add plastic flowers, a cash register, and play money.

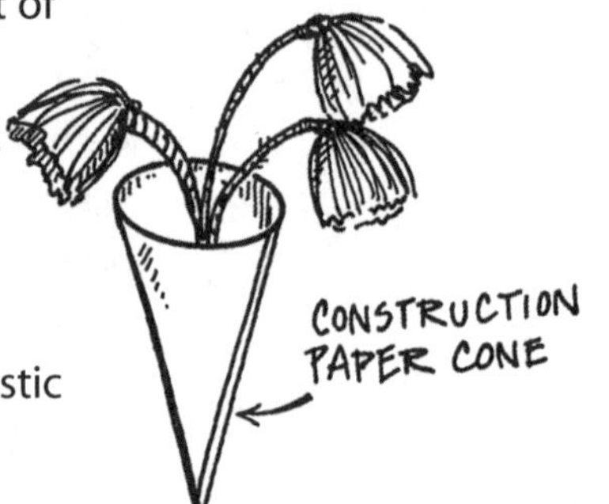

Related books *ABC Book of Flowers for Young Gardeners* by JoAnn Stoker
The Reason for a Flower by Ruth Heller
The Rose in My Garden by Arnold Lobel
Miss Rumphius by Barbara Cooney

Laura Durbrow, Lake Oswego, OR

These Are for You

Materials

small pieces of paper or index cards
colored pencils
plastic flowers
tissue paper (to wrap flowers in)
staplers (to secure the tissue paper and notes)

What to do

1. Visit a local flower shop to show the children what goes on in that type of business.
2. Ask someone to pretend to deliver flowers to the classroom with a note attached. Read the note to the group and discuss with them that when flowers are sent to people, they come with a little note from the person who sent them.
3. Put the materials in the dramatic play area. Encourage the children to write a note before they deliver any flowers. Be available to take dictation and assist the children with their notes.

Related books *Flower Garden* by Eve Bunting
Oh Say Can You Seed?: All About Flowering Plants by Bonnie Worth
Planting a Rainbow by Lois Ehlert

Ann Kelly, Johnstown, PA

What's That Smell?

Materials

cotton balls
several cups
variety of floral scents (potpourri oils work well)
two pictures of each floral scent
masking tape
pen
piece of poster board
glue

What to do

1. Place two cotton balls in the bottom of each cup.
2. Pour enough potpourri oil on the cotton balls to saturate. Make two cups of each scent.
3. Write the names of the floral scents on masking tape and stick to the bottom of the matching cups.
4. Ask the children to match the scents by finding two that smell the same.
5. For added difficulty, trace the cups onto a piece of poster board. Glue one floral picture (one for each scent) in each circle so that each scent has a picture that it can be matched to. Also, write the name of the flower under the appropriate picture. After a small group has had an opportunity to smell the scents and discuss their names, encourage the children to try and match the cups to the pictures they represent.

Related books

Flower Garden by Eve Bunting
Oh Say Can You Seed?: All About Flowering Plants by Bonnie Worth
Planting a Rainbow by Lois Ehlert
What's That Smell?: A Lift and Sniff Flap Book by Janelle Cherrington

Ann Kelly, Johnstown, PA

Garage Sale

Materials

garage sale signs
cash register
money
small tables and shelves
colorful sticker dots and price tags
play money
table with umbrella and chairs
lemonade stand

What to do

1. This is a great center for children to get creative. For a few weeks, let the children pretend to have a garage sale in the center. Then ask them if they would like to have a real sale.
2. Prepare for the sale by asking parents to donate old items they no longer want or need. Help the children make price tags for each item.
3. On the day of the sale, set up the classroom with signs, tables, and a lemonade stand. Encourage parents to shop at the sale when they pick up the children. Invite parents of children in other classes, too.
4. After the sale, help the children count the money. With the money they earn from the sale, buy the group a special treat.

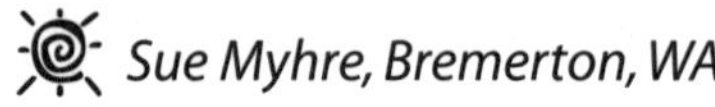
Sue Myhre, Bremerton, WA

How Much for That?

Materials

large piece of paper
markers
dramatic play items
price tags
pretend money
cash box

What to do

1. Write "What we know about a garage sale" at the top of a large piece of paper. During large group time, ask the children to tell you what they know about a garage sale. Write down their comments on the large sheet of paper. If necessary, steer the conversation toward pricing the items for sale.

2. Encourage the children to help set up the dramatic play area for a garage sale. Help them prepare price tags for the dramatic play items and display the items around the area.
3. Involve parents, if desired, by requesting they have their child choose an item from home to add to the garage sale. You can also organize a fundraiser by having the children and families sponsor a real garage sale.

Related book *Yard Sale* by Mitra Modarvessi

Ann Kelly, Johnstown, PA

Trash to Treasures

Materials

donated items from the children's homes
small round stickers
markers
craft paper

What to do

1. Take the children on a walk to a neighborhood garage sale. Encourage the children to look at all the items on sale and talk to the people having the sale.
2. Tell the children they will be having their own garage sale. Ask parents to let the children bring in one or two items that they are absolutely sure they no longer need or want. Ask the parents to contribute one or two items also.
3. When the items arrive, ask the children to sort them into different categories, such as stuffed toys, dolls, cars, action figures, books, women's clothes, men's clothes, children's clothes, and so on.
4. Let the children decide how much each item should cost. Keep the prices extremely low (between a penny and a quarter).
5. Help the children use stickers and markers to create a price tag for each item.
6. Arrange the items around the room according to the categories they were sorted into.
7. Ask the parents to give their child a dollar's worth of change. Make sure they have at least one quarter, one nickel, and one dime. The rest of the dollar can be in pennies.
8. Create a "Garage Sale" sign using markers and craft paper. Hang the sign on the classroom door.

9. Encourage the children to browse through the items for sale. Give them a lot of time during the day to browse the sales items and make their purchases. They can buy any item they choose as long as they have the right amount of money. Give LOTS of help with addition and subtraction. Use the actual money to demonstrate these principles.
10. Be prepared for children who want to take back the things they brought. Explain that they can certainly buy back their own items if they wish.
11. After the children have finished shopping, invite other classrooms to visit the garage sale. Give the visiting children a few coins so they can purchase something.
12. Continue the garage sale until all the items are purchased or the children's interest wanes. Give the remaining items back to the children who donated them or give them to a local charity. You may want to keep the women's and men's clothes for your dress-up center.
13. Collect the money the children spend on the items so you can give it back to the parents at the end of the activity.

More to do Hold a toy drive. Encourage the children to bring in new and gently used toys, which they can donate to a local children's charity.

Outdoors: In good weather, take some tables outside and turn your garage sale into a yard sale.

Related books *Arthur's Honey Bear* by Lillian Hoban
Caps for Sale by Esphyr Slobodkina

Virginia Jean Herrod, Columbia, SC

What's My Function?

Materials variety of tools (such as carpenter and household tools)

What to do

1. Assemble a variety of tools. Gather the children in a circle around the pre-assembled items.
2. Ask them to look at the items from where they sit in the circle.
3. Choose an item and talk about it, focusing on the function of the item. For example, if you choose a hammer, you might say: "I would use this tool to pound nails into walls. From the other end, I might use it to take nails out of the wall, too. Maybe I could use it to pound on a rock to break the rock into smaller pieces. Does anyone know what the name of this tool is?"
4. Choose one child to find an object to discuss. Tell the child to take a moment to look at it carefully.
5. First offer to have the child describe the tool as you did the hammer. If the child is quiet or resistant, ask probing questions, such as, "Where do you think you might use this tool? Is there something else you might use with the tool? What do you do with this tool?"
6. Give all children in the circle a chance to choose a tool and explain its use.
7. After all children have had a turn within the circle activity, place the items in an area of the room that will become the garage sale.
8. Encourage the children to pretend to go shopping at the garage sale. One child will be the seller, and the rest of the children will be the buyers. They enter the garage sale, look around, and approach the seller with questions about a particular object. Again, guide the children to focus on the function of the tool.

Related books *If You Hopped Like a Frog* by David M. Schwartz
Solomon the Rusty Nail by William Stieg

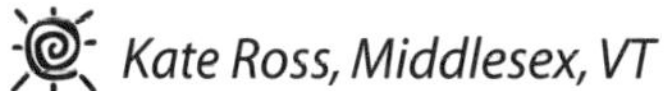
Kate Ross, Middlesex, VT

Diagnostics

Materials

dry-erase board and markers
table
hoses
tape
tools
scooters

What to do

1. Ask the children if they have any ideas about how to fix a broken-down car. Write down all of their ideas and make a list of supplies the children think they would need to fix problems on the underside of a car.
2. Provide as many of the materials from the children's list that you can. Tape a few hoses to the underside of a table and label it a broken-down car.
3. Add tools and scooters and show the children how to lie on their backs and scoot under the "car" so they can work on it.
4. During free play, assume the role of the customer and have the children verbalize the work they are doing. Expand their sentences and define new vocabulary words.

Ann Kelly, Johnstown, PA

Gas Station

Materials

two or three refrigerator boxes
two or three lengths of strong rope
two or three hose nozzles
pretend cash register
pretend money
mechanical tools such as wrenches, pliers, and screwdrivers (real or play)
work gloves
baseball caps
work shirts
cardstock paper
markers and crayons
buckets
sponges
paper towels

What to do

1. This center may be created indoors or outdoors, depending on your indoor space and the children's needs.
2. Let the children help paint and decorate the refrigerator boxes to represent gas pumps. Attach a length of rope to each box. Make sure the rope is long enough to reach the riding toys. Attach a hose nozzle to the free end of each rope.
3. Place a table near the gas pumps. Place the cash register and pretend money on the table.
4. Place the tools and work gloves on another table near the pumps.
5. Add baseball caps, work gloves, and work shirts to the dress-up clothes.
6. Open the gas station for business!
7. Encourage the children to drive the riding toys up to the gas station. They can pretend to pump their own gas and fix their "cars" with the tools. Remind them to check the oil, too!
8. If outside, add a car wash to the fun. Put some buckets, sponges, and paper towels near the gas station and let the children really wash the tricycles and riding toys.

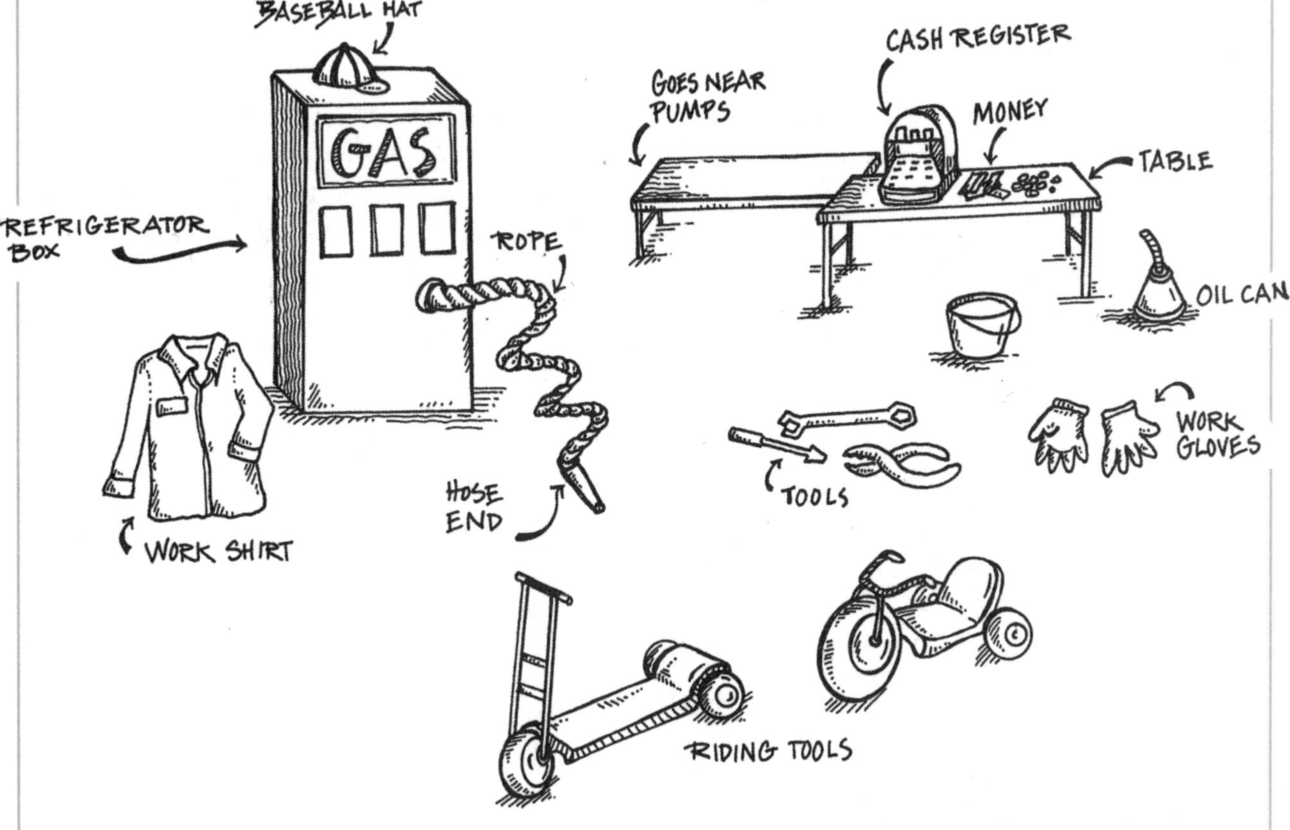

Field Trip: Take a field trip to a gas station. Have the attendant show the children around. Make sure they see the gas pumps, air pumps, and displays of car care products. Or, ask a real gas station attendant or mechanic to visit the classroom, making sure he or she brings along some tools for the children to explore.

Related books *Car Wash* by Sandra Steen and Susan Steen
Five Little Monkeys Wash the Car by Eileen Christelow
How Georgina Drove the Car Carefully From Boston to New York by Lucy Bate
Mr. Grumpy's Motor Car by John Burningham
My Car by Byron Barton
Uncle Wizzmo's New Used Car by Rodney A. Greenblatt

 *Virginia Jean Herrod, Columbia, SC*

License Rubbings

Materials

several license plates
paper
unwrapped crayons

What to do

1. Demonstrate how to make crayon rubbings by putting a piece of paper on top of a license plate and rubbing the side of a crayon over it.
2. As the children work, talk about the numbers that appear in the rubbings.
3. Tape the rubbings on the back of the classroom vehicles (such as bikes, wagons, and cars made out of boxes).

 *Ann Kelly, Johnstown, PA*

Magnet Play

Materials

hot glue gun (adult only) or tape
various toy cars, planes, or things that move
round or square magnets
magnet wand

What to do

1. Hot glue or tape round magnets to the backs of various toy vehicles with wheels.
2. Place the vehicles and magnet wands on a tray and show the children how to put the wand close to the magnet to repel or attract the car.
3. By using a variety of vehicles, you can teach children about friction, as the vehicles will move at different speeds.

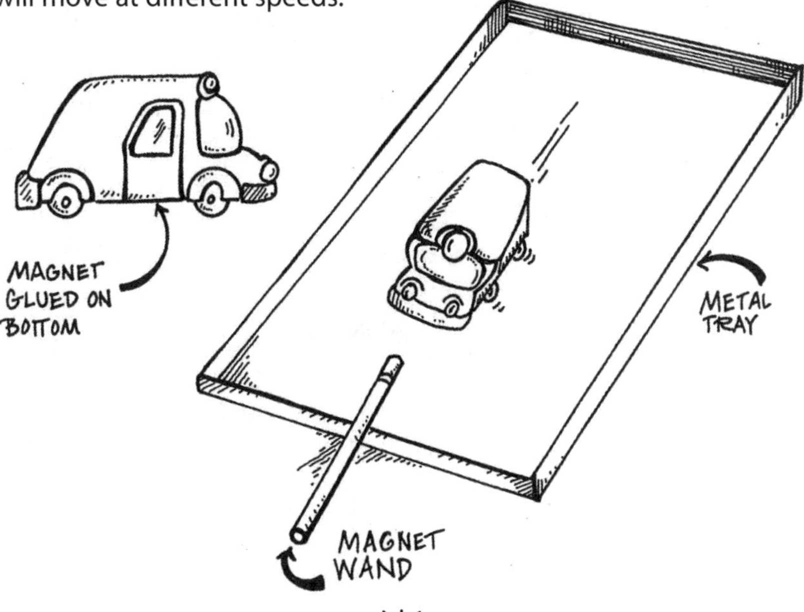

Melissa Browning, Milwaukee, WI

Out of Gas

Materials

water table or tubs
water
clear tubes
siphon pumps
large sheet of paper
marker

What to do

1. Fill the water table with water and add clear tubes and siphon pumps.
2. Show the materials to the children and ask them to guess what the siphons are for. Make a list of their guesses.
3. Encourage them to explore the materials during free play.
4. Regroup after free play and have the children share what they discovered.
5. Have the supplies close by to show the group what the siphon pumps can do.

Ann Kelly, Johnstown, PA

Please Get Me a...

Materials

tools
items used with the tools (such as screws with a screwdriver)

What to do

1. Set up the learning center as a gas station.
2. Explain to the children that this area is the part of the gas station where cars are fixed or repaired.
3. To demonstrate, give a child one of the smaller items and ask him to find the matching tool. For example, give a child a nail, and he should find a hammer. Give a child a bolt, and he might find a wrench.
4. Let the children explore and match independently.

Related books

Raffi Songs to Read™ Wheels on the Bus by Raffi
Truck by Donald Crews

Kate Ross, Middlesex, VT

Squeegee Art

Materials

window-washing squeegees
trays (big enough to put the sponge end of the squeegee in)
paint
paper
Plexiglas
squirt bottles filled with water
paper towels

What to do

1. Add squeegees, large trays, Plexiglas, paint, squirt bottles of water, and paper to the art area. Add some interest to the sponge painting by cutting unique shapes into the sponge ends of the squeegees.
2. Encourage the children to explore the materials as desired. For example, they could paint with the sponge end of the squeegees dipped in paint, scrape their work with the rubber end of the squeegee, clean the Plexiglas using water, paint on the Plexiglas with either end of the squeegee, and make a print by placing the paper on the Plexiglas and rubbing the back of the paper.

Ann Kelly, Johnstown, PA

Blooming Fingers

Materials

fingerpaint
paintbrushes
construction paper
tissue paper
glue
markers

What to do

1. Paint the palm side of the children's hands or help them paint their own hands. Give each child a sheet of construction paper.
2. Help the children press their hands on the paper with their fingers pointing straight up. These will be "stems."
3. Ask children to tear pieces of tissue paper and glue them to the top of the fingertips to make "flowers."
4. Add the words that children dictate about their flowers.
5. If desired, make a large classroom mural of a spring or summer garden by having the children make handprint flowers on large paper.

More to do

Holidays: These make great Mother's Day, Father's Day, or Valentine's Day cards. Fold a piece of construction paper in half. Have the children make flowers on the front of the folded paper. Open the paper and write phrases inside the card such as, "I'm blooming with love for you," or "My love blooms in your care." Encourage children to decorate the card as desired and sign their names.

Related books

Miss Rumphius by Barbara Cooney
Planting a Rainbow by Lois Ehlert

Designing Our Own Flowers

Materials

Styrofoam balls, any size
various colors of tissue paper
glue
straws
vase

What to do

1. In the greenhouse center, give each child a Styrofoam ball. Encourage the children to tear tissue paper into pieces and glue it to their Styrofoam ball to make "flowers." Encourage creativity.
2. When the children finish, help them insert a straw into their Styrofoam balls.
3. Place all of the "flowers" into a vase for the class to enjoy.
4. If a special guest comes to the class, give him or her the bouquet of flowers as a special thank you.

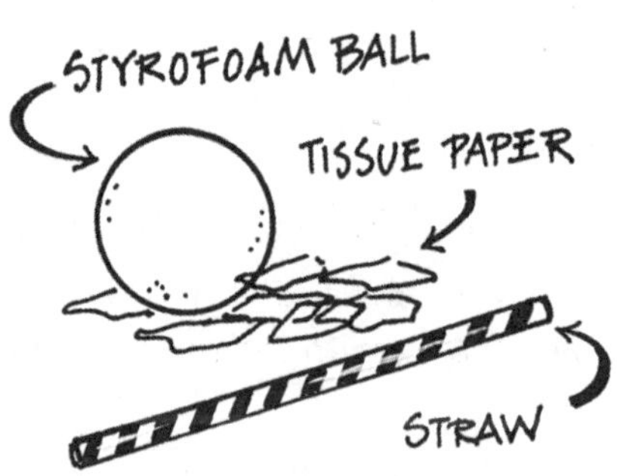

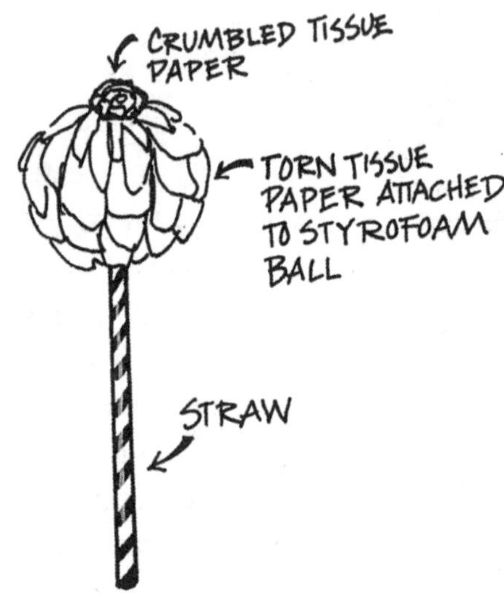

More to do

Math: Ask the children to count the flowers. Take one away, and ask how many are left.
Science: Study the parts of a flower.
Writing: Help each child write a note to someone she wants to give her flower to. Send the flower and note home with the child to give away.

Related books

Allison's Zinnia by Anita Lobel
Chrysanthemum by Kevin Henkes
Flower Girl by Laura Goodwin
The Gardener by Sarah Stewart
Oh, Say Can You Seed? All About Flowering Plants by Bonnie Worth
Planting a Rainbow by Lois Ehlert
The Tiny Seed by Eric Carle

Lori Dunlap, Amarillo, TX

Flower Fun

Materials

story about flowers
paper plates
scissors
yellow paint
construction paper
pre-cut construction paper flower petals
stapler
glue
empty paper towel rolls
green paint
bright colored crepe paper strips
pre-cut clock hands
brads

What to do

1. Read a story about flowers to the children. Do some of the following "flower" projects with the children.
2. Help children make flower masks from paper plates. Cut out the center of paper plates and give each child the outside rim of a plate. Let the children paint the plate rim yellow and paste pre-cut construction paper petals in any color to the mask.

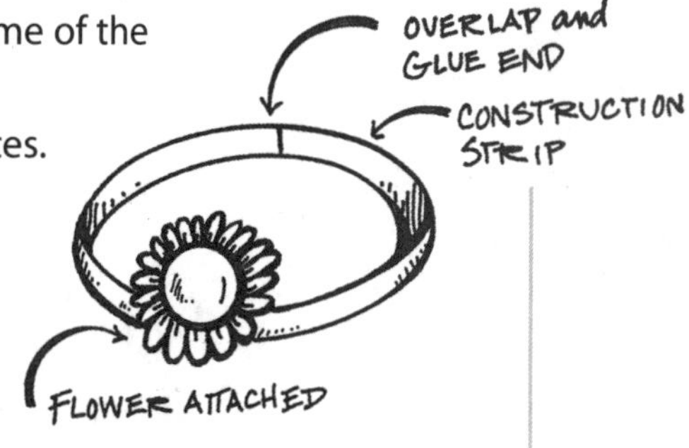

3. Make flower hats with the children. Cut out flowers from construction paper. Give each child a long construction paper strip. Fit it to the child's head. Encourage the children to glue flowers to the strip. Staple both ends together to make a hat.
4. Help the children make scepters. Give each child an empty paper towel roll to paint green ("stem"). Provide pre-cut flower centers and petals for them to glue onto one end of the paper towel roll. Attach bright colored crepe paper strips.

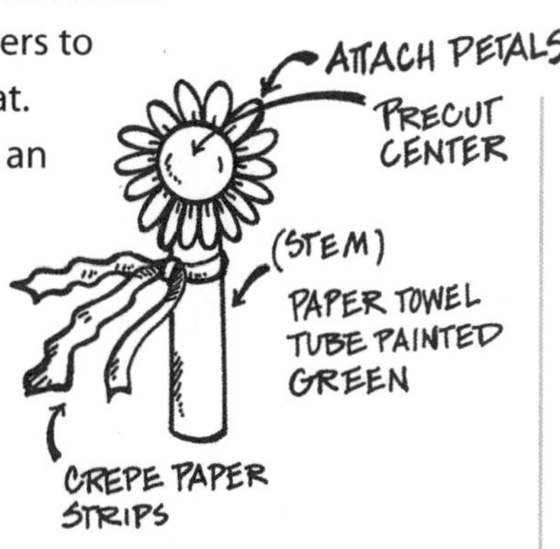

5. Help the children make a flower clock. Make a clock face on paper plates and give one to each child. Encourage the children to color the clock "face" or fingerpaint it with a bright color.
6. Provide pre-cut clock hands and help the children use brads to attach the hands to the clock face. Let the children finish their clocks by gluing on pre-cut flower petals.

Lisa Chichester, Parkersburg, WV

Garden Seeds

Materials

variety of hardy seeds (such as marigold, zinnia, sunflower seeds, and beans)
seed packets
egg cartons
tray
soil
2-liter plastic bottle

What to do

1. Place seeds, seed packets, and an egg carton on a tray for sorting.
2. Encourage the children to sort the seeds. They can sort seeds into appropriate seed packet or line them up by size in the egg carton.
3. When finished sorting, plant the seeds with the children.
4. As the seeds grow into small plants, encourage the children to observe the variety of leaves.

Note: If you plant the seeds in a two-liter plastic bottle with dirt and close the lid, there will be little need for watering in the beginning.

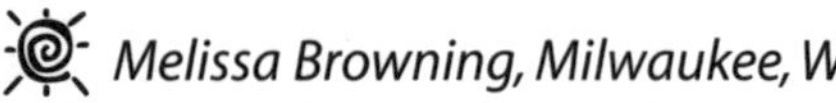

Melissa Browning, Milwaukee, WI

Garden in a Wagon

Materials

old wagon
rocks
potting soil
water
shovels
small plants and/or seeds (including grass seed)

What to do

1. Add a layer of rocks to the bottom of the wagon.
2. Cover the rocks with potting soil.
3. Help the children plant small plants and seeds.
4. Let the children take turns watering the plants each day.
5. Encourage the children to watch the wagon daily for signs of growth.
6. The wagon can be moved outdoors during the day for more direct sunlight.

Related books

A Gardener's Alphabet by Mary Azarian
Planting a Rainbow by Lois Ehlert

Sandy Scott, Vancouver, WA

Gardening Song

Materials none

What to do

1. Sing the following song to the tune of "Hokey Pokey."
2. If desired, use real props such as seeds and watering cans.

Gardening

We put our garden gloves on, (Pretend to put on gloves.)
We dig a hole in the ground, (Dig a hole.)
We put one seed in (Drop seed in hole.)
And we cover up the hole. (Cover hole.)
We sprinkle on the water (Sprinkle seed with watering can.)
And we watch it grow. (Move head from ground to sky.)
That's how we plant a seed! (Clap hands to rhythm of words.)

Related books

The Carrot Seed by Ruth Krauss
Flower Garden by Eve Bunting
The Tiny Seed by Eric Carle

 *Kaethe Lewandowski, Centreville, VA*

Green Thumbs

Materials

one 2-liter plastic bottle for each child
craft knife
flower bulbs
small flowerpots
potting soil
small trowels or spoons
water

What to do

1. To prepare, use a craft knife to cut off the lower ¼ of each plastic bottle. Discard the bottoms. Save the tops to use as greenhouses.
2. Give each child a small pot, a flower bulb, a small trowel or spoon, and some potting soil.
3. Show the children how to plant the bulb in the pot. Put the potting soil in the pot, place the bulb in the center (try to point the sprout end upward), and then add more potting soil on top. Ask them to press down gently with their fingertips.

4. Let the children lightly water their bulbs. Put the pots on a sunny shelf.
5. Invert the plastic bottles on top of the pots to create mini greenhouses. If desired, let the children decorate the greenhouses with small flower and leaf stickers. (Don't overdo it or the sun will not be able to reach the bulbs.)
6. Encourage the children to observe the bulbs over a period of several weeks. Use a journal to record the changes the plants undergo.
7. When the weather is right, take the bulbs outdoors and plant them in a garden.
8. You can do this activity using grass seed instead of bulbs, if desired. Put potting soil in the pots and sprinkle with grass seed. Gently water and put the pots on a sunny shelf. Cover with the plastic bottle greenhouses and watch the grass grow.

More to do

Field Trip: Take a field trip to a real greenhouse.

Related books

The Carrot Seed by Ruth Krauss
The Garden of Happiness by Erika Tamar
How a Seed Grows by Helene J. Jordan
Someday a Tree by Eve Bunting

 *Virginia Jean Herrod, Columbia, SC*

Designing Our Own Flowers

Materials

posters and books of growing cycle of plants
paper cups
soil
variety of seeds
water

What to do

1. Show the children books and a poster on the growing cycle of plants. Talk about seeds, soil, water, sun, and so on.
2. Invite the children to choose a seed and plant it in a paper cup.
3. Encourage the children to work with each other and create the growing cycle with their bodies (crouched as a seed, sprouting, waking up with the sun, peeking above the ground, and so on).

Related books

The Carrot Seed by Ruth Heller
How a Seed Grows by Helene J. Jordan
The Tiny Seed by Eric Carle

 *Margery Kranyik Fermino, Hyde Park, MA*

How Many Cubes High Will It Grow?

Materials

soil
cups
fast-growing seeds
permanent marker
journal or paper and stapler
pencils or pens
Unifix cubes or small cube-shaped blocks
date stamp and inkpad

What to do

1. After having a group discussion and/or reading a book about growing plants, let each child plant a few seeds in a cup. Write each child's name on her cup.
2. Encourage the children to water their own plant, or make watering the plants a classroom job for one or two children.
3. If a journal is unavailable, staple paper together to make a journal. Write each child's name on a page in the journal. If children cannot recognize their name yet, mark their pages with a special icon, sticker, or symbol.
4. After the plants start to grow, show the children how to measure the growth of their plants by stacking cubes next to their plant and counting the cubes. Encourage each child to record how high their plant has grown on their page in the Plant Growth Journal. Show them how to date their entry using the date stamp.
5. Some children may be interested long after their plant has outgrown its cup. Make sure you have materials (pots and soil) available to transplant the plants of those children who are interested in continuing to observe the growth of their plant. Or, send the plants home with a note encouraging families to continue the learning process with their children.

Related books

Flower Garden by Eve Bunting
Oh Say Can You Seed?: All About Flowering Plants by Bonnie Worth
Planting a Rainbow by Lois Ehlert

Ann Kelly, Johnstown, PA

Mystery Seeds

Materials

zipper-closure plastic bags
several packets of seeds (such as tomato, lettuce, marigold, and zinnia)
pictures of various flowers and vegetables from catalogs or seed packets
scissors
large construction or chart paper
glue
seed starter soil
peat pots
Popsicle sticks
markers
mini greenhouse (from a discount store)

What to do

1. Remove the seeds from their original packets and place them in the plastic bags.
2. Cut out several pictures of flowers and vegetables from seed catalogs or seed packets.
3. Divide the large construction paper into columns. Make a column for each picture of fruit or vegetable that you would like the children to consider.
4. Glue the pictures to the construction paper. Be sure to put only one picture per column. Hang the chart in the greenhouse center.
5. Demonstrate the activity as follows:
   - Each child fills a peat pot ¾ full with starter soil.
   - Each child chooses a bag of seeds to take a few seeds from and sprinkles two or three seeds on the soil.
   - Children cover the seeds with ¼" of soil, and water so the soil is thoroughly damp.
   - Each child writes her name on a Popsicle stick and push the stick into the soil.
   - Put the pots in a mini greenhouse and place it in the greenhouse center. (Don't forget to put the mini greenhouse in a sunny place for faster growth!)
6. Encourage the children to watch the growth and try to guess which plants they planted. Provide several books for them to look at. When they think they know what the plant is, they can write their name in the corresponding column on the chart.
7. Let the excitement over the mystery build until the plants are growing, and then reveal which plants the children planted.

Related books

ABC Book of Flowers for Young Gardeners by JoAnn Stoker
Anno's Magic Seeds by Mitsumaso Anno
A Kid's Guide to How Flowers Grow by Patricia Ayers
The Magic School Bus Plants Seeds by Joanna Cole

A Packet of Seeds by Deborah Hopkinson
Plant Fruits and Seeds by David M. Schwartz
Plant Packages: A Book About Seeds by Susan Blackaby
Plants Grow From Seeds by Rachel Mann
Seeds by Gail Saunders-Smith
Seeds! Seeds! Seeds! by Nancy Elizabeth Wallace
Seeds Travel by Elaine Pascoe
So Many Seeds: Learning the S Sound by Kerri O'Donnell
Ten Seeds by Ruth Brown

Mike Krestar, Latrobe, PA

Seed Puzzles

Materials

scissors
poster board
tacky glue
packets of seeds with photos of the product on the front
rubber cement

What to do

1. To prepare, cut poster board into 9" x 4" rectangles.
2. Use generous amounts of tacky glue to attach a pile of seeds to one half of each rectangle.
3. At the other end of each rectangle, use rubber cement to attach a picture of the plant or flower (cut from the seed packet) that grows from the seeds you glued.
4. When the cards are dry, cut through the center to make two-piece puzzles. Use a different cut pattern for each puzzle.
5. Encourage the children to match the pictures with the seeds. The puzzles are self-correcting because only correct matches should fit together.

More to do

Science: Place seeds in margarine containers and provide magnifying glasses for children to examine them closely.
More Science: With the children, find out where seeds come from. Cut open fruit to find the seeds, shell peas from their pods, examine a sunflower, and pop open a milkweed pod.

Related books

The Carrot Seed by Ruth Krauss
From Seed to Dandelion by Jan Kottke

Sandra Gratias, Perkasie, PA

The Surprise Garden

Materials

The Surprise Garden by Zoe Hall
variety of seed packets, including flower and vegetable seeds
large jar
small paper cups
small wading pool
potting soil
several small watering cans
eight pieces of straight PVC piping long enough to fit around the wading pool
four pieces of straight PVC piping about 3′ long
eight PVC elbows
heavy, clear plastic sheet
journal

What to do

1. Beforehand, save and label one seed from each packet. Save the seed packets. Mix the rest of the seeds together in a large jar.
2. Read *The Surprise Garden* by Zoe Hall to the children. Talk about the garden in the story and tell the children they are going to create their own surprise garden.
3. Place the wading pool in a sunny area of the playground and let the children fill it with potting soil.
4. Give each child a small paper cup of seeds from the large jar. Ask the children to sprinkle the seeds over the potting soil. Make sure they evenly distribute the seeds rather than dump them in large clumps. Help the children gently cover the seeds with more potting soil. Let them use the watering cans to gently sprinkle water over the seeds.
5. Ask the children to help assemble a cube-shape frame for the garden with PVC pipes. Attach four straight pieces with the elbows to create a square frame.

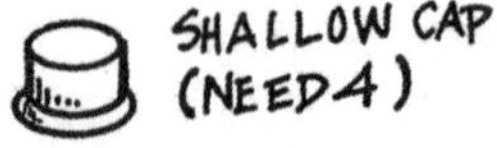

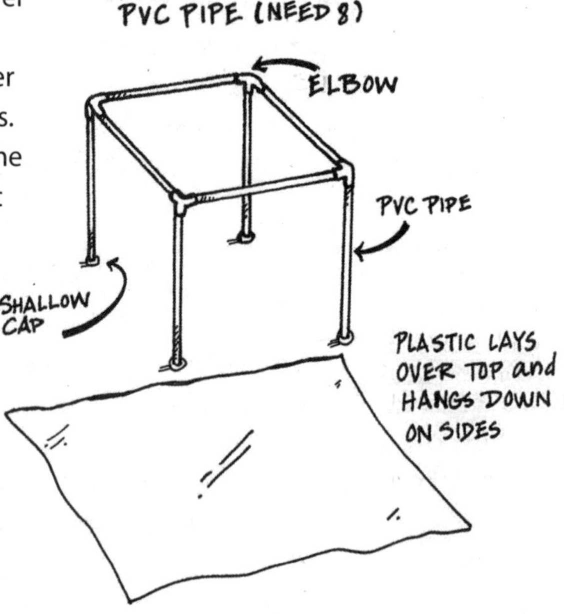

6. Put a 3′ long straight piece into each of the four elbow tops. Attach an elbow to the top of each of the four 3′ long sections.
7. Attach the four remaining straight pieces to the top of the frame.
8. Cover the frame with the clear plastic to create a mini greenhouse. If needed, secure the edges of the plastic to the ground by placing large rocks on it.
9. Water the garden as needed.
10. Show the children the seed that was saved from each pack. Ask them to predict what plant might grow from the seed.
11. Attach the empty seed packets to a piece of poster board. Put the saved seeds in a small container. Give the container to the children and challenge them to match the seeds to the correct packet. When the plants have reached maturity, challenge the children to match them to their seed packets.

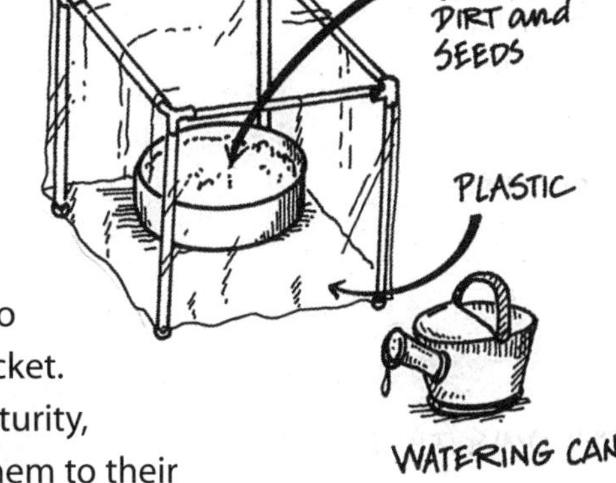

12. Let children observe the garden over a period of a few weeks. Keep track of the garden's progress in a journal.
13. When the seedlings are sturdy, remove the greenhouse cover. Show the children how to care for the garden. Remember to weed and water it on a regular basis. Enjoy the fruits (and flowers) of your labor!

Related books *The Gardener* by Sarah Stewart
Vegetables, Vegetables! by Fay Robinson

Virginia Jean Herrod, Columbia, SC

Stock Children

Materials

empty food cartons and cans
fruits and vegetables
boxes or baskets
paper and markers for labels

What to do

1. Bring empty food cartons and cans, fruits and vegetables, and boxes to a large or small group setting.
2. Ask the children to decide how the food should be grouped (or sorted) for display on supermarket shelves. Accept the criteria from the children, such as color, shape, texture, and food group.
3. Help the children make labels for the baskets or boxes so that they now where to put the materials during clean-up time.
4. Add all the materials to the dramatic play area for a supermarket theme.

Ann Kelly, Johnstown, PA

Buying Things

Materials

pictures of merchandise labeled with price tags
8 ½" x 11" tagboard or medium cardstock
picture of a grocery cart
paper cutter
pictures of coins
laminate
pocket chart

What to do

1. Look through old books or workbooks for brightly colored pictures of merchandise labeled with price tags, such as an orange for 30 cents, scissors for 5 cents, an apple for 26 cents, and so on.
2. Write directions for the activity on a piece of 8 ½" by 11" piece of tagboard turned horizontally. Print the title "Buying Things" at the top and the following directions underneath: "Place the coins next to the correct price tags." Embellish with two pictures of a grocery cart or similar picture.
3. Make copies of the merchandise pictures on tagboard. Use a paper cutter to cut around each card so that all of the cards are the same size.
4. Make another set of cards with pictures of coins needed to purchase each item.

5. Laminate the directions sheet, merchandise cards, and coin set cards for durability and cut them out.
6. Hang a pocket chart at children's eye level. Insert the directions in the top pocket of the pocket chart. Seat the children in a circle around the pocket chart. Place the merchandise cards in the pocket chart, leaving room for the coin set cards. Pass out the coin set cards to the children.
7. Ask if anyone has a coin card with the correct change to purchase each item. One at a time, let a child place a coin card in the pocket chart next to the corresponding merchandise card.

Jackie Wright, Enid, OK

Setting Up the Aisles

Materials

actual or play items found in a supermarket (such as foods, soaps, cleaners, brooms, and so on)
pictures of items

What to do

1. Assemble the supermarket materials in one location in the room.
2. During circle time, explain to the whole group that everyone will work together to set up a supermarket. There will be four to five aisles. Explain that similar items should go in appropriate aisles. Aisle setups might be:
   - fruits and vegetables
   - meats
   - drinks
   - desserts
   - soaps and cleaning products
3. Place pictures representing the materials for the aisles in the room or area so children can match the items to the pictures.
4. Depending on the dynamics of the group, either send one person at a time to choose an item and place it in the appropriate aisle or ask that the whole group work together.
5. Provide guidance as needed to children who need help finding objects that match the pictures.
6. When children seem to understand the concept, encourage them to explore and play independently in the supermarket learning center.

Related book *Pickles to Pittsburgh* by Judi Barrett

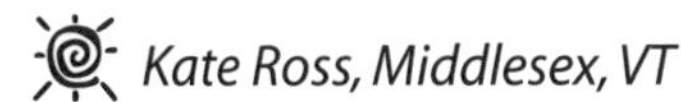
Kate Ross, Middlesex, VT

Shelf Stockers

Materials

empty food containers (boxes, cans, and bags)
markers
small pieces of paper

What to do

1. Visit a grocery store and talk to a person who stocks shelves about his or her job.
2. Back in the classroom, remove the blocks from the block area and replace them with empty food containers. Be sure to label the shelves: "boxes," "cans," and "bags."
3. Encourage the children to build structures with the containers.
4. Write "shelf stocker" on small pieces of paper. When it is time to clean up, motivate the children by giving them a "shelf stocker" badge to wear as they restock the shelves.
5. Remind them to sort the containers to match the labels on the shelves.

Related books

Let's Visit the Supermarket by Marianne Johnston
Supermarket Managers by Mary Firestone

Ann Kelly, Johnstown, PA

Supermarket Sorting

Materials

large piece paper
markers
newspaper and magazine ads with supermarket items
scissors
two paper grocery bags

What to do

1. Ask the children to describe the last time they were at a supermarket. As they tell their stories, note the things they saw at the supermarket on a large piece of paper. Talk about the items. For example, if a child says he saw a mop, ask what a mop is used for.
2. Ask the children to cut out newspaper or magazine photos of the things they saw at the supermarket. Try to find at least four examples of each item.
3. Label one paper grocery bag "Food Items" and the other "Non-Food Items."

Simpler labels might be "Food" and "Not Food."

4. Ask the children to sort their pictures into the correct bag. As they sort, talk about each item.
5. For an older group of children, increase the number of sorting bags. For example, have four bags labeled "Fruit," Vegetables," "Meat," and "Cleaning Items." Ask the children to sort their pictures accordingly. Add more bags and labels according to the children's skill levels.

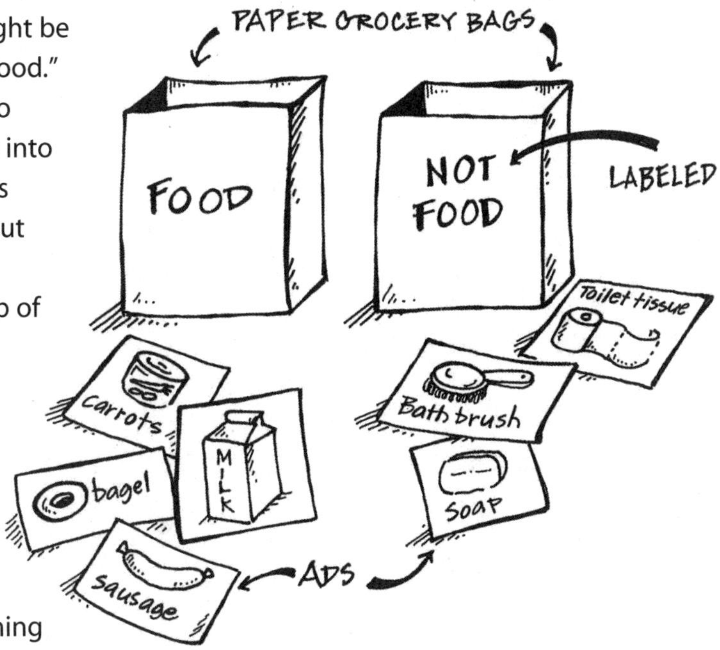

More to do **Art:** After the children finish sorting, let them use the cutouts to create a supermarket collage.

Related book *Papa Small* by Lois Lenski

Virginia Jean Herrod, Columbia, SC

Classroom Cereal Box Book

Materials

empty cereal boxes
hole punch
yarn or hinged metal binder rings

What to do

1. Cut out the front panel of empty cereal boxes. The more cereal boxes you have, the bigger your book will be.
2. Invite each child to your table to read the cereal boxes. Because most children learn to recognize common signs and print in their environment, they will be able to "read" the print on the cereal boxes.
3. Ask each child to tell you something about the cereal they read. For example, "It tastes sweet and crunchy," or "The box is red, like my favorite color!"

4. Write their statements on the back of the cereal box panels.
5. Using a hole punch, punch holes on the left side of each cereal box panel. With yarn or metal binder rings, put all the cereal box panels together to make a book.
6. Let each child take the book home to read to their family. When all the children have had a chance to take the classroom book home, place the book in the library corner for further reading.

More to do

Dramatic Play: Set up a grocery store in the dramatic play area using empty food containers and toy cash registers.

Related book

The Cheerios Animal Play Book by Lee Wade

 *Deborah Roud and Diane Reed, New Wilmington, PA*

Grocery Sort

Materials

labels from a variety of foods
glue
tagboard
laminate
poster of food pyramid (optional)

What to do

1. Mount labels from a variety of foods onto tagboard and laminate.
2. Ask the children to sort the items according to the category in which they belong, such as dairy, meat, fruit, vegetables, fats, and bread.
3. If desired, let children use a poster of the food pyramid to sort items.

 *Melissa Browning, Milwaukee, WI*

Grocery Bag Game

Materials

two or three large, brown grocery bags
basket or box
several sizes of empty grocery boxes (such as cereal box, fruit snack box, cracker box, box of rice, gelatin boxes, raisin boxes, and so on)
number cards labeled 1-12

What to do

1. Place an opened brown grocery bag in front of a child.
2. In a basket or large box next to the bag, place several different sized food boxes.
3. Ask the children to estimate how many grocery boxes they can fit in the grocery bag.
4. Ask a child to position the boxes in the bag to obtain a desired number of well-placed boxes.
5. Allow plenty of time for each child to experiment with spatial relationships. Ask questions such as, "Would this size box fit better on its side or up and down?" or "Is there a different way to arrange the boxes?"
6. Encourage the child to select the number card that corresponds with his guess. (Choose appropriate number identification according to age).
7. Have the children compare box sizes and arrange them from smallest to largest.

More to do **Literacy:** Cut out front portions of boxes and bind them together to make an environmental print book.

Related book *To Market to Market* by Anne Miranda

 *Deborah Roud and Diana Reed, New Wilmington, PA*

Grocery Store

Materials

empty boxes of food
empty cans of food with no sharp edges
cash register & play money
wallets and purses
child-size shopping carts
baskets
paper grocery bags
posters of fruit and vegetables

What to do

1. Set up an of the room area to resemble a grocery store. Put empty boxes and cans of food on the shelves, put a cash register with play money on a small table, and put child-size carts and baskets in the area. Decorate the area with posters of fruits and vegetables.
2. Encourage the children to choose food items and "purchase" them from the cashier.
3. Make a vocabulary word chart with words such as "food," "money," "cash," "cashier," "shopping cart," "credit card," and so on.

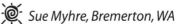

Sue Myhre, Bremerton, WA

Indestructible Food

Materials

labels from canned foods
2″ x 4″ pieces of wood cut into 4″ pieces
decoupage finish (such as varnish or lacquer) (adult only)

What to do

1. Remove labels from cans.
2. Decoupage the labels to pieces of wood that has been sanded.
3. Allow them to dry, then use them in the grocery store center.

 *Melissa Browning, Milwaukee, WI*

Let's Go Shopping

Materials

newspaper or magazine pictures of grocery items
brown grocery bags
markers

What to do

1. Label brown grocery bags with letters you are reviewing. Place bags in the center of a table.
2. Lay out pictures of grocery items.
3. Ask each child, in turn, to choose a picture, identify the beginning sound of the item, and place it in the bag with the correct beginning sound written on it. For example, a picture of a banana would go into the bag labeled "Bb."

Related book *Bear Wants More* by Karma Wilson

 *Suzanne Maxymuk, Cherry Hill, NJ*

Realistic Meat Tray

Materials

oak tag for meat patterns
pencil or pen
scissors
pink or tan craft foam sheet
brown permanent marker
bottle or pen of white correction fluid
clean Styrofoam meat trays
plastic wrap
clear tape

What to do

1. Make patterns for different shapes of meat on oak tag.
2. Use the patterns to cut out the shapes from craft foam sheets. Cut out pork chop and steak shapes from pink craft foam sheets, and chicken or fish shapes from tan craft foam sheets.
3. Use a brown marker to draw and color bone or skin. Use white correction fluid to draw fat.
4. Place the meat shapes in meat trays.
5. Cover each tray tightly with plastic wrap and secure on the back with clear tape.

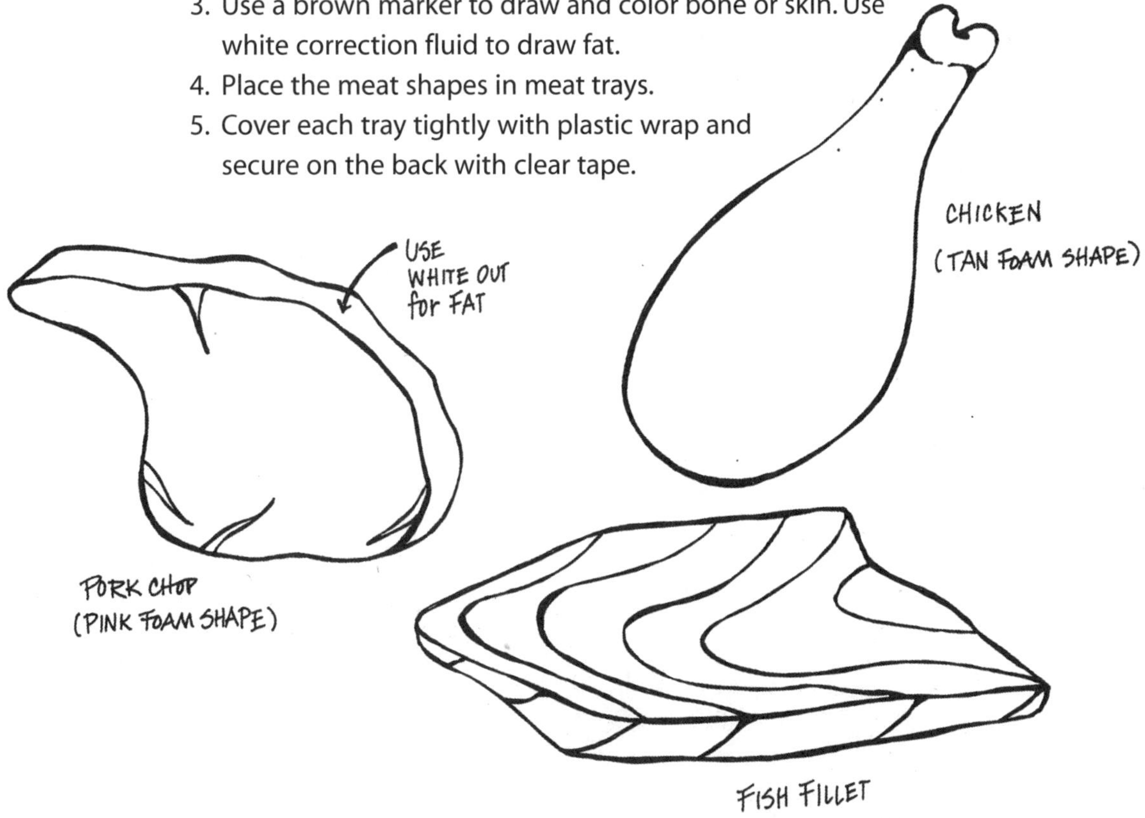

Related book *Eating the Alphabet* by Lois Ehlert

Mary Brehm, Aurora, OH

Swiss Cheese

Materials

yellow construction paper
scissors
slice of real Swiss cheese
hole punch
stapler

What to do

1. Beforehand, cut yellow construction paper into 3" squares. Make ten for each child.
2. Show the children a slice of Swiss cheese. Encourage them to count the holes.
3. Explain that they will make their own Swiss cheese counting books.
4. Give each child ten yellow squares. Help them write the numerals one to ten on the squares. Each square should have a different number.
5. Let them use a hole punch to punch as many holes as the numeral on the paper (slice of cheese) indicates. They continue until all ten cards have the correct number of holes.
6. Ask the children to line up their slices in numerical order, and then staple them together to make a Swiss cheese counting book.

Related books

Cheese Louise by David Michael Slater
Say Cheese Please by Leslie McGuirk

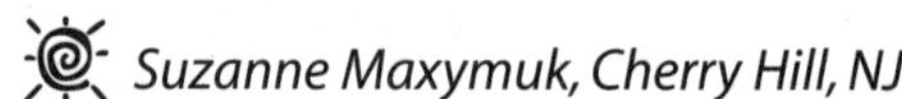
Suzanne Maxymuk, Cherry Hill, NJ

Bath Time

Materials

tubs or bins large enough to hold bathwater and babies
towels
baby dolls (not cloth)
soap
washcloths

What to do

1. Determine how many tubs you will need according to the space available and how many children will be in the area at one time. Think ahead to possible spills and wet floors and have plenty of extra towels available to put on the floor as needed.
2. In advance, fill the tubs halfway with water and place them on the floor or on a table. Place a washcloth and soap next to each tub.
3. Give each child a dressed baby doll to undress.
4. Show the children proper bathing techniques, such as holding the baby up and not letting soap get into the baby's eyes.
5. Encourage the children to give their baby doll a bath.
6. When children are finished, give them a towel to dry their baby and help them to redress the baby.

Related book *William's Doll* by Charlotte Zolotow

 *Barbara Reynolds, Galloway, NJ*

Beating Soapsuds

Materials

medium-size plastic bowls
plastic pitchers with tape to indicate one cup
liquid dishwashing detergent
manual rotary eggbeaters
large trays
sponge

What to do

1. Place a medium-size plastic bowl, plastic pitcher with tape to indicate one cup, and liquid detergent on each tray.
2. Let the children put one cup of water into their pitcher and pour it into a bowl. Put a small amount of detergent in the water.

3. Encourage the children to use an eggbeater to stir up soapsuds; let them go as long as they like!
4. Remove the eggbeater and tap it to remove suds.
5. Ask the children to rinse their bowl and return it to the tray. Wipe the bowl with the sponge and wipe up any spilled water.
6. This activity provides an opportunity to teach vocabulary such as "beat," "lather," "bubbles," and "eggbeater." It also helps develop hand-eye coordination and fine motor control.

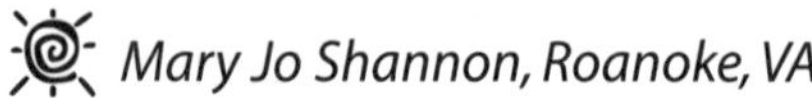
Mary Jo Shannon, Roanoke, VA

Learning About Babies

Materials

books about babies
baby photos of the children
photo album or bulletin board
paper
markers
baby clothing, shoes, and accessories (pacifiers, blankets, teething rings, and so on)

What to do

1. It is fun and helpful to start this unit when one of the children in the class has a new baby sibling, but it can also be done as part of a study of family life.
2. Tell the children that they are going to learn about babies. Read baby books together and discuss the uniqueness of each person born in the world.
3. Ask parents to send in baby photos of the children. Mount the photos on a bulletin board or put them in a photo album. Ask the children to dictate captions about their photos that you will write underneath the photos on the bulletin board or in the photo album.
4. Ask the children what they know about babies, and write down what they say. Let the children illustrate their quotes. Add these to the bulletin board or photo album.
5. Let children practice their lacing, snapping, and buttoning skills using baby garments and tiny baby shoes with laces.
6. If possible, ask a parent to visit the class with a baby and let the children ask questions about the baby.
7. Prepare typical baby foods to eat at snack time, such as applesauce, hot cereal, and pureed carrots.

8. Encourage the children to move like babies, for example, crawling, toddling, and rolling over.
9. Reflect upon how much the children have grown and learned since they were babies.

Related books *How Animals Care for Their Babies* by Roger B. Hirschland
Peepo! by Janet and Allen Ahlberg

 *Elisheva Leah Nadler, Har Nof, Jerusalem, Israel*

Let's Clean the Fridge

Materials
variety of plastic play foods
toy refrigerator
pictures of food representing different categories, such as meat, sweets, breads, fruits and vegetables, drinks, and so on

What to do
1. Assemble and display a variety of play food and pictures on a table in the housekeeping area.
2. Lead the children in this informal activity of organizing the foods into similar categories.
3. Ask a child to place one of the pictures of food, such as a hamburger, on a shelf in the toy refrigerator.
4. Encourage the other children to choose foods that would fit into the chosen category (meats) from the plastic foods.
5. When all items are chosen for that category, briefly discuss how the items are similar. Brainstorm other items that might fit on the shelf as well.
6. Repeat steps 3 through 5 using other categories of food. Continue until all the items are inside the refrigerator.
7. An alternative to this activity is to categorize food based on color, size, and so on.

Related books *The Beastly Feast* by Bruce Goldstone
Cloudy With a Chance of Meatballs by Judi Barrett
Tops & Bottoms by Janet Stevens

 *Kate Ross, Middlesex, VT*

Make-Believe Grocery Shopping

Materials

large variety of food pictures
oak tag cut into 3" x 6" strips
markers
glue
loose-leaf ring
hole punch
pencils
writing pads

What to do

1. Cut out pictures of foods commonly found at the grocery store, such as ice cream, celery, eggs, milk, bread, macaroni, fish, meat, and apples. Glue them to oak tag strips and write the word for each food on the strip.
2. Review the names of the foods with the class.
3. Punch a hole on one end of each strip and place the entire collection on a large loose-leaf ring. This allows children to fan out the items for easy reading.
4. Keep this as a reference list in the housekeeping area.
5. Encourage the children to refer to the collection so they can make a "shopping list" for a trip to the grocery center. They can write their chosen items on pads of paper.
6. Encourage the children to plan a pretend meal and choose the foods they need to buy at the grocery store.

Related books *The Hungry Thing* by Jan Slepian
More Spaghetti, I Say by Rita Golden Gelman
Pizza Kittens by Charlotte Voake

Related poem
Drink milk, drink milk,
That's the thing to do!
Drink milk, drink milk,
Milk is good for you!

Iris Rothstein, New Hyde Park, NY

Multicultural Housekeeping Area

Materials

empty containers of ethnic foods (such as cans of coconut milk, water chestnuts, chickpeas, grits, and taco boxes)
special kitchen tools (such as bamboo rice mats, ladles, pizza wheels, and spaghetti servers)
multicultural pictures, fabric, and books

What to do

1. Make sure your housekeeping area is diverse by stocking it with multicultural food items. Find items in the ethnic foods section of your local grocery store, or visit grocery stores specializing in ethnic foods. You can also ask parents for donations. Make sure empty cans are clean and child-safe.
2. Stock the kitchen area with special kitchen tools.
3. Display wall hangings, textiles, and so on.
4. Feature a multicultural theme. Read a related book and offer a related snack.

More to do

Science: Grow lemongrass, cilantro, rosemary, oregano, or other edible herbs in pots. Children can snip them and add them to snacks.
Sensory: Provide bowls or trays with different flours and grains, such as white, whole wheat, cornmeal, oatmeal, and grits. Punch holes in the lids of empty film containers, fill the containers with cumin, nutmeg, cardamom, and other spices, and let the children smell them.
Snack: Offer a snack of various breads, such as pitas, puppodums, matzah, tacos, pizza, foccacia, croissants, bagels, and tortillas. Serve with plantain chips, salsa, or chickpeas.

Related books *Big Moon Tortilla* by Joy Cowley
Bread, Bread, Bread by Anne Morris
Magda's Tortillas by Becky Chavarría-Cháirez
Moishe's Miracle: A Hanukah Story by Laura Krauss Melmed

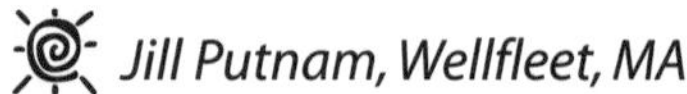
Jill Putnam, Wellfleet, MA

Number Clothesline

Materials

pictures of various articles of clothing
marker
sturdy string or clothesline
clothespins

What to do

1. Label each picture of an article of clothing with a numeral from one to ten.
2. Hang a clothesline in the housekeeping center.
3. Ask a child to hang up the clothes in numerical order. You could also divide the pictures among the children and have them work together.

Suzanne Maxymuk, Cherry Hill, NJ

Soda Can Ring Weaving

Materials

plastic six-pack rings (up to 25)
tape or stapler
variety of string, yarn, ribbon, and so on

What to do

1. Connect six-pack rings with tape or staples to make one large rectangle or square shape.
2. Hang it up at children's eye level, possibly on a clothesline that holds wet paintings.
3. Let a few children at a time weave yarn, string, or ribbon back and forth through the holes, as if they are sewing: over, under, over, under, etc.
4. Leave it hanging for a few weeks until it is full of colors and textures. This makes a beautiful wall hanging and is great for hand-eye coordination.

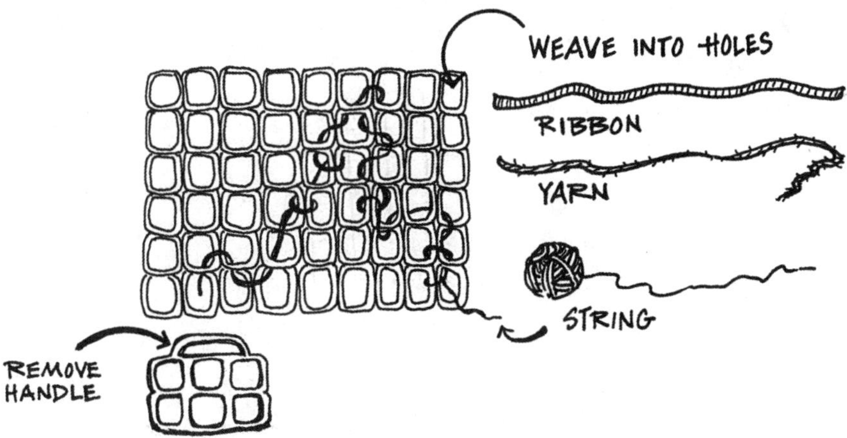

Audrey Kanoff, Allentown, PA

Springtime Cleaning

Materials

dust rags or mitts
water in spray bottle (no bleach)
cloths
paper towels

What to do

1. Tell the children that they are going to do a "spring cleaning" in their classroom. Explain that many people give their homes a thorough cleaning at the beginning of spring to make a fresh start.
2. Select a few children to help clean each center.
3. Encourage the children to clean using dust rags, water, and cloths. Ask them to remove toys from shelves, dust the shelves, and return the toys after cleaning.
4. An adult should oversee the cleaning to be sure there are enough cleaning materials in each center and to point out areas that still need to be cleaned.

5. The children may continue at outdoor time on this day or another day by bringing chairs outside and washing them in the play yard. They can rinse them with a hose and dry them with rags or cloth.
6. Add new plants or flowers to the classroom to welcome spring!

Jean Lortz, Sequim, WA

Toothbrush Holders

Materials

film canisters
X-acto knife or sharp scissors (adult only)
stickers or blank address labels
markers
toothbrush for demonstration

What to do

1. Cut an "X" into the lids of film canisters using an X-acto knife or scissors (adult only).
2. Give a film canister to each child. Encourage the children to decorate the film canisters with stickers, address labels, and markers.
3. Demonstrate how to use this as a toothbrush holder by placing a toothbrush bristle end down into a canister (with lid removed), and then pushing the lid down the handle of the toothbrush to close the canister.
4. Let the children bring them home to use as toothbrush holders.

Related books

Andrew's Loose Tooth by Robert Munsch
The Bear's Toothache by David McPhail
Franklin and the Tooth Fairy by Paulette Bourgeois

Related song

"Brush Your Teeth" by Raffi

Shirley Salach, Northwood, NH

Washing Clothes

Materials

manual tools (such as an eggbeater, broom and dustpan, frying pan, and metal spatula)
washboard
plastic dishpan
plastic pitcher
bar of mild soap
white cloth marked with pencil
sponge

What to do

1. Many manual tools are obsolete in today's homes. Introduce some of these items to the children and discuss their uses. Show the children a washboard and explain that before washing machines were invented, people used them to wash clothes.
2. Ask the children to pour 1 cup of warm water into the dishpan.
3. Place the washboard in the pan so it rests on one side of the pan.
4. Use a pencil to make marks on a white cloth. Wet the dirty cloth and spread it across the rough surface of the washboard.
5. Wet the soap and let children rub it across the pencil marks. Then they can rub the cloth against the rough washboard.
6. Ask them to rinse the cloth and check to see if the spots are gone. If not, repeat step five.
7. Introduce vocabulary, such as "washboard," "rinse," and "wring."
8. Remove the washboard and wipe it with the sponge. Wring the cloth and spread it on the washboard to dry. Empty the water and wipe the pan with the sponge.
9. To maintain interest, replace the cloth with doll clothes.

More to do

Science: Observe the difference in dry cloth and wet cloth. Explain how soap and water remove soil.

Mary Jo Shannon, Roanoke, VA

What's on the Floor?

Materials

bagless vacuum cleaner (vacuum cleaner with an empty bag can also be used)
newsprint
magnifying glasses
tweezers
several sheets of white construction paper
markers
large clear book tape
stapler or hole punch and yarn

What to do

1. After a period of free play, gather the children in a circle. Bring an empty vacuum cleaner to the circle and discuss its uses. Lead the discussion to kinds of things that dirty the classroom floor (things from the play that day). Make a list of what the children think they might find on the floor.
2. Quickly vacuum some particularly dirty parts of the floor. Make sure to vacuum an area that is not too damp or dangerous for the children.
3. Dump the contents of the vacuum cleaner on a few pieces of newsprint in the middle of the circle.
4. Divide the group into manageable numbers of children to investigate what is on the newsprint. Have magnifying glasses and tweezers available to assist in the exploration.
5. Let the children choose something they can identify or that interests them. Stick it to a large piece of clear book tape and tape it to a piece of white construction paper. Ask each child to write her name on her paper (write for those who can't).
6. Ask them to dictate what they found on the floor of the classroom. Write it underneath the item on the paper.
7. Staple or attach all of the pages together to make a class book and add it to the library area.

Ann Kelly, Johnstown, PA

Window Brighteners

Materials

materials that reflect the four seasons:

- summer: pressed flowers, fresh leaves, grass and weeds, pictures or drawings of the sun, pictures of swimsuits
- fall: colorful leaves, pumpkin, scarecrow, apples
- winter: pictures or drawings of a snowy day, mittens, hats, and coats
- spring: pressed flower buds, new grass and weeds, pictures or drawings of a sunny day, pictures of a kite

clear adhesive paper

thin paper

markers

dowel rod (available at home supply stores) as long as the window is wide

What to do

1. Make these colorful panels to brighten up your housekeeping center. The instructions for each season are the same except for the type of materials used.
2. For each season, go on a nature walk to collect as many natural items as possible. Remember to collect things that reflect the current seasonal theme.
3. Ask the children to draw pictures that depict the seasonal theme. Provide very thin paper, so when you hang your creation the light will shine through it.

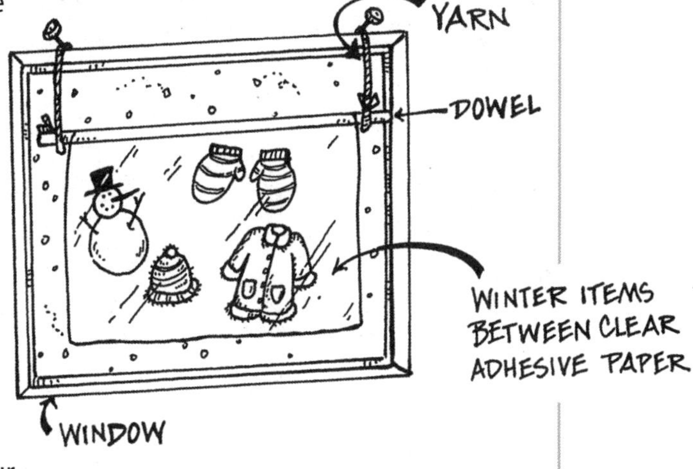

4. After collecting all the materials needed, cut a piece of adhesive paper large enough to cover the window you have selected for your panel. Make sure there is an equal amount of adhesive paper to cover the back of the panel.
5. Help the children apply the seasonal materials to one piece of adhesive paper in any manner they wish. Use this time to talk about the different things they have collected. Ask questions such as, "How does this colorful leaf show us what season it is?"
6. After the children are satisfied with the placement of the seasonal materials, apply the rest of the adhesive paper to the back, sandwiching the materials between.
7. Tape the dowel rod to the top of the panel. Tie whatever you have chosen to hang your panel with to both ends of the dowel rod.
8. Choose a window that gets a lot of light and hang the panel and illustrations in it.

More to do Let the children make individual panels to take home. Simply cut smaller pieces of adhesive paper for each child and let them use the seasonal materials to create a unique display. Edge with rick-rack or ribbon, if desired. Punch a single hole in the top, and help the child thread a piece of ribbon through it for hanging.

Related books *How Do You Say It Today, Jesse Bear?* by Nancy White Carlstrom
A Kitten's Year by Nancy Raines Day
Laughing Tomatoes and Other Spring Poems by Francisco X. Alarcon
Picasso and the Girl With the Ponytail by Laurence Anholt
A Prairie Year by Jo Bannatyne-Cugnet

Virginia Jean Herrod, Columbia, SC

How Fast Do I Have to Eat?

Materials

ice cream
ice cream scoop
cups
two large sheets of paper and a marker

What to do

1. At large group time, pass around a scoop of ice cream in a cup. Ask the children to describe what they see and feel in the cup. Talk about what happens to ice cream when it isn't in the freezer.
2. Write "How fast do I have to eat?" on one sheet of paper. Ask each child how long he thinks he has to eat an ice cream cone before it would melt and become a liquid. Write each child's answer on the sheet of paper and post it.
3. Put another scoop of ice cream into a cup. On another sheet of paper, note the time that you scooped the ice cream. Tell the class that the cup of ice cream will be on the science table during free play and they should check it often to see if it is completely melted.
4. One the second sheet of paper, write the time and what each child saw when he checked the state of the ice cream during free play.
5. When the ice cream is completely melted, calculate the time it took to melt completely. Write this time on both pieces of paper.
6. Review the results of the experiment and the observations with the group at the end of free play.
7. To extend this experiment, have the children put cups of ice cream in different locations (sun, shade, inside, outside, in the refrigerator, and so on) and observe and chart the differences.
8. Make sure you have enough ice cream for everyone to have a taste while they work.

Related books

Freezing and Melting by Robin Nelson
From Cow to Ice Cream by Bertram Knight

Ann Kelly, Johnstown, PA

I Scream, You Scream, We All Scream for Ice Cream

Materials

felt
scissors
glue
letter stickers
ice cream maker
ingredients to make ice cream
paper cups
plastic spoons and bowls
toppings for ice cream: chocolate syrup, chocolate chips, granola, cherries, whipped topping, caramel, sprinkles etc.

What to do

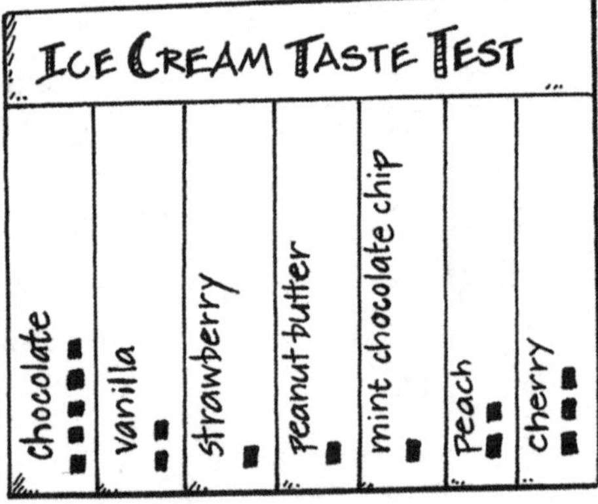

1. Cut out ice cream scoops from three different colors of felt (white, pink, and dark brown are nice) and cones from brown felt. Give each child three different colored scoops and a cone. Ask them to glue the felt ice cream to the cone and on top of each other. Then help them choose letter stickers to spell their names on their cones.
2. Using an ice cream maker and ingredients for homemade ice cream, make a variety of ice cream flavors with the children. Follow the instructions on the ice cream maker as the children watch. When the ice cream has formed, give each child a paper cup and plastic spoon to taste it. Graph the children's favorite flavor on a large piece of paper.
3. Have an ice cream party! Ask each child to bring a small container of their favorite flavor of ice cream to school. Set up a sundae bar on a table! Put chocolate syrup, caramel, whipped topping, cherries, chocolate chips, mini marshmallows, granola, sprinkles, chocolate candies, and so on into plastic bowls with spoons and let each child create his own ice cream sundae.

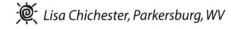

Lisa Chichester, Parkersburg, WV

Ice Cream Sundae

Materials

brown tissue paper
scissors
Styrofoam ball for each child
polyfill fiber
empty individual plastic applesauce containers or ice cream cups
red ½" or ¼" pompoms
white glue
yarn in pink, white, or brown
corrugated paper, construction paper, or oaktag
plastic sundae and banana split containers
plastic spoons
plastic fruit

What to do

1. Prepare "ingredients" for an "ice cream sundae." Cut out an imperfect, wiggly circle shape and thin wiggly strips to resemble chocolate syrup from brown tissue paper.
2. Give each child brown tissue paper "syrup," a Styrofoam ball, and fiberfill. The children glue the Styrofoam ball in a cup, glue tissue (syrup) on top of the Styrofoam, and fiberfill on top of the tissue for whipped cream. Provide red pompoms for a cherry.
3. To make "ice cream scoops," wrap yarn around cardboard at a width you want the yarn pompom to be (2" or more), until the yarn is wrapped about 1" thick.
4. Slip the yarn off the cardboard, tie the yarn tightly in the middle to make a bowtie shape, and cut the loops to make the pompom.
5. Put various colored pompoms in a cone, cup, or banana split dish. Add plastic fruit to make a split.
6. To make a cone, cut out a circle from corrugated paper, and then cut out one third of the circle. Twist into a cone and attach with glue or staples. This resembles a waffle cone. Paint the cone tan or brown, if desired.

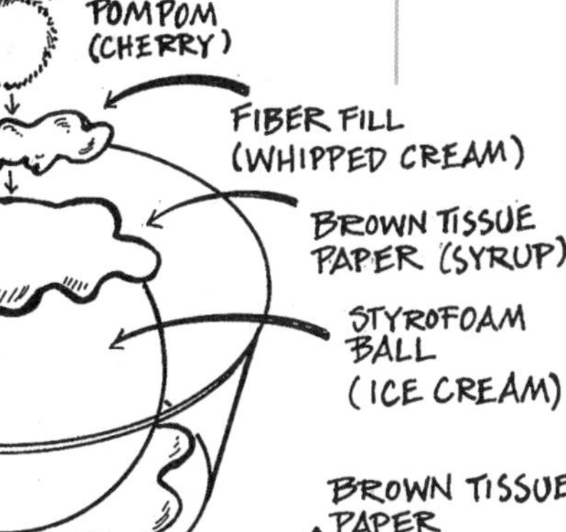

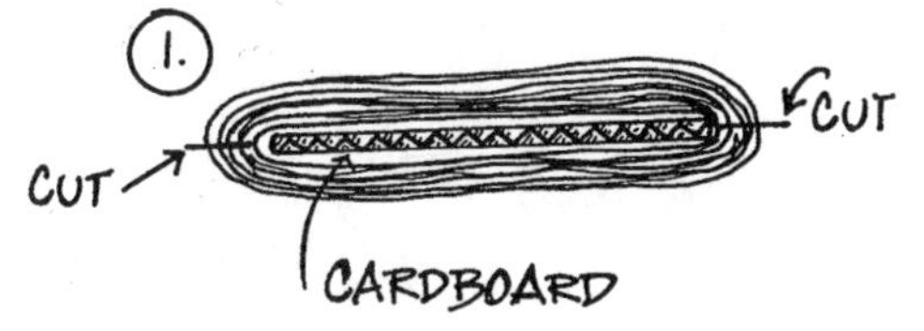

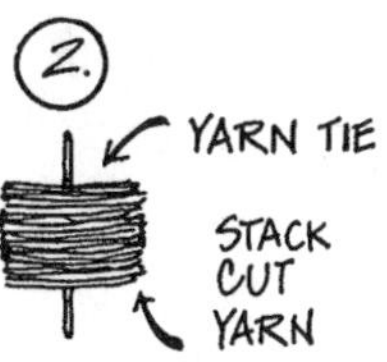

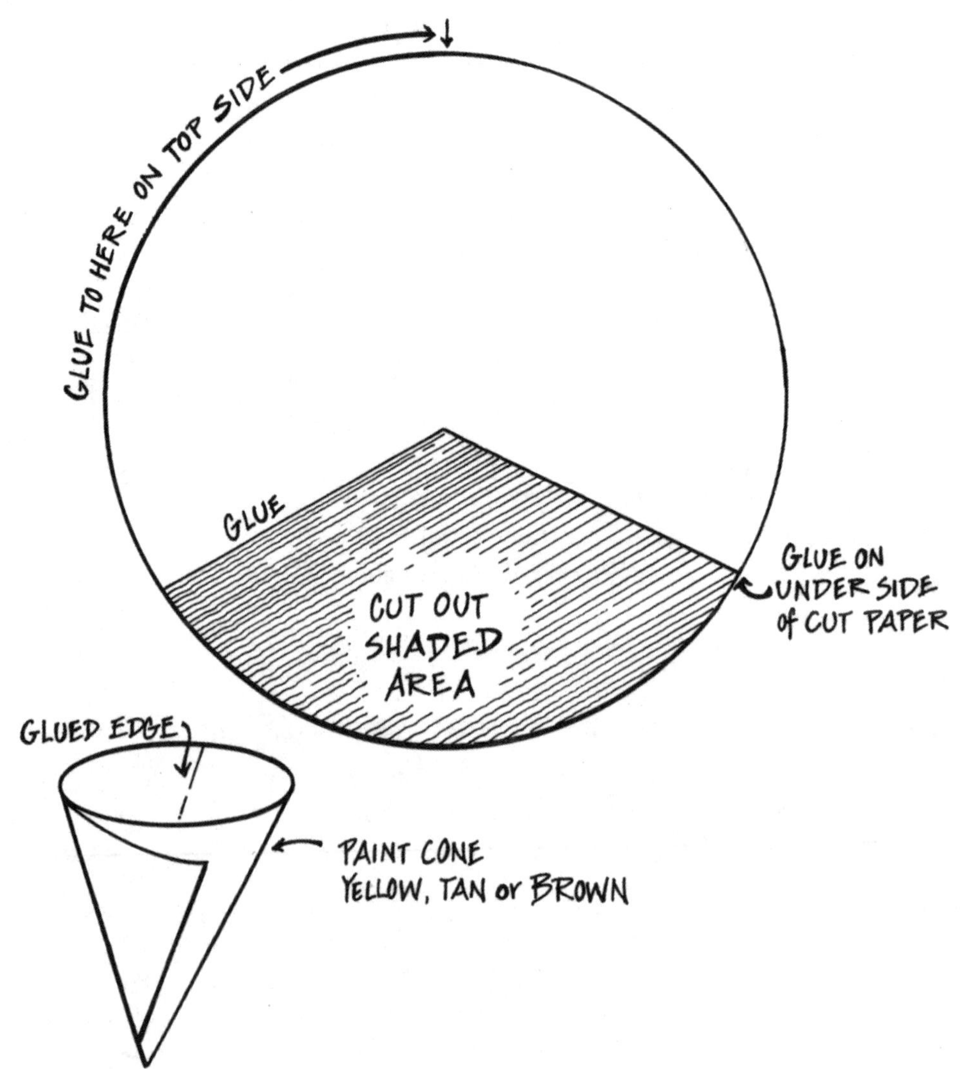

Related poem

Ice Cream Cones by Mary Brehm

When I am hot and sticky,
And don't know what to do,
I go to the ice cream store,
And get a cone or two.

Then I give one to my friend,
For it is fun to share,
And if it drips a little bit,
We don't really care.

For we enjoy the taste of it,
And it makes us cool.
And we can get the sticky off
in the swimming pool.

 *Mary Brehm, Aurora, OH*

Making Snow Cones

Materials

snow cone machine
ice cubes
flavored juice such as cranberry or lime (colors work great)
cups
spoons

What to do

1. Help each child make his own snow cone using the snow cone machine.
2. After turning on the ice machine, the child spoons some crushed ice into a cup and adds flavored juice on top.
3. Children can eat their snow cones for snack.

Sandy Scott, Vancouver, WA

Milkshake

Materials

12 oz. Styrofoam cups
pink, brown, red, and white tissue paper
pink and brown construction paper
tape
drinking straws
milkshake stickers

What to do

1. Give each child a Styrofoam cup.
2. Let the children choose which flavor "milkshake" they want to make (chocolate or strawberry). Give the children pink or brown tissue paper and construction paper accordingly. Also give each child white and red tissue paper.
3. Demonstrate how to cover the outside of the cup with the construction paper and tape it in place.
4. Ask the children to crumple the brown or pink tissue paper and put it in the cup, and then use white tissue paper for whipped cream. Children may roll red tissue paper into a "cherry" and put it on top of the whipped cream.
5. Give each child a straw to put in his cup. They may use stickers of ice cream to decorate their milkshakes, as well.

Barbara Cocores, Duarte, CA

Moo! Milk

Materials

story about cows and milking them
precut cow shapes on butcher paper
purple tempera paint
ice cream
purple soda
straws

What to do

1. Read a story about cows on the farm and how we get milk from the cow.
2. Say the following silly rhyme by Gelett Burgess with the children:

I never saw a purple cow,
I never hope to see one,
But I can tell you, anyhow,
I'd rather see than be one!

3. Provide pre-cut cow shapes and let children paint purple spots on them.
4. Explain that milk is a product from cows and that ice cream is made from milk.
5. Make purple cow milkshakes with the children. Mix three scoops of vanilla ice cream with purple soda in a large plastic cup. Add a straw and enjoy!

Lisa Chichester, Parkersburg, WV

We All Love Ice Cream!

Materials

two or three small tables and chairs
rectangular table
cash register and play money
playdough in several different colors
paper plates and cups
ice cream scoops
paper cones
napkins
plastic spoons
straws
serving trays
ice cream shop clothes (aprons, hats, visors and white shirts)
cardstock paper
markers

What to do

1. Take a field trip to a local ice cream shop and let the children order cones. Have an employee show the children around. If a field trip is not possible, ask someone who works in an ice cream shop to come in and talk to the children. Make sure they bring some samples!
2. Place two or three small tables and chairs in the housekeeping area for dining. Place a slightly larger table in the area for preparing ice cream treats.
3. Put different colored playdough in bowls on the preparation table. Add ice cream scoops, plates, cups, paper cones, and napkins.
4. Place aprons, hats, visors, and white shirts in the dress-up area. Ask children to name the ice cream shop and create a sign. Post the sign near the entrance to the area.
5. Create a menu of all the flavors available at the ice cream shop on a large piece of poster board. Post it behind the prep table.
6. Let the children use the materials freely during center time.
7. Have an ice cream truck visit the center. The children will enjoy seeing the truck and hearing the music. Let each child purchase an ice cream treat.

Related books

Big Mama by Tony Crunk
Garth Pig and the Ice Cream Lady by Mary Rayner
Ice Cream Larry by Daniel Pinkwater

Virginia Jean Herrod, Columbia, SC

A Chair for My Mother

Materials

A Chair for My Mother by Vera B. Williams
8 ½" x 11" paper in pink and white
photocopier
scissors
glue sticks
crayons

What to do

1. Before Mother's Day, read *A Chair for My Mother* to the children. Copy the phrase "We read *A Chair for My Mother* by Vera B. Williams" on white paper. Make a copy for each child.
2. Copy the chair pattern below on pink paper. Make one for each child.
3. Place the book, the pink chair patterns, and the white paper in the art center. Encourage the children to cut out the pink chairs and glue them to the white paper underneath the phrase.
4. Encourage them to use crayons to draw a picture of themselves with their mother or another important woman in their lives.
5. Compile the finished pages together into a book for the library area, or send them home as a gift for Mother's Day.

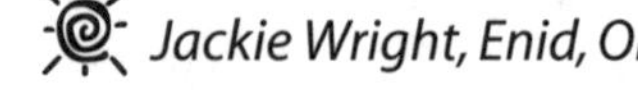
Jackie Wright, Enid, OK

Alphabet Hunt

Materials

cut-out or wooden letters
bag
variety of alphabet books
writing and drawing materials
large paper
glue

What to do

1. This activity works well with four or five children at a time.
2. Choose a letter for the day. A fun way to do this is to put letters in a bag and let a child choose one with her eyes closed.
3. Ask each child to look through an alphabet book for the letter of the day. When the children have found the letter, each child may talk about the items on the page. For example, if the letter is "B," the items on the page might be a bear, bee, baseball, balloon, baby, banana, and so on.
4. Ask the children to draw one of the objects in their book on a piece of paper and write the word (with your help, if necessary).
5. Combine these drawings into a classroom big book titled "Alphabet Book." Glue the drawings onto a large sheet of paper and write the alphabet letter at the top. Attach the pages together as they are finished.
6. The alphabet big book can become part of the class library. Children love to read books they have created.

More to do

Transitions: Hand out a few alphabet cards to the children (starting with the letter "A") or use the grab bag method and let children choose their own letters. Ask them to line up in alphabetical order. When they have lined up correctly, ask them to call out their letter, like the "Alphabet Song."

Related books

Alligators All Around by Maurice Sendak
On Market Street by Anita and Arnold Lobel

Author Study

Materials

basket
many books by one author
signs with author's name
photos of author

What to do

1. Every teacher has a few favorite children's authors. This is a good way to set up an author study in the library center to give children a chance to share in the experience.
2. First, gather many books by the same author. Some common children's favorites are Rosemary Wells, Maurice Sendak, Denise Fleming, and Eric Carle. Place these books in a special basket and attach a sign that says "Author Study" and the author's name.
3. Next, post a photo of the author. Children enjoy seeing photos of the authors with their children, pets, and at various ages in their lives. The Internet is a good source for these photos. If possible, also post a print of the author's work or the book jackets.
4. If stuffed versions or puppets of the characters in the books are available, display these to help the children re-tell the story.
5. If your classroom has Internet access, use it to go to author websites. These are great! They sometimes have video clips of the author at work, photos of family, pets, and the home of the author. The children are fascinated, and it helps them to see the author as a real person and see writing as something they can do. If you don't have Internet access, go to the library and check out videos or biographies of the authors.
6. This is a great way to help the children build the ability to really look at books' similarities and differences, to learn to love the characters, and develop affection for great authors.
7. Change the author study weekly, monthly, or as the children's interests change.

Book Match

Materials

children's books
camera or scanner
book pockets
glue
chart paper
markers

What to do

1. Take a picture of each book in the library center, or scan the cover and print out a small picture.
2. Glue each picture to a book pocket.
3. Glue the book pockets to chart paper. Leave enough room around the pocket so the children can put the library checkout cards into it.
4. Encourage the children to play Book Match to work on their observation skills. The children pick a book, find the pocket with that book's picture on it, and put the library checkout card in the pocket. Continue until all books have been matched to their corresponding pictures.
5. This is a great way to teach children how to borrow classroom library books as well.

Related books

D.W.'s Library Card by Marc Tolon Brown
I Took My Frog to the Library by Eric A. Kimmel
Jonathan Goes to the Library by Susan K. Baggette
Leila and the Library and the Letter L by Cynthia Fitterer Klingel
Let's Visit the Library by Marianne Johnston
Tiny Goes to the Library by Cari Meister

Mike Krestar, Latrobe, PA

Bubble Painting

Materials

water
liquid soap
food coloring or liquid water-soluble, non-toxic paint
small margarine tubs or small bowls
low-sided tub
straws
paper towels
light-colored paper

What to do

1. Place soap, water, and food coloring or liquid paint into a butter tub. Place it in a low-sided tub to catch any runoff. Make more than one small tub of bubbles to provide a choice in colors.
2. Let children use a straw to stir the mixture, and then blow into the mixture to make bubbles. Let the bubbles flow out over the top edge of the butter tub.
3. Ask them to remove the straw and place it on a paper towel.
4. Demonstrate how to place light-colored paper over the top of the small butter tub and bubbles. Leave for a few seconds. The bubble shapes will show through the paper.
5. Lift the paper and look at the bubble design.
6. After the bubble pictures have dried, encourage the children to dictate a few sentences about their bubbles. Compile all of the papers together to make a "Bubble Book" for the library.
7. Have the children throw away their straws after they finish the bubble painting.
8. If desired, let the children use a variety of items to make bubbles, such as paper or plastic tubes, slotted spoons, colanders, and so on.

Tip: If a child has difficulty blowing into a straw or sucks into it, let her practice with plain water. Or, an adult can hold the straw in the middle and pinch it closed after the child blows air into the bubble water each time.

More to do

Movement: Encourage the children to form their arms into large round circles and pretend to be bubbles. Play music as the children dance like bubbles!

Science: Blow bubbles and catch them on a sheet of paper. Encourage the children to measure the size of the bubbles using a ruler or another item of measurement.

Related song

Bubbles (tune: "Twinkle, Twinkle, Little Star")

Bubbles, bubbles up so high
Floating, floating, in the sky.
Filled with colors, filled with air,
Popping here, popping there.
Bubbles, bubbles up so high,
Floating, floating in the sky.

Sandra Nagel, White Lake, MI

Class Caterpillar

Materials

The Very Hungry Caterpillar by Eric Carle
tissue paper (at least red, yellow, and blue)
glue
paper plates

What to do

1. Read *The Very Hungry Caterpillar* to the children. Tell them that they are going to make a class caterpillar.
2. Help the children cut or tear tissue paper into small pieces.
3. Ask the children to glue tissue paper to a paper plate. As each child's creation dries, add it to make a giant caterpillar on the classroom wall.
4. Create the head of the caterpillar by adding eyes, mouth, and antennae to a paper plate.

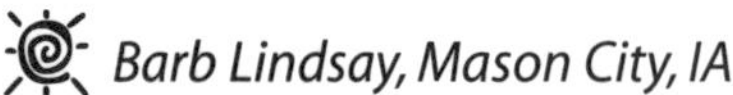
Barb Lindsay, Mason City, IA

Flags Around the World

Materials

pictures of children in full traditional costume
pictures of flags of different countries
scissors
photocopier
rubber cement
9" x 12" construction paper
marker
poster board
laminator
hole punch and yarn or binding machine
oak tag
felt flannel board

What to do

1. Find pictures and patterns of children from around the world dressed to express cultural diversity. Also find pictures of flags of different countries (corresponding to the children in traditional dress).
2. Enlarge and copy the patterns onto 8 ½ x 11" paper. Color the pages with brightly colored markers.
3. Mount each page on a separate sheet of 9" x 12" construction paper, using rubber cement (adult only). A border of paper will show around each page.
4. Label the name of the country on each page.
5. Make a 10" x 14" cover with the title "Around the World" and make a back cover out of heavy poster board.
6. Laminate the pages and the covers for durability, and cut them out. Assemble the pages and bind them in a binding machine or using a hole punch and yarn.
7. Create a flag on oak tag for each country depicted in the book. Color the flags, cut them out, and laminate them for durability. Back the flags with felt for flannel board use.
8. Work with the children to match the flags to the children in the book and display the flags on the flannel board. Show the children how to work with this book on their own, and challenge them to find a flag for every country in the book.

Hats, Hats

Materials

stories with a hat theme
paper plates
hole punch
glue or paste
ribbon
collage materials (such as tissue paper, crepe paper, feathers, and yarn)
camera (optional)

What to do

1. Read a few hat-theme books to the children. Some good hat stories include *Hats, Hats, Hats* by Ann Morris, *Jennie's Hat* by Ezra Jack Keats, and *Caps for Sale* by Esphyr Slobodkina.
2. Punch a hole on each side of a paper plate. Make enough for each child. Put paper plates, glue, ribbon, and collage materials in the art center.
3. Invite the children to create their own hats by gluing collage material all over one side of the paper plate.

4. Help the children thread ribbon through the holes in the plate and tie it under their chin.
5. If desired, take pictures of the children as they pose with their hats.
6. Find appropriate music for a hat parade, or have a hat fashion show.

Margery Kranyik Fermino, Hyde Park, MA

Instant Poster

Materials

The Trek by Ann Jonas
color photocopier
11″ x 17″ oak tag or poster board
glue stick
laminator
scissors

What to do

1. Sometimes children's books have pictures in the back that review the whole book. *The Trek* by Ann Jonas has these pictures.
2. Make a copy of the animals on the back two pages and enlarge them. Mount them on the oak tag or poster board using a glue stick.
3. Laminate for durability and cut out.
4. This is a very easy poster to make; the names of the animals and the title are already included on the pictures.
5. Read the book to the children and display it along with the poster.
6. Let the children visit this area in pairs or small groups. As they turn the pages, they can use the poster as a reference tool to name the animals hidden in the illustrations of the book.

Jackie Wright, Enid, OK

Make Your Own Books

Materials

paper in assorted sizes
scissors
long-arm stapler
drawing supplies
glue
sentence strips
magazines and catalogs

What to do

1. Fold a piece of paper into quarters. This will become a book with eight pages. Turn the folded paper so that the main "spine" fold is on the left. Cut off the bottom strip to separate the pages, keeping the main fold intact. Open it and staple at the main fold using a long-arm stapler. This makes a small eight-page book. Make one for each child.
2. Encourage the children to choose a topic and a title for their book. Examples of titles are: "Good Food," "Community Helpers," and "My Circus Book." Children could also make their own version of a favorite story such as "The Three Little Pigs." Let them illustrate their cover.
3. Ask them to illustrate their books by drawing pictures or cutting out pictures from magazines. Encourage them to dictate stories on sentence strips and glue them to the appropriate pages.
4. Write "the end" on the last page!
5. This project lets children practice in a variety of skills, such as number recognition (numbering the pages), sight word recognition, concepts of print (front, back of book, left to right progression), vocabulary words such as "author," "illustrations," "fiction," and so on.
6. Children love to read the books they created. Encourage them to read their books to their classmates. They may exchange their books to read to each other.

Iris Rothstein, New Hyde Park, NY

Making Wordless Books

Materials

paper
crayons
stapler

What to do

1. Ask the children to compile their drawings and paintings to make a wordless book. Tell them to put the pages together in any order that they like.
2. Staple the pages together.
3. Encourage the children to tell stories based on the pictures in the book.

Related books

An Ocean World by Peter Sis
Do You Want to Be My Friend? by Eric Carle
One Frog Too Many by Mercer Mayer
Pancakes for Breakfast by Tomie dePaola
Snowman by Raymond Briggs
Truck by Donald Crews

Liz Thomas, Hobart, IN

Memory Book

Materials

photographs of the children from home and school
pictures cut from magazines
small plastic photo album
stickers, glitter, buttons, charms, and ribbon
scissors
glue
colored paper

What to do

1. Place photos of children and pictures from magazines on a table. Also provide scrapbook materials, such as stickers, glitter, and so on.
2. Give each child a glue stick or glue, scissors, and a small photo album.
3. Encourage the children to create their own "memory books."
4. A variation is for children to create a "Friends Counting Book" by putting a photo of one child from the class on the first page, two children on the next page, and so on.

More to do

Music: Create a classroom songbook with the children. Ask them to cut out pictures from magazines that remind them of a song (for example, a barn for "Old MacDonald"). Put one song picture on each page then let the children take turns choosing a song to sing.

Our Animals A to Z

Materials

cookie cutters in animal shapes
white paper
pencils
stapler

What to do

1. Provide animal-shaped cookie cutters and encourage the children to trace their shapes on white construction paper.
2. Inside the shape, help the children print the letter that the animal's name starts with. For example, if the child traced a fox, she would write: "F is for fox."
3. If possible, try to find animal shapes in every letter of the alphabet. Staple the pages together to make a class alphabet book. Add it to the library center.

Related book

My Beastie Book of ABC by David Frampton

Sight Words for the Pocket Chart

Materials

old workbooks and children's magazines
6″ x 9″ oak tag
3″ x 5″ index cards or colored cardstock cut to 3″ x 5″
small pictures of sight words
glue stick
scissors
laminator (optional)
pocket chart

What to do

1. Cut out a set of pictures of sight words from a teacher supply catalog or workbooks (for example, pictures of different animals). Print the pictures on 6″ x 9″ oak tag to make picture cards.
2. Create a set of 3″ x 5″ flash cards with simple words to accompany the pictures.
3. Put matching pictures on the back of each word card so that the children can self-correct themselves. Laminate and cut out, if desired.
4. Place a pocket chart in the library center for word recognition. Ask the children to slip a word card into the chart, and then slip the matching picture in the slot that goes with the word. Children can look at the back of the word card to check their pairs.
5. Children enjoy working together so they can verify each other's answers. When one child has matched all the cards, they can switch roles and start again.
6. Change the cards weekly to keep interest fresh and to expand children's sight word vocabulary. Challenge older children to look at the picture side of a word card, spell the word, and then flip to the word to check their answers.

The Mitten

Materials

The Mitten by Jan Brett
large construction paper
scissors
animal-shape patterns
black construction paper
markers
glue

What to do

1. Read the story *The Mitten* by Jan Brett to the children.
2. Cut out a large mitten shape from construction paper.
3. Provide patterns of different animals and encourage children to trace them onto black paper to create "shadows."
4. Encourage the children to glue a variety of animal shadows on the mitten shape.
5. Let the children retell the story based on the shadows that they have glued onto their mitten.

Related books

My Shadow by Robert Louis Stevenson
The Snowy Day by Ezra Jack Keats

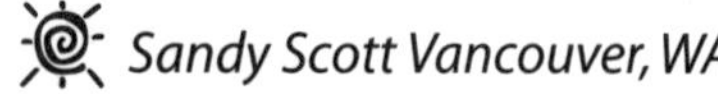
Sandy Scott Vancouver, WA

The Return Desk

Materials

paper
scissors
markers
26 books
contact paper
large table
alphabet written in order so children can refer to it

What to do

1. Take the children to the school library. Explain that they will help set up a book return desk in the classroom.
2. Cut paper into 26 small squares (2" x 2") and write a letter of the alphabet on each square. Choose 26 books from your class library, stick a letter of the

alphabet on each book using contact paper, and place the books in alphabetical order on the table ("library return desk").

3. Write the letters of the alphabet on chart paper and hang it close by so children may refer to it.
4. Encourage the children to borrow books and return them to their appropriate alphabetical spot on the table. If the children need extra help putting them in the correct spot, mark the location on the table with matching letters (use 2" x 2" pieces of paper and contact paper).
5. This is also great for children who need practice with numbers. Just replace the letters on the books with numbers. Choose a quantity of books that matches or challenges the skill levels of your group.

Related book *Jonathan Goes to the Library* by Susan Buggett

Ann Kelly, Johnstown, PA

The Shoes We Wear

Materials

Mary Wore Her Red Dress and Henry Wore His Green Sneakers by Merle Peek
paper in a variety of colors
markers
boots and shoe patterns
scissors
glue
mini stickers

What to do

1. Read *Mary Wore Her Red Dress and Henry Wore His Green Sneakers* by Merle Peek to the children.
2. Draw stick figures on paper (without faces), one for each child. On each paper write the words, "_______ is wearing _____ ______ with ______ on them."
3. Ask the children to cut out boot or shoe shapes using the patterns and any color paper she wants.

4. Encourage the children to glue the cut-out shoes to the feet of the stick person. They can decorate their stick person and shoes to look like themselves or someone they know.
5. Ask the children to dictate a sentence about the shoes on their stick figures, for example, "Mary is wearing red shoes with flowers on them." Write the child's words underneath the picture.
6. Make a classroom book by stapling all of the pages together. Let the children make a cover for the book and then add it to the classroom library.
7. Read *Mary Wore Her Red Dress and Henry Wore His Green Sneakers* again. Afterward, read the children's classroom book and sing the words using the same tune.
8. This can be adapted using other clothing items, such as coats, hats, mittens, pants, shirts, or socks.

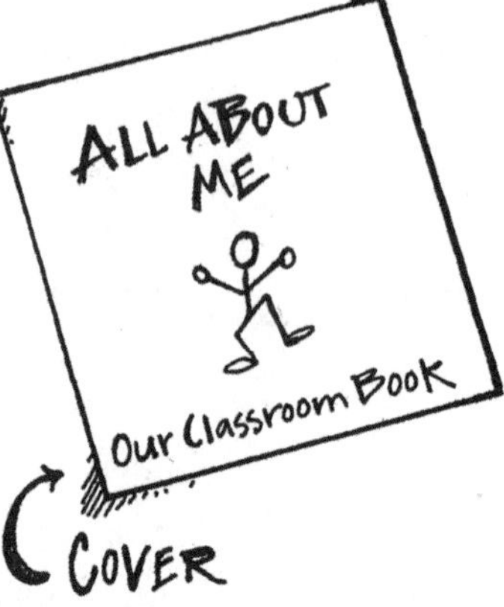

 *Sandra Nagel, White Lake, MI*

We Are Alike, We Are Different

Materials

We Are All Alike, We Are All Different by Cheltenham Elementary School Kindergartners
drawing paper
markers and crayons
glue
wool
buttons or wiggle eyes
large construction paper
photos of children's family members
magazine pictures
stapler or hole punch and yarn

What to do

1. Read *We Are All Alike, We Are All Different* to the children.
2. Ask each child to draw a self-portrait. Let them glue on wool for hair and wiggle eyes or buttons for eyes. Ask the children to dictate descriptions of themselves. Write the descriptions underneath the drawings. Older children can write their own descriptions.
3. Ask the children to glue their portraits on larger paper. Encourage them to decorate the paper by gluing pictures of family members around their portrait. They may also glue magazine pictures or draw pictures of things they like, such as foods and toys.
4. Ask children to dictate descriptions of their families or favorite things for you to write on the bottom of their construction paper page. Older children may write their own descriptions.
5. Ask for volunteers to help illustrate pictures for the cover. Glue the pictures on a large sheet of construction paper. Attach the pages together using a stapler or hole punch and yarn to make a large class book.

Deborah Litfin, Forest Hills, NY

Who's Who?

Materials

digital or 35-mm camera
computer and printer (if using a digital camera)
cardstock paper
glue
scissors
markers

What to do

1. Take a photo of each child showing the child's head and a bit of her shoulders. Try to make the child's face and hair fill the whole frame. Develop or print the photographs.
2. Glue each photo to the center of a piece of cardstock paper. Help each child print her name under her own photo. Place another piece of cardstock over the child's photo.
3. Mark a circle on the cardstock that, when cut out, will reveal only a small portion of the child's face. For instance, draw a circle so that it will reveal one eye and a nose; or one eye, one cheek, and the corner of the mouth. Cut out the circles.

4. Under the circle on each paper, print, "Who is this?" Attach the paper with the circle cutout over the paper with the photograph on it. You can attach it at the top or the sides. Either way is fine as long as the circle shows part of the child's face and the top paper can be lifted up or turned to reveal the child's whole face.

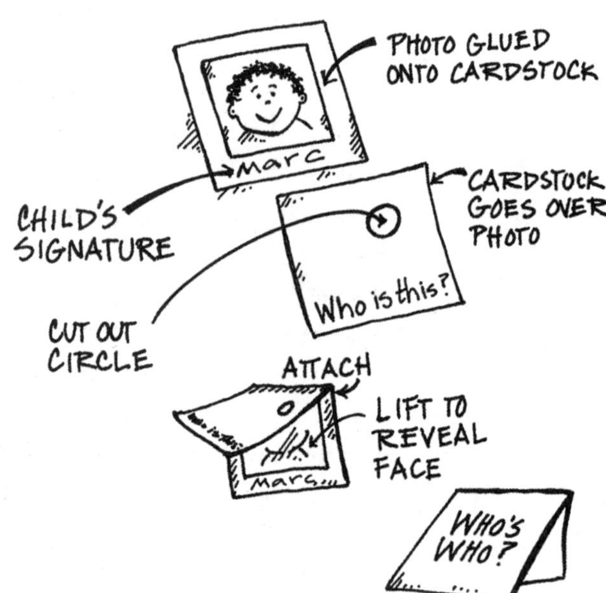

5. Create a front and back cover.
6. Bind the pages into a book. If you have a large class, you might want to make two or three books. Put the book in the library corner to read and enjoy.

More to do

Games: Make a guessing game for family members to enjoy. Using the same method described above, create a large poster with each child's photograph on it. Cut out a hole on another sheet of poster board so that a small part of each child's face will be revealed. Line them up carefully since there is more than one image. Attach the two poster boards together, making sure to leave a way to flip the top page up or turn it. Invite the children's family members to try to guess which photo shows which children.

Virginia Jean Herrod, Columbia, SC

Abracadabra!

Materials

black felt hat
scissors
small items of varied textures
magic wand

What to do

1. Cut a small slit into the top of a black felt hat, large enough for a hand to reach through it.
2. Place a variety of small items with a variety of textures in the hat.
3. Let the children take turns waving the magic wand and saying, "Abracadabra, I feel a..."
4. A child pulls out an item and shows the group.

Melissa Browning, Milwaukee, WI

Abracadabra Hat and Wand

Materials

black construction paper
tape
yellow construction paper
scissors
glitter
book on magic tricks
magic trick props
paper towel tubes
black paint
pipe cleaners

What to do

1. Let children make magician hats. Demonstrate how to roll black construction paper and tape into a large tube shape. Cut out a flat top and brim as shown in the illustration. Tape it together to make a hat.
2. Encourage the children to decorate their hats using pre-cut yellow stars and glitter.
3. Read a book about magic tricks and teach the children some easy tricks to do.
4. Make magic wands. Give each child an empty paper towel tube to paint black.

5. Ask the children to glue paper stars to two or three pipe cleaners and then tape the pipe cleaners so they are coming out of the wand as shown in the illustration.
6. Make a "stage" by spreading a blanket on the floor, or use a real one if possible. Put on a class magic show and let the children take turns going on stage to do a magic trick.

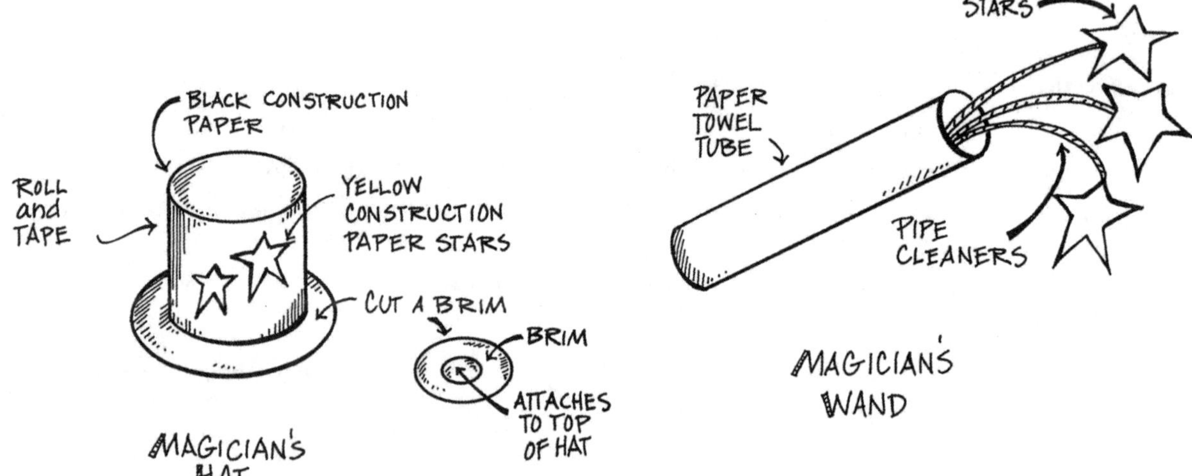

Lisa Chichester, Parkersburg, WV

Abracadabra Stage

Materials

two 4' long pieces of PVC pipe and one 6' long piece of PVC pipe
two PVC elbow joints and two PVC "feet"
one piece of thick colorful fabric (6' x 5')
large refrigerator box
scissors
paint, including gold or silver colors
12" slender dowel rod
two star cutouts
glitter
glue
metallic ribbon in at least two colors
magician's hat (top hat with sequins) and cape

What to do

Step One: Create a curtain on a frame for your magic show.

1. Attach one 4′ length of PVC pipe to each PVC "foot."
2. Attach an elbow joint to the top of each 4′ length of pipe.
3. Attach the 6′ length of PVC pipe to the two elbow joints, thus joining the two 4′ lengths together.
4. Drape the fabric over the 6′ length of pipe and use glue or any other means to attach it to the pipe.

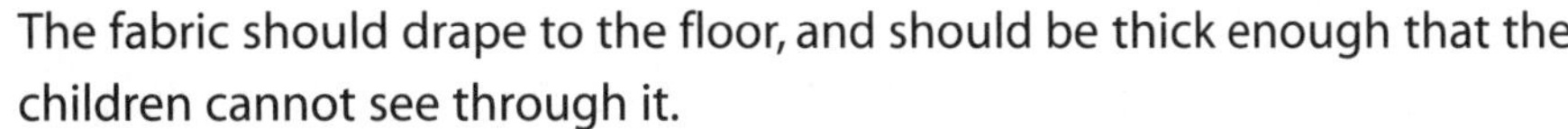

   The fabric should drape to the floor, and should be thick enough that the children cannot see through it.
5. Cut a slit up the center of the fabric almost to the top.

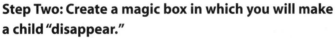

Step Two: Create a magic box in which you will make a child "disappear."

1. Place a refrigerator box on its side. Cut a door in one side of the box large enough so a child to crawl in and out of the box. Cut another door in what will be the top of the box. It is through this door that the child will enter the box in front of the audience.
2. Let the children help paint and decorate the box.

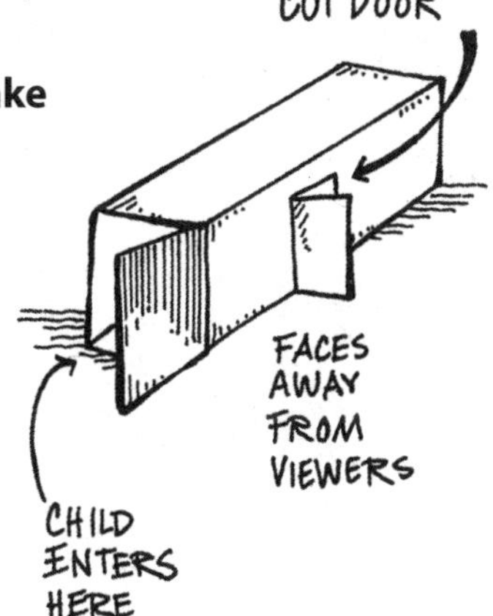

Step Three: Make a magic wand or purchase one from a dollar store.

1. Paint the dowel rod a bright gold or silver.
2. Sprinkle glitter on star cutouts and set aside to dry.
3. Attach the star cutouts to the top of the dowel rod with hot glue (adult only).
4. Attach several pieces of metallic ribbon to the base of the star.
5. Coat the dowel rod in glue and sprinkle with glitter. Set aside to dry.

Step Four: Time for the show!

1. Put the curtain and frame and the "magic box" in a predetermined area of the classroom. Make sure the curtain is directly behind the box. The "assistant" in the next steps will use this curtain as cover to escape from the magic box.
2. Put on the hat and cape and wave the magic wand around as you use your best ringmaster voice to invite the children to a magic show.
3. After the children have gathered in the area, explain that you are going to make a child disappear right before their eyes. Ask for a volunteer to be your assistant.
4. Open the top of the box and help the child inside.
5. Make a big show of talking to the child in the box. Tap on the box and say "Are you still in there?" Encourage the child in the box to answer you.
6. Wave the magic wand over the box as you chant a stream of your best magic words. While doing so, open the back of the box and help the child crawl out and hide behind the curtain.
7. Make a big show of waving the magic wand over the box. Say, "And now your friend is gone!" The more enthusiasm you show, the more fun the children will have.
8. Ask another child to come up and open the top of the box. Remember to encourage your "assistant" to be quiet through all this.
9. After a few moments, have the children seat themselves again. State that you are ready to bring their friend back to the classroom. Make sure the curtain is in place to hide the assistant's activities.
10. Wave the magic wand over the box and chant your magic words again. While doing this, open the back of the box and help the child crawl back inside.
11. Wave the wand over the box again and say, "And now, your friend is back!"
12. Open the top of the box and encourage the child inside to jump out.

Step Five: The children take over the show.

1. Show the children how the trick worked.
2. Let the children freely explore with the props. Encourage them to take turns being the magician and assistant.
3. Provide a variety of things for the children to pull out of the "magic hat." Show them how to stuff something in the hat, wave the magic wand over it while chanting magical words, and pull out the items.
4. Let the children take turns dressing up as a magician and posing in front of the magic curtain for a photograph.

Related Books *The Magical, Mystical, Marvelous Coat* by Catherine Ann Cullen
Milo's Hat Trick by Jon Agee

 *Virginia Jean Herrod, Columbia, SC*

Magician

Materials

basket of books about magicians and easy tricks
poster of magicians
dress-up clothes such as suit coats, fancy dresses, top hats, and white gloves
small table
box of small tricks
stuffed rabbit
child-size screen or room divider
colored sheer scarves
magic wands
playing cards
extra chairs for the audience
tickets

What to do

1. Turn an area of your classroom into a magic learning center. Hang posters of magicians and add a basket of books about magicians. Add dress-up clothes, small tricks, a room divider, magic wands, cards, and a table and chairs.
2. The area will glow with wonder as young magicians perform their magic tricks.
3. Be sure to use magic words with the children such as "alacazam," "abracadabra," and "behold!"
4. Encourage them to make tickets and set up the area to put on a magic show.

Sue Myhre, Bremerton, WA

Poof! A Pookah!

Materials

stuffed rabbit
magic wand
large hat
box
items representing one initial sound (such as pear, pants, puppy, pen, pepper, popcorn, pocket, and puzzle piece)

What to do

1. Place the materials in the designated learning center. Let the children explore the materials independently.
2. Present a magic show. Without the children seeing, place one of the items inside the large hat.
3. Wave a "magic wand" over the hat and say a few words of encouragement, such as "abracadabra," and begin making the targeted initial sound.
4. Encourage the children to repeat the targeted sound.
5. Ask, "What do you think is hidden inside the hat? It's something that starts with the sound /p/."
6. As the children guess, acknowledge their answers focusing on the initial sound. When the appropriate answer is given, say, "Poof! A pookah!"

Note: Explain to the children that a "pookah" is an invisible giant white rabbit that likes to make mischief in folk tales.

Related books

The Talking Eggs by Robert D. San Souci
Trouble With Trolls by Jan Brett

Kate Ross, Middlesex, VT

This Was Your Card

Materials

deck of playing cards or index cards
pictures of items relating to classroom theme

What to do

1. Use a deck of cards, or make a set of pair cards. If making cards, cut out pairs of matching pictures related to your current theme, such as colors, numbers, shapes, and so on. Glue the pictures to index cards. If using a deck of cards, choose enough pairs so that there is one for each child in the group and one for you. Put the remaining cards aside.
2. Give yourself and each child one card from a pair and spread the matching cards face down in the middle of the group where everyone can see them.
3. Let the children take turns turning over a card to try to find the matching card to the one he is holding.
4. Keep going around the group until every child has found his match.

Ann Kelly, Johnstown, PA

Wizard's Potion

Materials

large, clear plastic bowl
several small Styrofoam bowls or paper cups
plastic spoons and several large mixing spoons
flour
salt
sugar
cornstarch
baking soda
food coloring in water
gelatin
soap flakes
liquid detergent
ketchup
vinegar
chart paper

What to do

1. Place a large bowl and mixing spoons in the middle of a low table.
2. Surround the bowl with small portions of the listed materials in Styrofoam bowls or cups. Place a plastic spoon in each of the bowls.
3. Invite small groups of children to visit the center to create a "wizard's potion." Encourage them to add ingredients, one at a time, to the large bowl.
4. Ask questions such as, "How does this ingredient look? How does it smell? What do you think will happen when you mix it with _____?" "What shall we call the potion?" What happens when the vinegar is added to the potion?" (A chemical reaction with bubbling may occur).
5. Record the children's responses on chart paper and title it "Wizard's Wacky Potion."

More to do

Art: Make a whipped soap potion by gradually adding ½ cup soap flakes to ¼ cup water. Use an eggbeater to whip it to a fluffy consistency and use as thick paint on heavy paper.

Related books

Barney Bipples Magic Dandelion by Carol Chapman
Strega Nona by Tomie dePaola

 *Deborah Roud and Diana Reed, New Wilmington, PA*

Nights of Hanukkah

Materials

menorah pattern
candle pattern
tagboard
scissors
markers
hole punch
laminate
glue stick
Velcro or magnetic strip

What to do

1. Trace a menorah and candles on tagboard and cut out. Number the candles from one to eight (leaving the middle holder empty for the main candle, called the *shamash*). Laminate for durability.
2. On each candle except the shamash, punch enough holes to match the number on the candle.
3. Add Velcro (for Velcro boards) or magnetic tape (for cookie sheets or magnetic boards).
4. Encourage the children to practice numeral recognition and counting, and explore the tradition of Hanukkah at the same time!

More to do

This can be done with Kwanzaa, too. Use only seven candles, and no main candle. Use red, black, and green.

Jeanette Denning, Tinley Park, IL

Math

Materials

10 empty, plastic snack-size pudding cups
plastic counters
markers

What to do

1. Number each cup with the numbers 1-10.
2. Ask the children to put the correct number of counters in each cup.
3. As a variation, number the cups by twos, fives, or tens.

 *D'Arcy Simmons, Springfield, MO*

Count the Cats

Materials

colored picture of approximately 20 cats (animals, objects, etc.) hiding in different places
paper
tape
pencil

What to do

1. Build visual discrimination skills and fine motor skills with this variation of a tried and true activity. Find a picture from a children's magazine, activity book, or the Internet of approximately 20 cats (or other animals or objects) hidden in different places.
2. Tape the picture on a wall at child's height. Write each child's name on a piece of paper and draw a line next to each name. Tape the paper underneath the picture.
3. Invite the children to come to the center and count the number of cats they see in the picture. Ask them to write their answers next to their names.

Jackie Wright, Enid, OK

Count-a-Set Cards

Materials

colored cardstock or pegboard
scissors
old workbooks
glue stick
markers
glue stick
laminate
felt
rubber cement
flannel board

What to do

1. This easy-to-make center is perfect for reinforcing students' counting and sequencing skills. Cut cardstock to make 11 cards approximately 2" x 3 ½". These are for the pictures of the sets 0 to 10.
2. Look through old workbooks to find 11 colored pictures of sets with a similar theme (such as insects). For example, find an empty set for 0, one butterfly, two ants, three moths, four beetles, five caterpillars, and so on.

3. Glue each of the pictures to a 2" x 3 ½" card.
4. Cut 11 more cards from cardstock approximately 3" x 3 ½" for the numeral and number name cards. Write the numeral on the top of the card and the number name underneath it. For example, "0" and "zero," "1" and "one," and so on.
5. Laminate both sets of cards for durability and cut out.
6. Prepare the cards for flannel board use by gluing felt to the back of each card using rubber cement.
7. To do the activity, the child first sequences the numeral and number name cards on the flannel board. Then she matches each corresponding set card to the correct numeral and number name cards on the flannel board.

Jackie Wright, Enid, OK

It's Not Heavy, It's My Egg

Materials

large plastic eggs
different objects with different weights (such as quarters, large magnets, sticks of chalk, buttons, and rocks)
clear packing tape
permanent marker
Unifix cubes
box
balance scale
simple chart

What to do

1. Prior to presenting the center, fill each plastic egg with a set of each object. The eggs should vary in weight, so put varying amounts of objects in the eggs.
2. Tape the eggs shut and number them with a marker.
3. Demonstrate to the children how to predict weights using their hands as a scale. Ask them to sequence the eggs according to weight, from lightest to heaviest.
4. Show the children how to use the balance scale by adding Unifix cubes on one side to balance the weight of one of the eggs on the other side. Count the cubes and write the number on a chart. For younger children, ask them which objects used more cubes and which used less.
5. Ask the children to compare the numbers and determine which egg is the heaviest.

6. At the end of the week (or activity), ask the children to predict what they think is in each egg. Open the eggs and show the contents. Discuss why some eggs are heavy or light.

Chart Example:

Numbered Eggs	Number of Cubes Used
Egg 1	
Egg 2	
Egg 3	
Egg 4	
Egg 5	
Egg 6	

Marzee Woodward, Murfreesboro, TN

Jungle Bug Run Game

Materials

white foam board
black permanent marker
insect stickers
butterfly and ladybug cardboard cutouts
rubber butterflies and ladybugs
scissors
glue
two educational jungle/insect books
one die
several real bananas
two stuffed jungle animals

What to do

1. To prepare, use a permanent marker to draw a wavy line on a piece of foam board. Put various insect stickers and glue insect cutouts along the line to make a game board.
2. Put rubber insects (for markers), a few real bananas, one or two educational books

on insects and jungle/rainforest animals, a plastic storage jar to hold rubber insects, two stuffed jungle animals, and one die on a large table.

3. Make sure to lay out the materials in an interesting way so the children will want to come and play.
4. Gather a small group of children next to the table to participate in a math learning game. The goal is to encourage interest in insects found in the rainforest.
5. Let the children choose a rubber insect as a marker.
6. Explain that they will roll the die and move their marker along the game board to make it to the finish line. This helps the children learn math skills by counting and seeing the number of dots on the die itself.
7. Encourage the children to use the books on table to assist their understanding of rainforest animals and insects.
8. Ask questions about rainforest creatures after the children have completed the game.

Audrey Christo, Reseda, CA

Key Sorting

Materials

assorted keys
chart paper
marker

What to do

1. Collect a variety of keys. Ask for discarded keys at a hardware store or from a locksmith.
2. Ask the children to sort the keys. When they are done, ask them how they sorted them (shape, color, and so on).
3. Encourage the children to count the keys, as well.
4. Make a class graph depicting how many of each type or color keys there are.
5. Encourage the children to make patterns out of the keys.

Related books

Each Orange Had 8 Slices by Paul Giganti Jr.
Two Ways to Count to Ten: A Liberian Folktale by Ruby Dee

Barbara Saul, Eureka, CA

Learning Centers to Go

Materials

large, zipper-closure plastic bags
children's books (classroom theme oriented)
stamp and stamp pad
15 stickers (for each child)
paper numbered 0–5
coloring page
puppets
puzzles
class photos

What to do

1. "Learning Centers to Go" provides parents an extension of the classroom and involvement in the child's work at school. In a large zipper-closure bag, place a children's book that correlates to the classroom theme (for example, a book about doctors for a health theme). Add a stamp and stamp pad related to the theme for the children to use.
2. Include 15 theme-related stickers and a piece of paper numbered 0 to 5. Write directions on the paper for the children to coordinate stickers to the number value. (For older children, use larger number values.)
3. Add puppets, puzzles, and a coloring page. Also include any class photos that would relate to the theme.
4. Use your imagination when adding different items to the bag. Three or four items in the bag is usually sufficient. Include instructions for parents and let them know what needs to be returned the next school day.
5. Rotate the take-home learning centers through the entire class. This provides a great way for children to share their schoolwork with their families and it provides the home-to-school connection quality programs strive for. Children love carrying the bag home!

Diane Shatto, Kansas City, MO

Lucky Ladybugs

Materials

8 ½" x 11" tagboard or medium cardstock
scissors or paper cutter
construction paper
markers
pocket chart
laminator

What to do

1. Cut out ten cards from tagboard or cardstock. Make a set of ladybug cards by cutting out ladybug shapes from construction paper and gluing one to each card. On each ladybug, draw dots from one to ten, one number per ladybug. You will draw one dot on the first, two dots on the second, three dots on the third, and so on to ten.
2. Turn a piece of 8 ½" x 11" tagboard sideways and write "Lucky Ladybugs" at the top. Write the directions: "Place the numerals next to the correct ladybugs."
3. If desired, embellish with a colorful ladybug picture.
4. Print the numerals 1 to 10 on another sheet of tagboard.
5. Use a paper cutter or scissors to cut around the numerals and ladybug cards so that they are all the same size and fit nicely into the rows on the pocket chart.
6. Laminate the directions card, numerals, and ladybug cards for durability and cut out.
7. Hang the pocket chart at child's eye level. Insert the header card in the top pocket of the pocket chart. Place the numerals in the pocket chart, leaving room for the ladybugs cards.
8. Distribute the ladybug cards among the children.
9. Invite each child to count the dots on her ladybug and place her card next to the appropriate numeral on the pocket chart.
10. For added fun, make a file jacket with an answer key on the back. Use this to store the activity and for children to self-check when working individually in the center.

Jackie Wright, Enid, OK

Mail Call

Materials

red and blue construction paper
scissors
glue
markers
paper bags
envelopes with numerals on some and groupings of dots on others

What to do

1. Prepare mailboxes by cutting out and gluing a red rectangle to the top third of each paper bag and a larger blue rectangle to the lower two-thirds of the bag.
2. Write a numeral on each bag, and stapler the bags to a bulletin board or tape them to a shelf.

3. Write a numeral on some envelopes and a number of dots on others.
4. Encourage the children to take turns reading the numbers or counting the dots on the envelopes and placing them in the correct corresponding "mailbox."

More to do

Art: Make mail carrier bags with the children. Fold a 12" x 18" piece of construction paper in half, punch holes in the sides, use string to lace up the sides, and use the extra string to make a handle for the bag.

Sandra Nagel, White Lake, MI

Make a Graph

Materials

poster board
¾"-wide colored tape
airplane cutouts
scissors
laminate
double-sided tape

What to do

1. In advance, prepare a graph by dividing a piece of 14" x 28" white poster board in half to form two columns. Use colored tape to divide the columns.
2. At the top, write the question, "Have you ever flown in an airplane?"
3. Over the left column, write "yes" and over the right column, write "no."
4. Laminate the chart and a supply of die-cut airplanes and cut them out.
5. Print each child's name on an airplane.
6. Attach double-sided tape to the back of each plane.
7. Have each child place her airplane in the column that matches her answer.

Jackie Wright, Enid, OK

Math Boxes

Materials

one empty egg carton for each child
markers
counters (bingo chips, small buttons, colored paper clips, plastic eggs)

What to do

1. Help each child label the inside of the lid, the egg cups, or both by numbering them from 1 to 10.
2. Let the children decorate the outside of their boxes. Help the children write their names on their boxes.
3. Children can use their "counting boxes" to make patterns using plastic eggs, to count how many counters fit in each section, to use for hands-on addition and subtraction, sorting, and so on.
4. This is good for learning one-to-one correspondence, patterning, addition, subtraction, counting, sorting, numeral recognition, and early multiplication (10 cups holding 10 counters each equals 100).

Jeannette Denning, Tinley Park, IL

Pattern Bracelets

Materials

beads
small bowls or cups
pipe cleaners

What to do

1. Place a variety of beads in small bowls or cups so they don't roll around. Provide pipe cleaners.
2. Encourage the children to pick two or three bead colors to string on a pipe cleaner in an AB or ABC pattern. Older children can try more complex patterns.
3. When the bracelet is long enough to go around the child's wrist, the child can stop and twist the ends of the pipe cleaner together. It should be loose enough that children can slide it over their hand to put it on.
4. Make sure the ends of the pipe cleaner are turned under so the children do not get scratched or poked by the wire.

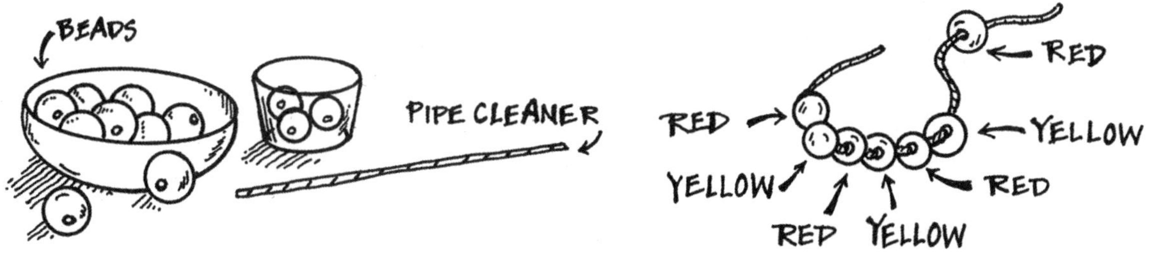

More to do

Holidays: The children can exchange bracelets for Valentine's Day or a Friendship Day activity.

More holidays: Use colors for specific holidays, such as red, white, and blue for July 4th.

Jeanette Denning, Tinley Park, IL

Patterns Everywhere

Materials

photos of patterns in buildings (parking lots, decks)
wrapping paper with patterns
paper strips
scissors
markers
magazines and catalogs

What to do

1. With the children, look for simple AB patterns in the photos and wrapping paper.
2. Look for patterns at school and in the classroom. Patterns can be found everywhere: brick-space-brick-space, glass-trim-glass-trim, coat space-wood divider-coat space-wood divider, and so on.
3. Encourage the children to make patterns using blocks, other children (tall-short, girl-boy), letters, numbers, anything and everything!
4. Expand the pattern to AABAAB and other fun, child-led patterns.
5. Have the children create patterns using pictures from catalogs and magazines or draw a pattern using markers on strips of paper.

Sandra Nagel, White Lake, MI

Polka-Dot Patterns

Materials

sentence strips
sticky colored dots
rubber stamps and stamp pad (optional)

What to do

1. Make several colored dot patterns on sentence strips. Have the pattern cover only half of the strip.
2. When the children go to the center, they pick up a pattern of dots and continue the pattern to the end of the sentence strip.
3. A variation is to use rubber stamps to make the pattern instead of sticky dots.

Barbara Saul, Eureka, CA

We Are Learning to Skip Count by Fives

Materials

8 ½" x 11" tagboard or medium cardstock
scissors
marker
die-cut goldfish
glue stick
pocket chart
laminate

What to do

1. This is a great activity for teaching children how to count by fives.
2. Print an activity title on a piece of 7" x 11" tagboard (turned sideways), such as "We Are Learning to Skip Count!" Draw a picture of a goldfish in a fishbowl, if desired.
3. Print the following rhyme on a piece of 8 ½ " x 11" tagboard turned sideways.

Skip count, skip count, count by fives,
Skip count, skip count, count by fives,
Skip count, skip count, count by fives,
We can count to 50.

4. Label ten die-cut goldfish shapes with a different numeral from 5 to 50 (5, 10, 15, and so on). Mount them on tagboard using a glue stick.
5. Use a paper cutter or scissors to cut the four lines of the rhyme into sentence strips and cut around each goldfish so they are all the same size and fit into the rows of the pocket chart. Laminate and cut out.
6. Insert the title card in the top pocket of the pocket chart. Place the four lines to the song under the title card, each line in a separate pocket in the pocket chart.
7. Hang the pocket chart at children's eye level.
8. Let children work individually or as teams to arrange the numbered goldfish in sequential order in the rows on the pocket chart.
9. Enjoy chanting the rhyme together in this fun center.

Jackie Wright, Enid, OK

Sorting: Stripes or Spots

Materials

pictures of objects with stripes and spots
pictures of wild animals or zoo animals with spots or stripes
felt or magnets
glue
flannel board or magnetic board
nature magazines
scissors

What to do

1. Show the children pictures of objects and discuss the differences in the stripes and spots. Look at the animal pictures and talk about the stripes and spots.
2. Glue felt on the backs of the pictures (for flannel board use) or magnets (for magnetic board use).
3. Divide a flannel board or magnetic board in half—one side for stripes and one for spots.
4. Give each child a picture to place on the correct side of the board.
5. Place the materials in the math center for children to explore and practice with during center time.
6. Do similar activities using other animal characteristics (such as fur or feathers, long or short necks, and so on) to help the children build their vocabulary as well as to focus on the similarities and differences.

Related books

Are You My Mother? by P.D. Eastman
Whose Tail Is It? by Peg Hall

Sandra Nagel, White Lake, MI

Star Walk

Materials

yellow paper
scissors
markers

What to do

1. Cut out ten 6″ stars from yellow paper. Draw a different shape on each one.
2. Review shapes with the children.
3. Tape the cutout stars in a line on the floor, close enough to each other so that the children can walk from one to the next.
4. Have the children line up behind the first star. Encourage them to walk down the line of stars, and name each shape as they step on it.
5. When one child finishes, ask her to sit on the floor while the next child does the "star walk."
6. Label the stars with numbers and do this activity again.

Related books

Draw Me a Star by Eric Carle
Little Star by Sarah Wilson
The Sky Is Full of Stars by Franklyn Branley

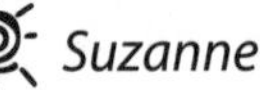 *Suzanne Maxymuk, Cherry Hill, NJ*

Telling Time to the Hour

Materials

pictures of clocks set to different times
oak tag clock with movable hands
scissors
felt
rubber cement

What to do

1. Search old workbooks for pictures of clocks that depict different hours of the day.
2. Use rubber cement to glue felt to the back of the pictures and an oak tag clock to use on a flannel board.
3. Use the clocks on the flannel board to teach telling time to the hour.

4. Invite a child to demonstrate how to set the hands on the clock to the correct hour as shown on the picture.
5. Put the clock and pictures in the math center so children can manipulate them during free choice time.

Related book *The Grouchy Ladybug* by Eric Carle

Jackie Wright, Enid, OK

Thanksgiving Counting

Materials

plastic or paper Thanksgiving dessert plates
clean milk caps
Thanksgiving theme stickers
permanent marker
craft glue

What to do

1. Number each plate 0 to 10, or to whatever number is appropriate for the children in your class.
2. Put one sticker on the inside of each milk cap. Use craft glue to keep them in place, if needed.
3. Ask the children to put the correct amount of milk caps onto each numbered plate.
4. Use these materials for a variety of math activities, depending on the ages and developmental level of the children.

Jeanette Denning, Tinley Park, IL

Tube Seriation

Materials

cardboard paper towel tubes
two colors of contact paper, material, felt, or paint
scissors

What to do

1. Carefully cut the cardboard tubes into various lengths, graduating from smallest largest.
2. Cover them with contact paper, felt, material, or paint. Be sure to alternate the two colors to make an AB pattern.
3. Encourage the children to explore, seriate, pattern, and so on. This activity is good for patterning, sorting, ordering, and sizing.

Jeannette Denning, Tinley Park, IL

What Time Am I?

Materials

clock

What to do

1. Ask two children to stand facing each other. Explain that they will take turns playing clocks.
2. One player holds one hand straight up (12:00). The right hand will be the 9:00 side of the clock; the left hand will be the 3:00 side.
3. The child puts her other hand at 3:00, 6:00 or 9:00.
4. The other child guesses what time it is.
5. Encourage them to take turns being the clock and guessing the time.

Cherra June Wilson, Norman, OK

Our Country's Flag

Materials none

What to do

1. Sing the following songs with the children. You can also sing the original songs to help the children remember facts and trivia about our country.

Related songs

Our Country's Flag by Deborah Stuck-Parker
(tune: "Yankee Doodle")
Our flag is red and white and blue
With stars and stripes real bold.
A star that represents each state
That shines just like true gold.
Fifty stars and thirteen stripes
Fifty stars and thirteen stripes
Fifty stars and thirteen stripes
Make up our country's flag.

I'm Glad I Have an American Flag by Deborah Stuck-Parker
(tune: "I Wish I Were an Oscar Mayer Wiener")
Oh, I'm glad I have an American flag.
One to hold and wave up in the air.
Red and white and blue are its colors,
That show freedom and pride everywhere.

Deborah Stuck-Parker, Eldon, MO

Equipping Your Movement Center

Materials

scarves and streamers
audio cassettes
CDs with varied cultural music
CD and tape player
rhythm instruments
masks
full-length mirror
appropriate costumes
posters of figures in various poses for children to imitate
hula hoops

What to do

1. Put the above materials in the music center. Invite the children to visit the center as part of their daily or weekly exploration activities.
2. Make choices depending on your movement objectives. You may wish to feature creative dramatics one day, and creative movement or rhythm and dance other days.

Margery Kranyik Fermino, Hyde Park, MA

Five Little Butterflies

Materials

felt pieces in pastel colors
scissors
flannel board
blank cassette tape
tape player

What to do

1. Cut out five butterfly shapes from various colors of felt.
2. Teach the children the following song. A wonderful version to help children learn the tune can be found on the record *Mockingbird Flight Songs for Kindergarten Keys* produced by The Economy Company.

Five Little Butterflies

Five little butterflies resting at the door.
One flew away and then there were four.
Butterfly, butterfly, happy and gay,
Butterfly, butterfly, fly away.

Four little butterflies sitting in a tree,
One flew away and then there were three...

Three little butterflies looking at you,
One flew away and then there were two...

Two little butterflies sitting in the sun,
One flew away and then there was one...

One little butterfly left alone,
He flew away and then there were none.

3. Make a recording of the children singing the song.
4. Put the butterflies and flannel board in the listening center along with a recording of the song.
5. Encourage the children to manipulate the desired number of butterflies on the flannel board as the song progresses.

Related book *The Very Hungry Caterpillar* by Eric Carle

Jackie Wright, Enid, OK

Five Little Chickadees

Materials

five pictures of chickadees
scissors
glue
tagboard or poster board
laminate
felt
flannel board
blank cassette tape
tape player

What to do

1. Find a picture of a chickadee and make five copies.
2. Glue the pictures to tagboard or poster board, laminate, and cut each one out.
3. Teach the children the words to the following rhyme.

Five Little Chickadees
Five little chickadees peeping at the door,
One flew away and then there were four.
Chickadee, chickadee, happy and gay,
Chickadee, chickadee, fly away.

Four little chickadees sitting in a tree,...
Three little chickadees looking at you,...
Two little chickadees sitting in the sun,...

One little chickadee left all alone,
It flew away and then there were none.
Chickadee, chickadee, happy and gay,
Chickadee, chickadee, fly away.

4. Make a recording of the children saying the rhyme. Put the chickadees and flannel board in the listening center along with a recording of the rhyme.
5. Invite the children to manipulate the desired number of chickadees on the flannel board as they listen to a recording of the rhyme.

Jackie Wright, Enid, OK

Five Little Pumpkins

Materials

Five Little Pumpkins by Iris Van Rynbach
pumpkin pattern
scissors
laminate
five craft sticks
hot glue gun or contact cement (adult only)
5" x 8" index card

What to do

1. As a follow-up to reading *Five Little Pumpkins*, provide stick puppets and a copy of the verse for the children to act out.
2. To make stick puppets, make a color copy of the pumpkins from the book, cut them out of construction paper, or duplicate a clip-art pumpkin from the Internet five times. You may number them one to five, if desired.

3. Cut them out, laminate them for durability, and cut out.
4. Attach a craft stick to the back of each using a hot glue gun or contact cement.
5. Print the following verse on an index card.
6. Put the book, stick puppets, and verse in the dramatic play center or puppet center. These are great to have available during the Halloween season.

NUMBER EACH

CUT FIVE

ATTACH STICK TO BACK OF PUMPKIN

PUMPKIN PATTERN

Five Little Pumpkins

Five little pumpkins sitting on a gate.
The first one said, "Oh, my, it's getting late!"
The second one said, "There are witches in the air!"
The third one said, "But we don't care."
The fourth one said, "Let's run and run and run."
The fifth one said, "We're ready for some fun!"
Oooo-oooo went the wind, and out went the light,
And the five little pumpkins rolled out of sight.

 *Jackie Wright, Enid, OK*

Five Little Speckled Frogs

Materials

colored picture of a frog and a log
marker
scissors
laminate
felt
rubber cement (adult only)
flannel board
blank cassette tape

What to do

1. Find a colored picture of a frog and another picture of a log. Duplicate the frog picture five times.
2. Number the frogs 1 to 5.
3. Laminate the frogs and the log, and cut them out.
4. Prepare the pictures for flannel board use by gluing felt to the back of each picture using rubber cement. Or, simply cut out five frogs from green felt and number them with a black, permanent marker.
5. Teach the children the words to the song. Record the children singing it.
6. Put the frogs, log, and flannel board, along with the recording of the song "Five Little Speckled Frogs" in the music center for the children to enjoy.

Five Little Speckled Frogs
Five little speckled frogs (hold up five fingers)
Sitting on a speckled log
Eating some most delicious bugs. (pretend to eat bugs)
Yum! Yum!
One jumped into the pool (one child jumps into circle)
Where it was nice and cool. (cross arms over chest and shiver)
Now there are four little speckled frogs.
Burr-ump!

Repeat, counting down until there are no speckled frogs.

Related book *Jump, Frog, Jump!* by Robert Kalan

Jackie Wright, Enid, OK

Homemade Rhythm Band

Materials see activity for ideas

What to do

1. Supply the music area with a variety of household items and challenge the children to create their own instruments. Encourage the children to discover as many ways as they can to create "music" with the items.
2. Items could include boxes, wooden spoons, spoons in various sizes, aluminum pie pans, large wide-tooth combs, plastic cups in various sizes, and so on.
3. Provide empty paper towel tubes. Cover one end with strips of masking tape, let children fill them with various small items, and seal the other end. The sound will change depending on the size and shape of the items. Be sure to seal the ends well.

Anne Slanina, Slippery Rock, PA

I've Got the Music in Me!

Materials

several small table easels
tape recorder and blank tapes
record player and CD player
instruments (cymbals, guitar, maracas, tambourine, xylophone, jingle bells, and rhythm sticks)
hats and headbands
oversize shirts
play microphones
music books

What to do

1. Show the children a variety of instruments and let them experiment with them. Demonstrate how to play each instrument for the children.
2. Place the instruments in an accessible area. Set up the table easels and put the music books or music sheets on them. Put the hats, headbands, and shirts in the dress-up area.
3. Encourage the children to dress up and form small bands. While the clothes don't make the musician, it's more fun to dress up for these special activities.

4. Encourage the children to use the music books and sheet music and pretend to play what is on them.
5. Play records or CDs of different types of music and encourage the children to join in!
6. Let them record themselves playing various instruments. Give each child a blank cassette tape. Make sure the children identify the instrument they are playing before recording the music. For example, "This is Mario and I'm going to play the maracas now."
7. Let the children use the play microphones for impromptu concerts as they sing along with the musicians.
8. Sing songs that everyone knows and encourage the children to play along on the instruments. Record it and play it back for the children. Play, sing, dance, record, listen and have fun!

Related book *Emmet Otter's Jug-Band Christmas* by Russell Hoban

 *Virginia Jean Herrod, Columbia, SC*

Lions and Lambs

Materials

paper plates
markers
scissors
orange yarn
cotton balls
fake fur
glue
masking tape
construction paper

What to do

1. Make lamb and lion paper plate masks as shown in the illustration. Use a marker to draw faces on paper plates. Give one to each child.
2. Encourage the children to color their plates. Help them cut out the eyes. Provide yarn and cotton balls for them to glue to their masks.
3. Teach them the saying, "March comes in like a lion and goes out like a lamb." Explain that this means the month of March starts out very wintry (windy and cold), and ends more spring-like (warmer and calm).
4. Play the game "lambs and lions." Half of the children are lambs and the other half are lions. Place tape on floor to mark the starting point. When you say, "Go," the lambs cross the base (tape) and the lions try to tag them. If a child is tagged, he is out. Play the game as many times as desired.

5. Make a wooly cotton ball lamb and a furry lion by cutting out shapes from construction paper (see illustration). Then let the children glue fake fur and yarn on the lion body and cotton balls on the lamb.

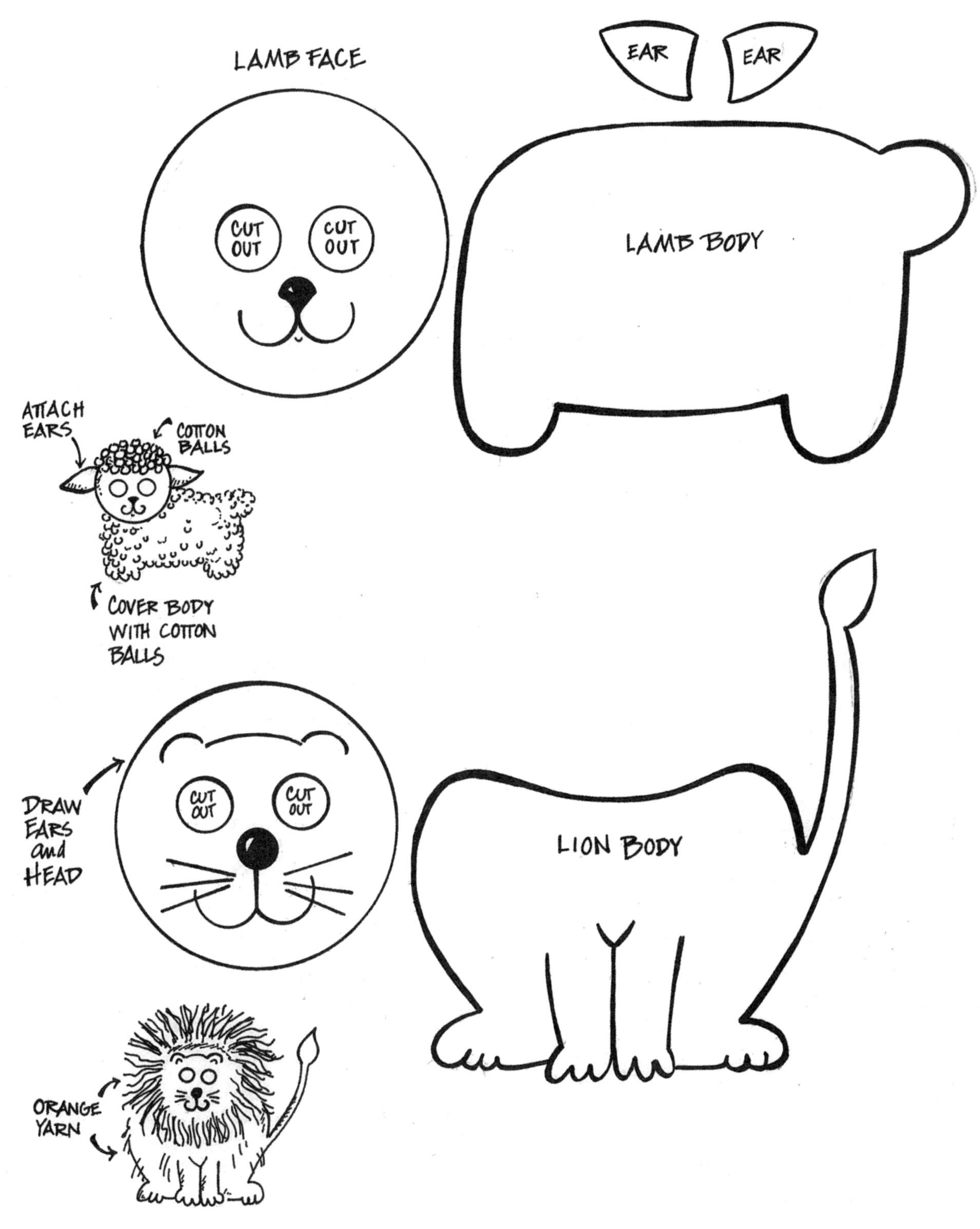

Lisa Chichester, Parkersburg, WV

Jack Jump

Materials

empty toilet paper roll
paint
small paper plate
glue
small piece of tissue paper
paint and brushes

What to do

1. Say the rhyme, "Jack be nimble, Jack be quick, Jack jump over the candlestick" with the children.
2. Have the children take turns jumping over a rope. Substitute the child's name each time (for example, "Mary be quick.").
3. Give each child an empty toilet paper tube. Encourage them to paint the tubes.
4. When the tubes are dry, the children put glue around one end of the tube and glue it in the middle of a small plate. At the opposite end, they glue a piece of tissue paper for the flame.
5. When the "candlesticks" are dry, the children can practice jumping and saying the rhyme.

More to do

At the beginning of the year, this can be a fun way to practice each child's name so everyone can recall their classmates' names.

Gross Motor: Some children may need to work on jumping over small objects at first; fortunately, the paper will not hurt them if it is kicked or jumped on.

Sandra Nagel, White Lake, MI

Making String Instruments

Materials

Styrofoam trays
rubber bands
triangle or xylophone (optional)
string instruments (optional)

What to do

1. Explain to children that not all artists create artwork to look at; some artists are musicians.
2. First, to demonstrate how vibration causes sound, strum strings on any string instrument or a musical triangle, but hold each instrument to prevent it from vibrating. There are many items that demonstrate this, including cymbals, xylophone, a glass, and so on.
3. Now release the strings and/or triangle so the instruments are now able to vibrate and make music and sound appropriately.
4. Show the children how they can make string instruments of their own by wrapping rubber bands around the Styrofoam trays. The rubber bands vibrate to cause sound.
5. Ask the children to predict whether or not the sound will be higher or lower if they make the rubber bands tighter. This is similar to what musicians must do to tune their string instruments. They make them tighter or looser for the exact right sound.
6. Provide children with rubber bands and trays and let them create their own string instruments.

Related books

Berlioz the Bear by Jan Brett
Zin! Zin! Zin! A Violin by Lloyd Moss

Related songs

"Old MacDonald Had a Band," on Singable Songs for the Very Young by Raffi
"The Orchestra" by Mark Rubin, narrated by Peter Ustinov

Shirley Salach, Northwood, NH

Mirror Images

Materials

full-length mirror
hand mirrors
large tagboard cards or poster board
markers
face cards or poster with facial expressions such as happy, sad, angry, frightened, silly

What to do

1. Draw stick figures in various positions on cards or poster board. Examples include standing on one leg, one arm raised, both arms raised, knees bent, arms out to the sides, kneeling, lying down, and so on.
2. Draw facial expressions (such as happy, sad, angry, frightened, and silly) on cards or poster board.

3. Show the full-length mirror to the children. Discuss or review how we show feelings (for example, smile when happy).
4. Invite children to visit the movement center and look in the mirror.
5. Show them the poster or cards of the stick figures and challenge them to look in the mirror and make their bodies look like the figures.
6. Provide hand mirrors. Encourage the children to make the same facial expressions on the poster or cards while looking in their mirrors.
7. Encourage the children to share their positions and expressions with friends at the center.

More to do

Circle Time: In the group setting, give mirrors to the children. Have them look at themselves and tell others the color of their hair, eyes, if they have freckles, and so on.

Related books

Here Are My Hands by Bill Martin Jr.
My Hands by Aliki

Margery Kranyik Fermino, Hyde Park, MA

Moth Greeting

Materials

white tissue paper, white silky scarves, or white crepe paper pieces (two pieces per child)

What to do

1. Explain to the children that moths and other bugs love to be around light at night, and if the light is turned off, the moths fly away and look for food.
2. Give each child two white "wings" (tissue paper, scarves, or crepe paper).
3. Invite the children to hold one piece in each hand as they dance around the circle greeting each friend to some "buggy" music.
4. When the lights go off, direct the children to stop and squat down.
5. Restart the moth movement when the lights are turned on.
6. Continue until everyone has had a chance to greet each classmate.

More to do

Outside: Go on a moth hunt outside.

Related books

Bugs, Bugs, Bugs by Bob Barner
Bugs by Nancy Winslow Parker and Joan Richards Wright
The Very Lonely Firefly by Eric Carle

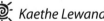

Kaethe Lewandowski, Centreville, VA

Musical Feelings

Materials

tape recorder and headphones
blank tape
assorted recordings of a variety of styles of instrumental music
construction paper
crayons

What to do

1. To prepare, record short passages of instrumental music, contrasting smooth, choppy, fast, slow, mysterious, happy, sad, and so on.
2. Encourage the children to put on headphones and listen to the recordings in the listening center.
3. While listening to the tape, encourage them to select colors of paper that they feel matches the music and move a crayon over the paper as the music dictates (fast, slow, smooth, choppy, bouncy). Remind them not to make a representational drawing, but a picture of mood and feeling.

Related books

The Banza by Diane Wolkstein
The Happy Hedgehog Band by Martin Waddell
Lizard's Song by George Shannon
The Musical Life of Gustav Mole by Kathryn Meyrick

 *Sandra Gratias, Perkasie, PA*

My Aunt Came Back

Materials

illustrations of the items mentioned in the song
tagboard
scissors
glue stick
colored markers
felt
rubber cement (adult only)
laminate
flannel board
tape player
blank cassette tape

What to do

1. Echoes of laughter will fill the room when children repeat not only the words but also the movements to the song. Set up a music center featuring the fun "echo" song, "My Aunt Came Back." This is a "call and response" song; the children repeat each line after the teacher says it. For example, say the first line, "My aunt came back," and the children repeat (like an echo) and say, "My aunt came back," and so on.
2. In advance, locate illustrations of a woman (the aunt) and a picture of each of the items mentioned in the following song.
3. Color the illustrations and mount them on colored tagboard. Laminate them for durability, and cut out. Prepare them for flannel board use by backing them with felt using rubber cement.
4. Teach the children the words, tune, and movements to the song. Record the children singing the song. Put the illustrations, the cassette recording, and flannel board in the music center. You may also want to challenge the children to continue each movement throughout the song, adding a movement after each verse.

My Aunt Came Back

My aunt came back (Children repeat.)
From Istanbul (Repeat.)
And she brought with her (Repeat.)
Some taffy to pull. (Repeat.)
(Pretend to pull taffy.)

My aunt came back (Children repeat.)
From Tokyo (Repeat.)
And she brought with her (Repeat.)
A mosquito. (Repeat.)
(Pretend to swat a mosquito.)

My aunt came back (Children repeat.)
FromTimbuktu (Repeat.)
And she brought with her (Repeat.)
Some gum to chew. (Repeat.)
(Pretend to chew gum.)

My aunt came back (Repeat.)
When she was able (Repeat.)
And she brought for me (Repeat.)
A ping-pong table. (Repeat.)
(Pretend to hit a ping-pong ball.)

My aunt came back (Children repeat.)
From old Algiers (Repeat.)
And she brought with her (Repeat.)
A pair of shears. (Repeat.)
(Pretend to cut something.)

My aunt came back (Children repeat.)
From old Japan (Repeat.)
And she brought with her (Repeat.)
A paper fan. (Repeat.)
(Wave hand in a fanning motion.)

My aunt came back (Children repeat.)
From the county fair (Repeat.)
And she brought with her (Repeat.)
A rocking chair. (Repeat.)
(Pretend to rock back and forth.)

Nursery Rhyme Rap

Materials

cardstock
variety of rhythm instruments
cassette tape
tape recorder

What to do

1. Write some of the children's favorite nursery rhymes on large cardstock cards.
2. Put the nursery rhyme cards, rhythm instruments, and tape recorder in the music center.
3. Encourage the children to select a rhyme and explore instruments for accompanying the rhyme when recited.
4. When children agree on the instruments and where and how they will be played, they may record their own musical nursery rhyme composition.
5. Play this for everyone to hear.

People in Motion

Materials

magazines and periodicals
scissors
glue or paste
8″ x 10″ construction paper

What to do

1. Have a discussion about body parts and movement.
2. Invite the children to cut or tear pictures from periodicals that show people moving in some manner, such as bicycling, running, swimming, walking, playing, and so on.
3. Have them glue their pictures to construction paper to make a collage.
4. Ask the children to choose a favorite picture from the collages and tell others why they like it. Encourage them to talk about the movements they have done.

 *Margery Kranyik Fermino, Hyde Park, MA*

Piano Pizzazz

Materials

piano or child's keyboard
someone who can play piano or a recording of piano music
black and white paper
black marker
white glitter

What to do

1. Use a real piano or a child's keyboard to teach the children about the white and black piano keys and basic notes.
2. Let the children take turns experimenting and trying out different sounds.
3. Play different kinds of music, such as jazz, classical, and pop, on the piano. (If

you are unable to play, play recordings of piano music.) Discuss the different styles. Challenge the children to identify the type of music they hear.

4. Using a piano key pattern, have the children use black and white paper to create their own paper keyboards. Help them name the notes and write them on their keyboard.
   Note: Look on the Internet or in resource books for a piano key pattern and notes.
5. Finally, let the children sprinkle white glitter on the keys for fun! Play a recording of piano music while the children work.

Lisa Chichester, Parkersburg, WV

Red-Eyed Loon

Materials

cardboard or tagboard for patterns
black construction paper 12" x 18"
marker
scissors
white pencil or white crayon
red construction paper
red sequins
white glue
gray tempera paint
white tempera paint
paintbrush
black crayon

What to do

1. Draw the entire loon and the cutaway wing on tagboard to make two patterns (see illustration). Cut out the patterns for children to trace.
2. Fold a piece of 12" x 18" black paper in half. Place the loon pattern at the bottom of the fold. Trace the loon on the doubled paper.
3. Cut out the loon, leaving the bottom fold area intact (this will make two loons that are connected at the bottom).
4. Trace the wing area on both loons using a white pencil or white crayon.
5. Cut out two red circles about ½" in diameter. Glue an eye on each bird.
6. Glue red sequins in the middle of both eyes.
7. Glue the head and beak area on both birds together. Paint the beaks gray on both sides.
8. Paint a white stripe on the neck, and around the wing to the bottom of the loon on both sides. Allow paint to dry.
9. Make wavy black stripes on the neck and near the wing using black crayon. Paint white dots on both wings.

10. Fold at the bottom edge of the bird. Push the fold of the double black paper up and in to make a three-dimensional bird.

Related book *Loon at Northwood Lake* by Elizabeth Ring

Mary Brehm, Aurora, OH

Row, Row, Row Your Boat

Materials pieces of rope, hose, tubing, and exercise bands

What to do

1. Let the children choose a partner and sit cross-legged facing each other. Ask them to hold hands with their partners and "see-saw" back and forth while singing, "Row, Row, Row Your Boat."
2. After repeating the song three times, have one child choose an "extender," such as a piece of rope or tubing.
3. With the pairs of children still sitting cross-legged and holding onto the shared extender, repeat the rocking back and forth movement while again singing, "Row, Row, Row Your Boat."
4. Let the children rotate the extenders they use and their partners. Encourage them to see-saw with a partner from varied positions, such as standing, sitting on chairs, and back to back.

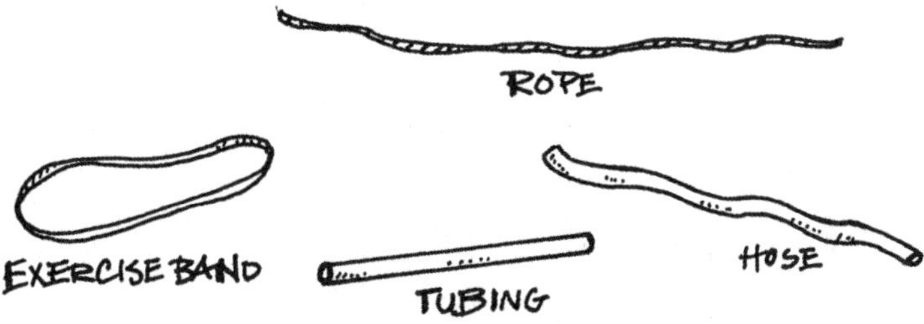

More to do **Transportation:** Use this motor activity with a boat unit or boat story.

 *Sandra Nagel, White Lake, MI*

Sing a Song of Greeting

Materials none

What to do

1. Ask the children to stand in a big circle. Choose one child to stand in the middle of the circle.
2. Sing the following song to the tune of "Frère Jacques." Insert the name of the child in the middle of the circle as indicated by parentheses.

Everyone sings: *Where is (Jennifer)? Where is (Jennifer)?*
Child in center sings: *Here I am, here I am!*
Everyone sings: *How are you today, (Jennifer)?*
Child in center: *Very well, I thank you.*
Everyone: *We're glad you're here, we're glad you're here!*

The Achoo Song

Materials box of tissues (optional)

What to do

1. When the children sneeze, sing the following song to remind them to cover their nose and mouth.

The Achoo Song
(tune: "The Mexican Hat Dance")
Achoo, achoo,
Achoo, achoo, achoo,
Achoo, achoo,
Achoo, achoo, achoo,
When you sneeze
Cover your nose, please.
Achoo, achoo,
Achoo, achoo, achoo.

2. Say the last "achoo" in the song with great drama. Say, "ah," pause, "ah" another pause, and finally a loud explosive "choo!" while you cover your own mouth and nose.
3. If desired, on the last "achoo" reach for a tissue while drawing the sneeze out. When you finally shout the last "choo," cover your nose and mouth with the tissue.

Related book *Stand Back, Said the Elephant, I'm Going to Sneeze* by Patricia Thomas

Virginia Jean Herrod, Columbia, SC

The Body Memory Game

Materials upbeat music

What to do

1. The goal of this activity is for the children to create and recall as many movements and sounds as possible.
2. Clear a space so the children can stand in a circle and have enough room to avoid tripping or bumping into objects.
3. Play upbeat background music that will not compete with the children's vocal level. Music can give the children a feeling of rhythm or encouragement to create more fun and outgoing movements or vocal sounds.
4. As children stand in a circle, the first child does something physical twice (with or without vocals). All movements and vocals should be done twice so that they are clear to all the participants.
5. The second child repeats the first child's movement and adds his own movement. The third child repeats the first child's movement and the second child's movement and then adds his own movement.
6. This continues until someone fails to repeat all the movements in order correctly. Then the game starts over again.
7. This exercise can be enhanced by having a theme for the game. For example, each child must create an animal movement with or without sound. The other children guess what animal the child is imitating. The next child in the circle repeats the previous animal movement and then acts out his own. The game continues until someone forgets the previous animal. Then it starts over again.

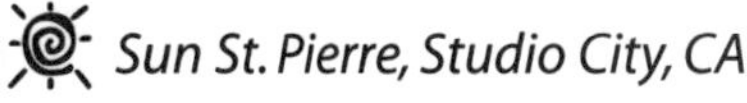
Sun St. Pierre, Studio City, CA

Your Music Center

Materials

rhythm instruments
xylophone or tone bells
keyboard
recorded music (CDs and audio tapes)
headsets for listening to tapes or CDs
prop box (scarves, streamers, pompoms)
puppets
song storybooks
cards with words to nursery songs and class favorites (flip chart)
full-length mirror
pictures of instruments, composers, and people playing instruments
markers
paper

What to do

1. Set up a music center with the materials listed above. Balance the center with materials for both active and quiet activities, but not at the same time.
2. Color code the keys on the keyboard to match word cards with favorite songs or nursery rhymes.
3. Provide opportunities for children to make choices. Change materials when interest wanes and according to your objectives.
4. Remove some of the noisier materials on days when quiet activities are more appropriate.

Margery Kranyik Fermino, Hyde Park, MA

A Bedtime Chart and Graph

Materials two large sheets of paper
markers

What to do

1. During group time, ask the children to talk about some of the things they do before bed each night.
2. List all the activities mentioned on a large sheet of paper. During free choice time, invite the children to illustrate the activities next to each one listed.
3. On a second sheet of paper, make a graph with numbers on the left side and bedtime activities on the bottom.
4. At the next group time, explain how to use a graph and what kind of information can be learned from them. Ask them to predict which bedtime activity will have the highest score (i.e., most of the children do the activity) and the lowest score (less children do the activity). For example, "Do you think more people brush their teeth each night or take medicine each night?"
5. Read each activity and ask the children to raise their hands if they do the activity before bed each night. Color as many squares as appropriate for each activity and compare your predictions.
6. If time allows, focus on the sequence of activities. For example, "Who brushes their teeth first?" "Who puts on their pajamas *before* their bath?"
7. If available, photocopy their illustrations several times and ask the children to cut and paste the sequence of events in whichever order they wish.

Related books *Bedtime for Frances* by Russell Hoban
Good Night Moon by Margaret Wise Brown
Good Night Owl by Pat Hutchins
Sleepy Bear by Lydia Dabcovich
There's a Nightmare in My Closet by Mercer Mayer

Related song "Brush Your Teeth" on Singable Songs for the Very Young by Raffi

 *Shirley Salach, Northwood, NH*

A Bedtime Story

Materials

black paper
chalk
stapler

What to do

1. Explain to the children that they are going to make a group bedtime story book. Let two or three children at a time work on the book during free play.
2. Ask each child to use black paper and chalk to draw a picture of something that makes her sleepy. Let each child describe her picture as you write down what she says.
3. Add a cover and bind the pictures together with staples. Read the book to the class at nap time or circle time.

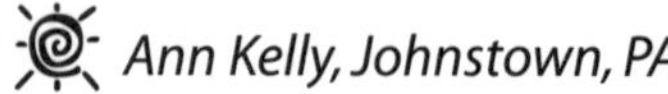
Ann Kelly, Johnstown, PA

It All Happened at Night

Materials

Night Driving by John Coy
tape recorder and audio tape
white construction paper
markers
purple plastic wrap
stapler

What to do

1. Read *Night Driving* by John Coy. Discuss the varying things the two characters in the book do and see as they travel at night.
2. Ask the children if they have ever traveled at night with their parents and encourage them to share their experiences. Use a tape recorder to record their thoughts. Explain that they are going to make a book about the experiences they have had at night.
3. Ask the children to draw a picture of something they saw while out at night.
4. Cover each child's picture with purple plastic wrap and staple in place. This will simulate a nighttime look.
5. Create a cover titled "It All Happened at Night." Bind the pages together into a book.
6. Let the children take turns taking the book home to share with their families.

More to do

Art: Have the children create large paintings of something they have done at night. After drying, cover them with purple plastic wrap and display them around the room.

Circle Time: If possible, darken the classroom so you can experience darkness together. Sit together and talk about the things they can still see and how different they look in the dark. Talk about things they can hear too.

Related books

And If the Moon Could Talk by Kate Banks
A Child's Good Night Book by Margaret Wise Brown
Goodnight Moon by Margaret Wise Brown
Night Driving by John Coy
Poinsettia and the Firefighters by Felicia Bond
Sleepy ABC by Margaret Wise Brown

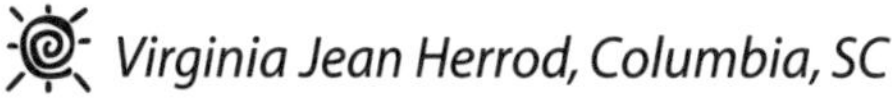

Nighttime

Materials

string of small blue holiday lights
soft, sheer material for decorating the ceiling
toddler nap pad or mattress
blankets and pillows
stuffed animals
lullaby tapes and CDs
tape player or CD player
basket of books about bedtime
night light
slippers, nightgowns, and robes

What to do

1. Set up a nap "nighttime" area by hanging small holiday lights and soft fabric on the ceiling. Put a toddler bed, blankets, and pillows in the area. Put a variety of bedtime books and lullaby tapes in the area.
2. This is a gentle way to help children feel comfortable and secure about nighttime. They can play and pretend, tuck each other into bed, read stories to each other, and listen to soothing music.

Night Sky

Materials

large black construction paper
yellow or gold paint or construction paper
scissors
glue
empty paper towel tubes
construction paper or wrapping paper
small sheets of black construction paper
sheets of gold and silver star stickers

What to do

1. Create a night sky by cutting out constellations, stars, and moon phases from yellow or gold paper and gluing them to large sheets of black construction paper, or painting stars and moon phases on the paper. Attach the pages to an easel or the back of a bookcase.

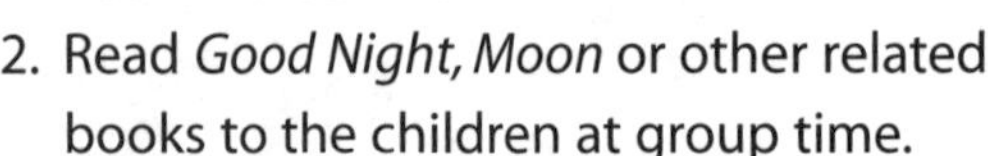

2. Read *Good Night, Moon* or other related books to the children at group time.
3. Encourage the children to make "telescopes" by gluing construction or wrapping paper on empty paper towel tubes.

4. Invite the children to look through their telescopes at the "night sky" pictures, identifying constellations, shapes, or moon phases.
5. Let the children create their own night sky with star stickers and small black construction paper.
6. Follow up by teaching the children "Star Light, Star Bright." Ask questions such as, "What would you wish for if you wished on a star?"

Star light, star bright
First star I see tonight.
I wish I may, I wish I might
Have this wish I wish tonight.

 *Margery Kranyik Fermino, Hyde Park, MA*

No Sun Equals More Fun!

Materials

photos of different nocturnal environments
glue
oak tag
6" x 18" and 12" x 18" white drawing paper
black permanent marker
regular and neon-colored crayons
diluted black tempera paint
½" flat paintbrushes

What to do

1. Collect photos from newspapers and magazines involving nighttime activities and nocturnal environments. Be sure to have a variety of photos, including city and country environments, animals, homes, people, and so on. Glue each photo to a piece of oak tag.
2. Introduce and display the cards. Ask the children to categorize the photos as desired and share with a friend or another adult.
3. Make a nighttime word list with the children. Ask each child to dictate nighttime words as you write the words on 6" x 18" drawing paper with a black marker. Have the children trace the words and decorate them with neon or light crayons, covering the marker lines. Encourage them to decorate the paper, too.
4. Let the children use diluted black tempera paint to paint over their paper, left to right. The crayon will resist the paint. Hang the papers to dry.
5. If desired, children can make their own nighttime book using their dictated words. Help them print their words on 4 ½" x 5 ½" sheets of paper using a bright-colored crayon. The children paint over the words as before. Let the paint dry and then staple the pages together to make a book.

Pajama Time

Materials

old slippers (one pair per child)
material scraps, pompoms, and ribbon
glue
fabric or felt
scissors
large beads
yarn
wiggle eyes
permanent markers
two baskets of night clothes (pajamas, slippers, and so on)

What to do

1. Give each child a pair of old slippers. Encourage them to decorate the slippers as desired using pompoms, old material, ribbon, and so on.
2. Make tiny "sleeping bags" by folding a 3" square of felt or fabric in half. Cut off the ½" of felt at the top of one of the folded sides. Glue the bottom and side together, leaving the top part open (like a sleeping bag).
3. Make "pajama kids" with the children. Give each child a tiny sleeping bag and a large bead. Demonstrate how to glue the bead at the top of the felt sleeping bag (at the opening). Encourage them to glue yarn "hair" and wiggle eyes to the bead and add facial features using a permanent marker.
4. Have a pajama relay. Gather in a large, open area and divide the children into two groups. Put two baskets of pajamas, slippers, nightcaps, and so on at the end of the relay area. When you signal them to start, one person from each team runs down to the basket, dresses for bed, and runs back. The child tags the next person in line. The tagged child helps the first take off the pajama items, and puts them on herself. This continues until all the children have run the race.
5. Have a pajama party day! The children wear their favorite pajamas and they bring a favorite sleep toy and sleeping bag to school. Pop popcorn and have an old-fashioned slumber party during the day or at naptime.

Playing in the Dark

Materials

blindfolds or masks with eye holes covered
simple four-piece puzzles
large beads and string
paper and pencils
old car license plates
instruments
4″ x 12″ rectangular frames with 2″ x 10″ center cut out

What to do

1. Talk about the dark with the children. "What kinds of things can you do in the dark?" Ask if they are ever afraid of the dark. Reassure children and try to help them overcome any fears.
2. Blindfold the children and encourage them to try the following activities:
   - Assemble a puzzle.
   - String beads.
   - Draw a smiling face.
   - Feel the raised letters and numbers on license plates and name them.
   - Listen to instruments and name sounds. Point to where they are.
   - Use the rectangular frame on top of a piece of paper as a guide to print their name.

Related books

The Goodnight Circle by Caroline Lesser
Grandfather Twilight by Barbara Berger
Night and Day by Catherine Ripley
The Sun's Asleep Behind the Hill by Paul O. Zelinsky
Teddy Bear Tears by Jim Aylesworth

What's in Your Night Sky?

Materials

one shoeboxes for each child (no lids)
scissors
aluminum foil
masking or duct tape
photos of starry nights
toothpicks
small flashlights
dark location

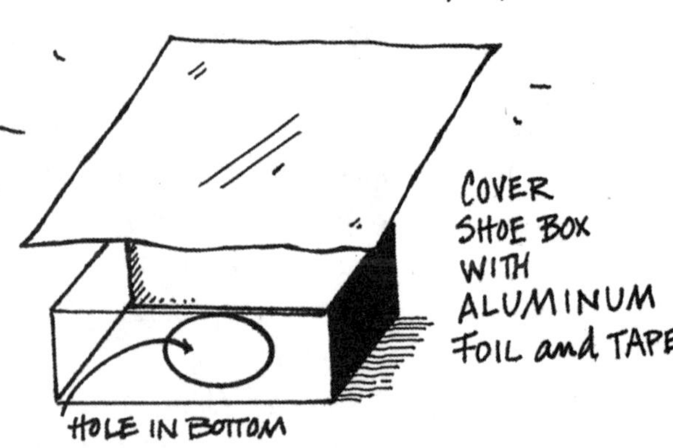

What to do

1. Prepare shoeboxes by cutting a hole in the bottom of each one large enough for a hand to fit through. Cover each child's box tightly with a piece of foil and secure it on all four sides with tape. Mark the boxes with the children's names.
2. Show the children a variety of night sky photos and pictures. Ask the children to talk about the night sky.
3. Let the children make their own "night sky" using the foil-covered boxes.
4. Demonstrate how to poke holes in the foil over the opening in the box with a toothpick. Each poke represents a star. Then show them how to put a flashlight inside the box and project their stars in a dark spot.
5. Encourage the children to talk about patterns or shapes that they see in their skies, and what they see in the skies that their friends made.

Related books

Night in the Country by Cynthia Rylant
Night Watch: A Practical Guide to Viewing the Universe by Terence Dickinson
Out and About at the Planetarium by Theresa Alberti

Ann Kelly, Johnstown, PA

Where Did the Moon Go?

Materials

black construction paper
scissors
white pencil or crayon
ruler
five index cards
broad black marker
3″ diameter white paper circles
glue sticks

What to do

1. Cut black construction paper into 6″ x 24″ strips. Divide each paper strip into five sections using a ruler and white pencil. Give one to each child.
2. Write the days of the week (Monday through Friday) on index cards. Encourage the children to copy each day of the week at the bottom of each section on their strip using a white pencil.
3. Ask the children to observe the moon every night for five nights. The following day, the children can cut out the shape of the moon from a white paper circle and glue it the appropriate section of the paper strip (Monday's moon in the Monday section, and so on).
4. On the nights when the moon is covered with clouds, children may color clouds or glue cotton balls in the designated space. If it rains or snows, children may use a white or light-colored crayon to record this.
5. Encourage the children to make a prediction on the back of the construction paper strip and draw a special nocturnal scene using crayons. "Which colors work better on the black paper?"

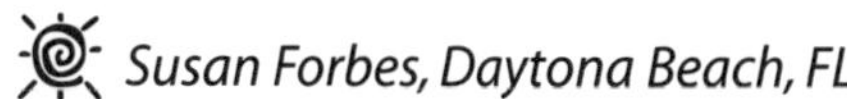

Susan Forbes, Daytona Beach, FL

"Whoo" Is Out at Night?

Materials stuffed toys or plastic toy representations of animals that stay awake at night (such as skunks, cats, owls, hamsters, bats, crickets, foxes, fireflies, and bobcats)

What to do

1. Place stuffed or plastic animals on a table in the designated learning center.
2. Talk about animals that stay awake at nighttime. Ask the children what the animals do at night. Encourage the children to engage in free play with the animals, exploring and creating scenarios.
3. Facilitate the play by asking questions such as, "What do bats do at nighttime?" "What kinds of things do crickets do at nighttime?"
4. If desired, write down or record the play scenarios created by the children and later share them during circle time.

Related books

Grandfather Twilight by Barbara Berger
Hedgie's Surprise by Jan Brett
Owl Moon by Jane Yolen

Kate Ross, Middlesex, VT

American Parade

Materials

flag stickers
small American flags
red, white, and blue streamers
tape or CD player
patriotic and marching music

What to do

1. Assemble the children in a few straight lines or some kind of parade formation outside.
2. Let the children stick flag stickers on their shirts or other clothing. Pass out streamers and flags to each child.
3. Explain to the children that they will be having a parade and that they should wave their flags and streamers as they march.
4. Play patriotic or marching music. Be sure to vary your marching pattern slightly from song to song so that the children may use a variety of muscles and skills. The parade is fun and the children really enjoy it!

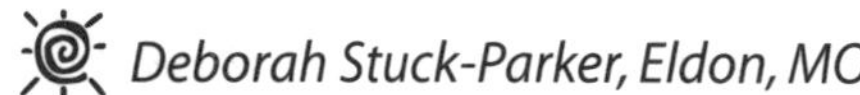
Deborah Stuck-Parker, Eldon, MO

Animals Hiding Everywhere

Materials

empty toilet paper tubes (two per child)
scissors
cardboard
animal skin print paper or assorted prints and colors of wrapping paper
glue

What to do

1. Prepare toilet paper tubes for each child as follows. Cut a slit down the length of one of the toilet paper tubes to open it. Cut a rectangle 2 ½″ x 1 ¼″ from each side of the tube as shown in the illustration. This creates a tube with four "legs." Cut a 1″-wide ring from the second tube (this will be the head).
2. Trace the open toilet paper tube (body) on cardboard to make a pattern. Also make a rectangle pattern 1″ x 4 ½″ to cover the ring.

3. Give the children their prepared toilet paper tubes. Let each child select a paper to use for the "skin" of his "animal." The children trace the cardboard patterns on the paper and cut out to cover the tubes.
4. Ask the children to glue the paper skin on the tubes. Demonstrate how to glue the ring onto the front edge of the body to create a head.
5. Encourage the children to add facial features to the head.
6. When all the animals are dry, divide the class in half. While one half waits (and doesn't look), the other half hides their animals where they will be "camouflaged." The waiting children search for the animals, and then the two groups switch roles.

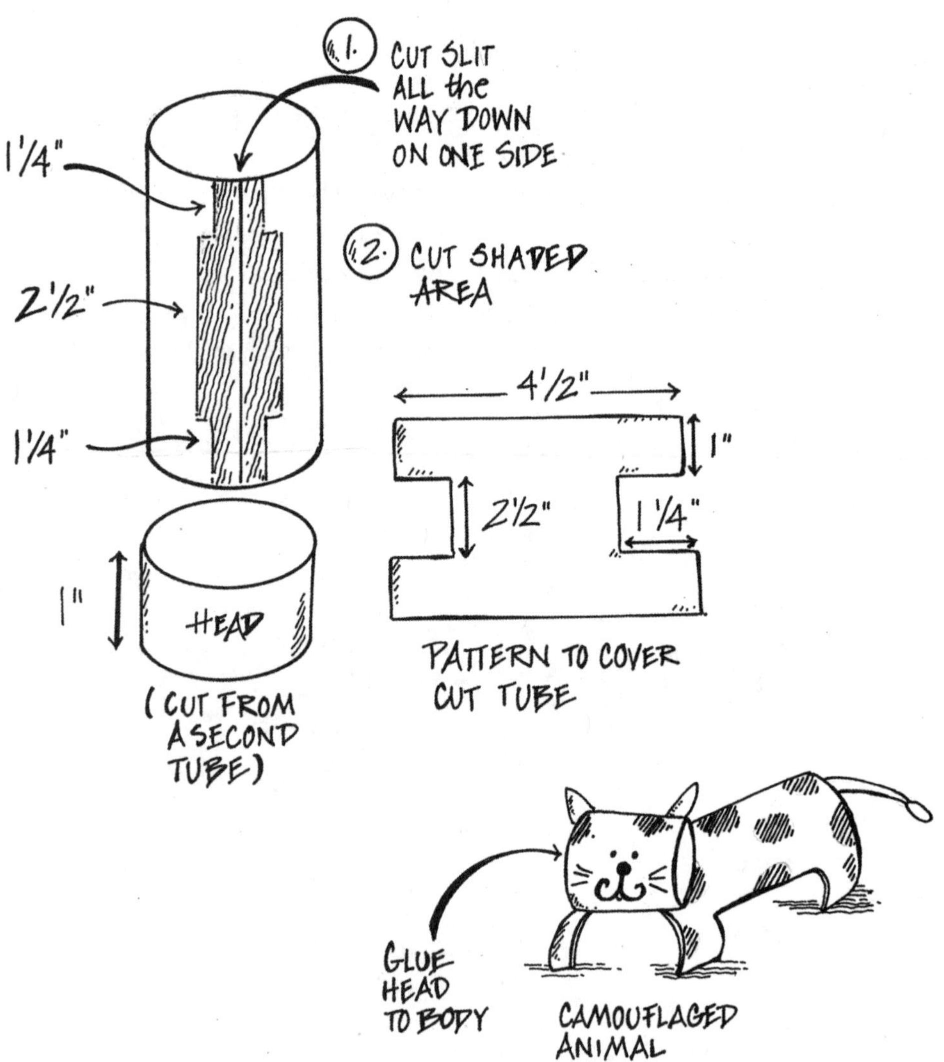

Related books *How to Hide a Butterfly* by Ruth Heller
Where's That Insect? by Barbara Brenner and Bernice Chardiet
Where's That Reptile? by Barbara Brenner and Bernice Chardiet
Where's That Spider? by Barbara Brenner and Bernice Chardiet

Sandra Gratias, Perkasie, PA

Autumn Leaves Collage

Materials

several bags of colored leaves
short-handled rakes
plastic storage bags
permanent marker

What to do

1. Collect a few bags of autumn leaves. Spread the leaves around an outdoor area.
2. Ask children to rake the leaves into a pile. Let the children jump into the pile and toss the leaves in the air, exploring how the leaves feel and sound.
3. Give each child a plastic storage bag with his name written on it. Invite the children to collect leaves of different shapes and colors and put them in the bags.
4. Discuss the different leaves and encourage the children to sort them according to size, shape, and color.
5. If desired, let children glue their leaves to construction paper to create a collage or attach the leaves to a "tree" bulletin board.

Margery Kranyik Fermino, Hyde Park, MA

Bug Discovery

Materials

digital camera or 35-mm camera
clipboards and paper (optional)
outside area with bugs
cardstock paper
scissors
glue

What to do

1. Lead the children in a bug hunt! Tell them they are not going to collect the bugs; instead they will photograph the bugs in their natural environment.
2. If desired, provide the children with clipboards and pencils so they can draw pictures of the bug in its natural environment. Include these drawings when you put the book together.

3. When they find a bug, assign a child to take its photo. Make sure to instruct the children on how to properly aim the camera or there will be many missed shots. With a digital camera, this is not much of a problem, but with a 35-mm camera, missed shots can be quite expensive.
4. As the child photographs the bug, talk about it. Ask what environment it is in. (Water? Sand? Dirt? Grass?) "What type of bug is it?" "What does the bug appear to be doing?" Give the children time to have a good conversation about each bug.
5. Try to find and photograph several different types of bugs.
6. If you used a digital camera, download and print the pictures on the classroom computer. Involve the children as much as possible in this step. If you used a 35-mm camera, let the children help you prepare them to be sent to the developer.
7. When you print out or get back the pictures, have the children glue each photo to a piece of cardstock paper.
8. Under each photo, write a brief description about the bug in the photo. Include the information that the children discussed when photographing the bug. Also mention which child took the photograph. For example, you might write, "This is the spider that Tommy photographed. It was spinning a web on the fence. You can tell it's a spider because it has eight legs." If desired, help the children use the computer or insect books to look up fun facts about each bug they found.
9. Repeat for each photo.
10. Create a front and back cover using more cardstock.
11. Bind the pages together in any manner you prefer. Put the book in your science area for all to enjoy.

Related books *A Firefly Named Torchy* by Bernard Waber
Grasshopper on the Road by Arnold Lobel
Hey, Little Ant by Phillip Hoose
In the Tall, Tall Grass by Denise Fleming
An Invitation to the Butterfly Ball by Jane Yolen
Miss Spider's Tea Party by David Callaway Kirk
One Hundred Hungry Ants by Elinor Pinczes
Some Smug Slug by Pamela Duncan Edwards
The Very Busy Spider by Eric Carle
Truman's Aunt Farm by Jama Kim Rattigan
Two Bad Ants by Chris Van Allsburg
Why Mosquitoes Buzz in People's Ears by Verna Aardema

Autumn Leaves

Materials colored construction paper or other colorful objects

What to do

1. Let the children choose a few pieces of colored construction paper or other colorful objects.
2. Bring the children outside to find objects in nature that match the paper or object.
3. This is a great activity to do in the spring. The children have fun matching the colors (it is surprising how closely colors can be matched). This activity helps with visual discrimination.

Related books *Color Dance* by Ann Jonas
Mouse Paint by Ellen Stoll Walsh
Red Leaf, Yellow Leaf by Lois Ehlert

Phyllis Esch, Export, PA

I'm Forever Blowing Bubbles

Materials

objects that are open and hollow or have open holes (sieve, colander, drinking straw, saltshaker top, toy car tires, hollow pipes and pipe fittings, large metal nuts and washers, screens, and funnels)
bubble solution

What to do

1. Bring in or ask the children to bring in a few objects that are open and hollow or have open holes.
2. Let the children bring the objects outside and dip them into bubble solution. Encourage them to blow through the holes in the objects, wave them around, or hold them up to the wind to make bubbles. Ask questions such as, "Do some objects work better than others?" "Do square holes make square bubbles?"
3. Make your own bubble blowers. Use a hole punch to punch holes on a plastic lid, make rings out of wire or pipe cleaners, cut off the bottom of a paper cup, and so on.

More to do

Art: Mix water, dish soap, and liquid tempera paint in bowls. Demonstrate how to lean over a bowl, insert a drinking straw, and blow gently to overflow the bowl with bubbles. Press a blank sheet of paper over the bubbles to create a bubble print. Add more colors.

More Art: Use the above mixture or commercial bubble solution mixed with food coloring to blow bubbles at paper hung on an easel or on a table to make bubble pictures. This makes pretty wrapping paper.

Related book *Bubbles* by Mercer Mayer

Sandra Gratias, Perkasie, PA

Let's Go Fly a Kite

Materials

lightweight paper
scissors
stickers, markers, and paint
glue
two dowel rods for each child
crepe paper streamers
yarn
twigs

What to do

1. Make a kite for each child by cutting lightweight paper into the shape as shown.
2. Let the children decorate their kites with paint, markers, and stickers. Help them write their names on their kites.
3. Help the children glue on dowel rods crisscrossed as in picture. Add crepe paper tails to the kites.

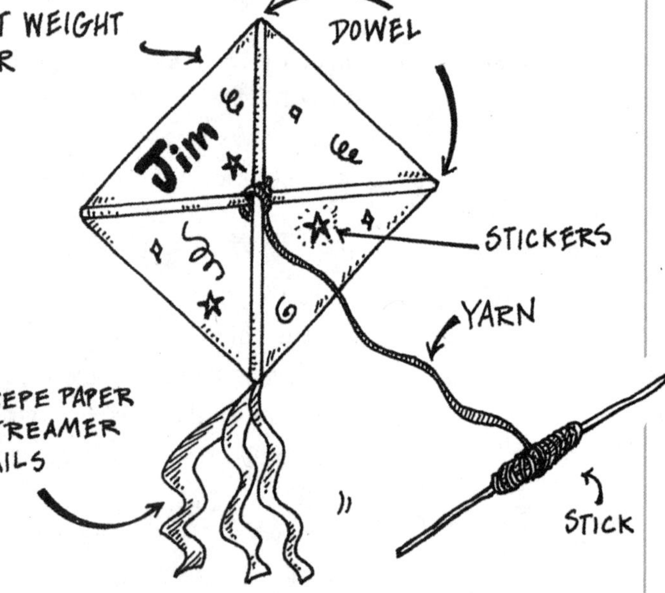

4. Attach yarn as shown and then help the children wrap the extra yarn around a twig. Go outside and try out the kites!

More to do

Music and Movement: Provide scarves. Play music and encourage the children to dance and pretend to fly kites using the scarves as kites.

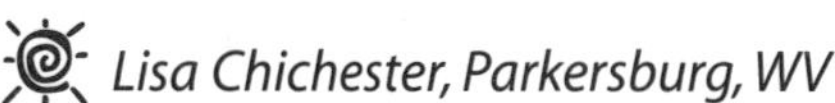
Lisa Chichester, Parkersburg, WV

Outdoor Art Fun

Materials

large sheets of paper
thumbtacks
paintbrushes
tempera paint in various colors
sidewalk chalk in various colors
spray bottles filled with water
glue
nature items
construction paper
pompoms, rickrack, and other scrap materials
old toothbrushes

What to do

1. On a nice day, go outside and hang painting paper on trees using thumbtacks. Provide paintbrushes and different colors of paint and encourage the children to look around and paint what they see in nature. Encourage them to talk about their paintings.
2. Have a sidewalk chalk party! Talk about how the chalk colors are "pastel." Encourage the children to draw chalk pictures on the concrete. Give them spray bottles full of water and let them "erase" their pictures and start again.
3. Take a nature walk and ask the children to collect leaves, nuts, twigs, and so on. Encourage the children to make nature pictures by gluing their finds to construction paper. Let them decorate the pictures by gluing rickrack and pompoms to the paper and splattering paint on with an old toothbrush.

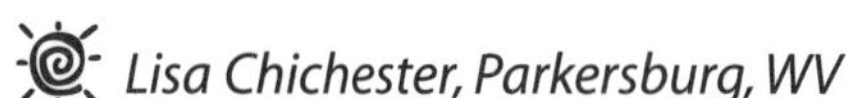
Lisa Chichester, Parkersburg, WV

Pool Party

Materials

three small plastic wading pools: small, medium, and large
hose
stopwatch
sprinkler
variety of water toys and containers for transferring water

What to do

1. In warm weather, have a Sprinkler Day!
2. Ask the children to help arrange the three empty pools in a line by size. Let them fill each pool using a hose. Predict how long it will take for each pool to fill. Use a stopwatch to keep track of the time.
3. After filling all three pools, compare how long it took to fill each one.
4. Ask the children to predict how many of them will fit in each pool. Let them sit in each pool, one at a time, until the pool is full of children. Count how many children are in the pools when full. Again, make a few comments that will lead to the children brainstorming about why each pool held different numbers of children.
5. Provide water toys and containers for transferring water. If the children show interest in transferring water, ask them to predict how many times they will have to travel back and forth in order to move all the water in the small pool to the other two pools. You will need LOTS of time for this!
6. Turn on the sprinkler and have fun!

More to do

Make some mini-pools for tabletop play when the weather is cold. Purchase three pie tins in three different sizes. Add small plastic dolls, some finely cut blue tissue paper, and some small rubber balls and have a pretend pool party!

Related books

All About You by Catherine Anholt
Better Not Get Wet, Jesse Bear by Nancy White Carlstrom
Dear Mr. Blueberry by Simon James
How I Captured a Dinosaur by Henry Schwartz

Virginia Jean Herrod, Columbia, SC

Springtime Kite

Materials

tempera paint in four or more colors
shallow bowl for each color of paint
thick string
scissors
9″ x 12″ white or pastel-colored construction paper
brown wood-grain craft foam or brown construction paper
yarn in pastel colors
white glue
scraps of craft foam sheets of various colors

What to do

1. Mix paint to a thin consistency and pour into separate bowls or flat cup containers.
2. Cut string into 16″ lengths. Put one string into each color of paint. Allow about 3″ of string to extend beyond the bowl to hold onto.
3. Choose one color of string and place it on a sheet of paper in a wiggly fashion. Fold the paper in half over the string.
4. Press down lightly on the paper as a child pulls the string out, wiggling it side to side as he pulls. Press the paper together firmly.
5. Open the paper and repeat the process with another color of wet string. This will form an interesting duplicate design.
6. Cut narrow strips of wood-design craft foam or brown construction paper. (This step can be done ahead of time.)
7. Let the painted paper dry. Trace the kite shape (see illustration) on the painted paper and cut out.
8. Glue the brown strips on the kite. Cut a strip of yarn and glue it to the back of the kite.
9. Cut bow shapes out of craft foam scraps. Cut at least three bows per kite. Glue the bows to the yarn on the back of the kite.

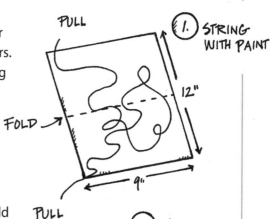

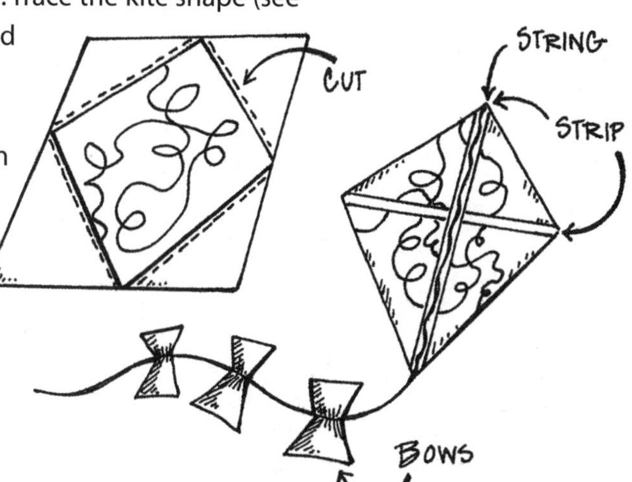

10. If desired, glue a loop of yarn for hanging the kite on a hook or door handle.
11. This makes a colorful spring bulletin board.

Related book *Curious George Flies a Kite* by H. A. Rey

Mary Brehm, Aurora, OH

What's Outside Our Classroom?

Materials

large sheet of paper
marker

What to do

1. At group time, ask the children what they might see if they took a walk outside the classroom.
2. Write all of their comments and guesses on a sheet of paper.
3. Take a walk outside.
4. Return to the circle and review the list. What did they see that was on the list and what did they forget or miss?

Ann Kelly, Johnstown, PA

Birthday Center

Materials

dinner plate
cardstock paper
colored pens or crayons
scissors
plain paper cups
laminate or clear adhesive paper

What to do

1. Trace a dinner plate on cardstock and cut one out for each child.
2. Encourage the children to decorate their circles for their own special birthday plates. Laminate the plates and save them.
3. Provide paper cups for them to decorate. Remind them to decorate the cups on the outside only.
4. Give each child a piece of 11" x 17" cardstock to decorate for a special place mat. Laminate or cover with clear contact paper.
5. On each child's birthday, she can use her special plate, place mat, and cup for snacks.

Related book *Happy Birthday, Moon* by Frank Asch

Barbara Saul, Eureka, CA

Angel Thoughts

Materials

white construction paper
scissors
white feathers
white and gold glitter
glue
hole punch
string
gold tinsel
empty toilet paper tubes (one for each child)
white paint
small construction paper wings
photo of each child's face

What to do

1. Cut out "angel wings" from white construction paper (see illustration). Let the children decorate their wings with white feathers and glitter.
2. Punch two holes in each side of the wings (as shown) and knot string through the holes so children can put them over the backs of their arms.
3. Make "halos" by tying the ends of gold tinsel together.
4. Make toilet paper tube angels with the children. Give each child a toilet paper tube. The children paint them white and glue construction paper wings to the back. Help the children cut out their faces from photos and glue to the front of the toilet paper tube.
5. Have an angel party. Cover the tables with white tablecloths, serve white angel food cake, and have them wear their angel wings and halos.

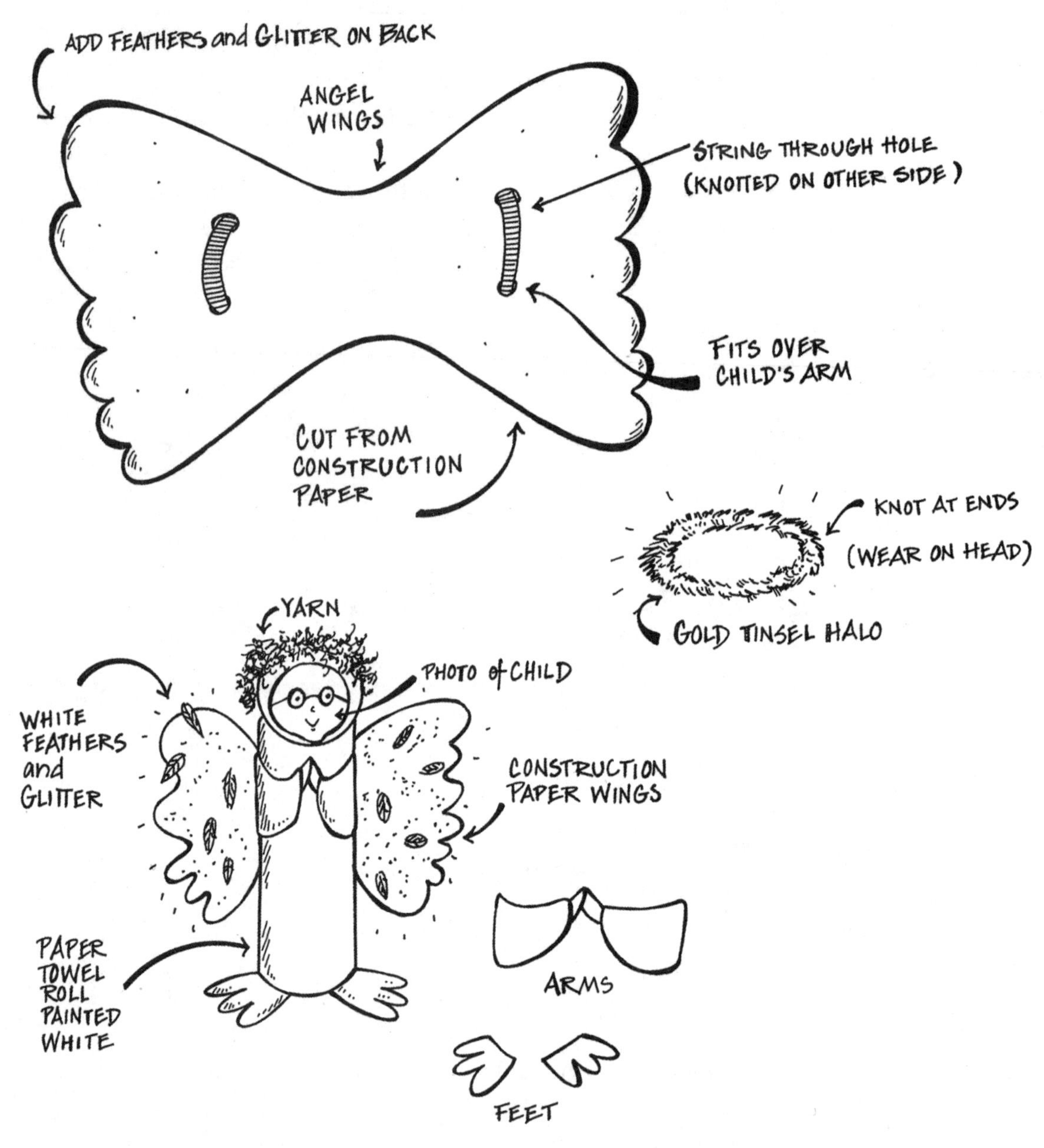

Lisa Chichester, Parkersburg, WV

At the Hop!

Materials

black poster board
scissors
music from the 1950's
pink, black, and white felt
glue
craft cord
T-shirts (one for each child)
scarves
vanilla ice cream, red soda, cherries, and whipped topping

What to do

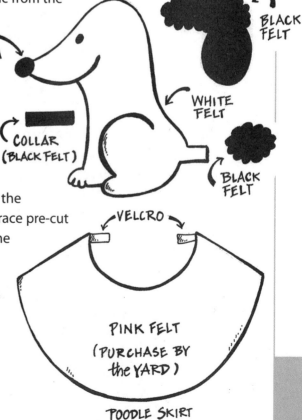

1. Talk about the 1950's with the children. Talk about the music, dances, fashion, and so on. Tell them they will be having a 1950's style hop!
2. Make "45s" (records) with the children. Cut out 5" diameter circles from black construction paper and cut out the middle (about 1" diameter) of each circle.
3. Teach the children the "twist" and other '50's dances (there are videos that you can watch ahead of time so you can teach these dances). Play music from the 1950's songs for the children to dance to.
4. Help the children make poodle skirts and initial shirts. To make a poodle skirt, cut a large circle from pink felt (as shown in the illustration), cut out the middle (big enough for a child's waist), and cut it apart. Sew Velcro where the closure will be. Help the children trace pre-cut poodles on black and white felt. The children cut out the poodles and glue them to their skirts. To finish, glue craft cord to make a leash for their poodle.

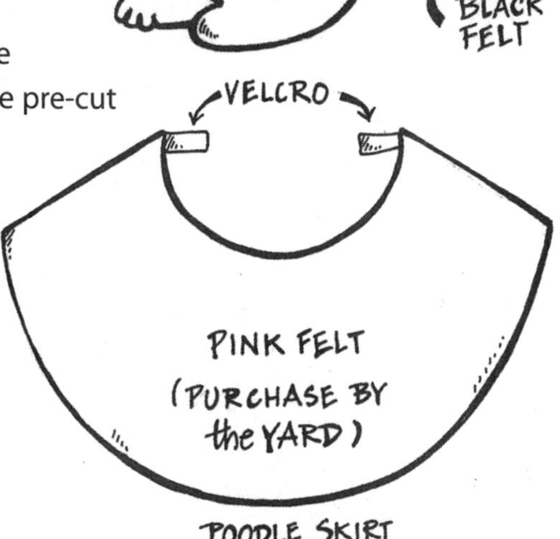

5. Make initial shirts with the children Give each child a pre-cut felt initial (the first letter of the child's name) to glue onto the front of a T-shirt as shown.
6. Provide scarves for the girls to tie around their necks.
7. Serve "cherry smashes," a popular drink from the '50's. Let each put two scoops of vanilla ice cream in a cup, fill the cup with red soda, and top with whipped topping and a cherry.

Lisa Chichester, Parkersburg, WV

Celebrating America

Materials

star-shaped rubber stamp
red and blue stamp pads
books about America
flag stickers
plastic drinking straws
red, white, and blue construction paper
glue
scissors
red and blue Jell-O

What to do

1. Prior to this activity, send home a note asking the children to wear red, white, and blue clothing on "Celebrate America Day."
2. On the day of the activity, stamp each child's hand with a red or blue star. Read books and sing songs about America. Some ideas for songs include "Twinkle, Twinkle, *Capitol* Star," "Yankee Doodle," "America the Beautiful," and "This Land Is Your Land."
3. Make small American flags with the children by taping straws to flag stickers. Help the children create "patriotic" headbands using red, white, and blue construction paper strips. Encourage them to decorate the headbands with red, white, and blue star cutouts.
4. When the headbands and flags are completed, have a classroom parade. Play patriotic music and let the children march around the room wearing the headbands and waving their American flags.
5. End the day with a snack of red and blue Jell-O jigglers.

Related books *Froggy Plays in the Band* by Jonathan London
God Bless America by Irving Berlin
McDuff Saves the Day by Rosemary Wells
Miss Mary Mack by Mary Ann Hoberman
Star Light, Star Bright by Susan Hood
Ten Wishing Stars: A Countdown to Bedtime Book illustrated by Sarah Dillard

Joan Bowman, Langhorne, PA

Frog Fair

Materials

tagboard or cardboard
sturdy paper
tempera paint
scissors
yarn
hole punch
green paper
frog stickers
paper towel tubes

What to do

1. Make "frog" necklaces. Use the illustration below (frog face pattern) to make a pattern on cardboard. Help the children trace around the pattern on sturdy paper and cut out. Encourage the children to paint their frog faces. Punch two holes in each face as shown and string yarn through to make a necklace.
2. Cut out a large letter "F" from green paper, one for each child. Encourage the children to decorate their letters with frog stickers.
3. Help the children make frog crowns and scepters. Cut out a headband from sturdy green paper for each child. Then cut out a frog from green paper (see illustration) for each child. Encourage the children to decorate their frog and glue to the top of the headband ("crown"). Fit the child's crown to her head and tape in place. Next, give each child an empty paper towel tube to paint green. Provide more green paper frogs for children to tape at the top of the tubes (as shown). Encourage them to decorate their "scepters" with green crepe paper strips.
4. Have a class frog festival party! Have the children wear their frog necklaces and crowns. Serve green drinks and "froggy" snacks.

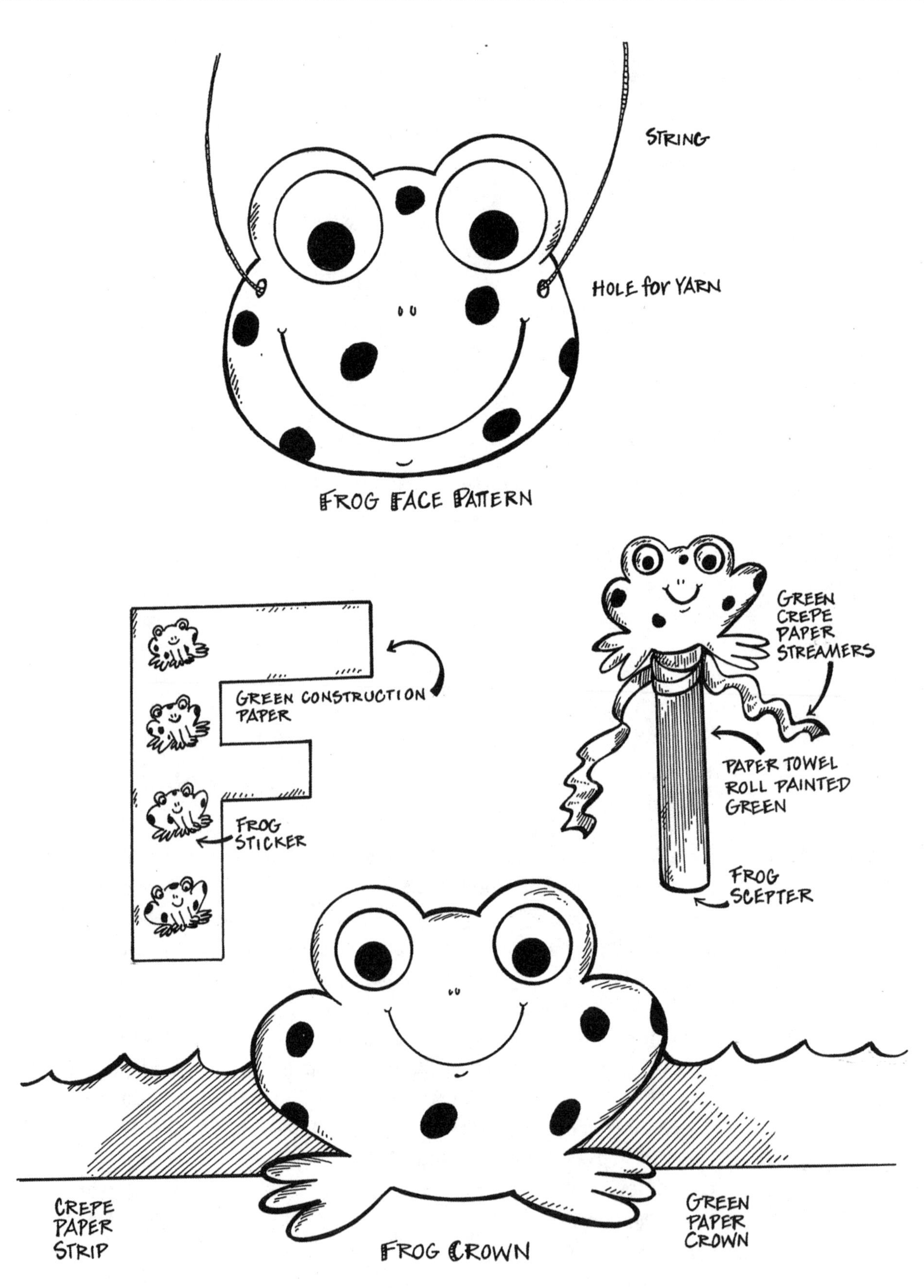

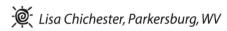

Lisa Chichester, Parkersburg, WV

It's a Surprise!

Materials

wrapping paper
scissors
tape
items to wrap

What to do

1. Put out wrapping paper, scissors, and tape in advance. Depending on the children's developmental level, you might want to precut different sizes of wrapping paper ahead of time or let them do it themselves.
2. Pre-select a basketful of toys and prizes for the children to wrap, or let them pick items from the shelves at the school to wrap.
3. Encourage the children to wrap the items, helping them as needed.
4. Let each child give a "gift" to another child, or save the gift for group time to play a guessing game. Let each child take turns holding up her wrapped item as the other children guess what it is. Whoever guesses what it is can unwrap it. Otherwise the child who wrapped it opens it up.
5. Any book about giving or friendship would be appropriate for this activity.

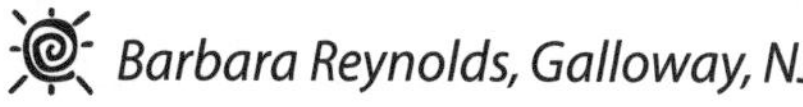
Barbara Reynolds, Galloway, NJ

New Year Celebration

Materials

refrigerated sugar cookie dough
slips of paper
baking sheet and oven
white T-shirts (one for each child)
fabric paint or fabric markers
black and white crepe paper streamers
number stickers
number cookie cutters

What to do

1. Make New Year's fortune cookies using sugar cookie dough. Beforehand, write "fortunes" on slips of paper. For example, "This year you will make a new friend." Cut the dough into small balls. Demonstrate how to flatten the balls on the baking sheet, stick the "fortunes" in the center, and fold the dough over. Bake according to package directions. Encourage the children to remove the fortunes before eating the cookies.

2. Make New Year's T-shirts with the children. Give each child a white T-shirt (purchased or donated by parents). Put newspaper or flat cardboard inside each shirt before writing on them. Help the children use stencils and fabric pens to write "I love _______ (insert the numerals of the new year)." Encourage them to decorate their T-shirts with fabric paint pens and markers.
3. Make New Year's hats with streamers and stickers. Help each child roll a piece of black of construction paper into a cone shape. Show them how to attach a black and white streamer at the tip of the hat. Let the children use number stickers to put the date of the new year on the front of the hat.
4. Have a New Year's party! Encourage the children to use number cookie cutters to cut out the date of the new year on leftover store-bought sugar cookie dough left from the fortune cookies. Let the children wear their T-shirts and hats, serve number cookies and fortune cookies, and celebrate!

Lisa Chichester, Parkersburg, WV

Olé, Olé! Mexico

Materials

colored scarves
sombrero
Mexican music
small plastic bowls
plastic knives and spoons
salsa ingredients (tomato juice, green pepper, onion, and small cherry tomatoes)
colored nacho chips
balloons
old newspaper
flour
glue
water
paint

What to do

1. Place a large sombrero in the middle of an open space. Play Mexican music and encourage the children to dance around the sombrero while waving colored scarves. Call it the "Mexican hat dance!"
2. Make homemade salsa. Help the children dice onions, cherry tomatoes, and green peppers. Give the children plastic bowls and help them mix tomato juice, onions, tomatoes, and peppers. Provide colored nacho chips and have a Mexican snack!

3. Help the children make small piñatas with balloons and papier mâché. Give each child an inflated balloon. Mix 2 cups flour, 1 cup glue, and ½ cup water in a bowl. Demonstrate how to dip newspaper strips into the mixture and wrap around the balloon. Layer the strips and let dry. Let the children pop their balloons by sticking pins into them. Encourage them to paint their piñatas. When they are dry, fill them with candy and so on.
4. Have a "Mexican Party!" Dance to Mexican music and break open the piñatas.

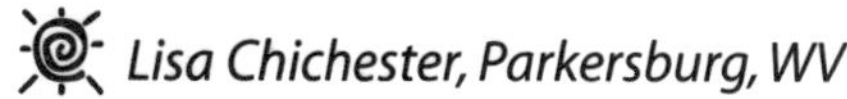

Lisa Chichester, Parkersburg, WV

Party

Materials

crepe paper
confetti
party hats, plates, napkins, and cups
party tablecloth
pretend or real birthday cake
candles
birthday crowns
birthday games and supplies

What to do

1. Tell the children that they are going to pretend it's their birthday and they are going to celebrate by having a big party! Talk about the children's experiences with birthdays.
2. Encourage the children to decorate the room with crepe paper streamers and confetti. Cover the table with a party tablecloth and put a party plate, napkin, and cup at each place setting. Put a pretend (or real!) birthday cake with candles in the middle of the table.
3. Let each child wear a birthday crown. Sing "Happy Birthday" and blow out the candles on the cake together.
4. Make a birthday vocabulary chart with the children. Include the words "birthday," "party," "prize," "cake," "candle," and "presents."
5. Put out a basket of books about birthdays, invitations, envelopes, and pictures of birthday parties.
6. Play games such as "Pin the Tail on the Donkey" and "Twister."

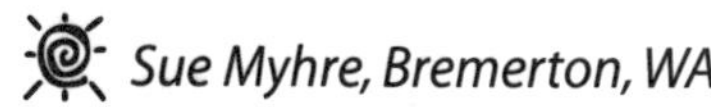

Sue Myhre, Bremerton, WA

Presidents' Day

Materials

pictures of George Washington and Abraham Lincoln
outline pictures of both presidents
crayons
clear contact paper
small, empty milk cartons
sticks
glue
straws
black watery paint
red paint

What to do

1. Show the children pictures of Abraham Lincoln and George Washington. Explain what a president does and talk about what each of these past American presidents did.
2. Give each child an outline (coloring-book style) of both presidents to color. Cover them with clear contact paper to make place mats.
3. Tell the children that Lincoln grew up in a log cabin (and that this is how "Lincoln Logs" got their name!). Let the children make their own "log cabins" by gluing sticks to small, empty milk cartons.
4. Tell the children the legend about George Washington and cherry trees. Encourage the children to make their own "cherry trees." Provide straws and watered-down black paint. Demonstrate how to use a straw to blow a spot of black paint on white paper until it forms a tree-like shape. After they have dried, let the children use red paint to make fingerprint "cherries" on the tree.

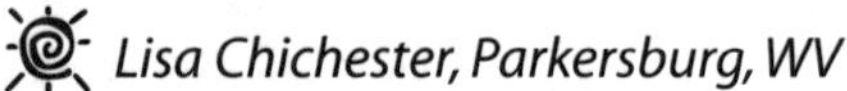
Lisa Chichester, Parkersburg, WV

Two-Way Birthday Play

Materials

playdough
collage materials (cotton balls, paper scraps, ribbon, confetti)
objects to press into playdough to make designs
fancy birthday plate for base of cake
variety of paper and card-making supplies (doilies, old birthday cards, used wrapping paper, and stickers)

scissors
glue
tape
stapler
pens
markers and crayons

What to do

1. Encourage the children to explore two complementary birthday activities in the art center. These could be for a special birthday celebration, an imaginary friend, or the class mascot. Or have a "just because" birthday for anyone and everyone!
    - **Play Cake**: Let the children use playdough to create little cakes. Encourage them to decorate their cakes with all kinds of collage decorations. Provide a variety of objects for them to press into the playdough to make designs (such as forks). Don't forget real candles! Or let them make candles by rolling up a scrap of paper and coloring the end yellow.
    - **Card Making**: Provide a large supply of paper and other card-making supplies for children to create unique birthday cards for someone special.
2. When the children are done, have a party!

Related books

A Birthday for Frances by Russell Hoban
Happy Birthday, Jesse Bear! by Nancy White Carlstrom
Happy Birthday to You by Dr. Seuss
Monster Birthdays by Sandra Boynton

Related song

Today Is My Birthday, Hip Hip Hooray by MaryAnn F. Kohl
(tune: "Zip-a-dee Doo-dah")
Today is my birthday, hip, hip, hooray!
My, oh, my, what a beautiful day!
I see surprises heading my way.
Today is my birthday, hip, hip, hooray.
Ready, COUNT!
1, 2, 3, 4!
Hip, hip, hooray!
(Ask everyone to count out loud with and use fingers to show how many years to celebrate for the birthday person.)

 *MaryAnn F. Kohl, Bellingham, WA*

Matching Pet Prints

Materials

pictures of several pets such as a cat, dog, guinea pig, rabbit, turtle, and pony
glue
tagboard
markers
laminate (optional)

What to do

1. Cut out several photos of pets from magazines. Glue the pictures on tagboard and cut them out.
2. Cut the remaining tagboard into 4" x 18" strips.
3. On each strip draw animal footprints in a repeated pattern across the strip that corresponds to the animals' photos.
4. Laminate the pet photos and corresponding footprints.
5. In the pet learning center, present the pictures of pets and ask the children to match them to the corresponding footprints.
6. Follow up with questions such as, "How do you know this print is made by this animal?"

More to do

Art: Ask the children to draw pictures of pets, real or imaginary (unicorns, "wild-things," dinosaurs), and create corresponding footprints.

Related book *Pet Show!* by Ezra Jack Keats

 *Deborah Roud and Diana Reed, New Wilmington, PA*

Pet Classification

Materials

pictures of assorted pets or plastic birds, fish, and animals

What to do

1. Encourage the children to sort the pictures or plastic animals according to animals that walk on the ground, fly in the air, and swim in the water.
2. Let the children sort the pictures or plastic animals any way they want (color of animal, two legs, no legs, or four legs, and so on).

Related book *Pet Show!* by Ezra Jack Keats

Pet Classification II

Materials

pictures of various animals or plastic animals
two large grocery bags
picture of a baby
picture of an egg
glue

What to do

1. Cut out pictures of a variety of animals from magazines. Or gather a variety of plastic animals. Glue a picture of a baby on one large bag and a picture of an egg on the other bag.
2. Encourage the children to sort the pictures or plastic animals according to whether they are born from mothers (babies) or hatched from eggs. Ask them to put them into the appropriate bag.

Phyllis Esch, Export, PA

Pet Grooming Salon

Materials

two toilet paper tubes
one small margarine container
duct tape
stuffed and plastic cats and dogs with long and short hair
milk crates
plastic tub
towels
mild shampoo (tear-free)
brushes
barrettes and ribbons
curlers
collars
plastic scissors
milk crates
play money and cash register

What to do

1. To prepare, create a "blow dryer" by duct taping two toilet paper tubes to the sides of a margarine tub at 6:00 and 9:00 positions. Cover with tape to create a blow dryer (see illustration).
2. Prepare the area by filling a large tub ⅓ full of water (to bathe animals), and put grooming accessories on a table nearby. Place stuffed animals in milk crate "cages."
3. Encourage the children to put on smocks and "groom" the animals. They can brush and comb stuffed animals, put accessories and curlers in their fur, and pretend to cut hair and nails.
4. The children can bathe plastic animals in the tub with the shampoo. After bathing the animals, they can towel them dry and "blow dry." (Make sure the children only put plastic animals in the water; stuffed animals get too soggy.)
5. When finished, the animals can wait in the cages for their owners to pick them up and "pay" the groomers.

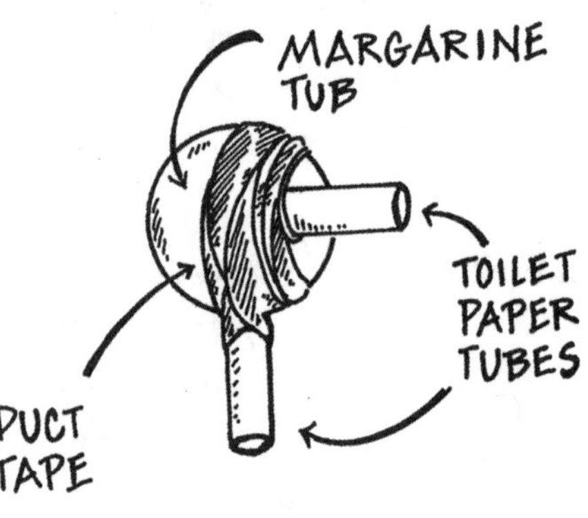

HAIR DRYER

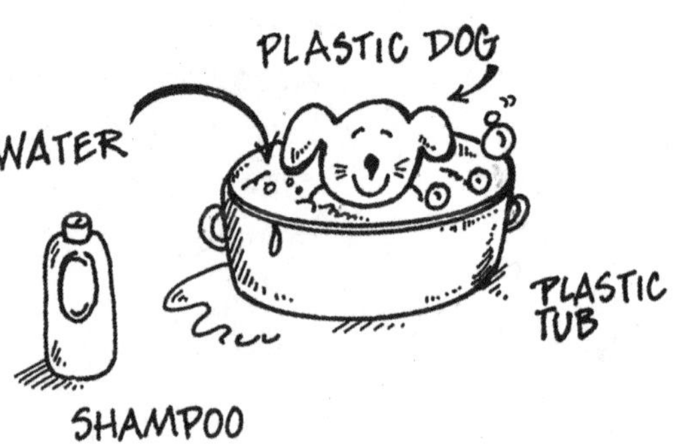

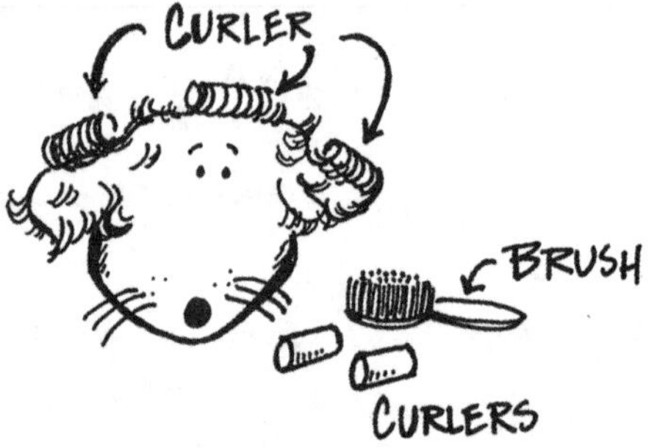

Related books *I Want a Dog* by Dayar Kaur Khalsa
My New Boy by Joan Phillips
Uses for Mooses and Other Popular Pets by Mike Thaler

Sandra Gratias, Perkasie, PA

Pet Paradise

Materials

graph paper
markers
pet beds
pet bowls
dry dog and cat food
leashes
large variety of stuffed animals (such as cats, dogs, fish, lizards, turtles, and snakes)
feeder goldfish (cheap at your local pet store)
fish food
a variety of plastic pets (such as lizards, snakes, and turtles)
collage materials (fake fur, plastic scraps, fabric scraps, yarn, and leather scraps)

What to do

1. Ask the children if they have any pets at home. Let each child tell about his pet (or a pet of a neighbor or relative). Make a graph of the results.
2. Turn your classroom into a "pet paradise."
3. Add pet carriers, bowls, food, pet beds, and leashes to the house area. Encourage the children to take care of the stuffed pets by feeding them, bathing them, and walking them.
4. Thoroughly clean the sensory table. Fill it half full with water and let it sit for one day. Add "feeder" goldfish. Encourage the children to observe the fish, but remind them to keep the fish in the water. Assign one child each day to be the "fish feeder." Add a plastic sand-filled basin. The top of the basin should be just above the water level. Put plastic lizards and turtles in the basin.
5. Encourage the children to use the science area materials to explore the pets. They can use magnifying glasses to get a close-up view of the goldfish, and scales to weigh the animals.
6. Add animal books to the reading area and encourage the children to look at them.
7. Put a variety of materials (such as fake fur, plastic, yarn, felt, fabric, and so on) in the art center for children to make collages and sculptures of their pets.
8. At the end of the day, discuss what they learned about pet care.

Virginia Jean Herrod, Columbia, SC

Animal Shelter

Materials

cardboard boxes
pens
paper
clipboards
leashes
collars
pet food dishes

What to do

1. Talk about animal shelters with the children. Explain what they are and why there is a need for them. Ask the children if any of them have ever adopted an animal from a shelter.
2. Set up a pretend animal shelter with a front desk, pretend application forms, collars, cages (cardboard boxes), and resource books with pictures of pets, and pet supplies (leash, brush, dish, and food).
3. Ask the children to choose their roles, such as volunteers, people searching for pets, or the animals themselves. Be prepared to model and explain the roles.
4. Guide children as needed to play their roles and let them refer to the books as needed. Provide space for "owners" to play with their pets once they have filled out an application form.

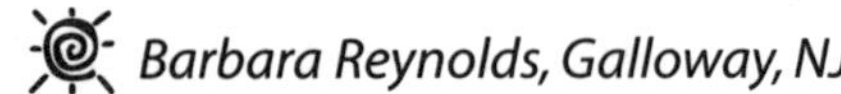
Barbara Reynolds, Galloway, NJ

Pet Shop

Materials

wooden, plastic, or cardboard blocks
beanbag, wooden, or plastic domestic animals
real or toy pet foods
play money
cash register (optional)

What to do

1. Encourage the children to set up a pet shop in the block area using a variety of blocks and animals.
2. After the children set up the pet shop, they can take turns being the salespeople and customers.

Related book *How Much Is That Doggie in the Window*? by Iza Trapani

 *Deborah Litfin, Forest Hills, NY*

Pet Show

Materials

magazines with pictures of pets
scissors
paper
glue
markers
felt in various colors
rickrack and pompoms
material scraps

What to do

1. Tell the children they will be making a group pet book. Encourage them to look through magazines and cut out pictures of a type of pet they would like to have. Ask them to glue the pictures to paper and dictate a couple sentences about the pet. Assemble the pages into a book by stapling them together and adding a cover.
2. Cut out a variety of pet shapes from felt (dog, cat, bird, and so on).
3. Let the children choose a felt pet and decorate using rickrack, scraps of material, ribbon, and so on.

 *Lisa Chichester, Parkersburg, WV*

Vet's Clinic

Materials

chairs and desks
stuffed animals
books or magazines
telephone
keyboard
date book
clipboard with pencil
paper
posters of doctors, pets, and so on
table
play medical tools (stethoscope, blood pressure pump, thermometer, and other tools)
nurse and doctor jackets, surgery scrubs, and shoe covers
stretch bandages and tongue depressors for splints
small plastic bandages

What to do

1. Set up a reception area with chairs, desk, and office equipment.
2. Behind the reception area, arrange medical diagnosis, treatment, and surgery areas.
3. Explain to the children what the areas are used for. For example, in the reception area, they may wait their turn, schedule appointments, and pay for services.
4. Encourage the children to take on different roles, such as pet owner, receptionist, doctor, and nurse.

Jean Lortz, Sequim, WA

All About Oranges

Materials

oranges
plastic knives
juicer
two wooden crates

What to do

1. Give each child a plastic knife and a peeled orange. Encourage them to cut the orange in half and explore what's inside. After exploring, encourage them to eat their oranges. Show them how to make an "orange grin" by putting a slice of orange in front of their teeth.
2. Help the children squeeze fresh orange juice using a juicer. Pour the juice into small plastic cups for them to taste.
3. Have an "orange gathering" relay. Divide the children into two groups and have them stand in two lines behind a masking tape start line. At the other end, place two wooden crates and scatter oranges in and around each crate. When you say "go," the first person on each team races down to the other end and picks up all the oranges. Then they race back to the next person in line and dump the oranges for the next team member to gather. This continues until all the children have had a turn.

Let's Have a Picnic

Materials

picnic basket
four to six place settings
plastic cups
picnic tablecloth
magazines
scissors
paper plates
glue
snacks (optional)

What to do

1. Put place settings, cups, and a tablecloth inside a picnic basket and place it in the picnic center.
2. Encourage the children to use the items in the picnic basket to set a place for each other at a pretend picnic. By setting a place for each child at the center, the children will be learning one-to-one correspondence.
3. Discuss healthy foods to take on a picnic. Encourage the children to cut out pictures of healthy foods and glue them to a paper plate.
4. If desired, let the children eat healthy snacks at their picnic.

Related books

Little Red by Sarah Ferguson
A Picnic in October by Eve Bunting
Picnic by Emily Arnold McCully
Teddy Bears' Picnic by Alexandra Day

Lori Dunlap, Amarillo, TX

Library Picnic

Materials

books about picnics
plastic insects (novelty stores)
picnic basket
butcher/bulletin board paper
scissors
green construction paper
markers
blanket

What to do

1. Beforehand, gather books about picnics, a picnic basket, and plastic insects.
2. Also in advance, make a tree out of butcher or bulletin board paper. Add construction paper leaves.
3. Place a blanket on the floor with the picnic basket. Place plastic insects on the floor next to the blanket.
4. Put books in the picnic basket and encourage the children to read the books while sitting on the blanket.

Quazonia Quarles, Newark, DE

Packing a Picnic Lunch

Materials

cards (cardstock or index cards)
markers
bread
peanut butter
jelly
cheese
mayonnaise
mustard
plastic baggies
celery and carrot sticks
individual boxes of raisins
cookies
juice boxes
paper lunch bags
large picnic basket

What to do

1. Let the children take an active part in the preparation of their picnic food.
2. In advance, prepare sequence cards for making a cheese sandwich and peanut butter and jelly sandwich. Put bread, peanut butter, jelly, mayonnaise, mustard, and cheese on a table.
3. On the same table, place small plastic baggies, celery and carrot sticks, boxes of raisins, cookies, and juice boxes.
4. Provide cards that indicate how many of each food item the children should take.
5. After the children make their sandwiches and put the rest of the items in a lunch bag, help them write their name on the bag.
6. Pack all the lunches in a large picnic basket. If it is nice outside, go outside and eat. If not, have a classroom picnic!

Note: Be aware of any food allergies to peanuts and plan accordingly.

Quazonia Quarles, Newark, DE

Picnic

Materials

tape player and nature sounds tape
plastic plants
photos of nature
books
pillows and blankets
bowls and cups
red and white checkered tablecloth
picnic basket
plastic food items

What to do

1. Transform your area into the great outdoors!
2. Play a tape recording of nature sounds. Decorate the walls with photos of nature and put plastic plants around the area.
3. Put books about picnics in the area and encourage the children to lie on blankets to read.
4. Encourage the children to pack a basket with plastic food and a tablecloth and have a picnic.

Sue Myhre, Bremerton, WA

Picnic Alphabet

Materials

pictures of picnic items representing letters A to Z
laminate or clear contact paper
large picnic basket
plastic letters
container

What to do

1. In advance, collect pictures of picnic items each starting with a different letter of the alphabet (see below). Laminate the pictures for durability.
2. Place the pictures in the picnic basket.
3. Put plastic letters (A to Z) in a container. Let the children take turns choosing a letter from the container.
4. Encourage the children to search in the picnic basket for something that starts with their chosen letter.

5. Some examples of picnic items from A to Z include apple or ant ("A"), blanket ("B"), fork ("F"), grapes ("G"), napkin ("N"), strawberries ("S"), umbrella ("U"), and yellow peppers ("Y"). Picnic items can be food, games, insects, or anything else one would see at a picnic.

Quazonia Quarles, Newark, DE

Picnic Time

Materials

large checkered tablecloth
plates
white napkins
red markers
ant stickers
black markers
colored lunch bags
letter stencils
peanut butter and jelly
bread
plastic knives
baggies
picnic foods (apples, pretzels, raisins)

What to do

1. Spread a checkered tablecloth on the floor of the housekeeping center. Encourage the children to put plates on the tablecloth and have a "teddy bear" picnic or another type of picnic.

2. Let children make their own picnic napkins. Demonstrate how to use a red marker to make checkers on a white napkin (as shown). Encourage the children to add ant stickers or draw ants on the napkins. Help each child write his name on the napkin.

3. Help the children use stencils to write their names on their lunch bags.
4. Let the children help make peanut butter and jelly sandwiches and put picnic items in their lunch bags. Have a class picnic inside!

Note: Be aware of any food allergies to peanuts and plan accordingly.

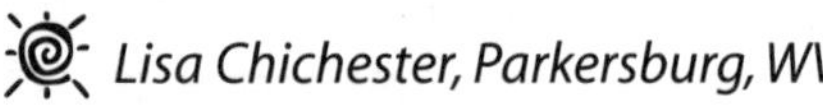

Lisa Chichester, Parkersburg, WV

Watermelon Fun

Materials

letter-size file folder
white paper
scissors
green, pink, red, and black markers
glue stick
laminate or clear contact paper
Velcro

What to do

1. Cut out 20 watermelon slices from white paper. Color a green rind and pink center on each one.
2. Draw a different number of seeds on ten of the slices (1 through 10). Write a different number on the remaining ten slices (1 through 10).
3. Glue the 10 watermelons with seeds on an open file folder. Glue the 10 watermelons with numbers on tagboard and cut each one out. Mount to the remaining 10 watermelons (with numbers) onto piece of tag board and cut out.
4. Laminate the inside of the file folder and watermelon slices. Add a small piece of Velcro to each watermelon on the file folder and the other side of the Velcro to the back of the watermelon slices. Store the pieces in an envelope.
5. Encourage the children to match the watermelon slices (with numbers) to the watermelon slices with seeds.

Jackie Wright, Enid, OK

When I Go on a Picnic I Will Bring...

Materials none

What to do

1. Play this memory language game during large or small group time.
2. Have the children sit in a circle. Start the game by saying, "When I go on a picnic, I will bring…." Name an object. Limit the items, if desired, by explaining that the objects need to be from a certain category (such as food or the name of a friend in the class).
3. Continuing around the circle, each child repeats the sentence and items already said and add a new item.
4. Bring literacy into this activity by writing a list of the items at the end of the game.
5. This activity can be simplified by asking the children to find an item in the classroom to bring to a picnic and bring it to group time. This helps the children build their vocabulary with less focus on memory and recall.

Related books *Picnic With Monet* by Julie Merberg
We're Going on a Picnic by Pat Hutchins

Ann Kelly, Johnstown, PA

Old Fashioned Bread and Butter

Materials

ingredients to make bread
bread-making machine or oven
clean glass jar
heavy cream
pictures of pioneer living (optional)
Little Red Hen story

What to do

1. Ask the children if they know how bread is made or how butter is made. Explain that ways of life continue to change. For instance, there are many machines that have been invented in the past few hundred years, and many more are invented every day. Tell them that people used to grow and raise their own food and did not have grocery stores to buy everything.
2. Tell the children that they are going to make their own bread and butter. While they will learn a little more about how things used to be done, it will be much easier for them than pioneers (who had to grow the wheat and milk the cow!).
3. Ask the children to wash their hands. Put out bread-making ingredients (use any favorite recipe) and heavy cream.
4. Encourage the children to measure and mix the ingredients for homemade bread while they take turns shaking a jar filled with heavy cream. The cream will thicken and turn to butter right in front of them!
5. Bake the bread and serve with fresh butter.
6. Read the story *The Little Red Hen* as children eat.

Related book *Little House on the Prairie* series by Laura Ingalls Wilder

Pioneer Center

Materials

small tent
blankets
cooking utensils

What to do

1. Set up a small tent in the classroom or outside. Talk about pioneers with the children.
2. Encourage the children to pretend to be pioneers. They can use blankets to set up inside the tent and use the utensils for "cooking."

Related book *Little House on the Prairie Picture Books* adapted from Laura Ingalls Wilder

Barbara Saul, Eureka, CA

Panning for Gold

Materials

small rocks (found at landscaping stores)
gold spray paint
aluminum pie pan

What to do

1. Away from the children, spray paint some of the rocks gold.
2. Talk about mining for gold. Explain how people used to look for gold in creeks by sifting rocks in pans.
3. Encourage the children to sift through rocks in aluminum pie pans to try to find "gold."

Related book *A Prairie Boy's Winter* by William Kurelek

Barbara Saul, Eureka, CA

Wanted Posters

Materials

gray or white construction paper
construction paper crayons or markers
lighter (adult only)

What to do

1. If you have a computer with a clip art program, print out pages with the border of a "Wanted" poster. If not, draw a border on white paper and make copies for each child. Title the poster "Wanted for ________."
2. Give each child a blank "wanted" poster with a border.
3. Encourage the children to draw self-portraits.
4. Ask each child to tell you his best quality (for example, great artist, good friend, or good runner). Write the quality (or let the child write it, if able) on the poster.
5. When the children all finished, use a lighter (away from the children) to burn the edges of each poster to give it an old time or rustic look.

Safety Note: Do the last step after children have left for the day to discourage any interest in playing with lighters!

Wanda Guidroz, Santa Fe, TX

Simple Pilgrim Hats, Collars, and Apron

Materials

white lunch bags
rectangular lace paper place mat
paper cutter or scissors
white tissue paper or crepe paper (20" x 14")
12" x 18" white construction paper, drawing paper, or butcher paper
white and black yarn
black construction paper (12" x 18" and 9" x 12")
gold or silver paper
stapler
white glue

What to do

1. Show the children (girls) how to make a Pilgrim bonnet by laying a paper bag on its side and cutting out the bottom of the bag. Fold back the bag 2″ on the front edge. Glue yarn inside the fold along the entire length, and then glue it to the bag. Glue a 2″-wide piece of lace to the folded band. Help the children as they work.

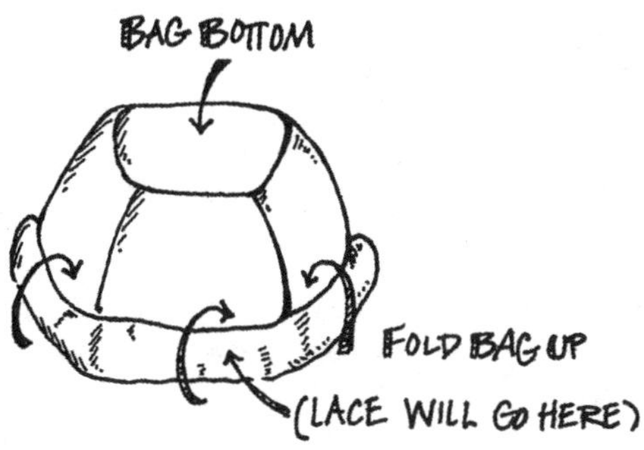

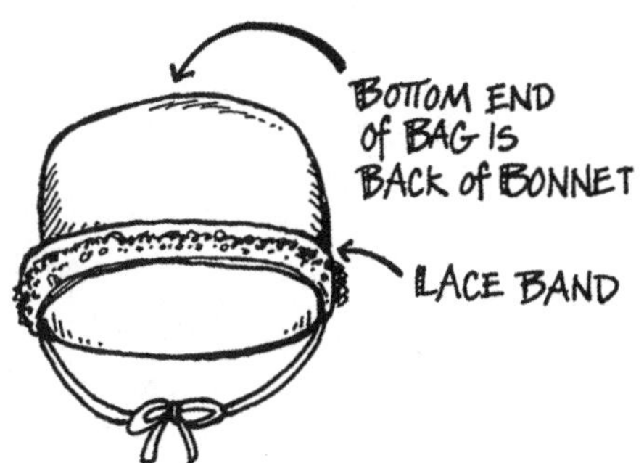

2. Help the children make collars. To make a girls' collar, draw a round collar shape on white paper, about 10 ½″ wide and 9″ from top to bottom. Cut out. Glue 6 ½″ lengths of white yarn to the back of the collar edge by the neck area.
3. To make a boys' collar, draw a square-shaped collar on white paper, about 13 ¼″ wide and 12″ from top to bottom. Cut out. Glue two 11″ lengths of black yarn to the back of the collar edge by the neck area. This looks like a shoestring tie.

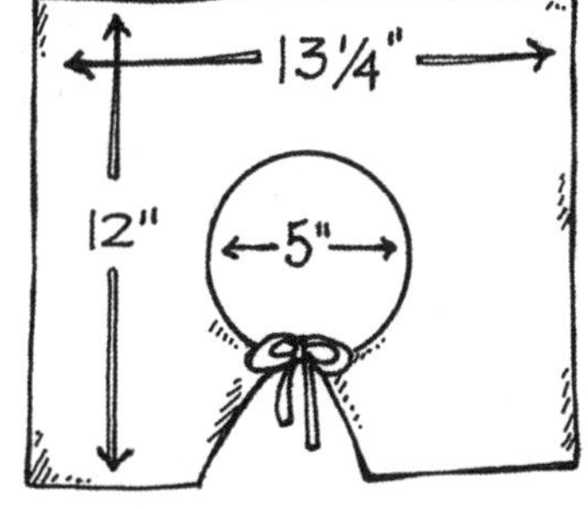

4. Make Pilgrim hats (boys). Draw a Pilgrim hat on 9″ x 12″ black construction paper and cut out. Cut out a rectangular buckle from silver or gold paper. Cut a headband strip 2″ wide and 18″ long. Measure to each child's head and staple into headbands. Staple the hats to the headbands.

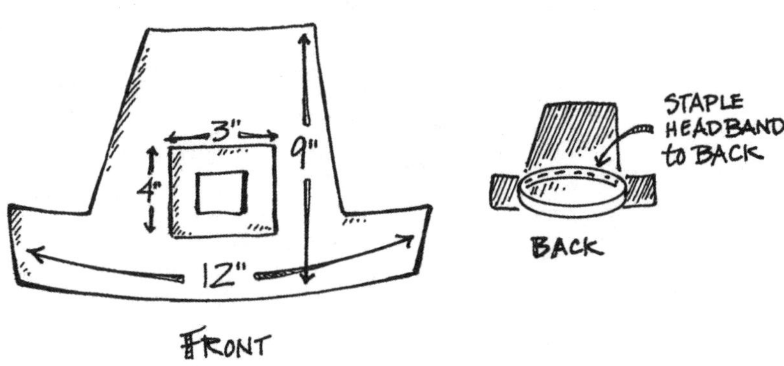

5. Make Pilgrim aprons with the children. Cut tissue paper or crepe paper 20″ x 14″. Cut construction paper into pieces 12″ x 4″, and fold the 4″ width in half. Put white glue about ¾″ from the bottom edge of the waistband. Gather cloth, tissue, or crepe paper onto glued area. Cut white yarn into 55″ lengths. Put glue along the folded edge of the waistband. Push yarn down on the glue, leaving an equal length to tie on each side. Glue the top 2″ of the paper waistband over the gathered paper or cloth.

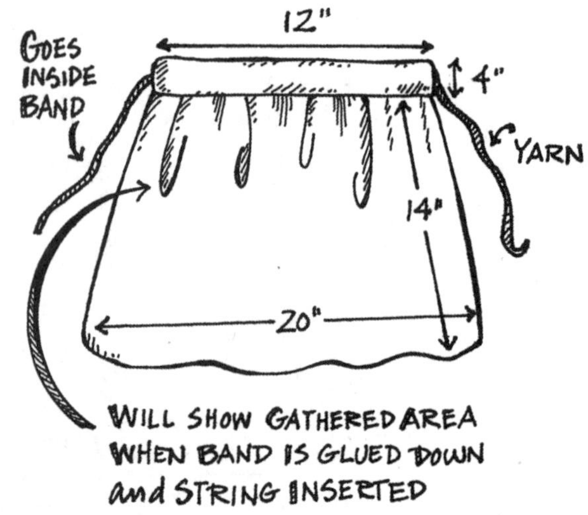

6. Dramatize the first Thanksgiving with the children.

Related book *The First Thanksgiving* by Lou Rogers

Mary Brehm, Aurora, OH

Yonder! A Pioneer's Life

Materials

Yonder by Tony Johnston
large refrigerator box
craft knife (adult only)
two hollow plastic hula hoops
large hollow blocks
tape
white canvas fabric or a large off-white blanket
several cardboard boxes
two hobbyhorses
sturdy rope
several small wooden chests
old pots and pans
tin cups
pioneer clothes (bonnets, floppy straw hats, cowboy hats, old dresses, old dress pants, suspenders, and flannel shirts)
several medium-size sticks

What to do

1. Read *Yonder* by Tony Johnston to the children. Talk about the story. Ask questions such as, "How would you feel if you and your family moved to a new and strange place?" Encourage the children to tell their own stories about moving.
2. Let the children help create a covered wagon. Choose an area in the room to put the wagon. Once it is assembled, it cannot be moved.
3. Start by removing the top and bottom flaps of a refrigerator box using a craft knife (adult only). Place the refrigerator box on its side and use the craft knife to cut several small windows in the two sides. (While this is not historically accurate, it lets the children see out while maintaining the strength of the box.)
4. Use a craft knife to cut two plastic hula hoops in half.
5. Use large hollow blocks to build a platform for the refrigerator box. Tape the blocks together securely so they will not fall over. Place the refrigerator box on top of the platform.
6. Securely tape the hula hoop halves to the top of the refrigerator box.
7. Drape the white canvas fabric or large blanket over the hoops to create the covered wagon top. For a more historically accurate look, paste the fabric to the hoops.
8. Cut out four wheels from the cardboard boxes. Affix the wheels to the sides of the refrigerator box so they just touch the floor.
9. Use a couple of large blocks to prop the hobbyhorses up in front of the covered wagon.
10. Create a set of reins from the horses to the wagon using the sturdy rope.
11. Put the small wooden chests, wooden crates, old pots and pans, and tin cups in the wagon. Add pioneer clothes to the dress-up area.
12. Scatter sticks around the room. When the children "stop their wagon for the night," they can gather the sticks to make a "campfire."
13. Let the children use the materials freely during center time.

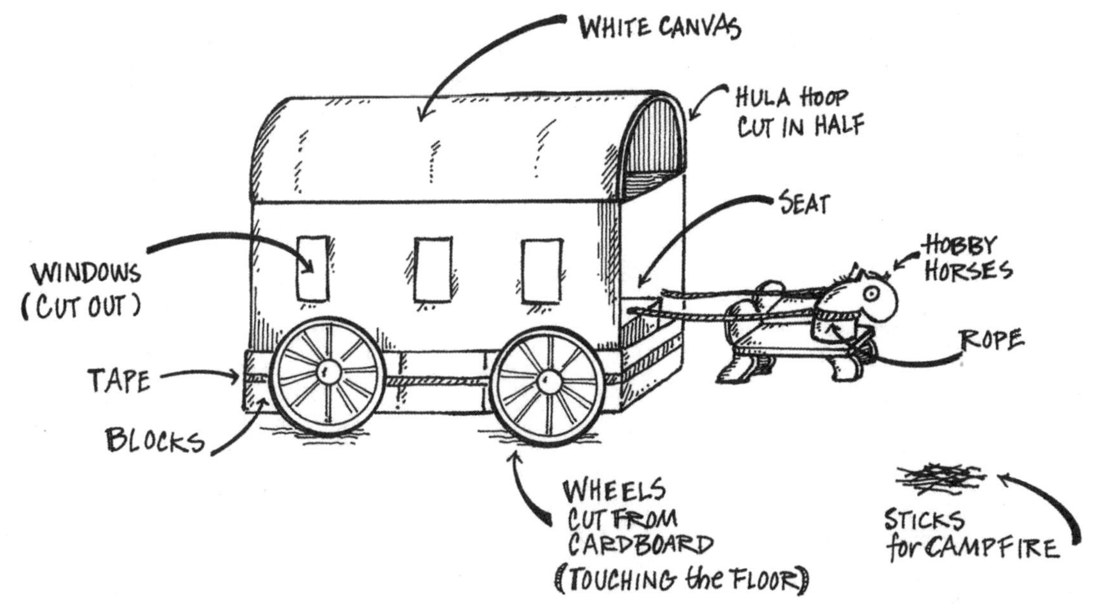

Related books *Dakota Dugout* by Ann Turner
Johnny Appleseed by Reeve Lindbergh
The Josefina Story Quilt by Eleanor Coerr
Kindle Me a Riddle: A Pioneer Story by Roberta Karm
The Long Way Westward by Joan Sandin
My Prairie Christmas by Brett Harvey
Three Names by Patricia MacLachlan
Yonder by Tony Johnston

Virginia Jean Herrod, Columbia, SC

Letters

Materials

medium cardboard box
red, white, and blue paper
glue
craft knife
index cards
children's photos
paper
pens, pencils, crayons, and markers
envelopes
stickers for play stamps
paper scraps, magazines, catalogs, and junk mail

What to do

1. Before doing the activity, decorate a medium cardboard box to look like a mailbox. Cover the box with red, white, and blue paper. Write "MAIL" in large capital letters on the box. Cut out a mail slot for letters to fall into the box.
2. Make address cards by printing each child's name clearly on a large index card. Glue a photo of the child underneath her name. The children can use these cards when addressing mail on envelopes.
3. To introduce the activity, tell the children they will be exploring letter writing with paper, envelopes, stamps, and a mailbox. Explain that all of the children will have a name card with a corresponding photo so others can address mail to them. Mail is delivered to individual cubbies or mailboxes each day.
4. Encourage the children to come to the postal center and write letters to their family, someone in the class, or anyone they choose. Any method of sharing information on paper is fun, including drawings, actual writing, cutting out pictures and gluing on paper, and artwork.
5. Help the children address the envelopes using the address cards. If the child is very young, she can let an adult know whom the letter is for. Provide stickers for stamp and let the children "mail" the letters using the cardboard mailbox.
6. Choose a class helper to distribute the mail each day to individual cubbies or mailboxes in the room. Other mail can go to the child to take home for Mom, Dad, or Fido.
7. Encourage the children to read their mail at school or at home.

Related books

Community Helpers From A to Z (Alphabasics) by Bobbie Kalman, Niki Walker
Dear Annie by Judith Caseley
Dear Mr. Blueberry by Simon James
Dear Peter Rabbit by Alma Ada
Here Comes Mr. Eventoff With the Mail (Our Neighborhood) by Alice K. Flanagan

The Jolly Postman by Allan Ahlberg
The Jolly Christmas Postman by Allan Ahlberg
Jonathan Goes to the Post Office by Susan K. Baggette
The Mail and How It Moves by Gail Gibbons

Related song

Write a Letter by MaryAnn F. Kohl
(tune: "Mary Had A Little Lamb")
Write a letter to my friend,
To my friend, to my friend.
Write a letter to my friend
And send it with a stamp. (WHAM!) (Emphatically stamp one fist on the other palm of the hand, like pressing a stamp in place.)

Write a letter to my mom,
To my mom, to my mom.
Write a letter to my mom
And send it with a stamp. (WHAM!)

Continue to substitute any words children choose.

MaryAnn F. Kohl, Bellingham, WA

Letters to Friends

Materials

pre-addressed and stamped envelopes for each child
paper
pencils and crayons
books about post offices

What to do

1. Depending on your time and budget, ask each family to send in an envelope, stamped and addressed to their child, or prepare all the envelopes yourself.
2. Tell the children that they will be sending a letter to a friend in the class, and in a few days, each of them will receive a letter at her house!
3. Randomly pass out the envelopes to the children, either in a small group setting or to a few at a time during free choice time. To avoid hurt feelings, children should not select whom they want to write letters to. Encourage them to keep their letter a surprise so the recipient will have to wait until the letter arrives at her house.
4. Encourage the children to write the name of the child they are sending the letter to and draw a picture. Help them write a message if they'd like to include one.

5. Mail the letters together, if possible.
6. Read a story about the post office, or show a video clip of your own post office.
7. Invite a postal worker to visit your classroom to describe his or her work, show his or her mailbags and bins, and explain the machines in a post office.
8. Ask children to let you know when they receive their letters and see if there are any differences as to when children get their letters. "Why would some take two days, and some take three days?"

Related books *Frog and Toad, The Letter* by Arnold Lobel
Ira Says Goodbye by Bernard Waber

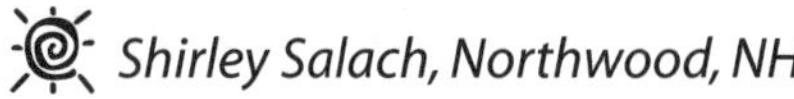
Shirley Salach, Northwood, NH

Mailbags

Materials
large brown grocery bags
scissors
stapler
blue paint
markers
American flag stickers (optional)

What to do
1. Cut off a 2" strip from the top of a large brown grocery bag.
2. Staple each end of the strip to the sides of the bag to make a shoulder strap.
3. Paint the bag and strap with blue paint.
4. When dry, write "U.S. Mail" on both sides and add American flag stickers for decoration.
5. Children can make their own bags to bring home or use in the postal center.

Andrea Hungerford, Plainville, CT

Main Post Office, USA

Materials

long low table
three child-sized chairs
three tri-fold display boards
three working calculators
three shoeboxes
stamps (free stamps from junk mail)
pretend money
cardstock paper
markers
four 3′-long dowel rods
four coffee cans
sand
lightweight rope
working baby scale
envelopes of varying sizes
small square table and small rectangular table
writing paper
pens and pencils

What to do

1. Ask the children if they have ever been to a post office with their parents. Talk about the things they might have seen there. Discuss the counter, the stamps, the workers, and anything else they might have seen.
2. Set up a postal center with the children. Place a long, low table in the area with three chairs behind it.
3. Cut the front of the three tri-fold display boards down to almost the bottom, making sure you don't cut them apart. Place them on the table to serve as dividers for each post office station. For stability, tape the top of the display boards together and tape the bottoms to the table.
4. Place one calculator and one shoebox at each station. Put stamps in one part of the shoebox and pretend money in the other.
5. Use the cardstock paper and markers to create badges for the post office workers. You can pin or tape these to the children as they play.
6. Pour sand into each coffee can and place a dowel rod in each one. Use these to create a walkway up to the table. Tie the rope to the dowel rods to complete the walkway.
7. Remove the top from a baby scale, exposing the square platform. Place the baby scale on the small square table and explain to the children that they can use it to weigh oversize items.
8. Place envelopes of varying sizes, writing paper, pens, and pencils on the rectangular table and place several small chairs around it.

9. Encourage the children to take turns "working" at the bank. Those who aren't working can use the writing paper, pens, and pencils to write letters to friends or family. Show the children how to fold the paper so it fits in the envelope, and encourage them to visit the post office to weigh their letters and buy stamps.
10. Have extra money on hand to refill the money boxes at each station. Invite children and teachers from other rooms to visit and buy stamps at your post office.

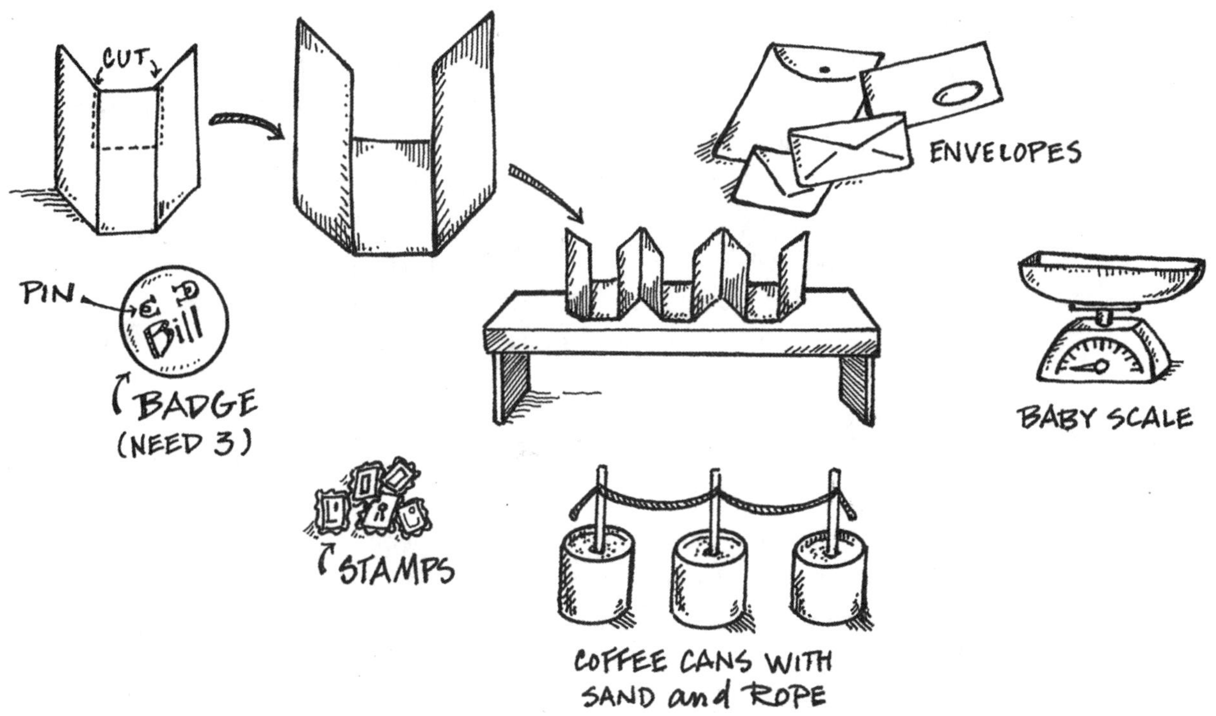

Related books *Hi!* by Ann Herbert Scott
The Jolly Christmas Postman by Allan Ahlberg
The Jolly Postman or Other People's Letters by Allan Ahlberg

Virginia Jean Herrod, Columbia, SC

Opposite Stamps

Materials variety of stamps (old and new)

What to do

1. Preparation: Collect a variety of stamps from all over the world. Perhaps a post office will be willing to donate stamps for this worthy educational cause.
2. Place the stamps in a box or container in the post office learning center.
3. Let the children explore the stamps. Stay in the center to guide the children. Ask probing questions such as:
   - "Can you find stamps that look like they came from a hot place?" (For example, a desert might be represented by a palm tree.) "What would be the opposite of a hot place? If it's not hot, it's ______."
   - "Can you find stamps that look like they came from a cold place?"
   - "Can you find a picture of a woman?" "What would be the opposite of a woman?" "If you're not a woman or girl, you're a _____ or ______."
   - "Can you find pictures of men?"
   - "Can you find a stamp that looks like nighttime?" "What would be the opposite of nighttime? If it's not night, it's _____."
4. If desired, encourage the children to work independently to make pairs of opposite representations with the stamps. (This will depend on the skill level of the group.)

Related books *Clifford's Opposites* by Norman Bridwell
The Jolly Postman or Other People's Letters by Allan Ahlberg
Olivia's Opposites by Ian Falconer

Kate Ross, Middlesex, VT

Post Office

Materials

junk mail
envelopes
pads of paper
pretend stamps
handheld tools (such as hole punch, stapler, and calculators)
large metal rubber stamp
ink pad
mailboxes
cardboard shoe dividers (for mail sorting)
mailbag
mail carrier coat and hat
markers
pretend money
cash register

What to do

1. It is fun for children to pretend to be mail carriers. Set up an area of the room to be a post office. Add the materials from the list above.
2. Write each child's name on the cardboard shoe divider. Encourage them to write letters to each other and "mail" them. It is fun to mail and receive letters.
3. Ask your local post office for a donation of coat and hats from mail carrier uniforms.

Postman, Postman!

Materials

books on postal workers
mail carrier hats
mail bags
pretend letters (junk mail)
envelopes
postcards
small pretend mailboxes
shoeboxes
pens and pencils
paper

What to do

1. Read a story about postal workers and what they do on the job.
2. Provide post office materials in the postal center. Encourage the children to dress up like postal workers, put mail into mailbags, and deliver letters.
3. Explain why mailboxes have flags and what they are used for. Children can put letters into the small mailboxes and raise the flag. The mail carrier will know to pick up the letters inside.
4. Provide a variety of pens, markers, pencils, old stamps, envelopes, paper, and postcards. Encourage the children to write, pretend to write, or dictate a letter to someone they know. Show them how to address an envelope and add a stamp.
5. Let the children write different states on the envelopes, and then help them sort the mail in boxes or baskets according to the state on the envelope.

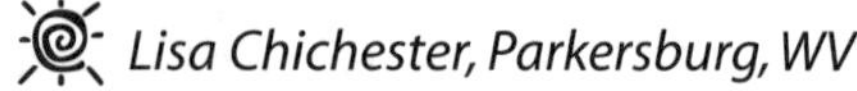

Lisa Chichester, Parkersburg, WV

Setting up a Mail Center

Materials

table and chairs
paper
markers, pencils, and crayons

What to do

1. Inform parents (ideally at the beginning of the year) that their children will be welcome to send mail from school with the help of teachers.
2. Invite parents occasionally to send in addressed and stamped envelopes with their children, including the return address. Also ask them to let you know when there is a specific occasion, such as a grandmother's birthday, and aunt's new baby, or a friend who is sick, so their child can mail out appropriate letters or cards.
3. Let the children visit the mail center during their free choice time and at least complete a picture for their letter. Encourage them to also write their names and a short message. You might want to suggest that they dictate a message for you to write for them.
4. Children may need help folding their letters carefully to fit them in the envelopes.
5. Walk with the children to a nearby mailbox or outgoing mail slot in your center so they can mail their letters.

Related books

Frog and Toad, The Letter by Arnold Lobel
Ira Says Goodbye by Bernard Waber
Little Bear by Else Holmelund Minarik

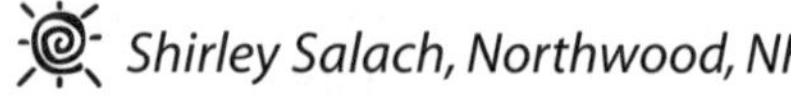

Shirley Salach, Northwood, NH

Stamp Collecting

Materials

variety of stamps
magnifying glasses
paper
colored pencils
clear tape or glue

What to do

1. Send home a note asking parents to bring in old stamps. These can be postmarked and cut from mail.
2. Bring the stamp collection and other materials to an area of the classroom set up for post office play.
3. Encourage the children to make observations about the different stamps. Ask questions about the shapes, sizes, and colors. Ask open-ended questions about the pictures. Discuss what stamps are for and how they are used as payment to have items delivered to any place in the world.
4. Let the children choose their favorite stamp and attach it to a piece of paper.
5. Encourage them to use their imaginations to draw a picture of where the stamp is from, where the mail came from, or what was inside the envelope or letter. Ask the children to describe their drawing and write the description on their project.

Ann Kelly, Johnstown, PA

Valentine Delivery

Materials

shoe divider boxes
envelopes
pens and pencils
paper
stamps and inkpads
stickers to use as stamps
plastic mailbox

What to do

1. Transform the dramatic play area of the classroom into a post office.
2. Include a low table for the children to create letters.
3. Label each of the boxes with a child's name (for younger children use a picture of each child).
4. Children can take their letters to the "post office" to purchase stamps and mail their letters. Postal workers can cancel the stamps on the letters using a stamp and inkpad.
5. Encourage the children to create letters to bring home to parents.

Related book *The Post Office Book* by Gail Gibbons

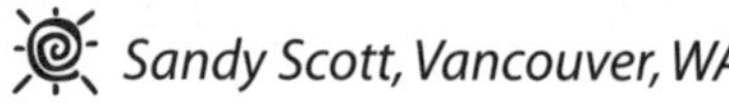

We Can Write Letters

Materials

word wall
stationery
pens and pencils
envelopes
stickers
mailbox

What to do

1. Create a word wall in your classroom of words the children are learning or have learned. Encourage the children to use the word wall to write letters to anyone they choose. The children may use any of the supplies at the post office center to do their writing.
2. Encourage children to use words they know from the word wall and to sound out words they do not know to complete the letters.
3. Let the children put their letters in envelopes, address them, and place them in the classroom mailbox.
4. As a class, explain what happens to letters when they are placed in the mailbox.
5. Arrange to have a class pen pal. As a class, write a letter to your new pen pal.

Related books

Clifford's First Valentines Day by Norman Bridwell
Let's Visit the Post Office by Marianne Johnston
The Post Office Book by Gail Gibbons
To the Post Office With Mama by Sue Farrell

Restaurants

Materials

menus
small tablets
pencils
clothesline
clothespins

What to do

1. If possible, visit a restaurant, including the kitchen area. If not, read books about restaurants and ask some restaurant employees to visit your classroom.
2. Set up the dramatic play or house area to represent a restaurant. Place a table and chairs behind the kitchen appliances so that the food prep area is separate from where the "customers" eat. Tie a clothesline over the food prep area to clip food orders. Put out the menus, tablets, and pencils.
3. Encourage the children to take turns playing different roles (cooks, food servers, customers). Model for or encourage the "food servers" to use the tablets to write down what their "customers" order. The food server can clip the orders to the clothesline for the cooks to refer to it as they prepare the food in the kitchen.

Related books

Froggy Eats Out by Jonathan London
Monsterlicious by Erik Jon Slangerup

Ann Kelly, Johnstown, PA

Chinese New Year

Materials

chopsticks or paper and rubber bands
rice
rice cooker
soy sauce
small bowls

What to do

1. Make chopsticks out of rolled paper and rubber bands or use real chopsticks (donated from Japanese or Chinese restaurants).
2. Make rice with the children. Encourage the children to feel the rice before it is cooked.
3. Cook the rice in a rice cooker. When the rice is done, let the children scoop rice into their bowls.

4. If desired, the children can add soy sauce or eat the rice plain.
5. Encourage the children to try to eat with chopsticks.

Related books *Cleversticks* by Bernard Ashley
The Dancing Dragon by Marcia Vaughan

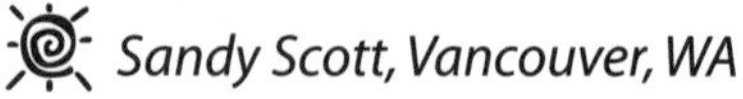

Sandy Scott, Vancouver, WA

Class Café

Materials

magazines
glue
paper
paper cups and plates
plastic cutlery
play cooking utensils
cash register (optional)
play money
play food
plastic tablecloth
pencils and paper
cookbooks
food donated from parents (such as pretzels, juice, crackers, and raisins)

What to do

1. Beforehand, make menus using magazine pictures and words.
2. Set up the house area like a café. Add menus, plates, cups, utensils, play food, and so on.
3. Let the children play "café" by taking orders, preparing play food, and serving it. The customers may use play money to purchase food.
4. At snack time, encourage the "waiters/waitresses" to take orders from the "customers." Make sure that the servers wash their hands before putting the food on plates and pouring juice. Let them switch roles so the waiters and waitresses eat, too.

Related books *Bread and Jam for Frances* by Russell Hoban
If You Give a Mouse a Cookie by Laura Joffe Numeroff
Pete's a Pizza by William Steig
There Was an Old Lady Who Swallowed a Fly by Simms Taback

Barbara Saul, Eureka CA

Drive-Through Window

Materials

large refrigerator box
craft knife (adult only)
low table
black construction paper
masking tape
yellow chalk
house area equipment
headphones
two scooters
cash register
play food

What to do

1. Set up part of the house or dramatic play area with a "window." Do this by cutting out a window from a large box and placing it on a low table near the edge of the area.
2. Tape black construction paper on the floor in front of the "window" to simulate the road. Draw yellow dashed lines on the black construction paper.
3. Place two scooters on black construction paper for cars.
4. Put headphones and a cash register by the window to take orders.
5. Children can use play food from "to go" orders.

Andrea Hungerford, Plainville, CT

Spider Menus

Materials

stories about bugs, spiders, and grasshoppers
chart paper
markers
large cardboard paper with spider stickers and menu written on it
spider stickers
Styrofoam balls one for each child
black paint
black pipe cleaners
wiggle eyes

What to do

1. Read a story about spiders with the children.
2. Encourage the children to help create a "spider menu" to use in restaurant play. Ask them what a spider would want to eat if he could go to a restaurant. List their responses on a large sheet of paper.
3. Cut cardboard or sturdy paper into 6" x 9" rectangles. Give one to each child to make his own spider menu. Encourage them to copy some of the items from the chart paper and decorate with spider stickers.
4. Make Styrofoam spiders with the children. Give each child a Styrofoam ball to paint black. Provide black pipe cleaners for legs and wiggle eyes.
5. The spiders can "read" the menus!

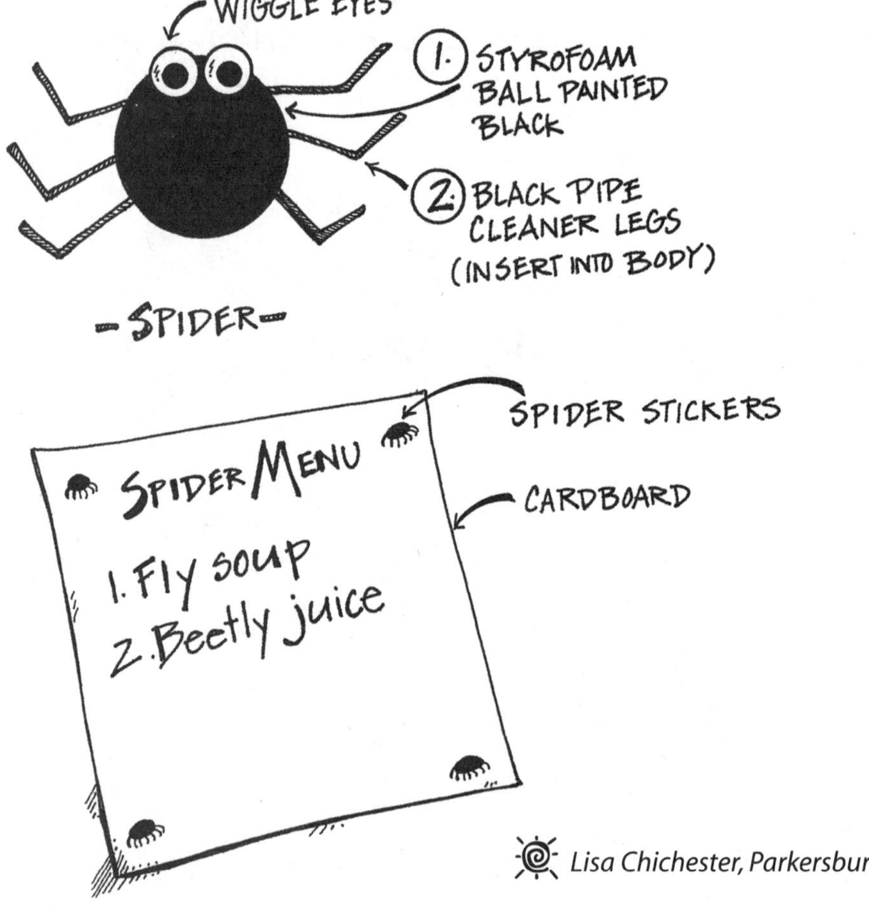

Lisa Chichester, Parkersburg, WV

Making Menus

Materials

food magazines and grocery store inserts
scissors
cardboard or oak tag
glue
pens and pencils
number stickers or price stickers (if available)

What to do

1. Encourage the children to cut out pictures of foods from magazines or inserts.
2. When they have cut out a few pictures, they can glue them to one side of a piece of oak tag or cardboard.
3. Encourage them to write the name of the food and the price next to each picture (help them as needed). Children can use number or price stickers, if desired.
4. Children can use their menus in restaurant dramatic play.

Related books

Chicken Soup With Rice by Maurice Sendak
Don't Forget the Bacon by Pat Hutchins
Pancakes for Breakfast by Tomie DePaola

 *Shirley Salach, Northwood, NH*

May I Take Your Order, Please?

Materials

picture menus (some restaurants have free picture menus)
grocery store inserts
laminating machine
scissors
glue
construction paper

What to do

1. If possible, get free picture menus from a few restaurants and laminate them. Keep a few intact, and cut apart the other laminated menus to get individual pictures of the various food products.

2. If you don't have picture menus, make your own. Simply cut out pictures of various food products from your local grocery store inserts and advertisements. Glue the pictures onto construction paper to make your menus. Make sure to cut out several pictures of the same food products, so that some are on the menu and some are not.

Tip: Ask parents to donate grocery store inserts from their newspapers. This way you will have multiple copies of the same food products.

3. Encourage the children to take turns playing the role of waiter or waitress while the rest of the children play the part of customers.
4. Customers place orders by pointing to food product on the menu. The waiter or waitress tries to remember what the customer orders, goes back into the "kitchen," and picks up the matching food product pictures.
5. The waiter or waitress delivers the food pictures to the customer. If the order is correct, the children switch roles. This continues until each child has had a chance to be a waiter or waitress.
6. This is a great way to help children improve their memory skills.

Related books

Big Jimmy's Kum Kau Chinese Take Out by Ted Lewin
Breakfast at Danny's Diner by Judith Bauer Stamper
Brown Foods by Patricia Whitehouse
Green Foods by Patricia Whitehouse
How Are You Peeling? Foods With Moods by Saxton Freymann
The Moon and Riddles Diner and the Sunnyside Cafe by Nancy Willard
My Favorite Foods by Dana Meachen Rau
Night of the Moonjellies by Mark Shasha
Orange Foods by Patricia Whitehouse
Red Foods by Patricia Whitehouse
Sorting Foods by Patricia Whitehouse
White Foods by Patricia Whitehouse
Yellow Foods by Patricia Whitehouse

Mike Krestar, Latrobe, PA

May I Take Your Order?

Materials

pictures of waitresses and waiters
aprons
small notepads
pens and pencils
small table and chairs

napkins
poster board
markers and crayons
paper

What to do

1. Talk with the children about waiters and waitresses and what they do in restaurants. If possible, show them pictures. Place aprons, mini notepads, and a table set with a vase, napkins, and chairs in the house center. Encourage the children to play "restaurant" as desired.
2. Make a menu of all the children's favorite foods. Ask the children to dictate foods to put on the menu for the class restaurant. Write them on a piece of poster board. Ask the children to think of what they might like to name the class restaurant. Take a vote, and write the winning name at the top of the menu. Encourage the children to illustrate the foods, if desired.
3. Ask the children to draw a picture of themselves and their family eating at their favorite restaurant.
4. Have a "class restaurant day!" Send home invitations asking parents to come to the class restaurant on a specific day. Also ask them to send in one of their child's favorite foods (from the class menu) on the big day. Copy the menu onto smaller sheets of paper for parents to order from. Encourage the children to "wait" on their parents!

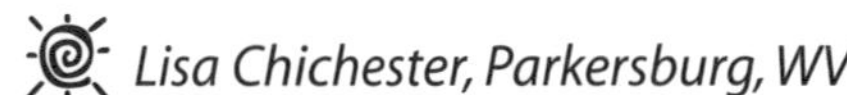
Lisa Chichester, Parkersburg, WV

Restaurant Menu Development

Materials

paper
pencils

What to do

1. When doing a restaurant theme, bring a group of children together. Talk about what happens when they go out to eat at a restaurant. Steer the children's conversation toward menus.
2. Talk about the classroom restaurant (in dramatic play area). Ask them if they should make a menu.
3. Help the children make menus and add them to the area. Let them illustrate the foods and add prices.

Ann Kelly Johnstown, PA

Please Wait to Be Seated

Materials

chart paper
markers
three small round tables
nine chairs
three small round tablecloths
real silverware (one fork and one spoon at each place setting)
paper or cloth napkins, paper plates, and paper or plastic cups
cash register
pretend money
cardstock paper
three clipboards and three pencils
child-sized aprons

What to do

1. Create a real restaurant in your own classroom!
2. Ask the children to talk about places they have eaten at. Ask specific questions such as, "Did you sit down and have a waiter take your order?" and "Did you go to a salad bar to get your food?"
3. Ask the children which type of restaurant they liked best. Keep track of their answers on a chart. Explain that they will be making their own in the classroom.
4. Decide what kind of food to serve at the restaurant. Since you will actually be serving real food, steer the children in the direction of something that can be prepared in your classroom. For example, they could make pizza and salad for a pizza restaurant.
5. Choose items to feature on the menu, keeping the choices down to one or two items.
6. Have the children use cardstock paper and markers to create menus. Make at least one menu for each table. If time permits, make one menu for each seat.
7. Choose a name for the restaurant and make a sign to post on the door.
8. Choose spot to set up the restaurant. Place the small round tables and chairs in the area. Put a tablecloth and a vase with plastic flowers on each table.
9. Ask the children to set each place with a plate, spoon, fork, and cup.
10. Place the small rectangular table with a cash register on it at the entrance. Put pretend money in the cash register. Place the menus on the table.
11. Ask the children to use cardstock paper and markers to make invitations asking their parents to visit their new restaurant. Since you will actually be cooking or preparing food, choose a special day for the restaurant to be open.
12. On the day the restaurant will open, spend the morning cooking whatever type of food the children chose. Make something to drink, too!
13. As people begin to arrive at the restaurant, let the children take turns seating them. Make sure the children give each patron a menu.

14. The children can don the aprons and pretend to be wait staff. They can use clipboards and pencils to "write down" what the patrons want.
15. As orders arrive, ladle out the food and help the children take it to the tables.
16. Provide each patron with pretend money so they can pay for their meal as they leave. Encourage the children to take turns working at the cash register.
17. As the patrons are done eating, have the children take turns clearing the tables. Put out a basin or tub to place the dirty dishes and throw away all disposable items immediately so they will not be accidentally used again.
18. Continue serving the patrons as they arrive until it is time to close your restaurant for the day!

Related books *D.W. the Picky Eater* by Marc Brown
Dinner at the Panda Palace by Stephanie Calmenson
The Edible Pyramid: Good Eating Every Day by Loreen Leedy
How My Parents Learned to Eat by Ina R. Freidman
The Paper Crane by Molly Bang
Pigs Will Be Pigs by Amy Axelrod
Rabbit Pirates: A Tale of the Spinach Man by Judy Cox
Sheep Out to Eat by Nancy Shaw
Spaghetti and Meatballs for All: A Mathematical Story by Marilyn Burns

Virginia Jean Herrod, Columbia, SC

Restaurant

Materials

menus
small tables and chairs
trays
cash register
play money
pads of paper
pencils
pretend kitchen area
pretend food
plates and utensils
posters of food
basket of books about food and nutrition

What to do

1. Set up your area to resemble a restaurant. Add the materials from the above list.
2. Introduce the children to words such as "menu," "order," "cook," "waitress," "waiter," and "tips."
3. Sit in the "restaurant" and let the children serve you. Take turns and wait on them as well.

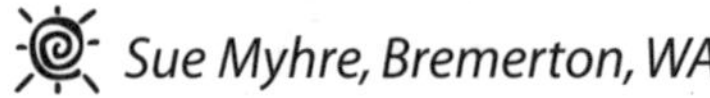
Sue Myhre, Bremerton, WA

Table Setting

Materials

table and chairs
four place settings

What to do

1. Bring four place settings to a small group of children. Place the items in front of the children, making sure the materials are mixed up and not grouped.
2. Use the materials for sorting activities. Encourage the children to sort the place setting by plates, forks, utensils, and so on.
3. Use the materials for one-to-correspondence activities. Ask the children to make complete place settings. Don't tell them what is missing; instead, help them solve the problem themselves.

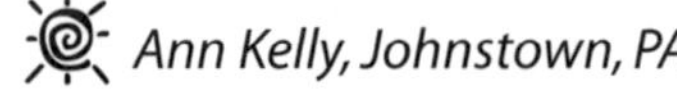
Ann Kelly, Johnstown, PA

African Safari

Materials pictures of safari animals

What to do

1. Talk about safaris. Explain that many different animals live in eastern and southern Africa, and that people visit these areas to see the animals.
2. Show the children pictures of animals typically found in Africa, such as a lion, zebra, elephant, gazelle, rhinoceros, hippopotamus, baboon, cheetah, leopard, crane, vulture, and hyena.
3. Encourage the children to sort the pictures in a variety of ways. For example, the children might sort the pictures into groups of large animals and small animals, striped/spotted animals and solid colored animals, land animals (lion) and water animals (hippo).

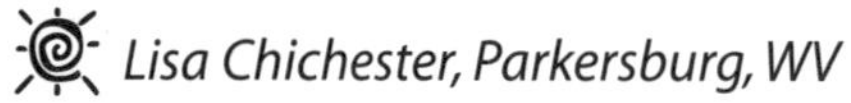
Lisa Chichester, Parkersburg, WV

Bird Watching

Materials

two empty toilet paper rolls per child
masking tape
string or yarn
hole punch
scissors
markers
pictures of birds and animals

What to do

1. Give each child two empty toilet paper rolls. Help them tape the paper rolls together.
2. Punch one hole in each of the toilet paper rolls, on the outside at one end. Help the children string the yarn through the holes and knot the ends to make a strap for the binoculars.
3. Encourage the children to decorate their binoculars with markers and stickers.
4. Hang bird and other animal pictures around the room for the children to look at with their binoculars.

5. Make a picture chart for each child with all of the bird and animal pictures. Each time a child sees the animal or bird, she puts a check next to it. Children can try to find all animals on the sheet.
6. Put the children into pairs to do some cooperative "bird watching" and work on social skills.

Sandra Nagel, White Lake, MI

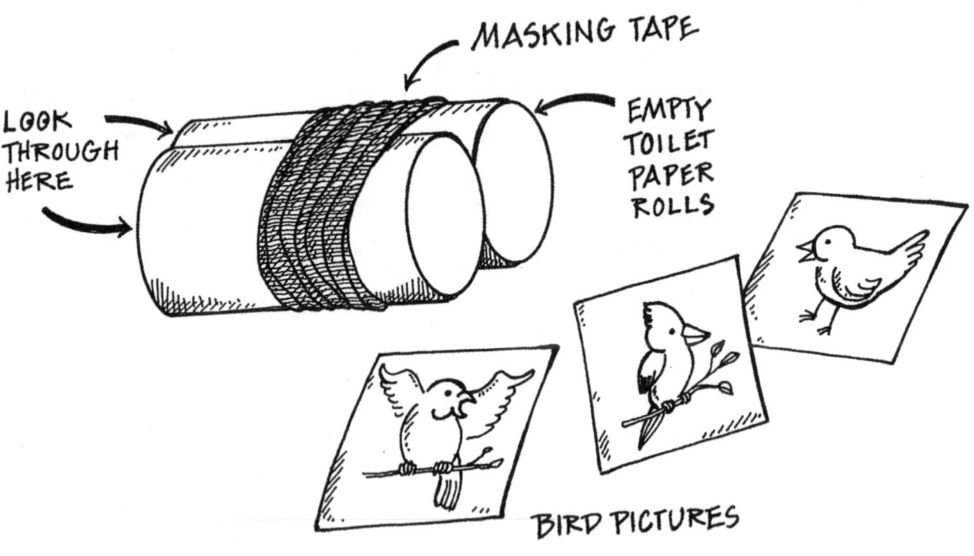

Dandy Desert

Materials

cardboard or tagboard
scissors
book about the desert and desert animals
paper
green fingerpaint
sand
brown or black clay

What to do

1. To prepare, make a cactus pattern on cardboard or tagboard and cut it out.
2. Read a story about the desert and its animal and plant life.
3. Let the children trace the cactus pattern onto paper and cut it out. Have them fingerpaint the cactus green and then sprinkle sand over it while it is wet.
4. Talk about rattlesnakes and how they live in the desert. Encourage the children to use brown or black clay to make their own rattlesnakes.

Lisa Chichester, Parkersburg, WV

Here Sits a Monkey

Materials

animal pictures (including a monkey)
scissors
tagboard or poster board
glue stick
laminate
hole punch
yarn
chair

What to do

1. Collect pictures of various animals from books, magazines, or the Internet. Be sure to include a monkey. Cut out enough so that each child gets one.
2. Glue the pictures to poster board or tagboard sized for the picture. Laminate for durability and cut out. Punch two holes in the top of each picture.
3. Insert yarn through the holes and tie the ends together to make a necklace.
4. Ask the children to choose necklaces to wear. Whoever chooses the monkey necklace sits in a chair in the middle of the circle. The rest of the children form a circle around "the monkey" and march or skip around it, singing the following American folk song.

Here Sits a Monkey
Oh, here sits a monkey in the chair, chair, chair,
She lost all the true loves she had last year,
So rise upon your feet and greet the first you meet,
The happiest one I know.

5. At the proper time, the monkey rises and chooses a child from the circle to take her place. The game is repeated and the name of the new animal is used in the song in place of "monkey."
6. Encourage the child in the chair to choose a child who hasn't been chosen yet so that everyone gets a turn.

Related song "Here Sits a Monkey" by Raffi, the Singable Songs Collection

Jackie Wright, Enid, OK

On Safari

Materials

book about safari animals
plastic sunglasses (one pair for each child)
black paint
paintbrushes
black and white feathers
glue
large blanket
stuffed safari animals

What to do

1. Read and discuss a book about safari animals.
2. Give each child a pair of plastic sunglasses (preferably white). Put newspaper and black paint on the worktable. Show the children how to paint black "zebra" stripes on the glasses. When the paint is dry, the children can glue black and white feathers on the top of the frames.
3. Go on a pretend safari trip. Spread a big blanket on the floor (if possible, find one with leopard or zebra stripes). Ask the children to sit on the blanket. Put a few large stuffed safari animals (zebra, lion, leopard, and giraffe) near the blanket.
4. As the children sit on the blanket, narrate a story about a safari.

Safari Exploration Center

Materials

brown and green bulletin board paper
variety of stuffed jungle animals
plastic bugs
large appliance box
craft knife (adult only)
chairs
steering wheel
cassette player and rainforest sounds tape
safari hats
binoculars
magnifying glasses
bug containers with tweezers
real or pretend cameras

What to do

1. If possible, set up this center next to a large window.
2. Twist brown bulletin board paper to resemble vines, and cut out large leaves from green bulletin board paper. Attach the vines and leaves to the ceiling and walls.
3. Put stuffed animals and plastic bugs around the "jungle" and hang some from the ceiling. If desired, place some of the bugs in the bushes outside the window.
4. Cut off one side of a large box and cut doors in two sides to make a safari "jeep." Place chairs and a steering wheel inside of the jeep.
5. Turn on a tape or CD of "rainforest sounds."
6. Encourage the children to put on safari hats and become explorers in the center. They can use binoculars or magnifying glasses to look at the "jungle creatures." Children can "capture" some bugs and put them in bug containers to examine them more closely.
7. If desired, provide a camera (or pretend camera) for children to photograph the jungle.
8. Sit back and watch and listen to their imaginations unfolding as they explore their safari center.

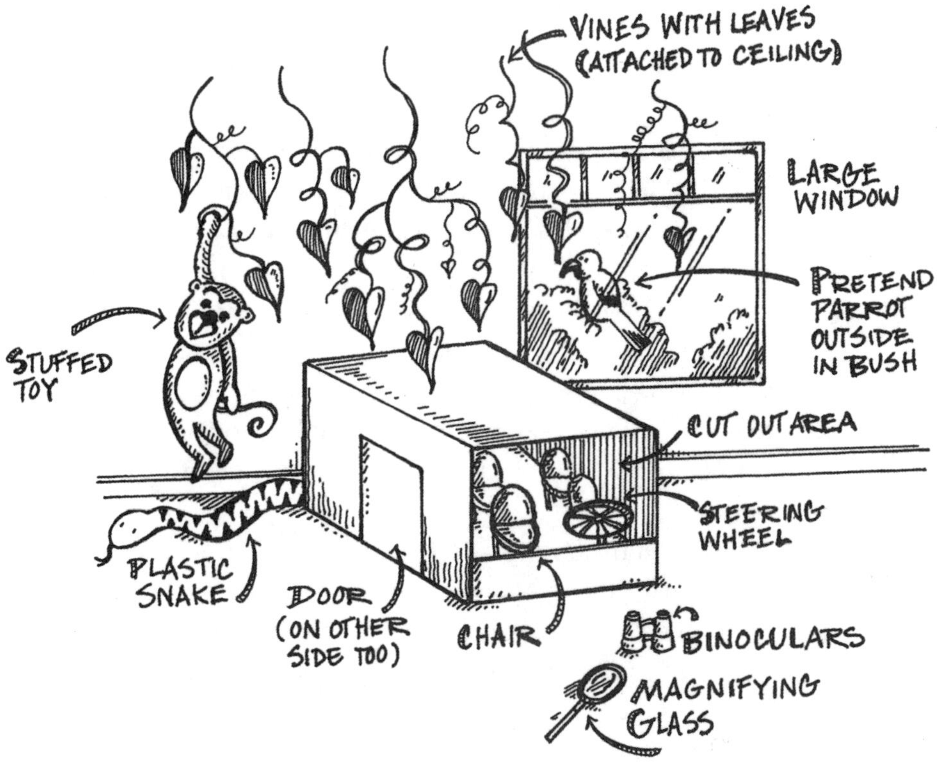

 *Wanda Guidroz, Santa Fe, TX*

There's a Rumble in the Jungle

Materials

Rumble in the Jungle by Giles Andreae and David Wojtowycz
cardstock paper
scissors
markers, crayons, and paint
felt pieces
yarn
glue
elastic bands
large cardboard boxes

What to do

1. Read the book *Rumble in the Jungle* to the children several times over a period of a week or more. The children will become more familiar with the story each time you read it, and they will start repeating parts as you read. Ask the children if they would like to pretend to be the animals in the book.
2. Using cardstock paper, cut out several simple masks representing the animals in the book. There are quite a few animals, so this step may take a few days. Let the children decorate the masks using felt, yarn, paint, markers, and so on.
3. Attach elastic bands to both sides of each mask and fit to the child's head.
4. Let the children use the masks freely for a few days. Continue to read the book each day. Explain to the children that they are going to act out the book.
5. Open and flatten the large cardboard boxes. Encourage the children to draw and paint a jungle background on the boxes. Instead of cardboard, you could also use large pieces of craft paper.
6. When everything is ready, gather the children together. Assign roles by giving each child an animal mask. Have everyone sit together facing the scenery.
7. Begin to read the book. As each animal is mentioned, encourage the children to go up in front of the scenery and pretend to be that animal. There are no lines for the children to repeat. They simply pretend to be the animal they represent. For example, they can stomp like a gorilla and beat their chests, or slither on the ground like a snake.
8. Continue reading until the story is done.

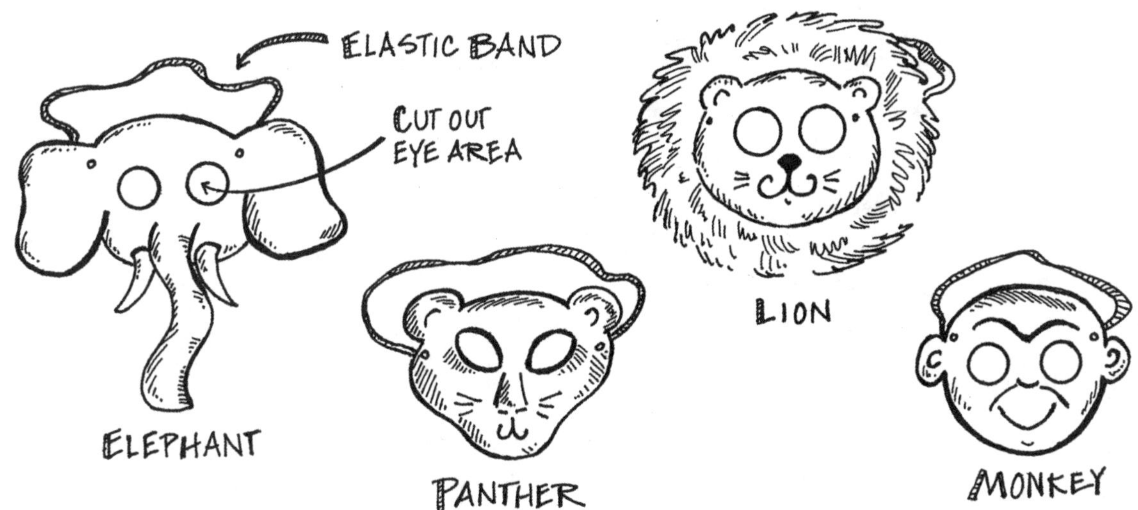

More to do **Dramatic Play:** Bring in a video camera and make a *Rumble in the Jungle* movie. Record the children as they act out the book.

Related books *The Bird, the Monkey, and the Snake in the Jungle* by Kate Banks
Deep in the Jungle by Dan Yaccarino

Virginia Jean Herrod, Columbia, SC

We're Going on Safari

Materials
The Wiggles: Wiggly Safari by Lauren Turnowski (ed.)
large sheet of paper
marker

What to do

1. Read the book *The Wiggles: Wiggly Safari* to the children.
2. As you read the book make a list of the different locations covered (desert, swamp, and so on).
3. Ask the children to recall what animals were found in each location and write the correct animals next to each location.
4. Assist the children in writing a chant similar to "Going on a Bear Hunt" where they go through the different safari locations and run into the animals. The children can create the hand movements and the ending to the chant.
5. As you repeat the chant throughout the safari theme, ask different children to create different endings to the chant.

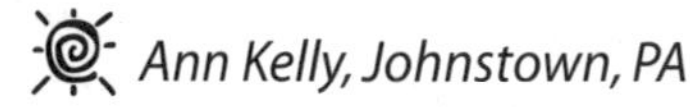
Ann Kelly, Johnstown, PA

Wild About Reading

Materials

markers
tagboard or cardstock paper
scissors or die-cut machine
laminate
pocket chart

What to do

1. On a piece of 8 ½" x 11" tagboard or cardstock, write "Wild About Reading" at the top and print the directions: "Place the cards with words you can read on the word wall."
2. Cut out elephants on a die-cut machine. Print sight words on each elephant. Mount each elephant on tagboard, laminate, and cut out.
3. Hang the pocket chart at children's eye level. Seat the children in a circle near the pocket chart. Insert the title/directions card in the top pocket of the pocket chart.
4. Place one elephant at a time in the pocket chart. Ask for volunteers to read the words. This fun center gives children an opportunity to learn many new words.

Jackie Wright, Enid, OK

Yoga Safari

Materials

non-skid surface for barefoot play

What to do

1. Children will discover their wild side as they go on a "yoga safari" mimicking animals and objects of nature.
2. Make sure the children are barefoot when practicing any type of yoga, especially active poses such as animals. Also make sure the children have plenty of room to spread out and move.
3. Tell the children that before they get "wild," they must first get to their destination. Start by having all the children sit on the floor with their legs straight out in front of them. Ask them to pretend to hold a steering wheel and "**drive** into the jungle."
4. After "arriving," start walking in place. Along the way, demonstrate movements and sounds of animals through yoga poses. Tell a story and stop

to do the poses. For example, "**Look up** in the trees and watch an **eagle** fly over your heads, looking strong and powerful." Encourage the children to copy your yoga poses.

5. Continue the story and poses: "We can hear the thunderous feet of the mighty **elephants** as they cross the caravan. Let's pitch our **tent** before we go any further. Can you hear the roar of the most feared animal—the **tiger**—sitting upon a large rock, stretching in the sun? Beyond the field, the fierce **lions** roar to protect their cubs from our caravan. Let's return to our tents for the night. Oh, I hear the hiss of the dangerous **cobra**. Let's crawl inside our tents and lay as still as a **mouse**."
6. More poses can be added depending on time restraints. This activity can be repeated many times by changing the animals and substituting different yoga poses.

Sherry Harper, Coventry, RI

Water Table

Materials

plastic eggs
plastic grass
plastic letters of the alphabet
alphabet sheet

What to do

1. Beforehand, put a plastic letter inside each plastic egg.
2. Add plastic grass and the letter-filled plastic eggs to the sand and water table.
3. Encourage the children to hunt for eggs!
4. When a child finds an egg, have him open it up and remove the letter inside. He then crosses off letter on an alphabet sheet.

D'Arcy Simmons, Springfield, MO

Create Sand

Materials

rocks
water
dishpan
coffee can
large sheet of paper
magnifying glasses

What to do

1. Ask the children to wash the rocks in a dishpan of water.
2. Let the rocks dry and place them in a clean coffee can. Put the plastic lid on the coffee can.
3. Bring the coffee can outdoors and ask the children to kick it around.
4. After the children kick and move the can for a while, bring it back inside and place it on a large sheet of white paper. Ask the children to sit around the paper.
5. Remove the large rocks first. Then, carefully empty the contents of the can onto the paper.
6. The contents of the can will now consist of small grains of sand. Ask the children where the sand came from. The children will discover that they made sand!
7. Give the children magnifying glasses to observe the grains.

Sandy Scott, Vancouver, WA

Dinosaur Dig

Materials

sand table
sand
cotton swabs

What to do

1. Bury a lot of cotton swabs in the sand.
2. Ask younger children to dig in the sand to recover as many cotton swabs ("dinosaur bones") as they can.
3. Record the number of cotton swabs each child finds on a daily chart.
4. Younger children really enjoy doing this daily especially because they like to find more "bones" than the day before. Children can also re-bury the cotton swabs themselves and dig over and over again.

 *Andrea Hungerford, Plainville, CT*

H2OH!

Materials

water table
several 16- or 20-ounce soda bottles
several 2-liter soda bottles
water
a glass eyedropper
food coloring
small objects such as dice, coins, or toothpicks
1"-diameter vinyl pipe
duct tape

What to do

Make the following three exploration bottles and keep them in the water table for exploration.

Color Bottles

1. Fill several 16 ounce bottles about ⅔ full with clear water. Slowly add a few drops of food coloring to the water.
2. Encourage the children to notice how the color mixes with the water. After a minute, cap the bottle and seal it with duct tape. Let the children shake the bottle until the color is completely mixed with the water. Put the color bottles in an accessible area.
3. Encourage the children to explore the bottles. Point out how the water moves when they shake the bottle. Ask them to notice the air bubbles. Ask questions such as, "How can you make a lot of bubbles in the bottle?"

Sink-and-Float Bottles

1. Fill a 2-liter bottle to the top with clear water.
2. Place a glass eyedropper in the bottle, making sure the bulb is up.
3. Tightly screw the top on the bottle. Wrap the cap with duct tape for additional waterproofing.
4. The eyedroppers should float at the top of the bottle.
5. Encourage the children to squeeze the sides of the bottle and observe what happens to the eyedropper. Ask questions such as, "What happens to the eyedropper when you squeeze the sides of the bottle?"
6. Put the sink-and-float bottle in an accessible area and let the children explore it freely.

Double Bottles

1. Fill one 2-liter bottle with clear or colored water. Drop a small object such as a coin, toothpick, or die into another 2-liter bottle.
2. Connect the two bottles by screwing the tops (with no lids) into the ends of a piece of vinyl pipe. Duct tape the ends for additional waterproofing.
3. Encourage the children to turn the bottles so the full bottle is on top and observe the action of the water as it flows from one bottle to the other.
4. Use a stopwatch to time how long it takes for the water to transfer from the full bottle to the empty one.
5. Observe and comment on the action of the object in the bottle. Ask questions such as, "How can you make the water flow faster/slower?"
6. Put the bottle in an accessible area and let the children experiment.

More to do

Outdoors: Go outdoors on a snowy day. Collect snow in three different size containers. Bring them indoors and place them in different areas of the room. Watch what happens.

Science and Nature: Put a pie pan on a table and draw a water line on the inside of the pan. Pour water into the pan up to the water line. Place the pan on a sunny shelf. Encourage the children to check the water level frequently. Ask questions such as, "What do you think is happening to the water in the pan?" Talk about *evaporation*.

Related books

Cocoa Ice by Diana Appelbaum
The Magic School Bus at the Waterworks by Joanna Cole
Sun Dance Water Dance by Jonathan London
Water Dance by Thomas Locker

 *Virginia Jean Herrod, Colmbia, SC*

Pepper Chase

Materials

pie pan
water
pepper shaker
bar of soap

What to do

1. Fill the pie pan with two inches of water.
2. Let the children shake pepper into the water.
3. Ask the children to dip a bar of soap into the pepper water and watch what happens. The pepper moves away from the soap. Ask the children why they think this happens.

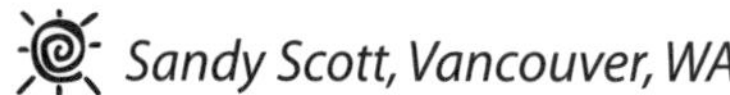
Sandy Scott, Vancouver, WA

Pond Building

Materials

children's books about ponds
sand and water table
water
large, shallow plastic bin
sand
watering cans or a hose
shovels
small sheets of plastic cut from garbage bags
small rocks or clean gravel

What to do

1. Read a few books about ponds and show pictures, if available. Have a discussion about ponds.
2. Fill the water table with water and place a large, low plastic bin filled with sand next to the water table.
3. Encourage the children to use water cans, shovels, and small sheets of plastic to create their own ponds. Show them how to dig a hole, line it with plastic, cover with gravel, and add water.
4. Help the children problem-solve if their pond leaks.

Related book *At the Pond* by David Schwartz

Ann Kelly, Johnstown, PA

Water Table Counting

Materials

permanent marker
bleached foam egg carton, or egg tray
ping-pong balls or other small floating objects (plastic toys or corks)
water table or a similar container to hold water
water
small fishing nets

What to do

1. Using a permanent marker, number the sections of the egg carton. Depending on the concept on which you are focusing or on the children's abilities, number the sections from 0–11 or 1–12, or number them by twos (2, 4, 6, and so on), fives, or tens.
2. Write numbers on the ping-pong balls or floating objects to match the numbers in the egg sections.
3. Fill the water table or container with water, and place the balls or floating objects in the water.
4. Encourage the children to "fish" for the objects and place them in the appropriate egg carton sections.
5. This activity can be easily adapted to practice letters, names, shapes, and so on.

More to do

Books: Use books and songs to support this activity. For example, if you use floating items such as fish, read the book *Swimmy* by Leo Lionni.

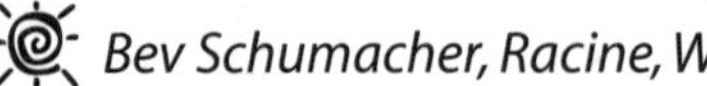

Oviparous Animals

Materials

pictures of animals that hatch from eggs
markers
scissors
oak tag or poster board
glue stick
laminate
felt
rubber cement
flannel board

What to do

1. Cut out pictures of animals that hatch from eggs (*oviparous* animals) from magazines or old workbooks. Oviparous animals include alligators, caterpillars, chickens, dinosaurs, fish, frogs, snakes, and turtles.
2. Label the name of each animal on the front of the picture.
3. Glue the pictures to oak tag or poster board using a glue stick. Laminate the pictures for durability, and cut out.
4. Use rubber cement to attach felt to the back of the pictures for flannel board use.
5. Explain to the children that oviparous animals are animals that produce eggs that hatch after they are laid. Ask the children to name some examples. As each is named, place the picture of the animal on the flannel board.
6. Put the pictures and flannel board in the science center for children to revisit during free choice time.

Related book *Chickens Aren't the Only Ones* by Ruth Heller

Seasonal Sort

Materials

poster board
markers
cutouts of different articles of clothing for all seasons

What to do

1. Use a marker to divide a piece of poster board into four equal sections. Write the name of a season in each square and draw or glue an item that is representative of the season (such as a snowman for winter, flowers for spring, beach ball for summer, and pumpkin for fall).
2. Ask the children to sort the cutouts of clothing by the seasons in which they are worn. For example, mittens are worn in the winter.
3. If desired, use doll clothes for this activity as well.

Vicki Whitehead, Satsuma, AL

Hibernating Bears

Materials

light blue construction paper
body pouf
white tempera paint
manila paper
scissors
tape
stamps of large bear and baby bear
brown stamp pad
large tables
sheets

What to do

1. Give each child a piece of light blue construction paper. Ask them to dip a body pouf into white paint and print "snow" all over their paper.
2. When the paint is dry, cut a semicircle in the bottom center of the page to resemble the mouth of a cave, creating a flap (don't cut the semicircle all the way to the other side).
3. Cut manila paper into 5" x 7" rectangles. Help the children tape the manila paper behind the flap, on the back of the paper.
4. While holding the flap open, ask the children to use the stamp pad and the bear stamps to put bears inside the cave.
5. When the flap is closed, the bears are "hibernating." The children can lift the flap to peek at them.
6. When the children are finished, sit in a circle and talk about why bears sleep in caves in the winter.
7. If you have large tables in your room, cover them with sheets to make caves and have the children crawl inside to "sleep." When you announce that spring has arrived, the "bears" wake up and all come out of their caves!

Related books *Copy Me, Copycub* by Richard Edwards
Time to Sleep by Denise Fleming

Diane Weiss, Fairfax VA

Earth Day Learning Center

Materials

large white paper
scissors
easel
green and blue tempera paint
rocks (one for each child)
paintbrushes
newspaper

What to do

1. Explain to the children that Earth Day is a day to celebrate our earth. You can do this activity any day of the year when you want to celebrate the earth.
2. Pre-cut a huge circle from white paper and place it on an easel. Encourage the children to work cooperatively to paint the "earth" green and blue. Show them a globe as an inspiration.
3. Go outside and let each child collect a rock. Make baby earth rocks! Place the rocks on newspaper and encourage the children to paint their rocks blue. Then they can add green spots (land).
4. Talk about how wonderful the earth is and the ways we can help keep it nice.

Lisa Chichester, Parkersburg, WV

Magnetic Personalities

Materials

photocopy of each child's face
colored construction paper
scissors
magnet strips
glue

What to do

1. Make photocopies of each child's photograph. Give each child a photocopy of her face.
2. Ask the children to cut out their faces and glue them to construction paper.
3. Glue a magnet strip on the back of each picture.
4. Talk to the children about magnets. Ask them how magnets work. Encourage them to try and stick their pictures on different surfaces to see if they stick.

Related book *The Biggest Boy* by Kevin Henkes

Barbara Saul, Eureka, CA

Anatomy Art

Materials

large roll of butcher paper
pencil
scissors
red construction paper
textured paper (such as cardboard or felt)
tissue paper
yarn
packing pieces (biodegradable)
scissors
glue
markers

What to do

1. Ask the children to lie down on butcher paper. Trace each child's body on a piece of large butcher paper.
2. Provide the following materials to represent internal body parts:
   - **Heart**: Cut a heart shape from red construction paper.
   - **Lungs**: Use textured paper and cut into two oval "lung" shapes.
   - **Stomach**: Crumple tissue paper (any color).
   - **Intestines**: Use yarn.
   - **Bones**: Use packing pieces.

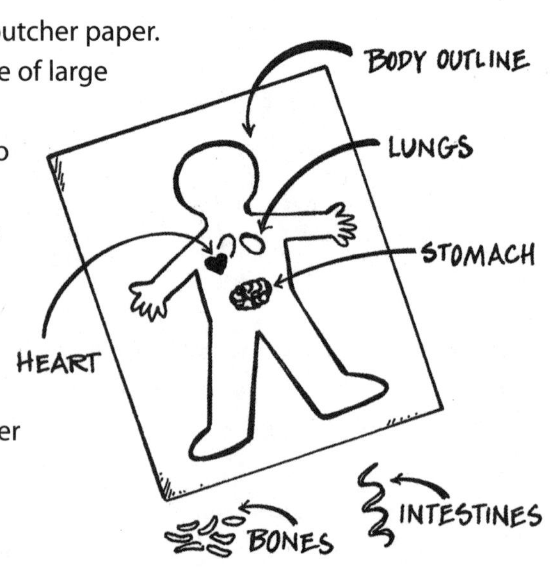

3. Show the children a picture of a body with internal organs. Encourage them to glue the different internal body parts on their tracing.
4. Help them label each inside body part.
5. Encourage the children to decorate other features such as hair, eyes, nose, mouth, and feet with markers.
6. Use your imagination and add other materials to represent the various internal organs.

Andrea Hungerford, Plainville, CT

Bird Feeders

Materials

newspapers
peanut butter or lard
vegetable oil
pinecones
string or yarn
wild birdseed mix
two bowls
plastic knives or craft sticks
large spoons
small plastic bags

What to do

1. Cover the working area with newspaper.
2. Mix peanut butter or lard with a little vegetable oil to make it easier to spread.
3. Tie a string onto each pinecone. Place the birdseed in a bowl.
4. Give each child a pinecone. Ask her to spread the peanut butter and oil mixture all over the pinecone, and then place the pinecone in the bowl with the birdseed. She can use a small spoon to scoop more seeds onto the sticky parts of the pinecone.
5. Place each finished pinecone in a plastic bag with the string sticking out of the bag. This lets children carry it home with minimal mess.
6. Encourage the children to hang their bird feeders outside a window at home. The child can watch for the birds to come and eat. It may take a few days for the birds to discover the feeder.
7. While this sounds like a messy activity, it is actually an easy cleanup—just roll up the mess left behind in the newspapers.

8. Some home a note to parents about the activity. For example:

Dear families,
We made bird feeders today to help the birds during the cold winter months. Please carefully hang it on a branch outside so that the birds can find the seeds. If there is a place where your child can watch from a window, it would be ideal. Thank you for your help.

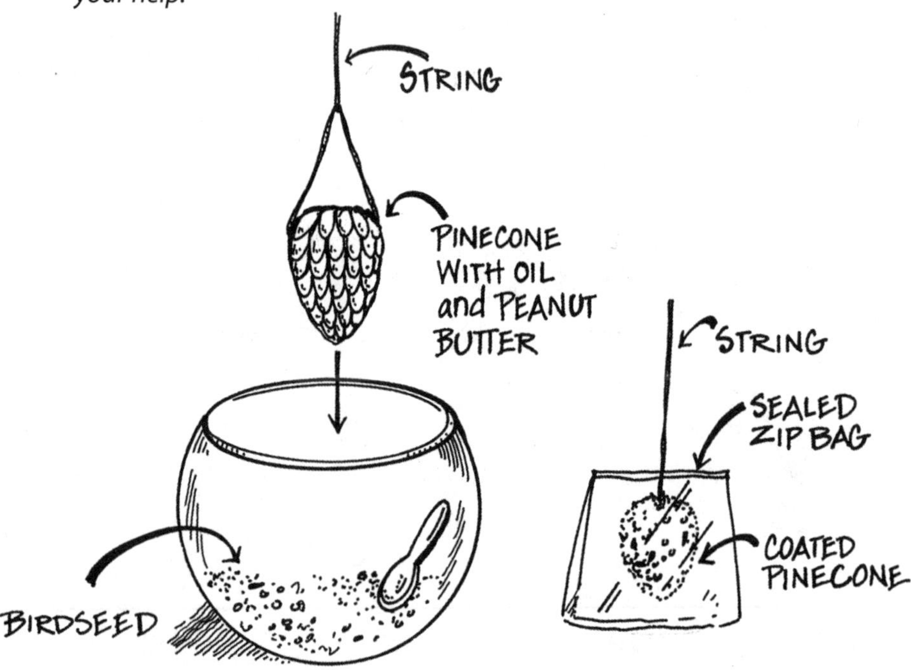

Sandra Nagel, White Lake, MI

Bird in Its Nest

Materials

tagboard
brown or black marker
scissors
tan, red, or blue construction paper
yellow paper
light blue 9" x 12" construction paper
markers
white glue
shredded paper or plastic grass
wiggle eyes

What to do

1. Draw the wing and bird shape on tagboard (see illustration) and cut them out to make patterns.
2. Let each child choose a piece of red, tan, or blue paper to make her bird the desired color.
3. Help the children trace the bird and wing on construction paper and cut out.
4. Cut out a diamond shape from yellow paper for a beak. Fold in half and give one to each child.
5. Ask the children to turn the light blue paper the sideways. Encourage them to use a black marker to draw a branch across the 12" width of paper and draw green leaves on the branch.
6. They can use a marker to draw a yellow or orange sun.
7. Provide shredded paper or plastic grass for children to glue on the branch for a nest. Dab with brown watercolor paint.
8. Demonstrate how to glue the beak, wiggle eyes, and wing on the bird.
9. If desired, children may use a brown or black marker to add eyebrows, head lines, and feather lines on the tail and wing.
10. Glue the bird into the nest.

Related book *The Best Nest* by P.D. Eastman

Mary Brehm, Aurora, OH

Birdy Pick-Up Game

Materials
large tub
twigs, leaves, and grass clippings
yarn
feathers
spring-type clothespins

What to do
1. Fill a large tub with twigs, leaves, yarn, feathers, and grass.
2. Encourage the children to use clothespins to try to pick up the items in the tub.
3. The children can try to move the items from one area to the other or use them to build a bird's nest.

Related books
Birdsong by Audrey Wood
What Makes a Bird a Bird by May Garelick

Sandy Scott, Vancouver, WA

Bug House

Materials
eight small "Y"-shaped PVC joints
twelve equal lengths of straight PVC piping that fit the "Y" joints (not too long—the length you choose will determine the size of the bug house)
masking tape
mesh bag (large enough to go around the bug house)
yarn, string, or a rubber band

What to do
1. Let the children experiment with the mesh bag, the eight PVC joints, and the twelve straight pieces of PVC pipe. Explain that they will use these materials to make a "bug house" so they can observe a bug in the classroom.
2. Ask the children to arrange the pieces in a square box shape. Let the children do this themselves—it may take a while, but eventually they will figure it out. This step may take a few days.
3. After the children have arranged the pipes in a square shape, use masking tape to attach the pieces together.
4. Slide the mesh bag over the PVC pipe box.

5. Use yarn, string, or a rubber band to close and secure the opening of the bag. Whatever you use, remember you will have to open and close the top each time you put a bug in the box.
6. Keep the bug box handy, especially when outdoors. If the children find a bug they want to observe, let them put it in the box.
7. Keep the box in the science area. Encourage the children to observe the bug and note what is doing. If desired, have the children look up facts about the bugs they found.
8. After a day of discovery, return the bug to its own environment. The mesh bag can be removed and washed, if needed.

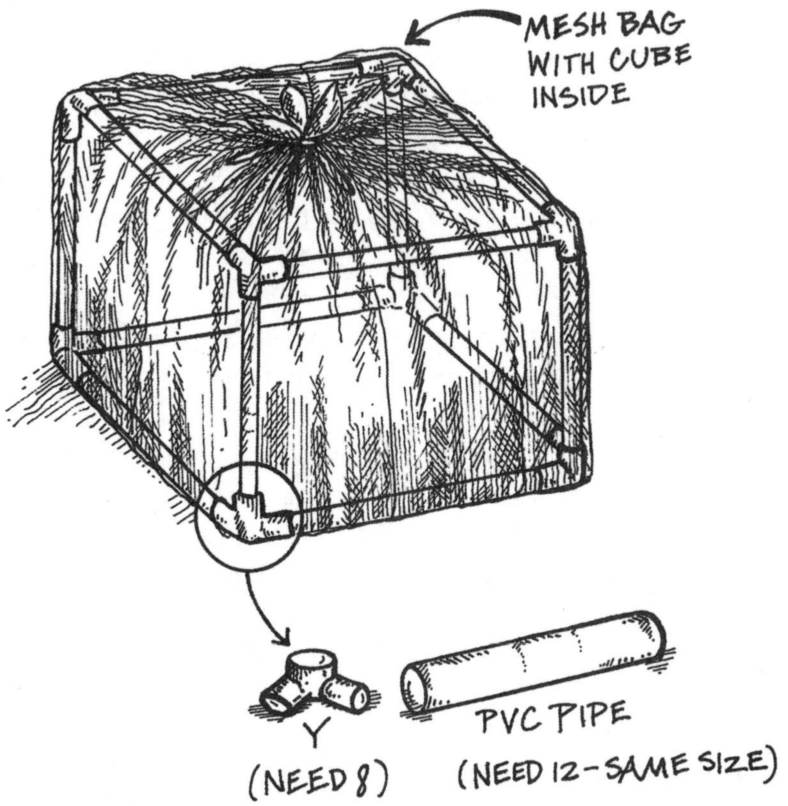

Related book *Bug Off!* by Cathi Hepworth

Virginia Jean Herrod, Columbia, SC

Bug Journal

Materials

spiral-bound notebook
pencils, pens, or markers
bug house (see "Bug House" on page xxx)
sentence strips
small container
camera (optional)

What to do

1. Place a spiral-bound notebook in the science area next to the bug house (see page 430). Explain to the children that they can use the notebook to draw pictures of the bugs in the bug house or write stories about them.
2. Ask the children to help create a notebook label that reads "Bug Journal."
3. Tell the children they can also use the bug journal to practice writing bug-related words, such as "bug," "insect," "grass," "wings," "legs," "eyes," and so on.
4. Print the bug-related words on sentence strips and put them in a small container in the science area. The children can refer to these when writing in the journal. Add a picture to each sentence strip to aid the children in reading the words.
5. When a child draws a picture of a bug, encourage her to write a story about it. Help the children write their stories in the journal.
6. If desired, use a digital or 35-mm camera to take photos of bugs in the bug house or in their natural environment. Add the photos to the journal and encourage the children to make up stories about them.
7. Take the bug journal outside so the children can record what they observe about bugs in nature.
8. Remember to always return bugs to their natural environment after a day of observing.

More to do

Art: Make "bug-eye" glasses. Cut child-sized eye masks from cardstock paper. Add an elastic band to fit each child's head. Give each child two chenille stems to create antennae. Add these to the glasses by punching a hole near the edge of each side and looping the chenille stem through the hole. Then let the children decorate their bug eyes as desired. Do not, however, let the children use glitter. This tends to fall off and might get in the children's eyes.

Related books

Breakout at the Bug Lab by Ruth Horowitz
Grasshopper on the Road by Arnold Lobel
Miss Spider's Tea Party by David Kirk
Roberto the Insect Architect by Nina Laden
Some Smug Slug by Pamela Duncan Edwards
The Very Busy Spider by Eric Carle

The Very Clumsy Click Beetle by Eric Carle
Wally the Wordworm by Clifton Fadiman
Why Mosquitoes Buzz in People's Ears by Verna Aardema

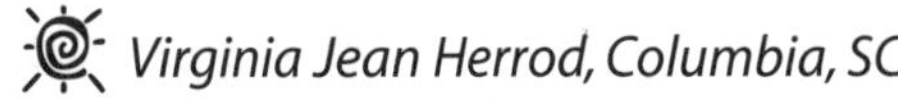

Virginia Jean Herrod, Columbia, SC

Caterpillar to Butterfly

Materials

The Very Hungry Caterpillar by Eric Carle
green pompoms
glue
wiggle eyes
pipe cleaners
balloons
plaster of Paris
newspaper
green paint
yarn
sticks
tagboard
markers
scissors
construction paper
crepe paper

What to do

1. Read *The Very Hungry Caterpillar* to the children.
2. Give each child six green pompoms and demonstrate how to glue them together to make a caterpillar (see illustration). Encourage them to glue on wiggle eyes and attach pipe cleaners for antennae.

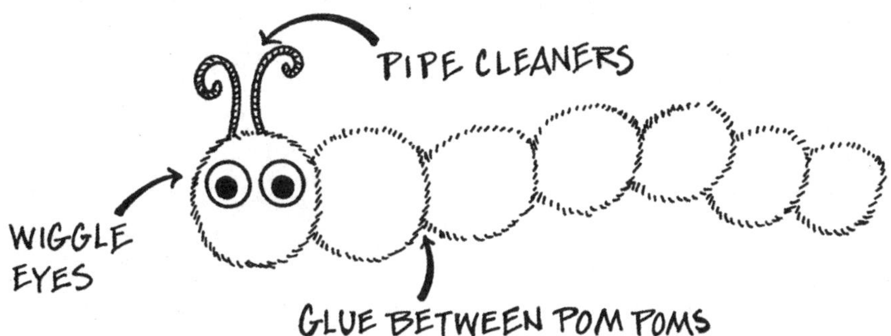

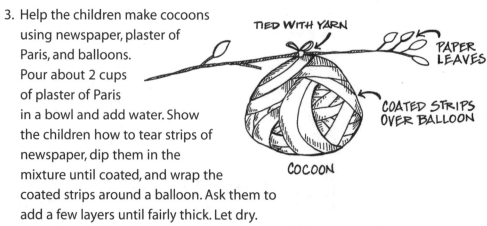

3. Help the children make cocoons using newspaper, plaster of Paris, and balloons. Pour about 2 cups of plaster of Paris in a bowl and add water. Show the children how to tear strips of newspaper, dip them in the mixture until coated, and wrap the coated strips around a balloon. Ask them to add a few layers until fairly thick. Let dry.
4. After the cocoons have dried, let the children paint them green. Help the children use yarn to tie their cocoons to a stick.
5. Trace the butterfly pattern (see illustration) on tagboard and cut out. Help the children to trace the butterfly pattern on construction paper and cut out. Encourage the children to decorate their butterflies with crepe paper "spots" and markers.
6. Have a "hungry caterpillar" party! Provide fruit and other foods from the story and let the "hungry caterpillars" munch away!

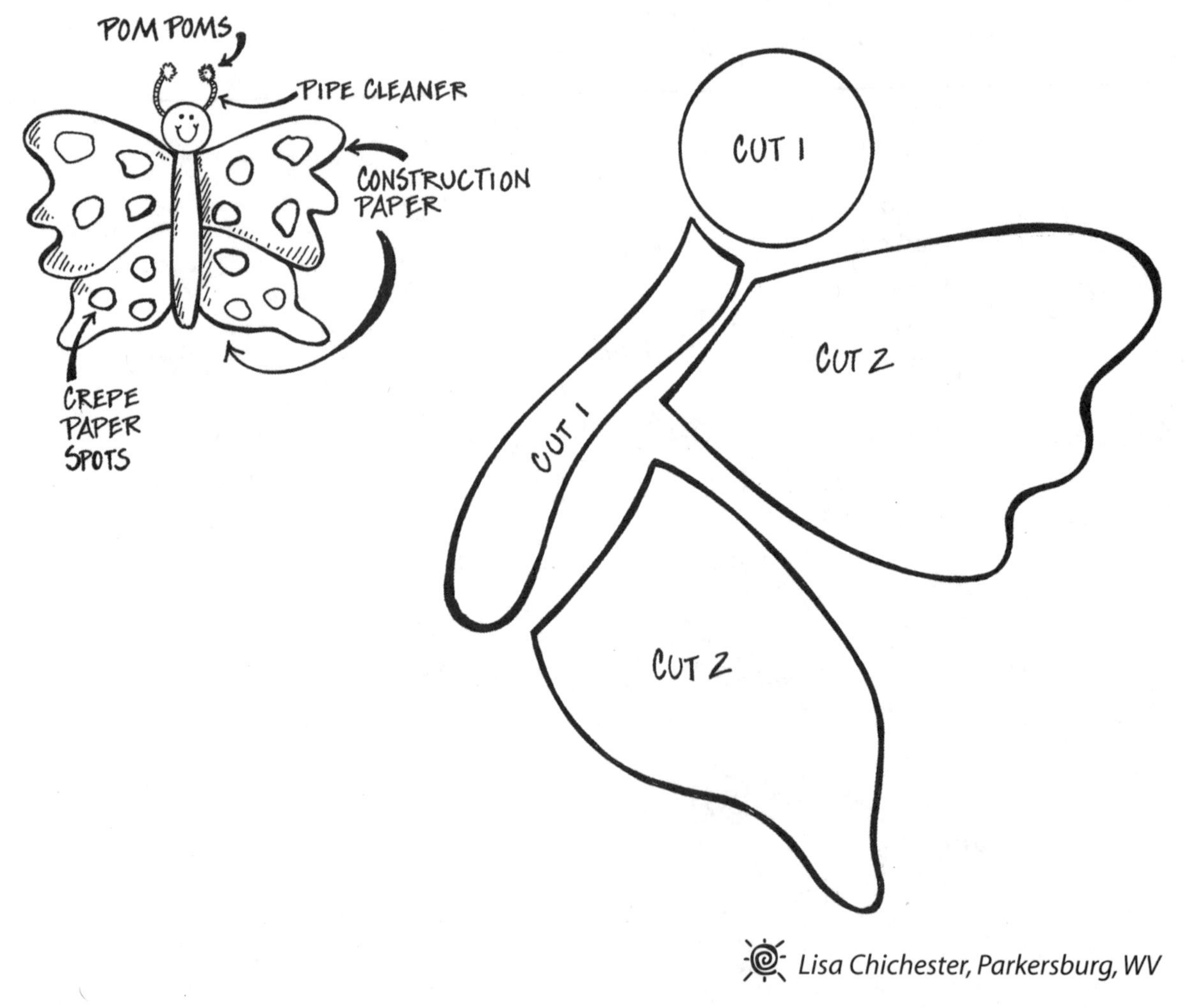

Lisa Chichester, Parkersburg, WV

Hot and Cold Classification

Materials

pocket chart
markers
old workbooks or magazines
scissors or paper cutter
8 ½" x 11" tagboard or medium cardstock
glue
laminate

What to do

1. Print the title "Classification" across the top of a piece of tagboard. Underneath the title, print "Hot Things" on the left side and "Cold Things" on the right side.
2. Cut out eight pictures of hot items (fire, iron) and eight pictures of cold items (snowman, ice cube) from old workbooks or magazines. Enlarge or make them smaller so they are a size appropriate for the pocket chart.
3. Glue the pictures on tagboard squares. Use a paper cutter to cut around the pictures so that the picture cards are all the same size and fit into the rows of the pocket chart.
4. Laminate the picture cards for durability and cut out. Hang the pocket chart and title card at children's eye level along with the title card.
5. Talk about cold and hot items. Give each child a picture card. Ask one child at a time to place her card under the correct heading in the pocket chart.

Discoveries on a Hike

Materials

plastic animals of varying sizes and types

What to do

1. Gather three to four children in a small group. Explain that they will pretend to go on a hike and see lots of animals.
2. Encourage the children to explore the plastic animals. Let each child choose three of the animals.

3. Ask the children to display the animals in front of them according to size—smallest to largest. As they set up the animals, prompt them with questions such as, "Which animal is largest?" " Which animal is smallest?" "Which animal is in between the others?"
4. Continue the discussion by asking them to think of similar animals that could be ordered by size, for example, a mouse, dog, and elephant.
5. Mix up the animals and redistribute them. Repeat the activity.

Related books *The Grouchy Ladybug* by Eric Carle
The Mitten by Jan Brett

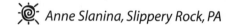

Anne Slanina, Slippery Rock, PA

Fall Finds

Materials
paper bags
fall nature items (leaves, pinecones, acorns)
magnifying glasses
water table

What to do

1. Begin this activity by asking families to help create this center. Send home a paper bag with a note attached. For example:

Dear families,
Please help us with this fall activity. Take a walk outside with your child and pick up some nature items. You might find leaves, rocks, nuts, and pinecones. As you walk with your child, talk about the weather, things you see, and things that change as the season changes. Place the items in the paper bag. Send in the bag when you have completed the walk.

2. As each child brings in her bag, let her share it at group time. Encourage the children to talk about their walk and what they found. This is a nice alternative to "Show and Tell."
3. After they show their items, ask them to place the items in the water table.
4. Encourage the children to explore the items using magnifying glasses. This is a nice activity to layer experiences and involve families.

Tracie O'Hara, Charlotte, NC

Go Buggy With a Matching Game

Materials

16 bug pictures from magazines or books
scissors
copy machine
11″ x 14″ tagboard
glue stick
laminate
self-adhesive Velcro
plastic zippered bag

What to do

1. Cut out pictures of sixteen different bugs. Make two copies of each bug to make two sets of identical bug pictures.
2. Glue one set of bugs to tagboard. Cut around the pictures to make game pieces.
3. Glue the other set of bug pictures to an 11″ x 14″ piece of tagboard to make a game board.
4. Laminate the game board and game pieces for durability and cut out.
5. Attach Velcro to the backs of the bug game pieces and to the bugs on the game board.
6. Store the game pieces in a plastic zippered bag attached to the back of the game board.
7. To do the activity, the child matches each bug game piece to the corresponding bug on the game board.

Jackie Wright, Enid, OK

I'm a Little Fishy

Materials none

What to do

1. Show the children pictures of fish. Talk about fish and where they live.
2. Sing the following song with the children to the tune of "I'm a Little Teapot."

I'm a little fishy, I can swim,
Here is my tail, here is my fin.
When I want to have fun with my friends,
I wiggle my tail and jump right in!

3. Create actions for some of the words.
4. Encourage the children to draw pictures of fish and dictate stories about them.
5. If possible, visit an aquarium to observe fish.

Related books

The Magic Fish by Freya Littledale
One Fish, Two Fish, Red Fish, Blue Fish by Dr. Seuss
The Rainbow Fish by Marcus Pfister
Swimmy by Leo Lionni

 *Kaethe Lewandowski, Centreville, VA*

Magnets

Materials

magnetic items (such as iron filings, iron nails, and paper clips)
non-magnetic items (such as toothpicks, pencil shavings, and crayons)
paper cups
magnets
markers
paper

What to do

1. Put each of the magnetic items and non-magnetic items into a separate cup.
2. Encourage the children to explore the items using magnets, observing which things the magnet picks up.

3. Draw a picture of each of the objects on a piece of paper. Make a copy for each child. As the children experiment with the magnets, ask them to write "yes" or "no" under each picture depending on whether or not the magnet picks it up.
4. Let the children explore classroom items to find magnetic items.

Related book *Mickey's Magnet* by Franklyn M. Branley

Barbara Saul, Eureka, CA

Match the Object to the Animal

Materials

pictures of animals focusing on a specific, unique body part (for example, an elephant's trunk)
objects that match pictured animal's specific body parts (see activity for ideas)

What to do

1. Collect a variety of animal pictures (focusing on specific body parts) and objects that match the body parts. For example:
   - anteater's nose—vacuum hose
   - camel's hump—water bottle
   - elephant's trunk—garden hose
   - spider's legs—knitting needles
   - sheep's wool—sweater
   - kangaroo pouch—baby carrier or pocket
   - chameleon—crayon/marker
   - crab claw—nutcracker
2. Gather a group of six to eight children in the science and nature learning center. Display the objects and pictures. Encourage the children to explore the items.
3. Have a brief discussion about how animals are all unique. Ask questions such as, "What is unique or special about a skunk?" "What can a monkey do that a dog cannot do?"
4. Ask the children to find match the animal pictures with the objects displayed on the table. They can help each other find the matches or work alone.
5. When the children have finished finding matches, reconvene in a circle.
6. Ask the children to display their matches and take turns describing them. Ask more questions such as "How does the object match the animal in the picture?" "Can you think of other animals that might have the same body part?"

Related books *The Foolish Tortoise* by Richard Buckley and Eric Carle
If You Hopped Like a Frog by David M. Schwartz
The Holes in Your Nose by Genichiro Yagyu, translated by Amanda Mayer Stinchecum

Kate D. Ross, Middlesex, VT

Nature Bracelets

Materials clear contact paper
scissors

What to do

1. Cut clear contact paper into strips and fit a strip around each child's wrist. Pull the paper from the contact paper so that the sticky side is facing out.
2. Go on a fall or spring nature walk. During the nature walk, encourage the children to find small nature items and stick them to their bracelets.
3. When you return to the classroom, ask the children to share what they found on their walk as they display their individual "nature bracelets."

Related books *Autumn Days* by Ann Schweninger
In the Tall, Tall Grass by Denise Fleming
Over in the Meadow by Ezra Jack Keats
Springtime by Ann Schweninger
When Autumn Comes by Robert Maass

Kaethe Lewandowski, Centreville, VA

Pumpkin, Pumpkin

Materials

pumpkins
yarn or measuring tape
chart paper
markers
water table
knife (adult only)
bowls
cards or chart and pen
magnifying glasses

What to do

1. Ask families to bring in several pumpkins of all shapes and sizes. Put them in the science center for several days so each child has a chance to touch, explore, and observe the pumpkins.
2. Introduce the idea of measuring the pumpkins using yarn or measuring tape. Help the children measure each pumpkin and record the results.
3. Ask the children to predict whether or not the pumpkins will float. Test them in the water table. Record the outcome.
4. Ask the children to predict which pumpkin will have the most seeds. Cut open the pumpkins and put each pumpkin's seeds into a separate bowl. Count the seeds with the children.
5. Ask each child to dictate a word that describes the outside of a pumpkin ("orange," "smooth," or "cold") and the inside of a pumpkin ("yucky," "wet"). Write their descriptions on chart paper.
6. Keep the pumpkins for a day or two so the children can study the decomposition. You may want to have a place outside where children can monitor this.
7. After the pumpkins are gone, the children can make a "pumpkin book" with all the information they gathered about pumpkins.
8. This activity can be extended to cooking (toasting the seeds), art (painting pumpkin pictures), books (reading the book *Pumpkin, Pumpkin* by Jeanne Titherington), and math (counting the pumpkins and placing them in order by size).

Related book *Pumpkin, Pumpkin* by Jeanne Titherington

Cotton Swab Skeleton

Materials

photocopies of the skeleton
scissors
9" x 12" colored construction paper
white glue
cotton swabs

What to do

1. Make photocopies of the skeleton (see illustration) for each child. Cut out the head and pelvic region of each photocopy.
2. Help the children glue the head and pelvic region onto construction paper in any color, trying to be anatomically correct.
3. Ask the children to dip the cotton swabs into white glue and glue them onto the construction paper with the skeleton head and pelvis, making the bones of the body. Display a finished skeleton to help guide them, and help them as needed.
4. As an extra counting exercise, write this sentence on the finished project: "I have 206 bones in my body, but this skeleton has ___ bones." Ask the children to count the cotton swabs on their pictures and write the number in the space provided.

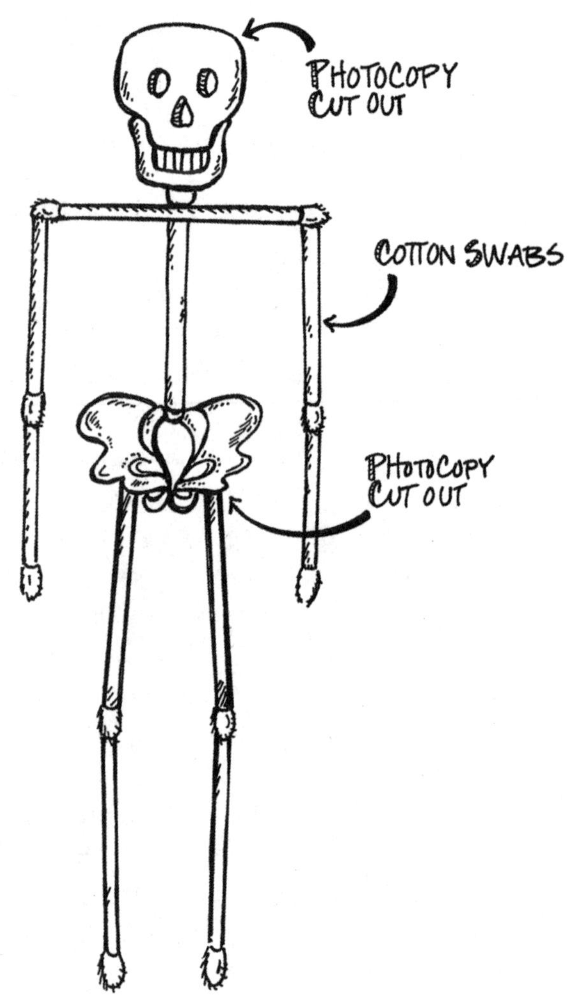

 *Andrea Hungerford, Plainville, CT*

Rock Crystals

Materials

plastic containers
permanent marker
water
food coloring (optional)
two rocks for each child (granite works best)
Epsom salt
pictures of rocks and minerals formed from water evaporation (such as quartzite, aquamarine, and emerald)

What to do

1. Give each child two plastic containers. Help them write, "light" on one and "dark" on the other. Ask them to put their names on their containers using stickers.
2. Explain that if they add salt to water and let the water evaporate, the remaining salt forms *rock crystals*. (Explain what *evaporation* means.) Ask the children to pour a small amount of water in each container and add food coloring, if desired.
3. Ask the children to place a rock in the bottom of each container. Help them spoon Epsom salt on top of the base rock until just a little stands above the water level.
4. Place one container in the dark and one in the light.
5. Show the children pictures of different colored stones and explain that the salt they added to their containers will eventually look a little like the rocks in the pictures.
6. Encourage the children to watch the containers each day and describe the changes they see.
7. Compare the results of the containers in the dark and the containers in the light.

Lisa Chichester, Parkersburg, WV

Science Backpack

Materials

large backpack
a variety of small science items to fit into the backpack (such as magnifying glass, compass, tweezers, unbreakable mirrors, bug catchers, play telescope, binoculars, pinwheels, bubbles, and flashlights)
paper
pencils and markers

What to do

1. Fill a large backpack with a variety of science items, paper, and markers.
2. Introduce the backpack to the children during circle time and explain what each item inside the bag is used for. Tell them that the backpack will be used outside as an "outdoor science center."
3. Bring the backpack outside during outdoor time and let the children use the items to explore the great outdoors.
4. If desired, include plastic bags and tape for collecting nature items and antibacterial wipes for cleaning hands.
5. Encourage the children to use the paper and markers to draw pictures of the natural environment outdoors.

Gail Morris, Kemah, TX

Science Center

Materials

silverware tray
variety of science tools (such as magnifying glass, binoculars, plastic kaleidoscope, eyedroppers, and tweezers)

What to do

1. Place all of the science tools in a silverware tray and place the tray on a shelf. This will allow the children to use and care for the tools properly.
2. You can use silverware trays to place items different items for viewing and weighing, such as rocks, shells, feathers, bones, and so on.

Melissa Browning, Milwaukee, WI

Science Slides

Materials

plastic sleeves for each child
nature items
tape

What to do

1. Purchase a plastic sleeve for each child. The best kind to use are the ones used for collecting baseball cards (heavy, plastic 3" x 4" sleeves with one of the four sides open).
2. Send home the plastic sleeves with a note for parents. For example:

Dear parents,
Please help your child find a nature item (leaf, stalk of grass, flower, and so on) and put it in this sleeve to make a "slide." Have your child bring it back to school. I will put these items in our science center for the children to examine and explore.

3. When the children return the "slides" (sleeves), write each child's name on her slide. Use tape to secure the open end closed so the children cannot remove the item.
4. Ask the children to show and tell about their slide. Encourage them to talk about where and how they collected their items.
5. Put different slides in the science center throughout the year. Encourage the children to explore the items with a magnifying glass. They get especially excited because they each have contributed to this collection.

Gail Morris, Kemah, TX

Science in a Jar

Materials

shovel
ruler or yardstick
large plastic jar with a tight-fitting lid
water
coffee filters
fine mesh strainer
magnifying glasses
wax paper
white craft paper
crayons or markers

What to do

1. Find a place outside where you can dig a hole at least one foot deep. Before digging, carefully remove the grass in a large piece so it can be replaced when you are done.
2. Show the children how to use the shovel. Let them take turns digging.
3. Occasionally stop digging and use the ruler to measure the depth of the hole. Help them to determine if they need to keep digging.
4. When the hole is one foot deep, ask the children to collect some dirt from the hole and place it in the plastic jar about halfway full.
5. Put the remaining dirt back in the hole and carefully replace the grass, tamping it down lightly.
6. Fill the rest of the jar almost to the rim with water. Screw the lid on tightly.
7. Let the children take turns shaking the jar vigorously. Encourage them to observe the materials in the jar. Record their thoughts.
8. Place the jar where the children can observe it, yet where it will not be jostled.
9. Encourage the children to draw pictures of what they see in the jar. Label the pictures "Day One" and display them for a day or so, (keep them for later use). Let the water in the jar settle for one day.
10. One the second day, encourage the children to note any changes in the jar. By now, the dirt and water should have separated into two definite layers, and the dirt should have separated into two or three layers, depending on the type of soil.
11. Ask the children to draw pictures of what they observe in the jar. Label the pictures "Day Two" and display them for a day or two (keep them for later use).
12. Put a coffee filter in the fine mesh strainer. Ask a child to open the jar. Most likely, there will be an odor to the water. Encourage the children to smell the water and comment on the odor. Record the children's thoughts.
13. Carefully pour off the top layer of water through the coffee filter. Try not to jostle the jar. Replace the lid and put the jar back in its place. Remove the coffee filter from the strainer and straighten it out on a flat area.
14. Let the children use magnifying glasses to explore what is on the coffee filter. Encourage them to talk about what they see through the magnifying lens.
15. Ask the children to draw pictures of what they see. Label the pictures "Through the Magnifying Glass" and display them for a day or two (keep them for later use). Let the jar sit for another day.
16. On the third day, encourage the children to note any changes in the jar. Have them draw pictures of the jar, label them "Day Three," and display for a day or two (keep them for later use).
17. Remove the jar lid and use a spoon to scoop out the top layer of dirt. Try not to disturb the remaining layers. Spread the dirt on wax paper. (Do not use newspaper or paper towels as they wick the water out of the dirt too quickly.)

18. Replace the lid and put the jar back in its spot. Encourage the children to explore the dirt. Talk with them about what they find in the dirt.
19. Let the children draw pictures of what they find in the dirt. Label the pictures "Dirt Layer One" and keep them for later use.
20. On the fourth day, repeat steps 17 through 19 for the remaining layers of dirt. Label any pictures the children draw with the appropriate dirt layer number.
21. Gather all the pictures the children have made. Ask the children to sort the pictures by the day they drew them.

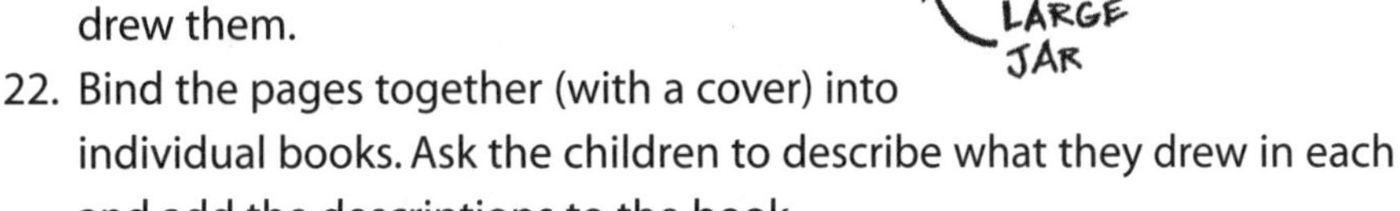

22. Bind the pages together (with a cover) into individual books. Ask the children to describe what they drew in each picture and add the descriptions to the book.

Related books *Harry the Dirty Dog* by Gene Zion
Mud Puddle by Robert Munsch

Virginia Jean Herrod, Columbia, SC

The Sky Moon Craters

Materials

pictures of the moon
floor covering (newspaper or plastic shower curtain)
small container (margarine tub or 4"-deep pan)
flour
cinnamon in shaker
small rocks and marbles

What to do

1. Talk about things in the sky, such as the sun, moon, stars, planets, and clouds. During the moon's third quarter phase, it can be viewed in the morning.
2. Encourage the children to look at the night sky at home (especially when the moon is full). Explain that planets do not "twinkle" and do not stay in the same place in relation to the stars. Ask children to look at the moon using binoculars or a telescope, if available.

3. Show the children pictures of the moon. Explain that the spots on the moon are either flat plains or craters (holes on the surface). Objects that hit the moon a long time ago made the craters.
4. Tell them that they are going to make their own craters.
5. Cover the floor with newspaper or an old plastic shower curtain. Fill a tub or pan with flour and place it in the middle of the floor covering.
6. Sprinkle cinnamon on top of the flour to make surface "dirt." This helps make the results easier to see.
7. Let the children take turns dropping or throwing rocks or marbles into the flour. Keep the other children away from the area as each child does this.
8. After each rock hits the flour, remove it. Encourage the children to look for the crater left behind.
9. When the surface is disturbed enough, smooth out the flour and add more cinnamon. This can be repeated as many times as desired.
10. For more information, go to NASA's main website at http://www.nasa.gov. You can visit the children's and educator's page at http://library.gsfc.nasa.gov/KidsPage/KidsPage.htm. From the mid-Atlantic and New England, write to NASA at:

NASA Teacher Resource Laboratory/130.3
NASA Goddard Space Flight Center
Greenbelt, MD 20771-0001
Telephone: (301) 286-8570

For addresses of centers in other regions go to http://ares.jsc.nasa.gov/HumanExplore/Exploration/EXLibrary/docs/BeyondLEO/Leo1295/Facility.htm.

Related books *Arrow to the Sun* by Gerald McDermott
Do Stars Have Points? by Melvin Berger and Gilda Berger
Draw Me a Star by Eric Carle
How Many Stars in the Sky? by Lenny Hart
Regards to the Man in the Moon by Ezra Jack Keats
The Moon Book by Gail Gibbons
The Sun Our Nearest Star by Franklyn Branley
Wait Till the Moon Is Full by Margaret Wise Brown

Mildred Simpson, Tampa, FL

Springtime or Autumn Tree

Materials

sponges
scissors
9" x 12" white construction paper
black, pink, and green tempera paint (for spring tree)
black, brown, orange, yellow, red, and green tempera paint (for autumn tree)
small shallow containers to hold paint
paintbrushes

What to do

1. Cut sponges into blossom shapes and leaf shapes. Make several of each.
2. Pour each color of paint into a separate container.
3. Ask the children to use a paintbrush to make a black tree on white paper. Allow the painting to dry.
4. For a spring tree, encourage the children to paint small green leaves on the tree and grass underneath. Show them how to dip a blossom-shaped sponge into pink paint and dab onto the tree.
5. For an autumn tree, the children dip the leaf shape sponges into the desired color and tap them on the tree, with some falling and some on the ground.

Mary Brehm, Aurora, OH

The Ants Go Marching

Materials

ants
magnifying glasses
chart paper
paper
markers

What to do

1. Go outside with the children and look for anthills on the school grounds. Discuss the importance of approaching an anthill carefully, so they don't step on it or disturb it.
2. When they find an anthill, ask the children to crawl carefully to it. They may lie on the grass or squat to look at the ants. Have the children watch the activity with and without magnifying glass.

3. Return to the classroom to discuss and chart their observations.
4. Encourage the children to draw pictures of ants and label their parts (with help). Children can create ant stories too.

Related books *The 512 Ants on Sullivan Street* by Carol A. Losi
The Ant and the Elephant by Bill Peet
How Many Ants? by Larry Dane Brimner
One Hundred Hungry Ants by Elinor J. Pinczes
Sarah's Story by Bill Harley
Want a Ride? by Bill Gordh

Sandra Nagel, White Lake, MI

Water Cycle Role Play

Materials

blue painter's tape
clear plastic cup of water
white, blue, or gray tulle scarves, about 18" square
music that evokes running water, water vapor, and thunderstorms (Beethoven's "Sixth Symphony" and Debussy's "Snowflakes Are Dancing" work well)

What to do

1. Starting at one end of the room, put blue tape on the floor in a pattern that resembles streams and rivers flowing from different directions towards each other, merging into a single large river. Make an "ocean" by taping parallel lines across the end of the "river."
2. Introduce the activity by holding up a clear, plastic cup of water. Explain that water travels a very long way to reach us. Point to the tape on the floor and tell them it represents rivers, streams, and the ocean. Water travels from mountains in little streams that flow together into bigger streams and rivers, which flow all the way to the ocean.
3. Talk about the "water cycle." Explain that when sunshine warms the water it *evaporates*, which means it turns into water vapor (an invisible gas) that floats up through the air. High in the sky the vapor cools and turns back into water droplets. Water droplets and vapor gather together to form clouds. When the drops get too heavy, they fall to the ground as rain. If the air is very cold, the water vapor turns into snowflakes made of ice crystals.
4. Demonstrate water vapor, cooling, condensation, and freezing using hot water and ice cubes, if desired.

5. Encourage the children to imagine they are raindrops falling from the sky into a little stream in the mountains. Wiggle your fingers and lower your arms to suggest rain. Play gently flowing music, such as "The Moldau" by Bedrick Smetana.
6. Now the children are water drops flowing along in the lively stream, bouncing around the rocks and spinning in whirlpools. Have them move closer as all the "streams" flow into a big "river." Tell them the sun is shining down on them, and they are getting warmer and lighter.
7. Change the music to "Snowflakes Are Dancing" or other ethereal music. Give each child a tulle scarf. Encourage them to twirl the scarves as they rise, moving slowly and gracefully and waving their arms.
8. Now they are "water vapor" floating up into the sky. Move close together and form big, puffy "clouds." As they "cool off" they get heavier and form raindrops.
9. Have the children move closer together and bunch up their tulle to look like a big cloud. Change the music to suggest a thunderstorm.
10. Tell them they are very heavy and are falling from the cloud, down to the earth in a big storm. The children move faster as the music gets exciting. Encourage them to jump and spin as they pretend to be blown by the wind.
11. Lead them in moving slowly and quietly as you change the music to the peaceful, flowing music from the beginning. The sun comes out and the storm is over. The river flows smoothly again.

More to do

Sand and Water: Build mountains and valleys in the sandbox or sand table. Pour water to show stream flow patterns.

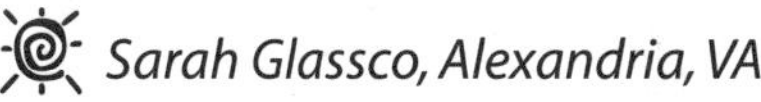
Sarah Glassco, Alexandria, VA

Weigh In

Materials

bathroom scale
chart paper
balance scales
two small gift bags
feathers
rocks
sticks
grass
wood chips
sand

What to do

1. Ask the children to guess how much they weigh. Write each child's name and guess on a piece of chart paper.
2. Show the children the bathroom scale and explain how it works. Weigh each child and record each child's actual weight on the chart next to her guess. Talk about the difference in guessed and actual weights.
3. Use the bathroom scale to weigh other things in the room. Be creative! Experiment!
4. Show the children the balance scale and explain that it doesn't show how much something weighs but shows which of two objects weighs more.
5. Show the children the feathers and rocks. Ask them to guess which one weighs more. Ask them to fill one small gift bag with feathers and the other bag with rocks.
6. Place the bag of feathers on one side of the balance scale and the bag of rocks on the other side. Talk about the result.
7. On a large piece of paper write, "Which is heavier?" Under the heading, write, "Rocks are heavier than feathers."
8. Weigh other objects the same way, such as sticks and grass, wood chips and sand, and grass and sand. Remember to record each result on the paper.
9. Let the children experiment with the materials during center time.

Virginia Jean Herrod, Columbia, SC

Learning About Food Quality

Materials

poster of food pyramid
clean, empty food packages

What to do

1. Talk about nutrition and healthy foods with the children. Talk about the food pyramid and show a poster, if available.
2. Discuss vitamins and minerals and how they are important for good health. Explain that food packaging contains information for the consumer, such as expiration date, weight, servings per containers, nutritional value, and ingredients.
3. Show the children a few empty food packages and point out the nutritional information, ingredients, expiration date, and so on.
4. Encourage the children to explore the packaging.

Cherra June Wilson, Duarte, CA

A Sense of Home

Materials items from home related to each sense
tape recorder
feely box

What to do

1. Have "senses week" by learning about a different sense each day of the week (Monday: sight, Tuesday: touch, and so on).
2. Send a note home to parents describing the week and asking them to send in an item from home to match each sense. For example:
   - **For Sight Day**, parents can ask their child to describe something they see in the house. Parents write down the description for children to bring in and share with the class.
   - **For Sound Day**, children can choose a sound at home (dishwasher, birds outside, dog barking) and describe it to their parents. Parents can write the description or tape-record the sound for children to bring in and share.
   - **For Touch Day**, children can choose an item from home to bring in and place in a "feely box" (box with a hole that a child's hand will fit through). The children in the class will take turns feeling the items.
   - **For Smell Day**, parents can send in something with a scent or odor. Ask them to put the scented item (if liquid) on a tissue and put it in a zipper-closure bag, or put the item in a jar. At school, the children guess what they smell.
   - **For Taste Day**, parents can send in a snack. Encourage them to bring something unique for children to taste. This could be as simple as a seasoned cracker or sweet and sour pickle. Encourage the children to taste at least one item, and describe what they taste.

Safety Note: Ask parents to list all food items that their child has an allergy to, and notify all parents of allergies.

Related books *My Five Senses* by Margaret Miller
What's That Smell? A Lift and Sniff Flap Book by Janelle Cherrington

Ann Kelly, Johnstown, PA

Alphabet Snow Hunt

Materials

white packaging peanuts
sensory table
Avalanche by Michael J. Rosen
plastic alphabet letters
plastic shovel
plastic buckets

What to do

1. Prepare the sensory table in advance by disinfecting it. After it dries, fill it with packaging peanuts.
2. Read the story *Avalanche* to prepare the children to hunt for missing letters in the "snow."
3. Empty uppercase and lowercase letters in the sensory table. Cover the letters with packaging peanuts.
4. Encourage the children to shovel out specific letters, such as all the letters of the alphabet, letters of their name, or letters that come before and after certain letters.

Quazonia Quarles, Newark, DE

Autumn Fun

Materials

large garbage bag
autumn leaves
sheet or tarp for the floor

What to do

1. Collect a large bag of autumn leaves.
2. Spread a sheet or tarp on the floor and dump the leaves in the center of the sheet.
3. Encourage the children to sit in the middle of the leaves and toss them in the air.
4. Encourage the children to notice and enjoy the variety of shapes and colors.

Related books

Red Leaf, Yellow Leaf by Lois Ehlert
Why Do Leaves Change Color? by Betsy Maestro

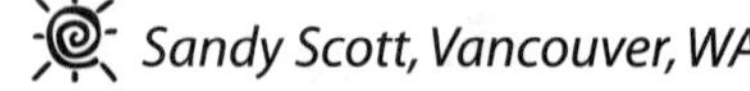
Sandy Scott, Vancouver, WA

Birdseed Discovery

Materials

sensory table or large tub
birdseed
funnels, scoops, and shovels
small plastic animals
plastic scale
bowls

What to do

1. Fill the sensory table about one third full with birdseed. Place small plastic animals on top of the birdseed.
2. Encourage the children to explore the birdseed using funnels, scoops, and shovels.

Related book *Quick as a Cricket* by Audrey Wood

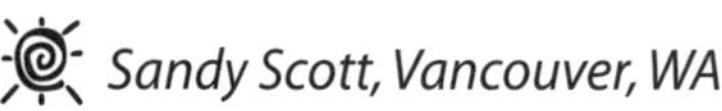
Sandy Scott, Vancouver, WA

Color and Shape Boxes

Materials

shoeboxes (plastic or cardboard)
hands-on materials (see activity)

What to do

1. Place colorful hands-on materials or materials in a variety of shapes in different boxes. Label each box as appropriate. For example:
   - **Color Boxes**—add paint sample cards or Formica samples (from the hardware store), color paddles, colorful rocks and shells, or other small objects. Make one box per color or one box with color activities.
   - **Shape Boxes**—add blocks, cookie cutters, puzzle pieces, books on shapes, and so on.
2. Keep these boxes on a shelf for the entire year, and change the contents often.
3. Use this idea to make nature boxes, such as shells and rocks. Children can sort, count, and examine the contents using a magnifying glass. Some of the children return to these boxes again and again, enjoying the cool smooth stones, or the beauty of the shells.

Tracie O'Hara, Charlotte, NC

Dry Winter Wonderland

Materials

large tub or sensory table
large bag of cornstarch
small plastic animals
smocks
wet towel
small shovels
bowls

What to do

1. Fill the sensory table one third full with cornstarch.
2. Hide small plastic animals in the cornstarch.
3. Make sure children wear smocks while playing in the cornstarch. Also, cornstarch becomes very slippery when spilled on a floor so have a wet towel nearby for the children to wipe their feet when they are finished.
4. Encourage the children to search for animals, build "homes" for the animals out of cornstarch, and explore as desired.
5. If the area is carpeted, it is fun to watch the creation of white footprints! Just vacuum the floor when done.

Related books

Look! Snow! by Kathryn O. Galbraith
The Snowy Day by Ezra Jack Keats
White Snow, Bright Snow by Alvin Tresselt

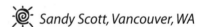

Sandy Scott, Vancouver, WA

Glitter Playdough

Materials

glitter
homemade playdough
rolling pins
seasonal-shaped cookie cutters

What to do

1. Add new sparkle and vitality to your playdough center by sprinkling glitter into your favorite playdough recipe.
2. Provide rolling pins and seasonal-shaped cookie cutters for children to cut out dough shapes.
3. Children will rush to the sensory center with new enthusiasm!

Jackie Wright, Enid, OK

Miniature Snowmen

Materials

fresh snow
large tubs
large towel
mittens
small twigs
1" x 6" scraps of material
muffin liners
beads or pebbles
baby carrots

What to do

1. Gather fresh snow in large tubs and bring it into the classroom. Spread large towels on the table and put the materials in separate bowls.
2. Ask the children to put on mittens before working with the snow. Help them mold snowballs to make a snowman's body.
3. Encourage them to decorate their snowmen using small twigs for arms, material scraps for scarves, muffin cups for hats, beads or pebbles for eyes and mouth (watch for choking hazard), and baby carrots for noses.
4. Follow up with observations of the melting snow.
5. If snow is unavailable, use white modeling dough (see recipe below). Children can use Mr. Potato Head accessories to decorate the snowman.

Modeling Dough Recipe

1 cup flour
½ cup salt
2 teaspoons cream of tartar
1 cup water
1 tablespoon oil
¼ cup white powdered tempera paint

Combine all the ingredients and cook over medium heat, stirring until it forms a ball. Remove from heat, let it cool, and knead.

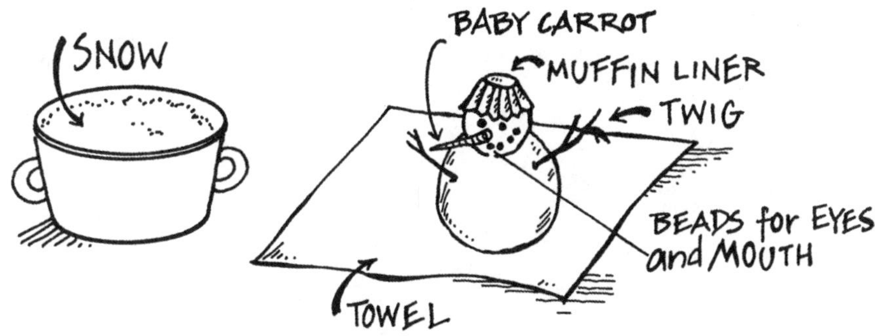

Related books *Fun in the Snow* by Laura Damon
Snow by Nancy Elizabeth Wallace
Snowballs by Lois Ehlert

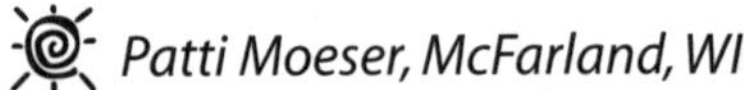
Patti Moeser, McFarland, WI

Packing Peanut Creation

Materials

biodegradable packing peanuts
squirt bottles filled with colored water
large tub or sensory table

What to do

1. Place biodegradable packing peanuts in a large tub or sensory table. Place squirt bottles filled with colored water nearby.
2. Encourage the children to squirt the peanuts. When the peanuts get wet, they will dissolve slightly and stick to other peanuts.
3. Encourage the children to make their own "peanut creations." Allow the creations to dry and display them in the room.

Related book *Moon Cake* by Frank Asch

Sandy Scott, Vancouver, WA

Playdough Mats

Materials

plain vinyl placemats
permanent markers
stencils and/or cookie cutters of letters and shapes
playdough

What to do

1. Trace stencils or cookie cutters on plain placemats to create desired designs. For example, use letter stencils to make the children's names or use holiday themed cookie cutters.
2. Invite the children to make shapes out of playdough using their hands or cookie cutters, and match the shapes to the ones on their placemat.
3. This is a good activity for matching, one-to-one correspondence, pre-reading, and sequencing.

Jeanette Denning, Tinley Park, IL

Practice With Favorite Color

Materials

sensory table or large tub
scraps of colored construction paper
scissors
yarn
masking tape

What to do

1. Fill the sensory table or large tub half full with paper scraps.
2. Attach scissors to the edge of the table using yarn.
3. Encourage the children to practice cutting their favorite colors of paper.
4. Let the children cut the paper into as many small pieces as they want. Each day the pieces will get smaller and smaller as their fine motor skills increase.
5. This is great for color recognition and cutting practice.

Related books

Hooray for Me! by Remy Charlip
Quick as a Cricket by Audrey Wood

Sandy Scott, Vancouver, WA

Sensory Bags

Materials

small plastic zipper-closure bags
sensory materials (such as sand, shaving cream, and dirt)
colored plastic chips or buttons
masking tape

What to do

1. Partially fill each plastic bag with a different sensory material and hide a plastic chip or button in each bag.
2. Close the bags and reinforce the bag closure with masking tape.
3. Invite the children to squish the bags to discover the chip or button.
4. The children will have fun shaking, squeezing, and rolling the bags to discover the hidden item.

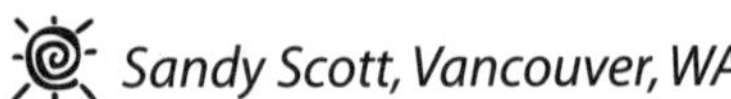

Sandy Scott, Vancouver, WA

Sensory Cards

Materials

heavy poster board
scissors
sandpaper
fabric with varying textures
glue
markers

What to do

1. Cut poster board into cards.
2. Make sensory cards by gluing different textures on each card.
3. On the back of each card, write a word that describes how it feels to the touch (rough, smooth, bumpy, soft, and so on).
4. Let the children take turns feeling the cards. Encourage them to write their own descriptive word or tell you or a friend.
5. If desired, extend the activity by asking the children to find an object in the room that feels similar to the card they felt.

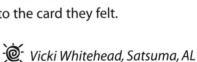

Vicki Whitehead, Satsuma, AL

Sensory Table Playdough

Materials

sensory table
4 cups flour
1 cup salt
1 ¾ cups warm water
small containers with lids
large empty bowl

What to do

1. Make playdough with the children using the sensory table.
2. Put 4 cups of flour in a large container, 1 cup of salt in a container, and 1 ¾ cups warm water in a container. Place the containers and a large empty bowl in the sensory table.
3. Encourage the children to look at the ingredients. Don't give them any instructions on how to make the playdough. Simply say, "Here's what you need to make playdough."
4. Give the children a few minutes. Watch and see what they do. They may dig in and start mixing the ingredients together.
5. If, after a few moments, the children don't start mixing the ingredients, offer some encouragement. Offer hints as needed. However, try not to lead the children too much. Give them ample time to figure things out on their own. Sooner or later, they will realize what needs to be done and start mixing away.
6. After the children have mixed the playdough and played with it for a while, offer containers for storage.
7. If desired, double or triple the recipe and let the children make the playdough as described. Then give each child a small zipper-closure bag to bring home some playdough.

More to do

Add a flavorful twist by letting the children add a package of unsweetened drink mix to the playdough.

Related books

Don't Touch by Suzy Kline
Josefina by Jeanette Winter

Virginia Jean Herrod, Columbia, SC

The Five Senses in Boxes

Materials

five cardboard or plastic shoeboxes
books on the five senses
objects representing each of the senses

What to do

1. Label each box with one of the senses. Fill each box with materials that represent the sense. For example:
   - **Sound**—bell, headphones or earplugs to muffle sound, music box, and rattles
   - **Touch**—piece of fur, sandpaper, smooth rock, and rubber band
   - **Smell**—sachets, scratch-and-sniff stickers, and plastic film cans with cotton balls soaked in different scent oils
   - **Sight**—binoculars, magnifying glasses, and color paddles
   - **Taste**—photos of favorite foods, or actual foods for tasting

   Safety Note: If you choose to add real foods to the taste box, check for any food allergies and monitor use closely.
2. Put a book about each sense in each box. Use class-made books, if available.
3. Introduce each box separately at circle time, and then put it in the science or sensory center for the children to explore independently. Keep these boxes on the science shelf all year.
4. Change the contents of the boxes occasionally. Change them according to classroom theme, if desired.

Tracie O'Hara, Charlotte, NC

The Eyes Have It

Materials

magazines
scissors
small baskets
glue
paper

What to do

1. Talk about the different parts of our bodies. Focus on similarities and differences, senses, or identifying body parts.
2. Have the children work in groups, each focusing on a particular body part. Ask each group to cut out pictures from magazines of the body part they are working on and keep them in their basket.

3. When they finish cutting out pictures, ask them to glue their pictures onto paper. Ask each group to share what they found during a show and tell time.
4. Help the children notice what they found. Talk about similarities, differences, and things that are fun about the pictures.

Touch Box

Materials

shoebox
scissors
variety of items (textured items or items with interesting shapes)

What to do

1. Cut out a hole in the lid of the shoebox and place it on the box.
2. Without the children seeing, put an item in the box.
3. Ask a child to guess what the item is by feeling it through the hole. Let the children take turns adding items and guessing what they are.
4. The items can correspond with the theme of the week.

Related book *My Five Senses* by Margaret Miller

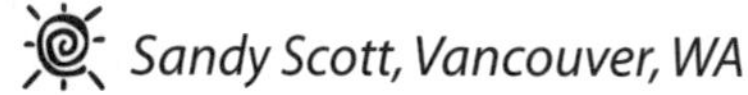

Touch and Feel Book

Materials

variety of fabrics and materials (such as felt, fur, feathers, and vinyl)
glue
oak tag pieces
hole punch
fasteners (brass brads or silver snap rings)
markers

What to do

1. Glue each piece of fabric to a piece of oak tag.
2. Punch two or three holes along one side of each piece of oak tag and fasten them together to make a book.
3. Write the name of the material on each page.
4. Encourage the children to explore the touch and feel book.

Related books

Pat the Bunny by Dorothy Kunhardt
Pat the Cat by Edith Kunhardt
The Touch Me Book by Pat and Eve Witte

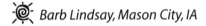

Barb Lindsay, Mason City, IA

Touching

Materials

disposable rubber gloves
textured materials (such as pebbles)
cotton
string

What to do

1. Fill each glove with a textured material and cotton.
2. Tie the opening of each glove tightly with string.
3. Put the gloves in the sensory learning center. Encourage the children to describe the texture of each glove by feeling, poking, and manipulating the gloves.

Related books

My Fingers Are for Touching by Jane Belk Moncure
Touching by Helen Frost

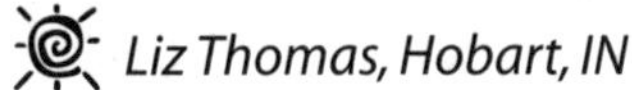
Liz Thomas, Hobart, IN

A Bag of Shoes

Materials

various pairs of shoes, slippers, and boots
grocery bags

What to do

1. Gather a variety of shoes for this activity (check yard sales and second-hand stores). Send a note home asking for donations of old pairs of shoes that are clean enough for classroom use. With large shoes, children are more willing to leave their socks on while trying on the shoes.
2. Place the shoes in a pile and ask the children to find matches or "pairs."
3. Ask them to do a variety of sorting activities. For example, ask them to put all of the shoes that could be worn in the snow in one pile and all of the shoes that could be worn in the summer in another pile.
4. Children can sort shoes by size, color, marks on the soles, or by those with laces, Velcro, or buckles.
5. Encourage the children to count how many shoes, slippers, and boots there are and compare the results.
6. At the end of the activity, have the children find pairs of shoes and put them in grocery bags.
7. Put the shoes in the dress-up so the children can try them on.

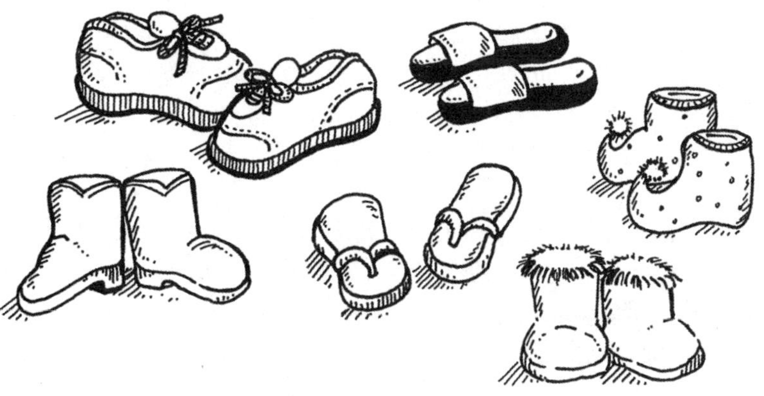

More to do

Read *The Shoemaker and the Elves* to the children. Set up a "shoe-making" area with shoes and toy hammers. The children can pretend to be elves making shoes.

Sandra Nagel, White Lake, MI

Gone Shoe Shopping Rhyme Play

Materials

magazines
scissors
glue
note cards or shoeboxes

What to do

1. Ask the children to talk about some of their shoe shopping experiences. These may include why they got new shoes, where they went, and how they were measured for shoes.
2. Tell the children that they will pretend to visit as they participate in the following rhyme and movements.

Going Shoe Shopping

My old shoes don't keep out water very well, (Shake head no.)
And when they're wet, mom says they smell! (Hold nose.)
We went to the shoe store and walked in the door,
There were boxes of shoes stacked from ceiling to floor. (Point up, then down.)

Shiny shoes that look good to dance in, (Dance a few steps.)
Big black boots to direct traffic in, (Wave arms or point.)
High-heeled shoes, worn with best clothes, (Raise up on tiptoe.)
Tall, furry boots to warm cold toes. (Stamp "cold" feet and hug body.)

There! Bright orange sneakers—bouncy and light! (Bounce gently.)
The shoe store clerk tied them to fit just right. (Hold out foot for tying.)
I waited so that mom could pay,
Then home I skipped, all the way! (Skip.)

3. Cut out pictures of all kinds of shoes. Glue the pictures to separate note cards or put each picture in a separate shoebox. Let each child choose a card and talk about who might wear the shoe, what kind of job the person might have, and what clothes the person might wear with the shoes.
4. Have the children sort the cards by color or type of shoe.

Theresa Callahan, Easton, MD

It's a Shoe-in!

Materials

variety of footwear (such as boots, high-heeled shoes, sneakers, cleats, sandals, swim shoes, slippers, men's dress shoes, and so on)
table
shoehorns
cash register
play money
shopping bags
full-length mirror
several small chairs
dot stickers
markers

What to do

1. Take a field trip to a local shoe store. Let the children look at all the different types of shoes. Talk about why people need different types of footwear.
2. If possible, invite a shoe store employee to visit the classroom. Ask him or her to bring along the instrument used to measure customers' feet and use it to measure each child's foot. Make a note of each child's shoe size.
3. Make a shoe size graph. Make a line graph that shows the children's shoes sizes from smallest to largest.
4. Set up a shoe store in the classroom. Put a variety of shoes on low shelves and place a table near the shoes. Place the shoehorn, cash register, and the shopping bags on the table. Put a full-length mirror near the shoes.
5. Give each child some play money.
6. Encourage the children to use the materials freely. They can take turns playing customers and shoe store clerks.
7. Ask the children how much each pair of shoes should cost. Let them use dot stickers to make small price tags for each pair of shoes.
8. Children can try on a variety of shoes and choose a pair to "purchase." The "customers" take their shoes to the register and pay for them. The "clerk" rings up the sale, takes money, makes change, and puts the shoes in a shopping bag.

More to do

Dramatic Play: Set up a shoeshine stand. Put empty polish containers, shoeshine cloths, and polishing brushes in a bucket. Encourage the children to use the materials to pretend to shine their new shoes.
Math: Measure each child's foot with a ruler and graph the information.

Related books *Father's Rubber Shoes* by Yumi Yeo
The Growing-Up Feet by Beverly Cleary
My Best Shoes by Marilee Robin Burton
New Shoes for Silvia by Johanna Hurwitz
New Shoes, Red Shoes by Susan Rollings
Red Dancing Shoes by Denise Lewis Patrick
Shoes, Shoes, Shoes by Ann Morris
Sounds My Feet Make by Arlene Blanchard
Whose Shoes? by Brian Wildsmith

Virginia Jean Herrod, Columbia, SC

Missing Shoes From the Shoe Store!

Materials assortment of real shoes or cardboard shapes of shoes
ruler

What to do

1. Before the children arrive, place one of each pair of shoes in the shoe store center. Hide the matching shoes in other areas of the room.
2. Invite a couple of children to take turns working in the shoe store. Their job is to use a ruler to measure the children's feet ("customers") and give each customer a shoe of her choice. The children do not need to put the shoes on.
3. When children have the correct size shoe of their choice, they leave the shoe store to search for the matching shoe hidden in the classroom.

Related book *Alexander and the Terrible, Horrible, No Good, Very Bad Day* by Judith Viorst

Shirley Salach, Northwood, NH

Shoe Lineup

Materials variety of shoes

What to do

1. Place a variety of shoes in the shoe store center.
2. Ask a small group of children in the center to sort the shoes according to when they are worn (for example, summer shoes, winter shoes, and rainy day shoes).
3. Demonstrate how to sequence the shoes according to the season. For example, sandals could represent summer, "school shoes" could represent fall, boots could represent winter, and rubber rain boots could represent spring.
4. Once the shoes are in line, ask the children to point to each shoe and say which season it could be worn in.
5. Discuss the similarities and differences between the shoes. Talk about why the shoes are made differently for different seasons.
6. If desired, research and discuss the differences between shoes from other cultures or countries.

Related books *A Busy Year* by Leo Lionni
Caps, Hats, Socks, and Mittens by Louise Borden

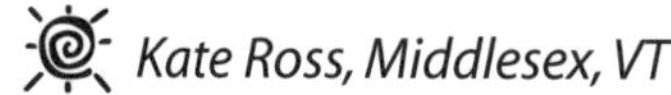

Kate Ross, Middlesex, VT

Shoes Galore

Materials

old pairs of shoes
rickrack, pompoms, ribbon, and scraps of material
glue
paint

What to do

1. Ask the children to bring in an old pair of shoes from home. The shoes could belong to a parent, sibling, or the child.
2. Put all of the shoes together and let each child pick a pair to wear in a "shoe parade!" Walk around the classroom wearing the shoes.

3. Encourage the children to decorate their shoes using paint, rickrack, old ribbon, pompoms, and so on to make "crazy shoes." Give a prize for the craziest shoe.
4. Help the children make a giant shoe sculpture using the shoes.
5. Read the story "The Old Woman Who Lived in a Shoe" with the children.

Lisa Chichester, Parkersburg, WV

So Many Shoes!

Materials

construction paper in a variety of colors
scissors
pencils, crayons, and markers
laminate
tape

What to do

1. In the shoe store center, ask the children to remove their shoes.
2. Help each child trace her foot onto a piece of construction paper the same color as the child's shoe.
3. Ask the children to cut out their traced shoe patterns and decorate them to look like their shoe.
4. Spread out all of the paper shoes on the floor. Encourage the children to group the shoes according to color, style, and so on.
5. Laminate the paper shoes, and tape them to the floor to make a pathway across the room.

Related books

Caillou: New Shoes by Marion Johnson
Pair of Red Sneakers by Lisa Lawston

Lori Dunlap, Amarillo, TX

Beginning Sounds

Materials

magazines and catalogs
scissors
index cards
glue stick
paper
markers
poster board or tagboard
rubber cement
laminate

What to do

1. Cut out about 12 pictures of common objects (such as a dog, banana, and cup).
2. Glue each picture to an index card and cut into the shape of a tulip (if desired).
3. Trace the outline of a butterfly (about 3" square) on paper and cut out. Cut out as many butterflies as there are pictures. Write the initial consonants corresponding to the picture cards on each butterfly ("d" for dog, "b" for banana).
4. Glue the picture cards and butterflies to poster board or tagboard using rubber cement (teacher only) and cut out.
5. Label the backs of the tulips with the names of the pictures on the front. Laminate for durability.
6. Encourage the children to match each letter (butterfly) to a corresponding picture with the same initial consonant (tulip).

Coconut Sound Shakers

Materials

plastic coconut cups (found in novelty stores and catalogs)
assorted materials for sounds (pebbles, marbles, sand, and confetti)
clear tape
labels
markers
laminate
self-adhesive Velcro
sensory table
green streamers

What to do

1. In advance, fill each coconut with a different sound-producing object.
2. Seal the containers closed with clear tape.
3. Draw a picture of each sound-producing object on separate labels and laminate.
4. Stick Velcro on each coconut cup and on each label.
5. Put a symbol on the labels and coconut cups so children can check their answers.
6. Fill the sensory table with green streamers and add the coconut cups.
7. Encourage the children to pick up coconut shakers, shake them, and guess the objects inside. The children can attach the matching label to the cup.

Quazonia Quarles, Newark, DE

Bells Are Ringing

Materials variety of bells
two cards
markers

What to do

1. Acquire a variety of bells in all shapes and sizes, such as jingle bells in various sizes, cow bells, hotel desk bells, and so on.
2. Write the word "loud" on one card and "soft" on the other card. Write the words as they sound—write "loud" in wide uppercase letters, and write "soft" in small, close together, lowercase letters. This will cue non-readers as to what the words say.
3. Ring each bell separately. Does it make a loud or soft sound? Ask the child to put the bell next to the card that describes its sound.

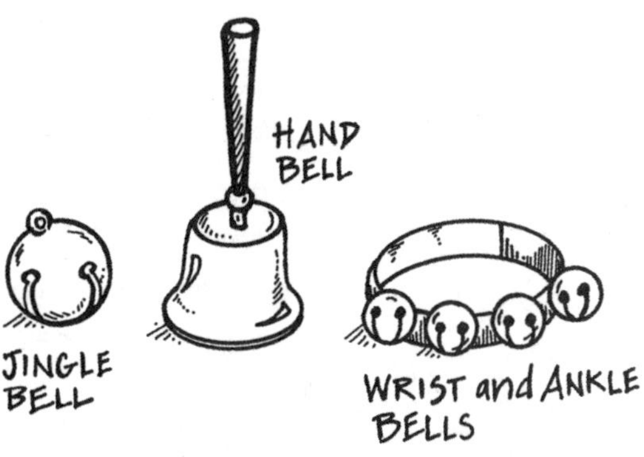

Tracie O'Hara, Charlotte, NC

Guess a Hum

Materials tape recorder and tape

What to do

1. Ask children if they know what humming is. Ask a child to demonstrate humming. If no one can, demonstrate for them and explain how to do it.
2. Encourage the children to take turns humming a tune. The rest of the children guess the tune.
3. Or, when the children are not around, tape yourself or someone else humming different tunes for the children to guess.
4. Tape record each child humming a tune. Play the tape at group time for the children to guess the tune and which child is humming it.

 *Jean Lortz, Sequim, WA*

Hearing Walks

Materials

paper or notebook
pen

What to do

1. Before going outside on a "hearing walk," explain to the children that they will be listening for sounds.
2. On the walk, ask the children to describe what they hear. Write down their observations.
3. After returning from the walk, ask the children to recall the sounds they heard. Compare their recollections with the list from the walk. This activity will help the children learn to listen and recall what was heard.
4. Sing a "call-and-response" song where you sing a phrase and the children repeat what you sing. Ella Jenkins' song, "Did You Feed My Cow?" from the album *You Sing a Song and I'll Sing a Song*, is an example of this type of song.

 *Phyllis Esch, Export, PA*

Music Shakers

Materials

small, empty water bottles with lids
funnels
small sound-producing items (such as beads or small buttons)
tape
markers
stickers
music tapes or CDs
sticks (tongue depressors, craft sticks, and 6-8" pieces of small dowel rods)

What to do

1. Open the empty bottles to let the insides dry completely. Give one to each child.
2. Show the children how to use a funnel to place the sound-making objects of their choice into their bottles.
3. Screw the lids on tightly and tape for extra security.
4. Let the children decorate the outside of their bottles with permanent markers and stickers.
5. Play music and encourage the children to shake their bottles with the music.

6. Provide small sticks for them to rub on the ridges on the sides of the bottle to make a different sound.
7. If desired, have the children make a classroom set by putting one type of item into each bottle.

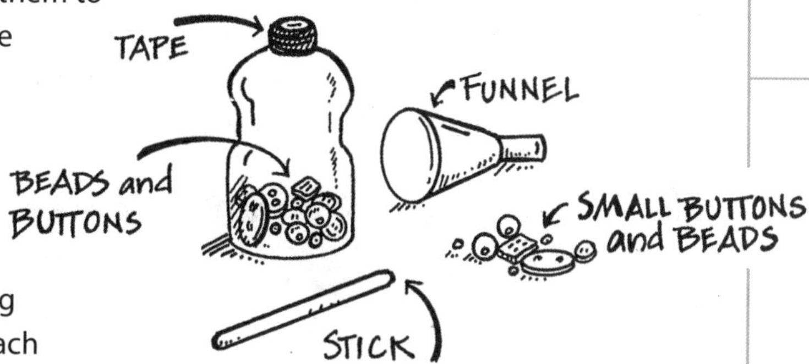

Sandra Nagel, White Lake, MI

Now Hear This!

Materials

plastic film canisters
objects that make different sounds (see activity)
duct tape
hot glue gun (adult only)
two or three shoeboxes
4″ x 6″ index cards

What to do

1. Ask for donations of empty film canisters from a film-processing store. Collect objects that make different sounds, such as pebbles, nails, cotton, corks, shells, sand, paper clips, water, dry cereal, nuts and bolts, jingle bells, raisins, keys, rice, and so on.
2. Fill two canisters with each object, making sets of two per sound. You also can use the same materials of different sizes or amounts. Seal the tops with glue or tape. Place the canisters in a shoebox for storage.
3. Print the names of each object on separate index cards. Glue a sample of the object on each card. Place the completed cards in another shoebox for storage.
4. Encourage the children to shake the canisters and match the sounds. Start with only a few canisters.
5. After the children have explored for a while, mix up the canisters and introduce the identification cards. Encourage the children to shake the canisters and identify the sounds by placing them on the cards.

6. Increase the number of canisters in each shoebox, as the children get better at identifying them.
7. By placing the same objects with varying sizes or amounts in one box (such as pebbles in different sizes), children's hearing acuity will improve.

More to do **Games:** Two children can play a version of the card game "Go Fish!" using the canisters.

 *Susan Forbes, Daytona Beach, FL*

Sensory Tape

Materials tape recorder

What to do

1. Make a tape of familiar sounds in the classroom. Tape environmental noises, such as the squeak of a door, toilet flushing, water running, children laughing, and so on.
2. Play the tape and challenge the children to identify the sounds. It is especially fun to tape each child talking and have the children try and identify the speaker.
3. This is a fun activity that will help develop children's auditory skills.
4. Read stories or sing songs that focus on sounds.

Related song "Old MacDonald"

Phyllis Esch, Export, PA

Sound Cans

Materials

one or more large cans (such as a coffee can) with a secure lid
various materials to put in cans (such as an eraser, cotton ball, cotton swab, paper clip, crayon, seashell, small rock, puzzle piece, and so on)

What to do

1. Put different items into each can and replace the lid. Decorate the cans, if desired.

2. Introduce the activity by shaking one can, listening to the sound, guessing what is inside, and removing the lid to check.
3. Sing the following song as the children explore the cans.

What Is in That Can? *by Jean Lortz*
(tune: "Where, Oh Where has My Little Dog Gone?")
Oh, what, oh, what is in that can?
Oh, what, oh, what can it be?
Oh, shake, oh, shake oh shake that can.
Oh, what, oh, what, can it be?
Oh, take, oh, take the lid off the can.
Oh, what, oh, what do you see?

Jean Lortz, Sequim, WA

Sounds Abound!

Materials

tape recorder
markers
craft paper
digital or 35-mm camera

What to do

1. Before going outside on a "listening walk," do the following activity with the children. Use a tape recorder to record a variety of sounds heard in daily life, such as water from a faucet, a toilet flushing, radio or television, lawnmower, car motor, airplane, dog barking, cat meowing, birds chirping, and people talking.
2. Use craft paper and markers to create a picture for each recorded sound.
3. At circle time, give each child a picture of a sound. Play each sound and ask the children to guess what the sound is. The child holding the picture of the sound stands up. Continue until all the recorded sounds have been identified.
4. Go on a listening walk outdoors to create your own sound recordings. Bring a tape recorder and a camera.
5. Walk around a designated area with the children. Every few minutes have the children stand still and listen. Ask them to identify a sound they hear.
6. Take a photo of the sound source. For example, if the children hear a truck passing by, take a photo of the truck. Record the sound with the tape recorder.

7. Continue doing this with other sounds until you have a variety of sounds recorded. Remember to take a photo of each sound source.
8. After developing the photographs, glue each photo to the top of a piece of white craft paper. Ask the children to dictate text for each photo. Keep the text simple. For example, under the photo of a truck print, "We heard a truck driving on the road."
9. Brainstorm to think of a title for the book. Create a cover and bind the photo pages together.
10. Read the listening book together, playing each sound as you read.

More to do

School-to-Home Connection: Let the children take turns taking the tape recorder home to record several sounds at home. When they return to school, play a guessing game in which the children try to identify the sounds.

Virginia Jean Herrod, Columbia, SC

Sounds Are Fun

Materials

magazines and catalogs
scissors
felt
rubber cement (adult only)
felt board
cassette tape and tape recorder (optional)

What to do

1. Help the children cut out pictures from magazines and catalogs of items that make sounds (such as a dishwasher, dog, and baby). Glue each picture to a piece of tagboard and print the sounds the item makes underneath.
2. Back the pictures with felt using rubber cement for later use on the felt board.
3. Cut the pictures apart to make two-piece puzzles (keep the picture on one piece and the sound on the other).
4. Put the pictures of the objects on half of the felt board and ask the children to identify the sound each one makes. As each sound is identified, place the sound piece of the puzzle next to the picture.
5. Put the puzzle pieces in the listening center with the felt board for use during free choice time. If desired, tape-record the sounds on a cassette tape for the children to use with the puzzles.

Jackie Wright, Enid, OK

Celestial Tubes

Materials

empty cardboard tubes (toilet paper, wrapping paper, paper towels)
black paper
tape or rubber bands
thumbtacks or pencils

What to do

1. Help the children, if needed, tape (or secure with a rubber band) a small piece of black paper over one end of each tube.
2. Help the children punch holes in the black paper as well as randomly on the tube using a thumbtack. If working with very young children, have them mark where they want their holes with a marker and make the holes for them. Or, use a pencil.
3. Encourage the children to put the tubes up to a window or light to see the beautiful "constellations!" (If working with older children, you may try to replicate patterns of actual constellations.)

Related book *The Magic School Bus Lost in the Solar System* by Joanna Cole

 *Shirley Salach, Northwood, NH*

Coffee Filter Parachutes!

Materials

coffee filters
markers
hole punch
scraps of paper
string
tape

What to do

1. Encourage each child to decorate a coffee filter with markers.
2. Assist the children in punching four or five evenly spaced holes around the edges of their filters ("parachute").
3. Encourage each child to draw a small person or animal on a small piece of scrap paper and cut it out. While they work on their figures, begin tying string through the holes in the coffee filters (to save time later). Each piece of string should be at least 1′ long.

4. Help the children use a small amount of tape to attach four or five equal lengths of string onto their person or animal.
5. After the "riders" are attached to the "parachutes," find a high place in the room to launch the parachutes!

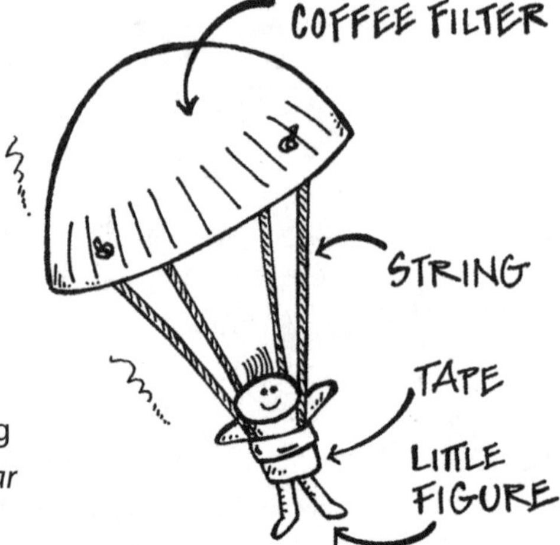

Related books *The Fallen Spaceman* by Lee Harding
The Magic School Bus Lost in the Solar System by Joanna Cole

 *Shirley Salach, Northwood, NH*

Me Constellations

Materials

digital or 35-mm camera
constellation charts
star stickers
thick, clear plastic sheets
tape
classroom window

What to do

1. Take a full-length photograph of each child. When printing or developing the photos, make them as large as possible (8" x 10").
2. Ask the children if they have ever looked up at the stars when outside at night. Explain that years ago, people who studied the stars (astronomers) decided that some stars made the outline of people or animals. These groups of stars are called "constellations."
3. Show the children some constellation charts. (You can obtain these at your local planetarium or online.)
4. Give each child her photo, a clear plastic sheet, and a sheet of star stickers.
5. Ask the children to place the clear plastic sheet on top of their photograph. Then have them outline their pictures using the star stickers.
6. When finished, the child removes the plastic sheet from the photo. She now has a personal "Me Constellation."
7. Help the children think up names for their constellations. For example, The Big Alex (Big Dipper) or Rachelopeia (Cassiopeia). Write the names under each child's constellation.
8. Tape the constellations to a window.

9. If desired, let the children use the plastic sheets and star stickers to make constellations of other familiar items they find in magazines or catalogs.

Related books *A Lot of Otters* by Barbara Helen Berger
Draw Me a Star by Eric Carle
Half a Moon and One Whole Star by Crescent Dragonwagon
How Many Stars in the Sky? by Lenny Hort
Watch the Stars Come Out (Mira como salen las estrellas) by Riki Levinson

 *Virginia Jean Herrod, Columbia, SC*

Old Gadgets to New Contraptions

Materials

parts of tools or objects (see activity for examples)
pieces of wire or twist ties
string
Styrofoam peanuts
toothpicks
buttons
plastic tableware (forks, spoons, knives)
material scraps
nails, screws, and bolts
glue

What to do

1. Put all of the materials at a learning center. Examples of parts of tools include a clothespin taken apart, the wheel of a toy car, a canning jar lid, the handle of a spatula, the wing of a toy airplane, a pan or bucket handle, a propeller, and parts of nail clippers.

2. Explain to the children that the learning center is set up for them to create gadgets or tools to use in "space." Perhaps the children could work together or independently to create a spaceship.
3. After the children have created an apparatus, share the item(s) at circle time. Facilitate the discussion by asking probing questions such as, "What is the name of the contraption?" "How is it used?" "How did you make it?" "What materials did you use to create it?" "How would it be used in space?"

Related book *Arrow to the Sun* by Gerald McDermott

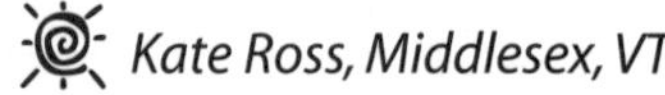

Outer Space Center

Materials

paper plates
crayons
globe

What to do

1. Show the children a globe and encourage let them to share what they know about it.
2. At the space center, provide paper plates for the children to make their own "globes." Encourage them to use crayons to color the ocean and the land.
3. Let them make their globes as desired; their globes do not need to look like accurate depictions!

Satellite Sculptures

Materials

Styrofoam balls of various sizes
packing peanuts
colored or plain toothpicks
glue
colored paper
scissors
paper circles

What to do

1. Explain to the children that pictures are "two-dimensional" because they are flat, and sculptures are "three-dimensional" because they have three or more sides.
2. Show the children a picture of a ball or circle, and then a real Styrofoam ball to illustrate the difference between two-dimensional and three-dimensional objects.
3. Put all of the materials in the space center.
4. Encourage the children to make "satellite" sculptures of their own design.

Barbara Saul, Eureka, CA

Space

Materials

large cardboard appliance box
paint
large butcher paper
string(s) of blue or white small twinkling lights
old helmets
several pairs of snow boots
walkie-talkies
vacuum cleaner hose
posters of space and astronauts
basket of books about space

What to do

1. Make a spaceship with the children using a large refrigerator box.
2. Encourage the children to paint and decorate the cardboard box to look like a spaceship.
3. Cover the walls in the designated area with large butcher paper. Let the children decorate the paper with stars and planets. Attach twinkling lights to the walls and ceiling.
4. Encourage the children to dress like space explorers by putting on helmets and boots.
5. Hang posters of space, add a basket of books about space, and encourage the children to play in the spaceship!

Sue Myhre, Bremerton, WA

Space Helmet

Materials

large brown paper bags
scissors
pens
glue
aluminum foil

What to do

1. Cut off 12" from the top of each bag so it will go over a child's head. Turn the bag upside down and cut out a "window" from either the front or back of the bag so that the child can see out of it.
2. Give each child a pre-cut paper bag. Encourage them to decorate their "helmets" using pens, glue, and aluminum foil.
3. When everyone has made a helmet, take a pretend to ride to outer space.

Related books

Happy Birthday Moon by Frank Asche
Papa, Can You Get the Moon for Me? by Eric Carle

Barbara Saul, Eureka, CA

Spaceship

Materials

large refrigerator box
craft knife or scissors (adult only)
paint
small chairs

What to do

1. Use a refrigerator box to make a spaceship.
2. Lay the box on its side and cut out windows in the front side (adult only).
3. Paint the box to look like a spaceship and put small chairs inside.
4. This center is open-ended. Children can play in the spaceship as desired.

Barbara Saul, Eureka, CA

A Trip to the Moon

Materials tape recorder

What to do

1. Convert your housekeeping area into a space shuttle ready to take off!
2. Beforehand, make a tape recording of a take-off count. Count down with the children to launch the space shuttle.

Related book *I Want to Be an Astronaut* by Byron Barton

Jackie Wright, Enid, OK

Twinkle, Twinkle, Little Star

Materials

book about constellations
markers
star-shaped cookie cutters
scissors
felt
yarn
construction paper
glitter

What to do

1. Read a book about stars and constellations to the children.
2. Help the children make star ornaments. Encourage them to trace a star-shaped cookie cutter onto a piece of felt and cut out. Help each child tie a piece of yarn into a bow and glue it on the star.
3. Encourage the children to trace the star-shaped cookie cutters onto construction paper and cut out. Provide glitter and glue to decorate them.
4. Sing "Twinkle, Twinkle, Little Star" using the glitter stars. Encourage the children to move the stars to the music.

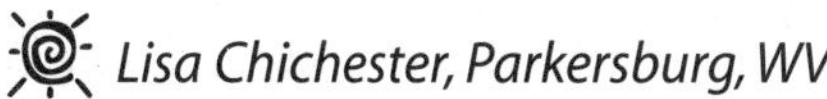
Lisa Chichester, Parkersburg, WV

A New Story

Materials

comic strips and comic books (age appropriate)
scissors
glue
paper

What to do

1. Display comic strips, old comic books, scissors, glue, and paper at the storytelling learning center.
2. Let each child choose two to four comic strips or one comic book.
3. Ask the children to cut apart the different comic strips or cut out individual pictures from the comic book. Keep any leftover pictures for other children to use.
4. Encourage the children to rearrange the pictures into a new strip with three or four frames. You may wish to prompt for logical sequencing as the children are setting up their strips. For example, ask, "If this happened first, what might happen next?" "What might happen before or after this part?" "How is this new story silly?"
5. Ask the children to glue their new comic strip onto a piece of paper.
6. Let the children explain the new story to a friend or the whole group, if desired.

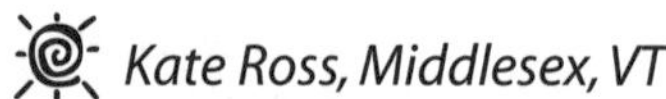
Kate Ross, Middlesex, VT

Be the Author

Materials

old calendars
scissors
three-ring binder
plastic protector sleeves

What to do

1. Ask parents or friends to donate old calendars to use to create child-made books for your classroom library.
2. Cut out calendar pictures and place them in plastic sleeve protectors in a three-ring binder.
3. Encourage each child to look through the pictures and select his favorite. Ask the child to dictate a story about his picture to you or another adult (parent volunteer). Write down the child's story and encourage him to sign his work.

4. Tape the dictated story to the picture in the plastic sleeve.
5. Children love to see their own stories, and the book will soon become a favorite.

More to do If you have a computer in your classroom, let the children dictate their stories on the computer as a supplemental activity to hand-writing their story. It is exciting for the children to see their words come to life when printed out.

Tracie O'Hara, Charlotte, NC

Class Newspaper

Materials

newspaper
paper
pencils and markers
glue
scissors
camera

What to do

1. During circle time, show the children a newspaper and point out the different parts. Talk about newspaper jobs, such as editor, columnist, reporter, sports writer, photographer, and so on.
2. Tell the children they are going to make their own class newspaper. Help them pick a name and write it on a large piece of poster board.
3. Talk about newspaper articles. Explain that a good story needs to answer these questions: who, what, when, where, why, and how (five "W's" and one "H").
4. Show the children how editors lay out a newspaper page. Cut out pictures and stories from a different newspaper and help the children put them together.
5. Assign each child a job for the class newspaper. Help them think of something they would like to write a story about. Remind them of the five "W's" and one "H".
6. Use an instant camera and take pictures to go with the story.
7. Encourage the children to dictate and illustrate stories, if desired.
8. Cut out the stories and lay them out like a newspaper.
9. If desired, make copies on a photocopier and send them home each week.
10. Rotate jobs each week and set aside time for them to work on the class paper each day.

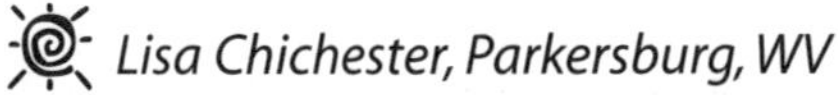
Lisa Chichester, Parkersburg, WV

Felt Board Center

Materials

favorite storybooks
markers
felt
scissors
felt board

What to do

1. Make felt board pieces to match favorite storybooks (such as *The Very Hungry Caterpillar* by Eric Carle). Draw characters and/or objects from each book onto felt and cut them out.
2. Use the felt board pieces at circle time. Have the children participate by putting the pieces or characters from the story on the flannel board as you read the book or tell the story. Make sure to have enough pieces for everyone in the class to have a turn.
3. Make a storytelling learning center by putting the felt board, books, and felt board pieces in an area of the room.
4. Children can take turns being the teacher and students during free play.

Audrey Kanoff, Allentown, PA

My Gingerbread Man Story

Materials

felt board
markers
felt
scissors

What to do

1. Cut out a gingerbread man and wolf from felt to make felt board props.
2. Read several different versions of the "Gingerbread Boy" to the children.
3. Provide a felt board in the storytelling center. The children can use the gingerbread man and wolf props to make up their own version of the story.

Related books

Gingerbread Baby by Jan Brett
Gingerbread Boy by Harriet Zeiffert
Gingerbread Boy by Richard Egielski
Gingerbread Man by Jim Aylesworth

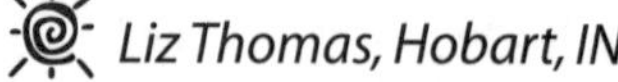
Liz Thomas, Hobart, IN

Once Upon a Fairy Tale

Materials

books about different fairy tales
scissors
construction paper
glue stick
laminate
container with lid
paper
crayons

What to do

1. Prior to presenting the center, cut out (or make copies of) five to ten pictures from each of the fairy tale books. Each picture should depict a fairy tale that is recognizable to the child. Make sure that some pictures show the main characters. Glue the pictures onto construction paper and laminate.
2. The week before doing this activity, read each of the books to the children so they are familiar with the stories.
3. Put all of the pictures in a box, making sure they are mixed up. Encourage the children to sort the pictures according to the story they come from.
4. After the pictures are sorted, let the children pick their favorite story to sequence by order of events.
5. Encourage each child to retell story using the sequenced pictures as props.
6. Ask the children to draw a picture of the story they sequenced.

Related poem

Say the following poem in the speaking pattern of *Brown Bear, Brown Bear, What Do You See?* by Bill Martin, Jr.

Cinderella, Cinderella, who do you see?
A fairy godmother to help me.
Snow White, Snow White, who do you see?
Seven little dwarfs friendly as can be.
Peter Pan, Peter Pan, who do you see?
Captain Hook after me.
Sleeping Beauty, Sleeping Beauty, who do you see?
A mean old fairy scary as can be.
Three pigs, three pigs, who do you see?
A big, old wolf huffing at me.

 *Marzee Woodward, Murfreesboro, TN*

Once Upon a Story

Materials

tape recorder
craft paper
markers, crayons, and colored pencils
heavy black marker

What to do

1. Do this activity a few months into the school year, after you have read many stories to the children.
2. Start to read a familiar story to the children. Read the first couple of pages and then put the book down. Ask the children if they would like to make their own new book to read instead.
3. Show the children the tape recorder and explain that they are going to work together to make up a whole new story.
4. Begin the new story by saying (into the tape recorder), "Once upon a time there was a …."
5. Choose a child and ask him to finish the sentence (for example, "turtle").
6. Repeat the phrase, adding the child's idea. "Once upon a time there was a turtle named …"
7. Choose another to fill in the blank ("Timmy").
8. Repeat the phrase, adding the child's idea. "Once upon a time there was a turtle named Timmy who lived in a …."
9. Once again, choose a child to fill in the blank ("hole").
10. Continue the story in this manner. Provide the basic ingredients of the story and let the children add the important facts as you go along. Try not to lead their thoughts into something that "makes sense." Let them think freely for themselves.
11. Continue until you feel the story is finished. This may take several days to complete it to the children's satisfaction.
12. Write the story down as dictated. Read it to the children.
13. Ask the children to draw illustrations for several of the scenes in the story.
14. Use a black marker to print the story on craft paper. Glue the illustrations to the appropriate pages.
15. Read through the story to make sure the pages are in the correct order.
16. Create a cover and bind the pages together into a book. Read the new story together and enjoy!
17. Let the children take turns bringing the book home to share with their families.
18. If desired, make a big book of the story by writing it on poster board instead of regular craft paper.

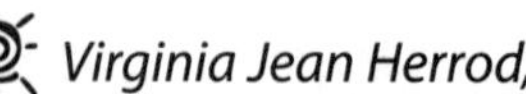

Virginia Jean Herrod, Columbia, SC

Four Puppets for Little Red Riding Hood Story

Materials

oak tag or tagboard
scissors
glue
construction paper (tan, pink, brown, blue, black, white, and gray)
markers and crayons
fabric or felt pieces
yarn
12-mm wiggle eyes
craft sticks or Popsicle sticks

What to do

1. Make puppets of Red Riding Hood, the grandmother, wolf, and woodcutter using the patterns on the follwing pages.
2. Make copies of the patterns and enlarge, if necessary. Cut out the outlines of each character and trace onto tagboard or oak tag.
3. Decorate the puppets as desired using markers, crayons, construction paper, fabric and felt pieces, wiggle eyes, yarn for hair, and so on.
4. Glue a craft stick or Popsicle stick to the back of each puppet. Use the puppets as you tell the poem on page 496.

WOODCUTTER

GRANDMA

LITTLE RED RIDING HOOD

FOLD IN
BACK OF HEAD
WOLF

The Red Riding Hood Story by Mary Brehm

There once was a girl named Little Red Riding Hood.
She was helpful and kind and very, very good.
Her Grandma made the hood that she wore every day
Whether she went to school or just out to play.

One day she heard that her dear Grandma was sick,
So she baked some goodies to take to her quick.
A path led from her house and through the wood.
Off with her basket skipped Little Red Riding Hood.

On her way she met a wolf that was as friendly as could be.
He asked where she was going, then he went to grandma's secretly.
Fooling Grandma with his voice sounding real high,
He went into grandma's house but she hid in a closet nearby.

Quickly the wolf donned her nightcap, and Grandma he pretended to be
When Red Riding Hood came in so very unsuspectingly.
"Grandma, what great big eyes you have," said she.
"All the better to see you, my dear," wolf replied hungrily.

"Grandma, what big ears you have!" she continued to say,
"All the better to hear you, dear, on this fine day."
"But Grandma, what a huge nose you have!" she queried more.
"So I can smell those goodies," wolf softly said as before.

"But Grandma, what big teeth you have!" Red Riding Hood said.
"All the better to eat you with!" yelled wolf as he jumped out of bed.
A nearby woodcutter heard Red Riding Hood call, "Help me!"
And he rescued Red Riding Hood and grandma very quickly.

They thanked the woodcutter and invited him to stay.
And they ate cookies and milk on that special day.

Sequence Stories

Materials

selection of stories with plots that have a definite sequence (such as *The Gingerbread Man, The Very Hungry Caterpillar, Caps for Sale*, and *The Mitten*)
cardstock
scissors
markers

What to do

1. Using markers and cardstock, make picture cards of a few stories with plots that have a definite sequence .
2. Read the stories with the class several times, encouraging them to help you read each one as they become more familiar with the sequence of the events. "Run, run as fast as you can..." Place the books in the library center where children can continue to enjoy them.
3. When they are thoroughly familiar with the stories, introduce four to seven picture cards (per story) depicting the actions of the story.
4. Make a numbered story map for each title on a large piece of cardstock. This is simply a piece of paper with the title of the book at the top and four to seven numbered columns.
5. Ask the children to place the picture cards on the story map in the order that events in the story happened.
6. To make this a self-correcting activity, number the cards on the back.
7. A variation of this activity is to choose one child to be "it." This child covers his eyes while another child removes one of the cards and pushes the cards together so there is no blank space. "It" must try to figure out which part of the story was removed.
8. Encourage the children to retell the story while following the picture prompts on the sequence cards.

Iris Rothstein, New Hyde Park, NY

Story Hour

Materials

plastic shoe holder
hand and finger puppets
chair

What to do

1. Hang a plastic shoe holder on the wall in the library center. Put hand and finger puppets in the plastic shoe holder.
2. Put a variety of picture books on a shelf in the center.

3. Encourage the children to take turns sitting on the chair and telling stories with the puppets.

Related books *Book! Book! Book!* by Deborah Bruss
A Day With the Librarian by Jan Kottke
D.W.'s Library Card by Mark Brown
Sam's First Library Card by Gail Herman

Liz Thomas, Hobart, IN

Story Retelling

Materials

1"-wide elastic
scissors
felt
yarn
needle and thread or hot glue gun (adult only)

What to do

1. Cut four pieces of elastic so that each piece fits around a child's head. Make four for each child.
2. Cut out three sets of sets of pig ears and one set of wolf ears (for "The Three Little Pigs") or three sets of bear ears and one pair of girl's ears (for "Goldilocks and the Three Bears") from felt.
3. Sew or hot glue each pair of ears to the elastic and sew the elastic closed.
4. Braid many pieces of yarn. Sew the hair to the elastic for Goldilocks.
5. Retell the story of "The Three Little Pigs or "Goldilocks."
6. Place the items in the dramatic play area to add a twist to the use of the area. This can be adapted for any other stories.

Melissa Browning, Milwaukee, WI

Storytelling Apron

Materials

homemade or purchased apron (felt, corduroy, or other fabric with nap)
needle and thread
old coloring books or felt
markers
scissors
Velcro

What to do

1. Make or buy an apron similar to one used for backyard barbecuing. This apron works best if made out of felt, corduroy, or other fabric with a nap. Sew pockets to the lower edge to hold materials.
2. Find pictures of a familiar story. Choose a story you like or want to use often, as the children will request it often. Make sure the pictures or symbols are brightly colored and large enough for all the children to see well. Coloring books are great to use because the pictures are already large and can be colored brightly. Pictures cut from felt are also good to use because they don't need Velcro.
3. Attach Velcro to the back of each picture so that it will stick to the apron.
4. Before you tell a story, put on the apron and put the pictures for the story in the pockets. As you tell the story, reach into the pockets for the appropriate picture and stick it to the apron. This helps make the story interesting.
5. The apron is also great for sequencing songs and fingerplays.

Phyllis Esch, Export, PA

What Else Happened in Nursery Rhymes and Fairy Tales

Materials

pictures depicting familiar nursery rhymes and fairy tales
writing paper
writing utensils

What to do

1. Display the pictures on a table in the storytelling center.
2. Share the pictures with the children and explain that they will use the pictures as a story starter.

3. Have each child choose a picture and expand upon it. For example, they could answer questions such as:
   - What were the three men in the tub doing as they sailed along?
   - What did Pinocchio do while he was inside the whale?
   - Why were Jack and Jill fetching a pail of water?
   - What did Sleeping Beauty dream about?
4. Encourage the children to write a story and illustrate it using the pictures. Younger children may need to dictate the story to an adult.

Related books *Goldilocks and the Three Bears* by James Marshall
Harold's Fairy Tale by Crockett Johnson.
The Jolly Postman or Other People's Letters by Janet and Allen Ahlberg
The True Story of the Three Little Pigs! by Jon Scieszka

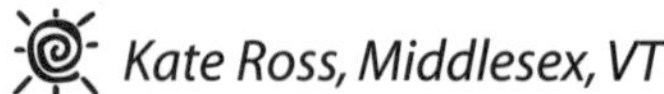

Kate Ross, Middlesex, VT

What If ______ and ______ Met?

Materials

pictures depicting different storybook characters
writing paper
writing utensils

What to do

1. Display the pictures on a table in the storytelling center.
2. Join children as they enter the storytelling center and share the pictures with them.
3. Ask each child to choose two different characters from two different stories.
4. With the two characters, the children will create a new story focusing on what might happen if the two characters met. For example, what if the giant from Jack and the Beanstalk met Cinderella? What would happen if Sleepy from Snow White met Sleeping Beauty? What if the Wolf from Little Red Riding Hood met the Gingerbread Man?
5. Provide ample time for children to write (or dictate) their stories. Encourage them to illustrate their stories when done.
6. When completed, ask for volunteers to share.

Related books *Babushka's Mother Goose* by Patricia Polacco
The Owl and the Pussycat by Edward Lear and Jan Brett

Kate Ross, Middlesex, VT

Ball Catcher

Materials medium-size beads
string
small paper cups
tray or bin
masking tape
hole punch

What to do

1. Place beads, paper cups, and pieces of string on a tray or in a bin.
2. Help the children punch a hole down near the bottom of their cup.
3. Help them thread string through the hole and tie a knot to the inside of the cup. Cover the knot and hole with tape.
4. Tie a bead to the other end of the string.
5. Let the children play with their new toy.

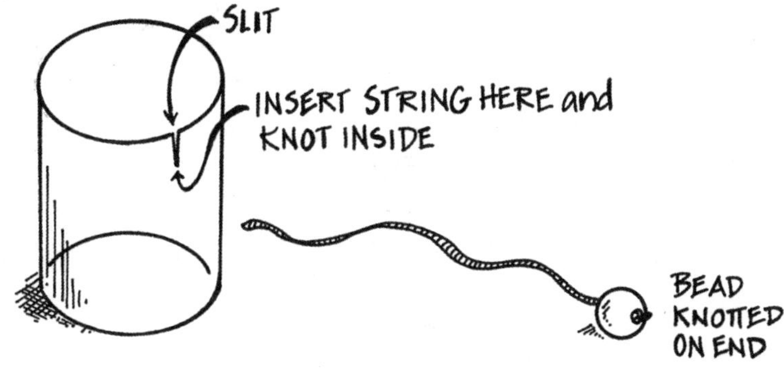

Melissa Browning, Milwaukee, WI

Juice Can Bead Toss Toys

Materials

yarn or string
X-acto knife, knife, or sharp adult scissors
plastic juice cans
plastic or wooden beads (about 1" diameter)
wallpaper scraps or tissue paper and glue (optional)

What to do

1. Precut pieces of string, approximately 1' long, one for each child.
2. Score a slit on the edge of each plastic juice can near the top.
3. Place beads, cans, and yarn on the table and let the children choose one of each. If children wish, they can decorate their juice can with scraps of wallpaper or tissue paper.
4. Challenge them to string their bead.
5. Tie the bead onto one end of their string and push the other end of their string through the juice can slit.
6. Make a knot on the end of the string that is now in the juice can. The bead should be out of the juice can, and the plain knot in the juice can.
7. Show the children how to hold the juice cans, toss the bead up, and attempt to catch the bead in their cans.
8. Shorten or lengthen string for varying difficulty levels.

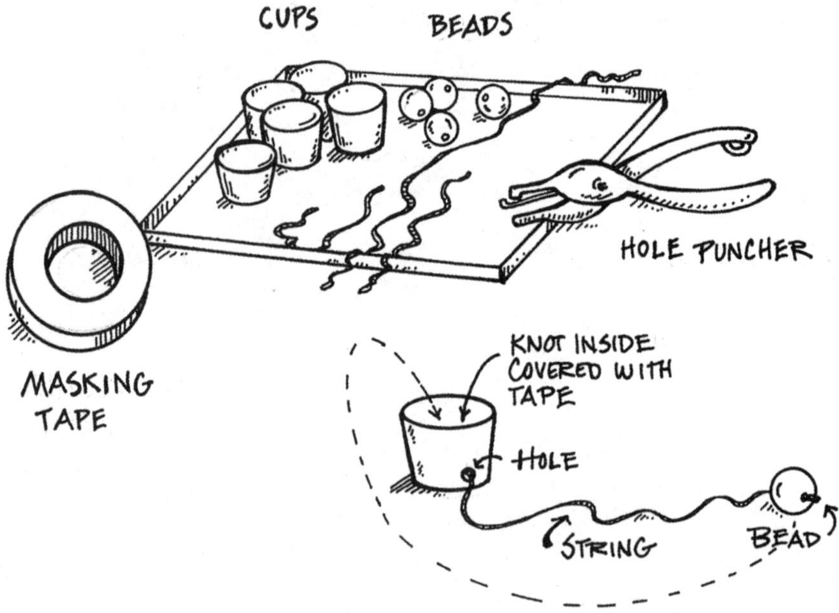

 *Shirley Salach, Northwood, NH*

Rainy Day Bucket

Materials

large container
small toys (such as from cereal boxes)

What to do

1. Collect a bunch of special toys that the children would not ordinarily play with on a daily basis.
2. Put these toys in a large pocket or container and label it "Rainy Day Bucket."
3. On rainy days only, take out the bucket for children to play with as a special activity.
4. You can also make one for "Snowy Days."

Andrea Hungerford, Plainville, CT

Repair Shop

Materials

broken toys
tools
tape
glue
small nails
safety goggles

What to do

1. Put the broken toys and other materials in the woodworking area.
2. Problem solve with the children working in the "Toy Repair Shop" and think of ways they may be able to repair a broken toy.
3. Encourage them to work on the broken toys.

Related book *The New Way Things Work* by David Macaulay

Ann Kelly, Johnstown, PA

Same Toy, But Different!

Materials requested toys brought from home

What to do

1. Send home a note to parents the night before the activity is to occur. Ask them to let their child bring one item from a chosen category (such as teddy bears or dolls). Suggested categories include teddy bears, dinosaurs, dolls, cars, pencils, and balls.
2. Gather the children with their toys or items in a circle. Ask them to place their object behind them as you give instructions.
3. Explain that they will be exploring like objects and finding out how they are the same and different.
4. Divide the children into groups of two. Remind the children that all items should be the same.
5. Ask the children to compare their objects. You may wish to prompt with the following questions:
   - Are the items exactly alike?
   - How are they the same? (Name at least two similarities.)
   - How are they different? (Name at least two differences.)
   - Even though two objects may be called the same thing ("teddy bear"), are they actually exactly the same?
6. After ample time, gather the children in the larger group. Ask them to share their discoveries.

Related books
A Pocket for Corduroy by Don Freeman
The Toy Brother by William Stieg
Where's My Teddy? by Jez Alborough

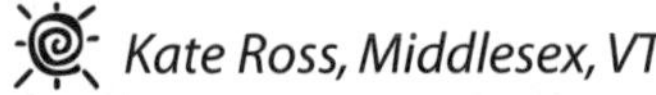
Kate Ross, Middlesex, VT

Something's Wrong

Materials
shoebox
wind-up toys

What to do

1. Place a variety of wind-up toys in a shoebox and put it in a learning center. Make sure that the some of the toys don't work (either because they are broken or missing a battery). Be sure that some of the toys are easier to operate than others.

2. No real preparation time is needed for this activity. The toys should "speak for themselves." The children will likely approach you or another adult to inquire how to get the toy to work.
3. The goal is to have children ask what's wrong, ask for assistance, and explore the toy to see why it doesn't work and yet others do.
4. If needed, model questions or requests such as, "Help me, please," or "I wonder why that doesn't work."

Related books *Albert's Alphabet* by Leslie Tryon
Alexander and the Wind-Up Mouse by Leo Lionni

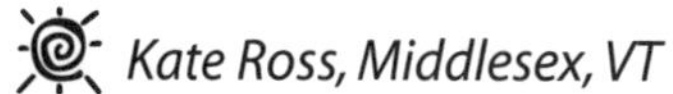
Kate Ross, Middlesex, VT

Toy Library

Materials

donated toys (one or two from each child's family)
index cards
pencil or marker
two index card boxes
craft paper
markers
small table and chair

What to do

1. Ask the children's parents to send in one or two gently used or new toys. Make sure that any of the used toys is not a child's favorite.
2. Explain to the children that they will be creating a "toy library." Tell them that they will be able to check toys out from the toy library and take them home for two or three days at a time. Make sure the children realize they cannot keep the toys, but must bring them back after the allotted time.
3. Ask the children to sort the toys into different categories, such as vehicles, action figures, stuffed animals, dolls and doll care, and electronics.
4. Have the children arrange the toys on the shelves according to the categories.
5. Help the children create colorful labels for each category of toy. Post the labels near the toys.
6. Using index cards, let the children help make a card for each toy. Draw a picture or paste a small photo of each toy on a card. Print the name of the toy under the picture. Put the cards in an index card box.
7. Label the other index card box "Checked Out." Put the index card boxes and a pencil or marker on a small table with a single chair. This is the librarian's station.

8. Create a sign for the toy library. Post the sign on the classroom door.
9. Encourage the children to design toy library cards for themselves. Print the name of the toy library on the card and each child's first name. (Do not put any personal information on the card, especially the name of your school.)
10. Open the toy library for business! Designate one child to be the librarian. At the end of the day, each child can choose one toy to take home for a few days.
11. Remind the children to show the librarian their toy library card. The librarian finds the card that matches the toy and prints the child's name on it. Put the card in the "Checked Out" box.
12. Each day, choose a different child to be the toy librarian. Have the librarian collect the returned toys and put them back on the shelves.
13. Continue the activity as long as the children's interest remains strong.
14. At the end of the activity, donate the toys to a local children's shelter or allow the children to take them home.

More to do

Books: Add books to the toy library. Find books that feature the toys in the library. Place the books near the toys and let children check them out with the toy. For example, place a book about cars near the cars.

Field Trip: Take a field trip to a real library. Attend a story time session and let the children choose a book to check out. Most libraries have teacher library cards, which allow teachers to check out many books.

Related books

At the Library by Christine Loomis
Harry in Trouble by Barbara Ann Porte
I Took My Frog to the Library by Eric A. Kimmel
Louie's Goose by H.M. Ehrlich
The Toy Brother by William Steig
Tomas and the Library Lady by Pat Mora

Virginia Jean Herrod, Columbia, SC

Mobility Equipment

Materials

scooter
wheelchair
walkers (with and without wheels)
canes and crutches
ramps

What to do

1. Ask a child's parent, grandparent, or friend to come in and talk about mobility differences and the related equipment. If possible, have the visitor demonstrate the techniques of using ramps when in a power chair scooter or wheelchair.
2. If a visitor is not available, take a field trip to a medical equipment store for demonstrations and comparisons between the types of chairs. Note the varying amounts and sizes of wheels there are.
3. This is a great activity to do as a follow-up. Add one or more of the following items to add to your transportation area: a scooter, wheelchair, walker, cane, crutches, and ramp.
4. Explain each piece of mobility equipment and how it enables a person to get from one place to another.
5. Encourage the children to explore the mobility equipment. Let them use non-motorized equipment to move from one center to another. Make sure the children understand the need to keep pathways between centers clear so they can move through freely.

Jean Lortz, Sequim, WA

All Aboard for Railroad Adventures

Materials

paper tickets
engineer hat
whistle
Freight Train by Donald Crews
construction paper in a variety of colors
scissors
markers and crayons
glue

What to do

1. Arrange the chairs in the room like a passenger car. Put on an engineer's hat, give each child a ticket, and blow a train whistle to announce the start of the activity.
2. When everyone is seated and comfortable in the "train," share train-related books, songs, and fingerplays with them. Read Donald Crews' *Freight Train*, which incorporates colors and train car recognition. A good poem to read is "Clickety-Clack" by David McCord. This wonderful poem makes an excellent knee-slapping chant that children will enjoy. Also do the fingerplay "Choo-Choo Train," which can be found in many fingerplay collections.
3. End the train activity by making train headbands.
4. Copy the pattern of the freight train cars (see illustration). Trace onto construction paper and cut out. Cut one out for each child.
5. Encourage each child to choose a train car cutout, color it, and glue it to a construction paper strip to make a headband.

Related books

Choo, Choo by Virginia Lee Burton
Dinosaur Train by John Gurney
Down by the Station by Will Hillenbrand
I Love Trains by Philemon Sturges
The Little Engine That Could by Watty Piper

The Little Train by Lois Lenski
Thomas the Tank Engine by Christopher Awdry
Train Song by Harriet Zeifert

Related songs "The Wheels on the Train" (sing to the tune of "The Wheels on the Bus")
"Down By the Station"

Joan Bowman, Langhorne, PA

How Would You Get There?

Materials

pictures of places (places in your town and around the world)
white construction paper
tape or glue
pen
hole punch
three-ring binder or folder

What to do

1. Show the children the pictures and photos. Talk about the places.
2. Let each child choose a picture of a place he would like to go. Ask the children to glue or tape their picture to a sheet of white construction paper.
3. Ask each child individually how he would get to the place in the photo. Encourage humor and creativity. Write what the child tells you next to the photo.
4. Punch three holes along the left side of each paper.
5. Let the children help make a cover for the book. Write each child's name on the cover as the authors.
6. Read the book at large group and add it to the library area.

Related books

Amazing Airplanes by Tony Mittin
Boats Afloat by Shelley Rotner
Freight Train by Donald Crews
Silly Sally by Audrey Wood
Trains by Byron Barton

Ann Kelly, Johnstown, PA

Police Officer Stick Puppet

Materials

cardboard
markers
scissors
construction paper in blue and black
white glue
silver or gold paper
6″ paper plate
20-mm wiggle eyes
1″ x 6″ craft stick

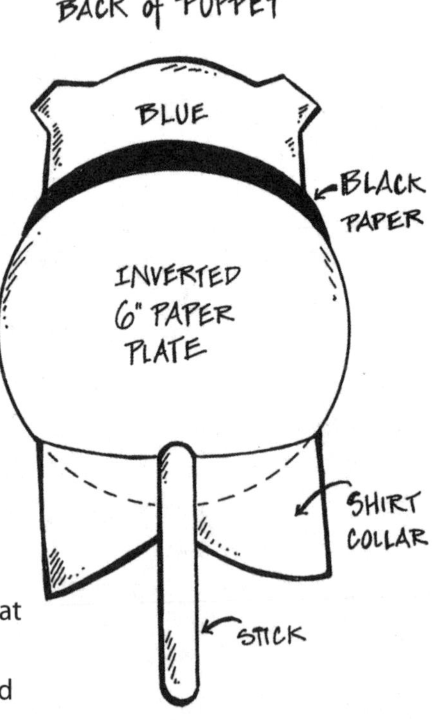

What to do

1. Make patterns for a police hat, collar, and shield badge (see illustration). Photocopy the illustrations. Trace the hat, collar, brim of the hat, and badge on cardboard and cut out to make patterns.
2. Ask the children to trace the hat on blue paper and cut out.
3. Ask the children to trace the brim of the hat on black paper and cut out. Help the children fold up the top ½″ of the brim and glue to the hat.
4. Encourage the children to trace the shield badge on gold or silver paper, cut out, and glue in the center of the hat.
5. Ask the children to trace the collar pattern on paper and cut out.
6. Give each child a 6″ paper plate. Encourage them to decorate a face on the paper plate by drawing hair, eyebrows, nose, and mouth. They can glue on wiggle eyes to complete the face.
7. Help them glue the hat to the top of the plate, and the collar to the bottom. Finish by gluing a craft stick to the collar and plate.
8. Encourage the children to play with their police officer stick puppets!

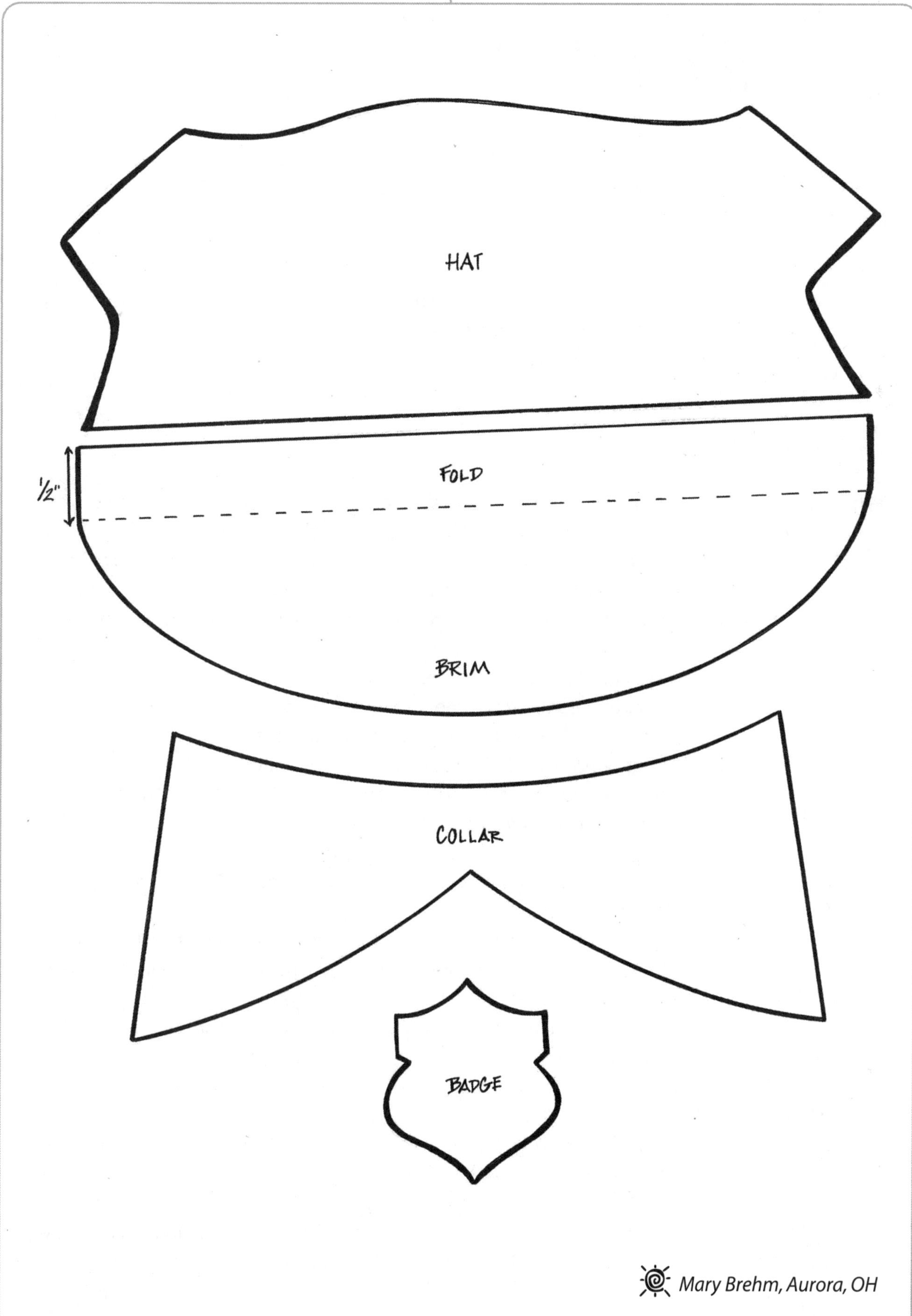

Mary Brehm, Aurora, OH

Riding the Bus

Materials

cash register
play money
large table
white shirt, vest, and visor
several small chairs and one large chair
real steering wheel or made from cardboard
bus driver hat and shirt
index cards
markers
yarn

What to do

1. Before setting up this activity, take a field trip on a real bus. Visit a real bus stop. Watch the people and talk about where they might be going.
2. Make a ticket counter by setting up a large table and putting a cash register on it. Put the white shirt, vest, and visor on the table.
3. Arrange several small chairs to represent the seats on a bus, putting them in rows of two with a small aisle in the middle.
4. Put the large chair in the front for the bus driver. Put a steering wheel (real or cut from cardboard) on the floor in front of the driver's chair.
5. Place the bus driver hat and shirt on the bus driver seat.
6. Make bus passes by printing "Bus Pass" on index cards. Punch a hole in the center of each card, thread a length of yarn through the hole, and tie a knot in the yarn. Put the bus passes on the ticket agent table.
7. Encourage the children to dress up before they depart on their bus ride. Provide purses, bags, and play money. Encourage the children to bring stuffed animals along for the ride.
8. The children can purchase tickets for their bus ride. Remind the ticket agent to ask the children where they are going and what time they want to leave. The ticket agent should give each child a bus pass.
9. Encourage the children to sing songs such as "The Wheels on the Bus" while riding on the bus.

Related books

School Bus by Donald Crews
The Seals on the Bus by Lenny Hort
The Wheels on the Bus by Maryann Kovalski

Trains

Materials

rectangular sponges
pie tins
paint in different colors including black
plastic cap
white construction paper

What to do

1. Pour different colors of paint and into individual pie tins.
2. Tell the children that they will be using the sponges to paint a train.
3. Show them how to dip the sponge into paint and press it onto construction paper to make a rectangle.
4. Encourage them to continue painting rectangles on their paper, making a long train.
5. When finished, show them how to dip a plastic cap into black paint and press it onto the paper to make wheels for the train.

Related books

Freight Train by Donald Crews
Trains by Anne Rockwell
Trains by Paul Strickland

Liz Thomas, Hobart, IN

Transportation Classification

Materials

pictures of (or plastic) cars, trucks, planes, boats, and so on
pictures of land or roads, sky, and water

What to do

1. Read books about transportation, cars, trucks, and so on.
2. Ask the children to sort the pictures or plastic objects according to whether they move on land, in the air, or in the water.
3. Provide pictures of land, water, and sky for the children to use while sorting.

Phyllis Esch, Export, PA

Twinkle, Twinkle, Traffic Light

Materials

red, yellow, green, and black felt
scissors
felt board
blank cassette tape
tape player

What to do

1. Cut out a traffic light outline from black felt. Cut out three 2" circles, one red, one yellow, and one green.
2. Find a recording of the song "Twinkle, Twinkle, Traffic Light" (found on the album *Piggyback Songs*). If this particular song is not available, substitute any of the versions of "Where Is My Red Light?" (sung to the tune of "Where Is Thumbkin?").
3. Make a recording of the children singing the song.
4. Put the traffic light, circles, and felt board in the listening center along with a recording of the song.
5. Encourage the children to listen to the song and manipulate the felt board pieces during free choice time.

Jackie Wright, Enid, OK

Vanity Plates

Materials

license plate or photocopy of a license plate
white-out
paper
letter cutouts
glue
pastel-colored marker
magazines
scissors

What to do

1. Make a photocopy of your state license plate. Use a real one, a toy one, or a photo of one (from the Internet or DMV). Then white out the letters and numbers on the photocopy. Make enough copies of the blank license plates for each child in the class.

2. Provide letter cutouts and help the children find the letters in their names. Ask them to glue the letters of their names on the plates. (You could also use sticky foam letters found at craft stores.)
3. Older children may like to write their own names on their license plates. If children are learning how to write their names, you may want to pre-write the names with a pastel-colored marker for them to trace over.
4. Display the license plates in the room, attach them to cardboard boxes for pretend cars, or compile them into a class scrapbook.
5. Locate photos of other state license plates in magazines and the Internet. Encourage the children to compare them. Challenge them to try and guess the states by their pictures. Suggest they watch for different plates as they are riding in their cars.

Related books *Big Book of Cars* by Trevor Lord
Cars and Trucks and Things That Go by Richard Scarry

Laura Durbrow, Lake Oswego, OR

Fingerpaint Drawing and Writing

Materials

paint smocks
large paper
tape
fingerpaint
paper towels

What to do

1. Have the children put on paint smocks and stand at the table.
2. Tape large pieces of paper to the table. Pour fingerpaint on the table and encourage the children to move the paint around with their fingers and hands.
3. Encourage the children to draw and write in the fingerpaint. They can try shapes, letters, numerals, names, and objects. Remind them that they can wipe their hands over the fingerpaint to smooth it out and start again.
4. Ask the children to verbalize what they are writing or drawing.
5. Encourage the children to use their arms and elbows to paint, too!
6. This is a good activity for children to practice keeping to their own space and respecting others' space and drawings.

Related book *It Looked Like Spilt Milk* by Charles G. Shaw

Sandra Nagel, White Lake, MI

A Diary of Our Day

Materials

paper
colored pencils
pens
hole punch
folders or yarn

What to do

1. Read several books from the book list below and discuss what a diary is. Tell them they will make their own diary by recording events of the day.
2. Ask each child to write her name on a few pieces of paper. Explain that they will use their paper to dictate or draw important things that they do that day.
3. Give the children several reminders throughout the day to take time to write or draw in their diary. Small group, recall, and transition times are good for reminders.
4. Ask the children to make covers for their diaries. Punch holes in each page and put them into three-ring folders or tie with yarn.
5. Review the books with the class.
6. These are great books to review with parents at parent conferences. The books provide insight into what each child feels is important as well as her skills in language development, writing, and drawing.

Related books

Dear Mrs. LaRue: Letters From Obedience School by Mark Teague
Dear Zoo by Rob Campbell
Diary of a Wombat by Jackie French
Diary of a Worm by Doreen Cronin
Letters From Felix: A Little Rabbit on a World Tour by Annette Langin

Ann Kelly, Johnstown, PA

Alpha Craze

Materials

white T-shirts
cardboard
fabric pens
alphabet stencils
paint
magnetic letters
clay
alphabet cookie cutters
sandpaper
scissors
paper

What to do

1. Give each child a white T-shirt. Put cardboard inside each T-shirt before the children paint on them. Encourage them to use fabric pens and stencils to make letters on their shirts.
2. Sing the alphabet song as the children make their alphabet T-shirts.
3. Encourage the children to place magnetic letters in order on a filing cabinet or other magnetic surface. Let them take turns singing the alphabet song and lining up the letters.
4. Provide clay and cookie cutters to make alphabet letters.
5. Trace the letters of the alphabet on sandpaper and cut them out. Ask the children to close their eyes and feel each letter. Challenge them to paint the letter they think it is.

Lisa Chichester, Parkersburg, WV

Black on White vs. White on Black

Materials

white gel pens, pencils, or crayons
black paper
black gel pens, pencils, or crayons
white paper

What to do

1. Beforehand, discuss how the print in books is black words on white paper.
2. Show the children a few books to demonstrate. Point out how print is read from left to right.
3. Explain to the children that they are going to reverse the color of the print and paper by writing with white gel pens or pencils on black paper. Encourage them to draw pictures on the black paper.
4. When they are finished, ask them to dictate what the picture is about. Write it underneath the drawing.
5. Let the children draw a picture using a black coloring pencil or crayon on white paper. Compare the two drawings.

Quazonia Quarles, Newark, DE

Name Center

Materials *Chicka, Chicka, Boom Boom* by Bill Martin, Jr.
small, white dry-erase boards
dry-erase markers

What to do

1. Read the book *Chicka, Chicka, Boom Boom* by Bill Martin, Jr.
2. In the writing center, encourage the children to use the markers and dry-erase boards to draw a coconut tree.
3. Ask the children to write any letters on the tree just like in the book. Provide an alphabet chart for them to use, if needed.

Related books *Black and White Rabbit's ABC* by Alan Baker
Clifford's ABC by Norman Bridwell
Eating the Alphabet by Lois Ehlert

 *Kaethe Lewandowski, Centreville, VA*

Envelope Book

Materials envelopes (if possible, use discarded or donated envelopes)
writing tools
glue sticks
hole punch
rings, brads, yarn, and bread twisters
scissors
pictures and other concept support materials

What to do

1. When children have a purpose for their writing, they are more easily engaged. Making a book can make the writing area more appealing. When children are participants of making a book they feel a sense of ownership and pride.
2. Start by sealing the envelope flaps to the inside of the envelopes (do not seal them closed) to make a permanent pocket to store things. On the outside of each envelope, write a concept, question, and so on (see suggested ideas below). The child puts the answer or response inside the envelope pocket
3. Bind the pages together as desired, and make a cover to support the books.

4. Following are some suggested ideas for books:
   - **Name Book**: Ask children to bring in a picture of themselves. Laminate for durability. The child's name is the title of her book. Page one is the first letter of the child's name, the second letter is the second page, and so on. Encourage the children to write each letter on separate index cards. Ask them to glue letter cutouts and pictures of things beginning with the letter sound to the cards. They finish by putting each index card into the correct pocket. The child's picture goes in the last pocket.
   - **Color Book**: Depending on the children's skill level, you can use colored envelopes, color white envelopes with markers, or write the color words. Prepare labels with each color word to be a tool for this book. Encourage the children to find objects, cut out things, insert pictures, and so on to represent the color page.
   - **Word Endings**: If children are at higher skill level, write word endings on each envelope. Children can use consonant or blend cards to spell words. The pages of specific objects may also go into the envelope pocket.

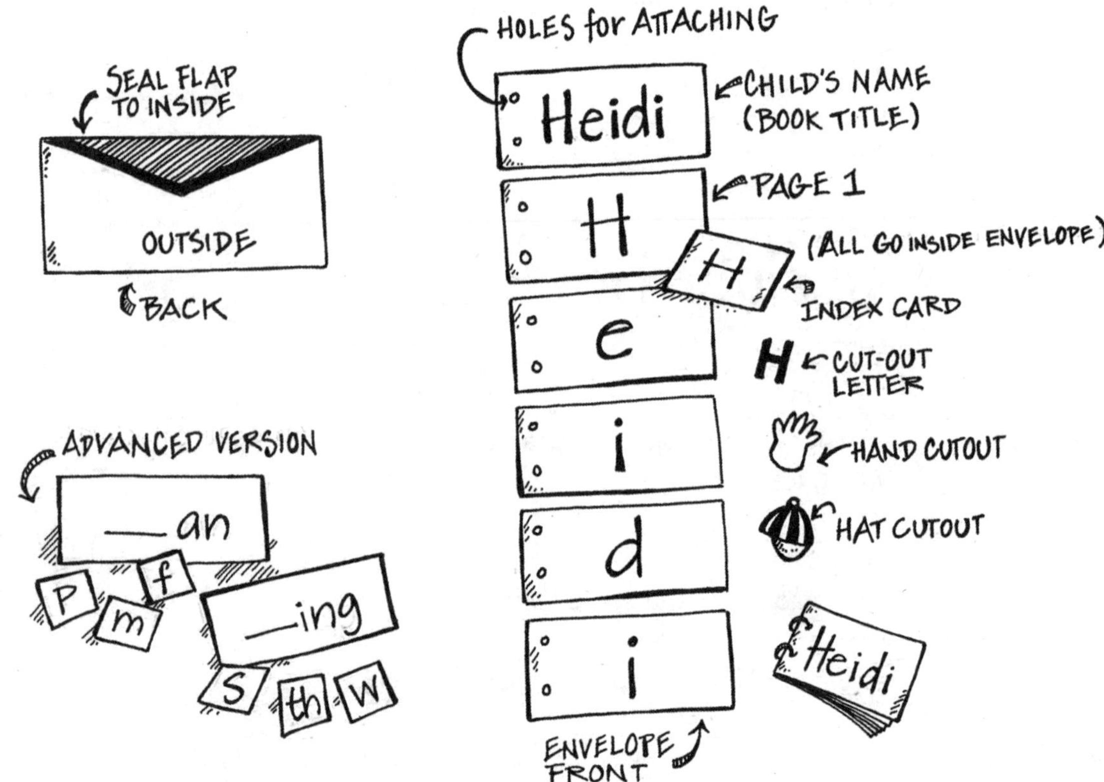

5. The possibilities for this kind of book are endless. For example, children could make "Me Books" to introduce themselves at the beginning of the year. These are also great for reviewing animals, community workers, different buildings, numbers, shapes, months of the year, dinosaurs, different textures, and so on.

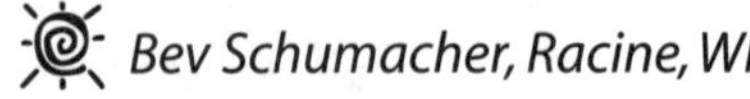
Bev Schumacher, Racine, WI

Flower Ink Stationery

Materials

long containers
variety of fresh flowers and ferns
paper towels
wooden cutting board or firm surface
scissors
cardstock paper
wax paper
hammer
construction paper

What to do

1. Place flowers in a long container with slightly damp towels to keep them moist. On a firm surface, layer a paper towel and cardstock paper.
2. Let the children choose flowers. Cut the flowers so there is very little stem.
3. Ask each child to arrange her flowers face down on the paper. Place wax paper over the flowers.
4. Hold the wax paper firmly so the flowers stay in place while the child taps gently on the flowers with a hammer. This makes the "ink" come out of the flowers and onto the paper.

Note: Supervise hammer use closely.

5. Remove the wax paper and gently pick off any flower or fern remains.
6. Allow the paper to dry.
7. Help the children fold the paper to make a card. Encourage them to sign their cards and give or mail them to someone.
8. This activity can also be done on cloth.

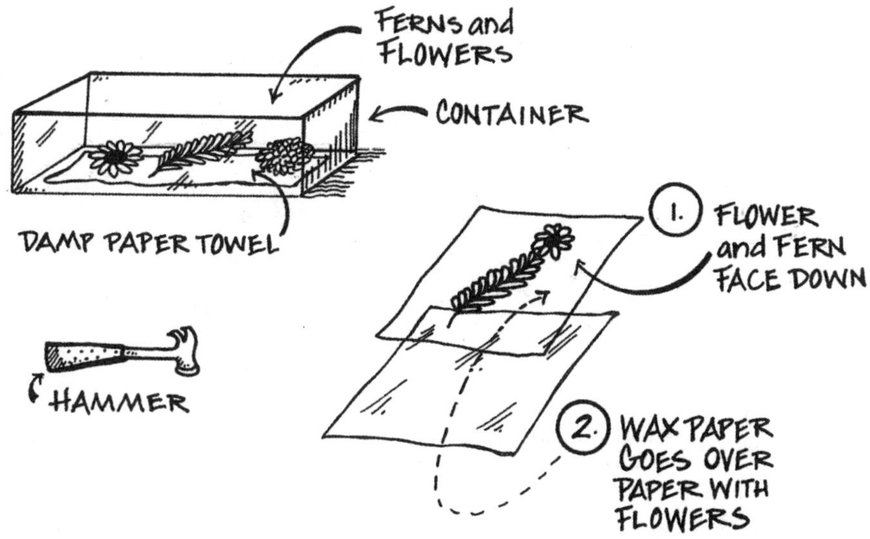

Penny Barsch, Meriden, CT

Friendship

Materials

tagboard
scissors
markers
rocks
old tin can (cleaned and dry)
branch
yarn

What to do

1. Talk about friends and what qualities make someone a good friend. Ask the children to talk about their good friends and what those friends do for them.
2. Make a "Friendship Tree." Cut out circles from tagboard. Draw a smiley face and write "My best friend …" on each one (see illustration).
3. Give a smiley face to each child. Encourage them to color their smiley faces and dictate or write what their best friend does or means to them.
4. Fill a can with rocks and stick a tree branch in it. Use yarn to hang the smiley faces on the friendship tree.

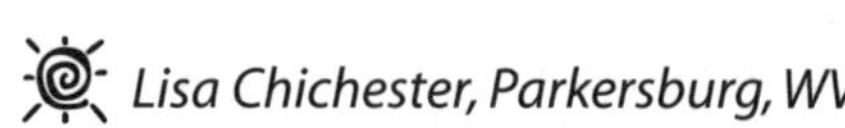

Lisa Chichester, Parkersburg, WV

Hello! My Name Is…

Materials

cardstock paper
digital or 35-mm camera
tape
markers
hole punch
yarn or string

What to do

1. Take a photo of each child in the class. Develop or print the photos.
2. Tape each child's photo to the center top of a piece of cardstock paper. Under the photo, print, "Hello! My name is ____________." Give each child her page.
3. Ask the children to print their names in the blank.
4. Next print, "I am __________ years old." Have each child print her age in the blank.
5. Finally, print, "I like to ____________."
6. Ask each child to dictate something she likes to do. Help the child to print her words in the blank.
7. Create a cover and bind the pages together into a book. Read and enjoy!
8. Let the children take turns taking the book home to share with their families.
9. Use a copier to make a black and white copy of the book for each child to keep.
10. If desired, make a "Hello" poster for each child to post around the room. Simply make a duplicate of the child's page in the book and hang it up for all to see.

Virginia Jean Herrod, Columbia, SC

Journal Bucket

Materials

spiral bound notebooks (one for each child)
craft paper
markers and crayons
scissors
glue
stickers
wide clear packing tape
large plastic bucket with a handle

What to do

1. Introduce the children to the idea of journaling by showing them the notebooks. Explain that each child will have her own notebook. They can use the notebooks to draw in, print words they know, or dictate stories in.
2. Give each child a piece of craft paper to design a label for her journal. Encourage the children to use markers and crayons to draw pictures on the paper. They can cut and paste the paper to make a collage for their notebook or apply stickers to the paper.
3. Ask the children to cut out their labels and apply them to the front of their notebooks using clear packing tape.

4. Show the children the bucket and explain that they can store their notebooks in it while they are not in use. (If possible, use a bucket that is more stylish than a regular mop bucket.)
5. Let the children use craft supplies and stickers to decorate the bucket. Create a label for the bucket ("Journal Bucket") and apply it to the bucket.
6. Keep the journal bucket in the writing center. Remind the children to use their journal during the day. They can write about things in which they are interested or they can draw pictures and make up stories. After a few days you won't have to remind them to use the journals. They will do it on their own.
7. Every few weeks, read the journals with the children and send them home for parents and siblings to read.
8. If desired, keep a class journal in the bucket in which you keep track of everyday and special events. Tape photos of special events to the pages and have the children dictate their thoughts to you. Record these thoughts on the pages.

Note: If you have a large class you may need to make two buckets.

More to do

More Writing: Print some simple questions on slips of paper and put them in a separate jar. Let the children take turns drawing a question out of the jar and answering it. Tape the question to the top of a page in their journal and write the child's answer below it. Sample questions are:

- "What do you like about school?"
- "Who are the people in your family? Tell something about each one."
- "Could you do without a TV in your house? Why or why not?"
- "Have you ever traveled on an airplane? Tell about it."
- "What is your favorite story or book? Tell about it."

Virginia Jean Herrod, Columbia, SC

Marker Caddy

Materials

2" x 4" piece of wood (10" long)
½" drill bits
power drill
hot glue gun
markers

What to do

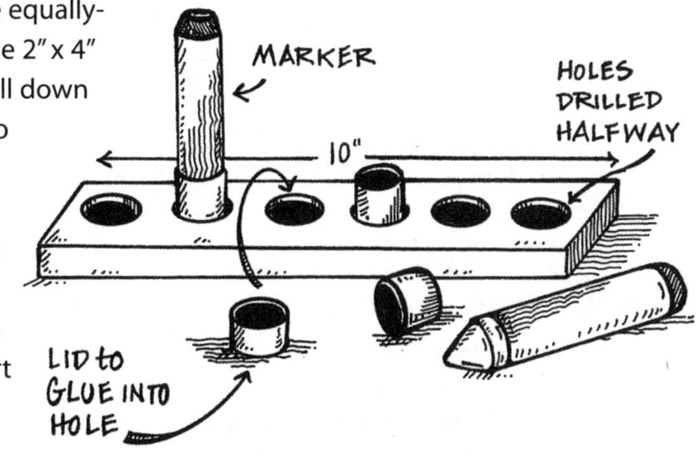

1. Using a drill, make equally-spaced holes in the 2″ x 4″ piece of wood. Drill down about halfway into the wood.
2. Using hot glue, place marker caps in the holes and allow them to dry.
3. Place this in the art center for long-lasting markers.
4. If desired, make a caddy for thinner markers or colored pencils by drilling smaller holes in a piece of wood.

Melissa Browning, Milwaukee, WI

Name Center

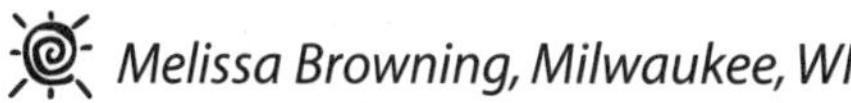

Materials

note cards
markers
magnetic letters
magnet board

What to do

1. Write each child's name on a note card. Place name cards, magnetic letters, and a magnet board in the writing center.
2. Ask each child to identify her name card and place it on the board.
3. Encourage the children to find the magnetic letters needed to spell their name.
4. If children are not yet able to identify their names, glue a photograph of the child next to her name.

Related book *ABC, I Like Me* by Nancy White Carlstrom

Suzanne Maxymuk, Cherry Hill, NJ

One Fish, Two Fish Poster and Book

Materials

One Fish, Two Fish, Red Fish, Blue Fish by Dr. Seuss
paint smocks or shirts
butcher paper
blue and yellow fingerpaint
paper
scissors
glue
black marker

What to do

1. Read *One Fish, Two Fish, Red Fish, Blue Fish* by Dr. Seuss.
2. Cover a table with butcher paper. Ask the children to put on paint shirts or smocks and stand at the table.
3. Place a bit of blue paint and yellow paint in front of each child. Encourage the children to move the paint around with their fingers and hands.
4. Encourage them to mix the two colors together. Ask them what happens when blue and yellow are mixed together.
5. Ask them to draw shapes, letters, and names. Challenge them to write as many letters as they can. Encourage them to describe what they are drawing in the paint.
6. When they are finished mixing and exploring the paint, help them place a piece of paper on top of the painted surface.
7. Help each child press the paper down onto the table, and then slowly peel the paper off, making a print of child's painted area.
8. Cut out patterns of fish (one fish, two fish, red fish, blue fish).
9. After the paintings are dry, encourage the children to glue fish cutouts to their paper. Using the marker, print the words by the fish.
10. If desired, do this activity on smaller paper (8" x 12"). Let the children dictate what they want on their page to make a classroom book.

More to do

Use different colors to get different effects and explore the various color combinations.

Related books

Brown Bear, Brown Bear, What Do You See? by Bill Martin, Jr.
Polar Bear, Polar Bear, What Do You Hear? by Bill Martin, Jr.

Reading Boxes

Materials

cube-shaped tissue boxes (one for each child)
paper
scissors
markers, crayons, and colored pencils
tape
sentence strips

What to do

1. Cut pieces of paper to fit around each tissue box. Give one to each child.
2. Encourage the children to decorate their paper and write their name on it. Help them tape it into place on their tissue box.
3. Cut sentence strips into word-sized pieces, and then cut in half horizontally.
4. With or without help, children can write on the sentence strips, creating various letters, numerals, words, and so on.
5. When they are finished, they can add their words and letters to their box.
6. Children can use their reading boxes to practice their reading skills.

Jeanette Denning, Tinley Park, IL

Simply Water

Materials

container (preferably clear, such a glass)
water
paper
writing utensils

What to do

1. Partially fill a container with water and place it on the table. Gather the children around the container.
2. Explain that they will look at the water in the container and then write about it. You may wish to move the water around in the container as the children quietly observe to give action to the substance.
3. Ask the children leading questions such as:
   - "How can you describe the water?" (adjectives)
   - "What are some objects you think about when you see water?" (nouns)
   - "What are some activities you think about when you think of water?" (verbs)
   - "Where are some places you find water?" (locations, prepositions)
4. You may wish to have an oral discussion before giving them time to dictate or write their thoughts. This may help reluctant writers get started.

5. Adults should engage in the writing process at the same time as the children.
6. Provide time at the end of the writing session for volunteers to share.

Related books *Kites Sail High, a Book About Verbs* by Ruth Heller
Many Luscious Lollipops, a Book About Adjectives by Ruth Heller
Rain by Robert Kalan

Kate Ross, Middlesex, VT

The Rhyming Game

Materials
drawing paper
crayons

What to do

1. Teach the children the following chant:

Rhyming is the name of the game,
Rhyming means it sounds the same.
When I say, "toy," then you say, "boy."
And that's how we play this game.

2. Practice the chant by inserting more sets of rhymes, such as "house/mouse."
3. When the children have mastered the rhyme, repeat the chant and leave out the second word as you point to a child. The chosen child supplies the missing word. "When I say 'hat' then you say ..."
4. Ask the children to go to the art or writing center, fold a piece of drawing paper in half, and draw their rhymes (one word on each side). Depending on the skill level of the children, you can provide the words to copy, let children dictate the spelling, or encourage them to spell the word like it sounds.
5. After everyone in the class has contributed a rhyming page, compile all the pages into a classroom rhyming book for the library.
6. Children need plenty of practice in mastering rhyming skills, so read a variety of children's literature that focuses on rhymes. After the children have enjoyed listening to the stories several times, they may help you "read" by supplying the missing rhyming words that you leave out.

Related books Anything by Dr. Seuss
Brown Bear, Brown Bear, What Do You See? by Bill Martin, Jr. (and other books by this author)
The Bunny Hop by Teddy Slater

 *Iris Rothstein, New Hyde Park, NY*

Time-Saving Idea

Materials computer and printer

What to do

1. If you have a computer, use it to do the monotonous task of making dotted letters. Simply download the desired font (National Dotted First Font) from the Internet and use it with your favorite word processing program to teach and reinforce correct writing forms with the children.
2. This is a great method to speed up time-consuming preparation for customized "trace the dotted letter" activities for your classroom.

Jackie Wright, Enid, OK

We Like Snow!

Materials

sentence strips
markers
scissors
11" x 17" dark blue construction paper
glue
white chalk

What to do

1. Write the following sentence on a sentence strip: "(Teacher's name) likes______snow." Read the sentence with the class.
2. Choose two or three children each day to make a sentence strip about what kind of snow they like. For example, "Sharon likes white snow." Each day, read the written sentences, and then do more sentences day after day until every child has a completed sentence strip.
3. Put all sentence strips in the writing center. Ask each child to find her sentence strip and cut apart the words in the sentence.
4. Ask the children to glue their sentences back in order at the bottom of a piece of 11" x 17" blue construction paper.
5. Encourage the children to illustrate their sentence using a piece of white chalk.

Related book *White Snow Bright Snow* by Alvin Tresselt

Lori Dunlap, Amarillo, TX

Writing

Materials

paper in different colors and shapes
markers, pencils, pens, and crayons
envelopes
pads of paper
stapler
hole punch
scissors
rubber stamps and inkpads
alphabet poster
rulers
journal books
new greeting cards or fronts of old greeting cards

What to do

1. Set up a writing area for two or three children to work together at a time. Decorate the walls with alphabet posters and a list of all the children in the class.
2. Encourage the children to use the writing center by rotating writing tools and paper frequently. Children are excited to see what's new in the writing area each week!
3. Encourage children to write their names by pointing to the name list. Add seasonal writing paper and decorations to the writing area to generate new interest.
4. Be sure to add a basket of books, including a child-size dictionary, laminated name cards, and vocabulary word list for that week.
5. Set up mailboxes for the children so they can "mail" each other cards, letters, and drawings.

Sue Myhre, Bremerton, WA

Desk Delights

Materials

variety of pens
basket
three-ring binders
paper
date stamp

What to do

1. To encourage children to write, "jazz" up the materials in the writing center.
2. Collect a variety of novelty pens and put them in a basket. These can be found at dollar stores, novelty stores, and in many stores during the holidays. Find pens that look like frogs, snakes, cartoon characters; soft pens with bears, monsters, snowmen, and dogs on the top; light-up pens; pens with feathers and flowers; and so on. Children love to use these pens.
3. To make it really special, save the pens for use during "Journal Time."
4. Make a journal for each child using a three-ring binder and paper. Binders are great to use because they are sturdy, and the children don't have to worry about slipping paper.
5. As the children draw or write, use a date stamp to let identify when the picture or writing entry was created.

Tracie O'Hara, Charlotte, NC

Writing Wheel

Materials

poster board
scissors
permanent marker
pictures of a particular subject (books, family, animals, food, holidays)
brad fastener
poster board arrow
paper

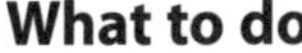

What to do

1. Cut out a large circle from poster board. Use a marker to separate it into equal sections.
2. Glue a picture that represents a subject area that is important to the children or what you want them to write about into each section.
3. Use a brad to connect an arrow in the middle of the circle.
4. Let the children take turns spinning the wheel. Whatever subject the wheel lands on, the children write a story or poem about it.
5. If the children are very young, they can draw pictures in a pre-made book and then dictate what the picture represents.

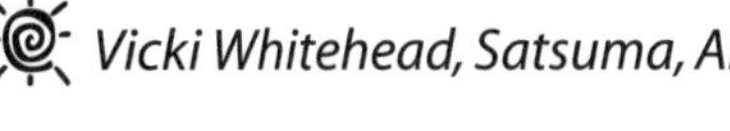

Vicki Whitehead, Satsuma, AL

Written in the Stars

Materials

yellow construction paper
scissors
markers
old magazines
tag board
glue
laminate
pocket chart

What to do

1. Cut out four stars from yellow paper, approximately 4" in size. Write a different letter on each star (preferably letters the children are familiar with or are learning).
2. Using old magazines, cut out three pictures that correspond to the beginning sound of each of the four chosen letters for a total of 12 pictures (for example, cut out a kangaroo, kite, and key to represent "k"). Glue each picture to a piece of 4" x 4" tagboard.
3. Laminate the four stars and the 12 picture cards for durability, and cut out.
4. Hang a pocket chart at children's eye level.
5. Discuss the names of the letters on each star. Randomly position each of the stars equal distance apart in the top pocket of the pocket chart.
6. Pass out the picture cards and encourage each child to determine its beginning sound.
7. Let each child place her picture under the correct star letter.

Jackie Wright, Enid, OK

Animal Stamps

Materials

rubber animal stamps
inkpad
paper

What to do

1. Place animal stamps, an inkpad, and paper in the zoo center.
2. Encourage the children to make animal books by using the stamps and copying the animal name or writing their own invented spelling of the name.

Melissa Browning, Milwaukee, WI

Animal Fun

Materials

animal paper plates or white paper plates and markers
hole punch
ribbon, yarn, or string
construction paper
scissors
glue
crepe paper
tape

What to do

1. Have a discussion about animals and their sounds and movements.
2. Let each child choose an animal paper plate. If these are not available, let the children draw animal faces on white paper plates.
3. Punch a hole on each side of the paper plate and thread ribbon or yarn through the holes to make a mask or necklace.
4. Cut out ears from construction paper. Encourage the children to glue the ears to their plates.
5. Tape crepe paper "tails" to the back of each child.
6. Encourage them to put on their masks and make the animal sounds and movements of their animal.
7. Children can recite animal poems, sing songs, or engage in creative dramatics with friends.
8. For added fun, let the children mix and match the animal parts to create a nonsense animal to name and share.

Related books *Animals, Animals* by Eric Carle
From Head to Toe by Eric Carle
Going to the Zoo by Tom Paxton

Margery Kranyik Fermino, Hyde Park, MA

Animal Habitat

Materials

shoeboxes
paint
felt and fabric paint
glue
pictures of animals or small rubber animals
tray

What to do

1. Make different habitats using shoeboxes. Paint the inside of shoeboxes to match each type of habitat, such as arctic, prairie, jungle, and farm.
2. Draw, paint, or use felt cutouts to decorate the habitats. For example, for a jungle habitat, use brown and green felt for a tree, blue for water lines, and light blue for a cloud or the sky. For a farm habitation, use red felt for a barn, white for a house, and green for grass.
3. Collect pictures of animals or small rubber animals and place them on a tray.
4. Encourage the children to sort the animals according to their habitat. They can place the animals in the appropriate shoebox.

DESERT HABITAT

PLASTIC SNAKE

PLASTIC SCORPION

Melissa Browning, Milwaukee, WI

Animal Lotto

Materials

two large, colorful identical zoo animal pictures
black marker
laminate
glue
heavy white paper or cardboard

What to do

1. This is a great game for encouraging children to notice details and also begin to learn to read maps.
2. Find two large, colorful identical zoo animal pictures. A good source for pictures is two identical zoo animal calendars. You can make twelve games from two calendars.
3. Mark each picture exactly the same with a heavy black marker, creating three rows of evenly spaced blocks down and three across. (This is a good number for young children, but adjust the number of blocks according to the children's ability level.)

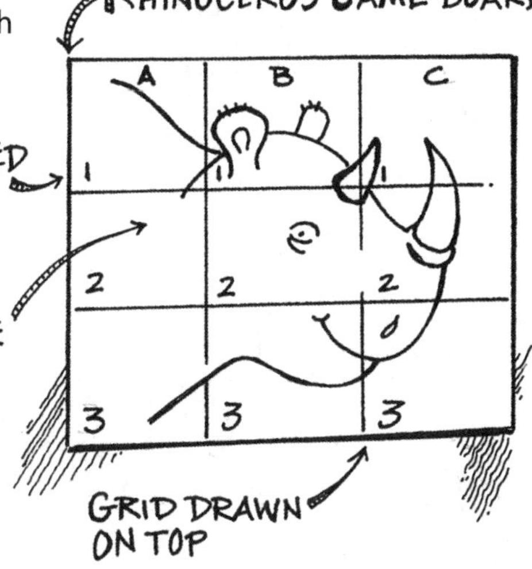

4. On one of the pictures, label each block with a letter at the top and a number on the left side (see illustration).
5. Laminate the game board for durability.
6. Glue the second picture to a piece of heavy white paper or cardboard. Draw identical blocks on the back (white paper) to match the front picture. On the back of the picture, label each block with the appropriate coordinate to match the first picture (A1, A2, A3, B1, B2, B3, and so on).
7. Cut out each square of the second picture and leave the first picture intact. Each square should have a coordinate on the back of it.

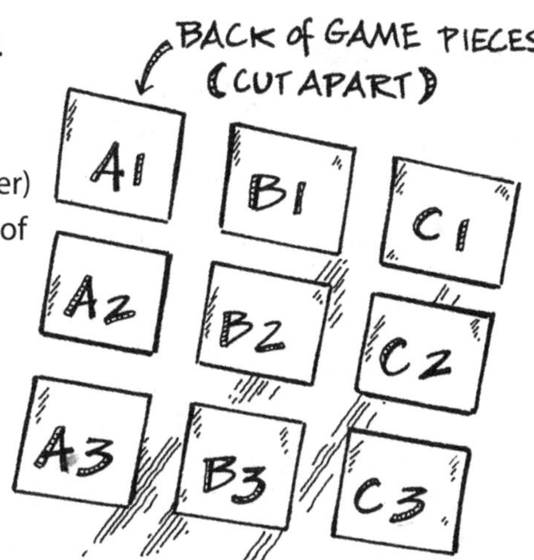

8. There are two ways to play the game, depending on the level of the children. The first way is to place the nine picture squares face up on a table. The children take turns placing the picture on the game board where it belongs.
9. The second way to play the game is more difficult. Place the game pieces face down with the coordinates showing. Children choose a piece and then try to determine where it belongs on the larger game board according to the coordinate. When a child determines where he is going to place the piece, he can check his answer by turning it over to see if the picture matches the square on the game board.

Anne Slanina, Slippery Rock, PA

Bugs for Lunch

Materials

small pictures of bugs, bug stamps, or paper and markers
tape
party blowers with rollout tongues (preferably silent)

What to do

1. Cut out small photos of bugs, use bug stamps, or draw pictures of bugs on small pieces of paper.
2. Place a loop of tape on the pictures of the bugs.
3. Put the bug pictures on tray or table, tape side up.
4. Give each child a party blower. Encourage them to blow out their "tongues" and catch bugs!

Related books

Frog Goes to Dinner by Mercer Mayor
Old Black Fly by Jim Aylesworth

Related song

"Five Green and Speckled Frogs"

Shirley Salach, Northwood, NH

Counting at the Zoo

Materials

paper
markers
stapler
pencils

What to do

1. Plan a field trip to the zoo.
2. Before the trip, make a ten-page animal counting booklet for each child.
3. On each page, draw a different zoo animal, starting with one animal on the first page, two on the second page, and so on. For example, page one might have one elephant, page two might have two lions, page three might have three giraffes, and so on. Make copies and staple them together so that each child gets a packet.
4. On the trip, give one packet to each child along with a pencil.
5. Ask the children to put a check on the page when they find the animal. Encourage them to count the number of animals in the packet and at the zoo.
6. They can color the animals in the packet at home or when they return to school.

Related books

1,2, 3 to the Zoo by Eric Carle
If I Ran the Zoo by Dr. Suess
My Visit to the Zoo by Aliki

Related song

"Momma's Taking Us to the Zoo Tomorrow" by Raffi

Sandy Scott, Vancouver, WA

Feed the Penguin

Materials

cereal box
scissors
picture of a penguin
paper
glue
blue paper plate
dice

What to do

1. Cut off the top of the cereal box and cover the box with paper.
2. Glue a picture of a penguin the size of the box on the front of the box. If you don't have a picture, draw one on the box.
3. Cut out goldfish shapes from paper and put them on a blue paper plate (to represent water). Put the box on a table along with goldfish cutouts.
4. To play the game, the children take turns rolling the dice. Whatever number appears on the dice, the child counts that many fish and "feeds" them to the penguin by putting them in the box.

Related books

Penguin Pete by Marcus Pfister
Penguins by Kathleen Zoehfeld
Tacky the Penguin by Helen Lester

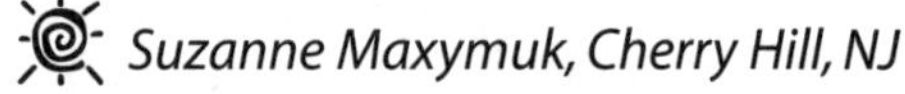

Suzanne Maxymuk, Cherry Hill, NJ

Giraffes

Materials

cardboard
yellow and brown construction paper
black markers
scissors
pencils
clip-on clothespins

What to do

1. Cut out a large "Z" pattern from cardboard.
2. Give each child a piece of yellow construction paper. Encourage them to trace the letter "Z" pattern on the paper and cut it out.
3. Show the children how to rip brown construction paper into pieces and glue them to their letter "Z" to make giraffe spots.
4. Encourage them to draw eyes and a mouth on their giraffes.
5. Clip two clothespins to the bottom of the "Z" to make the legs of the giraffe.

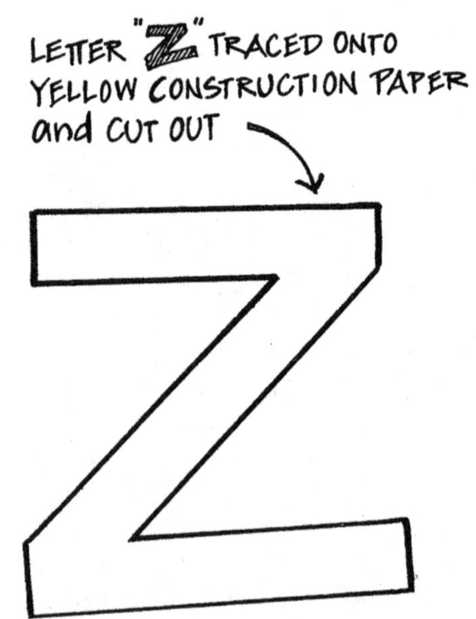

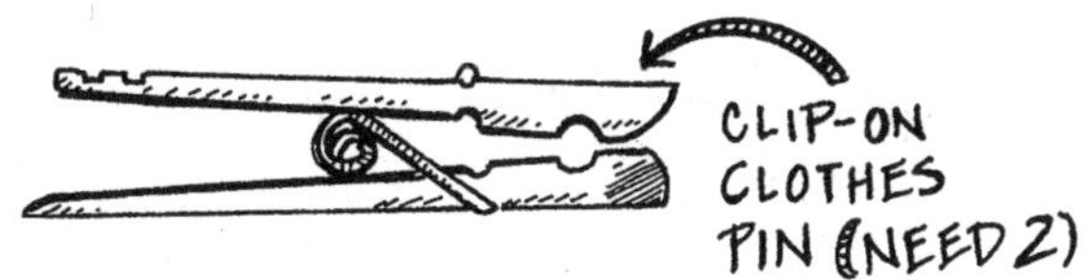

Related books *Going to the Zoo* by Tom Paxton
Zookeepers Care for Animals by Amy Moses

Liz Thomas, Hobart, IN

Happy Hippo Puppet

Materials

cardboard or oak tag
markers
scissors
tan, red, white, and black construction paper
small-print wallpaper
brown paper lunch bags
crayons
white glue
23-mm wiggle eyes

What to do

1. Make copies of the illustrations (see the next pages), trace onto cardboard or oak tag, and cut out to make patterns for a hippo face, hat, pants, teeth, shoes, and tail.
2. Help the children trace the patterns onto construction paper as follows: tan paper for the head, arms, jaw, and legs; red paper for the tongue; black paper for the hat and shoes; and white paper for teeth.
3. Give each child a paper lunch bag. The children glue two teeth under the hippo's tongue and two under the head. Then they glue the tongue to the jaw and slide it under the flap of the paper bag and glue to the bag.
4. Next, children glue wiggle eyes to the head. Encourage them to draw the hippo's facial features.

5. Ask them to glue the head and tail to the bag. They can add the hat, wallpaper pants, wallpaper hatband, and shoes. Or, add a red paper bow to one ear, wallpaper skirt, and pink paper shoes.
6. Finish by gluing arms and legs to the bag.

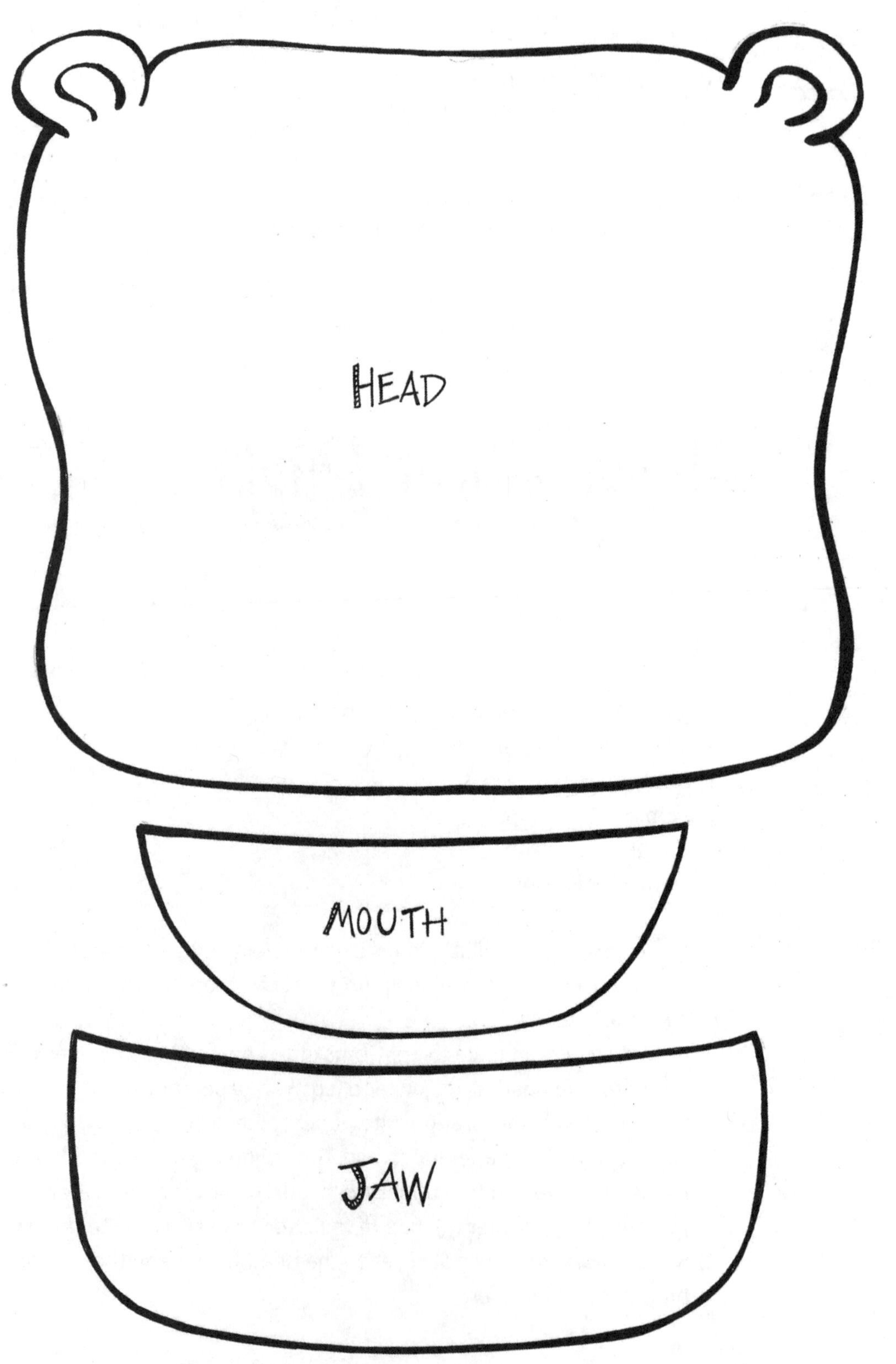

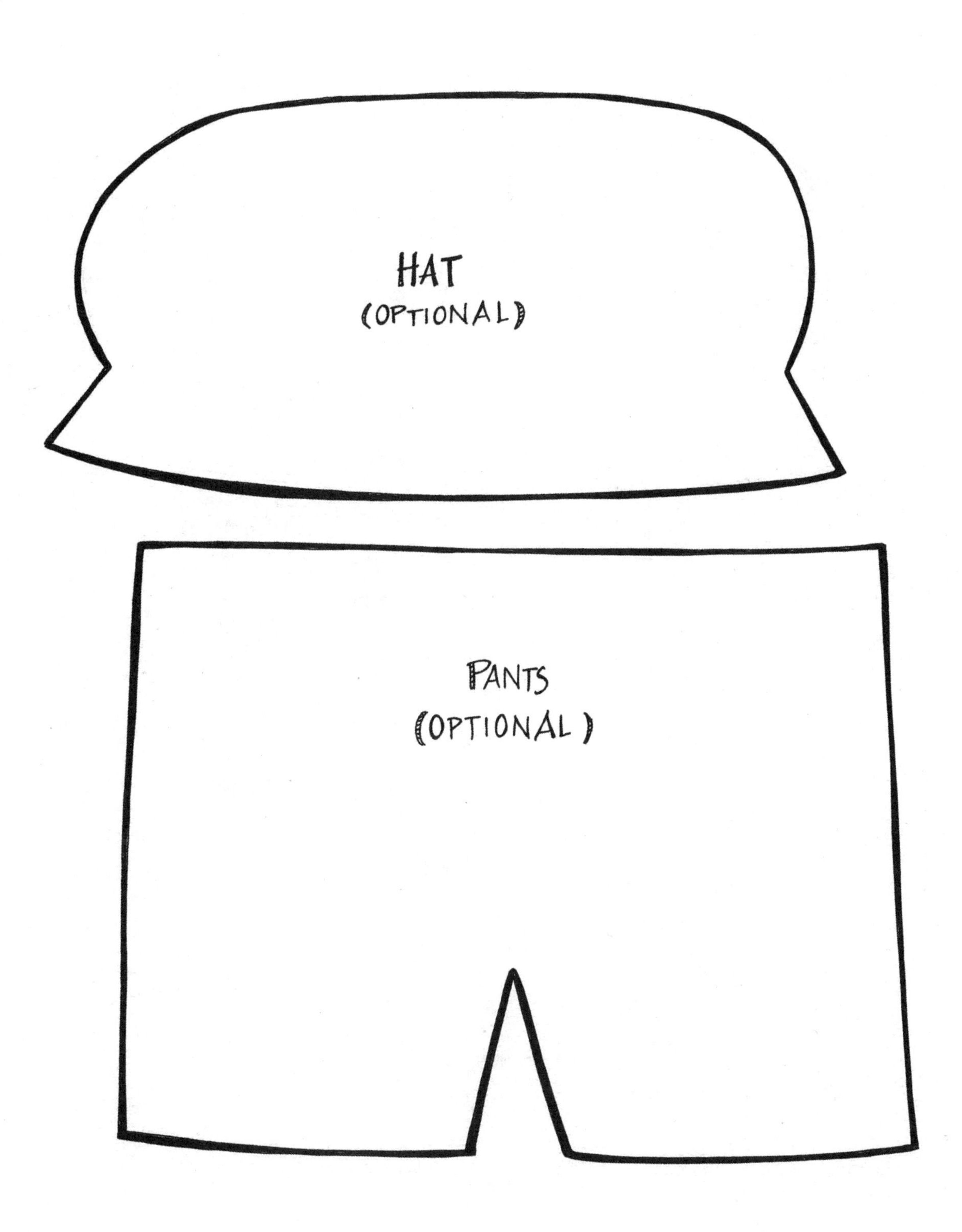
HAT
(OPTIONAL)
PANTS
(OPTIONAL)

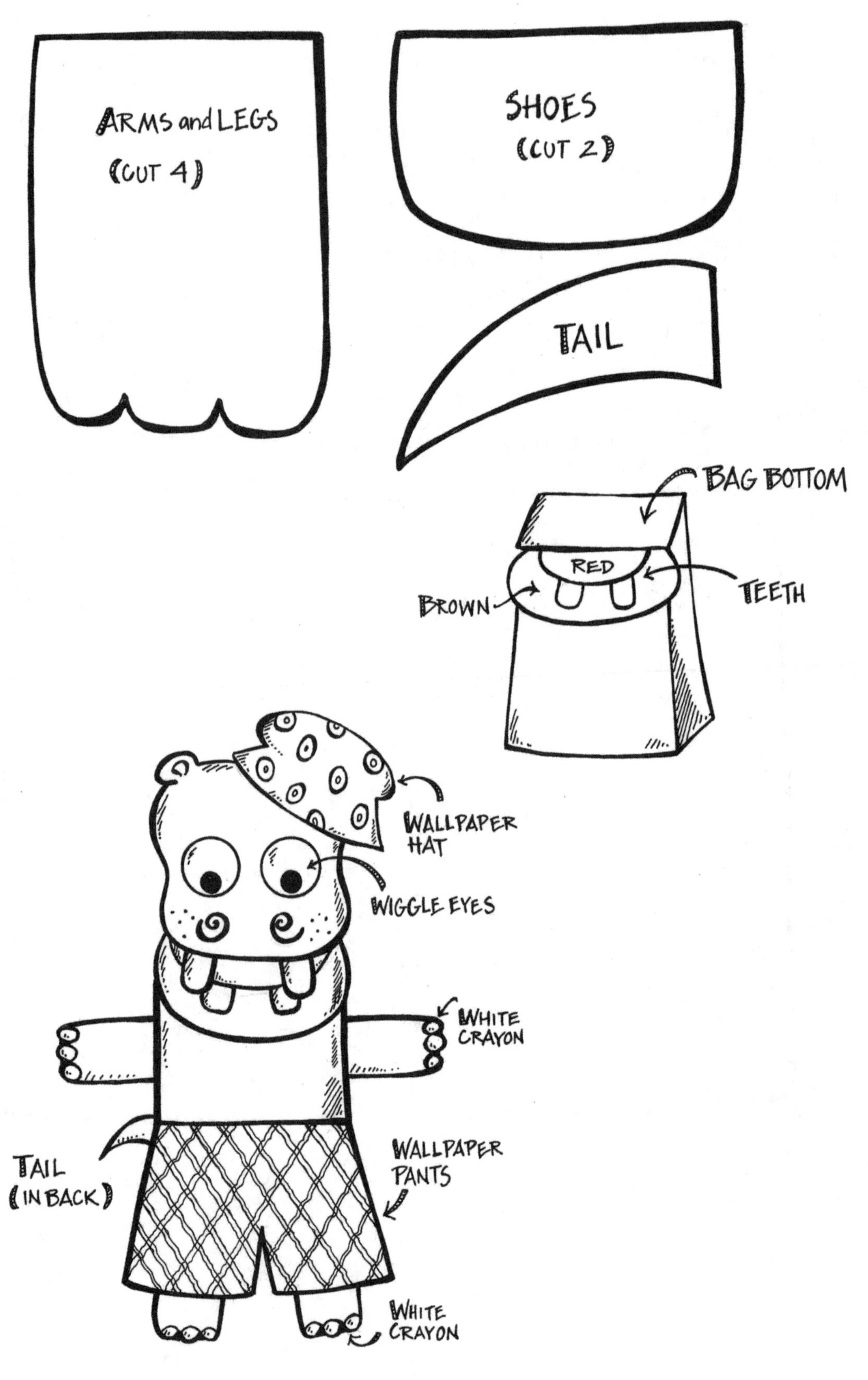
ARMS and LEGS
(CUT 4)
SHOES
(CUT 2)
TAIL
BAG BOTTOM
RED
BROWN
TEETH
WALLPAPER HAT
WIGGLE EYES
WHITE CRAYON
TAIL (IN BACK)
WALLPAPER PANTS
WHITE CRAYON

Related books *George and Martha, One Fine Day* by James Marshall
African Animal Giants (A National Geographic Action Book) by James Dietz

Related song **Happy Hippo** by Mary Brehm
(tune: "Frère Jacques")
Happy hippo, happy hippo,
Walking around, walking around.
He is very heavy, he is very heavy.
Thump, thump, thump,
Thump, thump, thump!

Hot, hot hippo, tired hot hippo,
Swimming around, swimming around.
He comes up for air, he comes up for air.
Splash, splash, splash!
Splash, splash, splash!

Mary Brehm, Aurora, OH

Jolly Octopus

Materials
12" x 18" white construction paper
pencil
crayons
watercolor paint
25-mm wiggle eyes
white glue

What to do
1. Draw a large circle with a pencil. Erase the bottom edge near the "chin" area and draw eight arms. Or, make a copy of the illustration on the next page and enlarge it.
2. Make one for each child and cut out.
3. Encourage the children to trace the octopus using brown, red, orange, or purple crayons.
4. Show them how to draw circles on the bottom edge of each octopus arm with black crayons. Draw a mouth with a red crayon.
5. Encourage the children to paint their octopus with tan, red, orange, or purple watercolor paint.
6. When dry, they can glue on wiggle eyes.

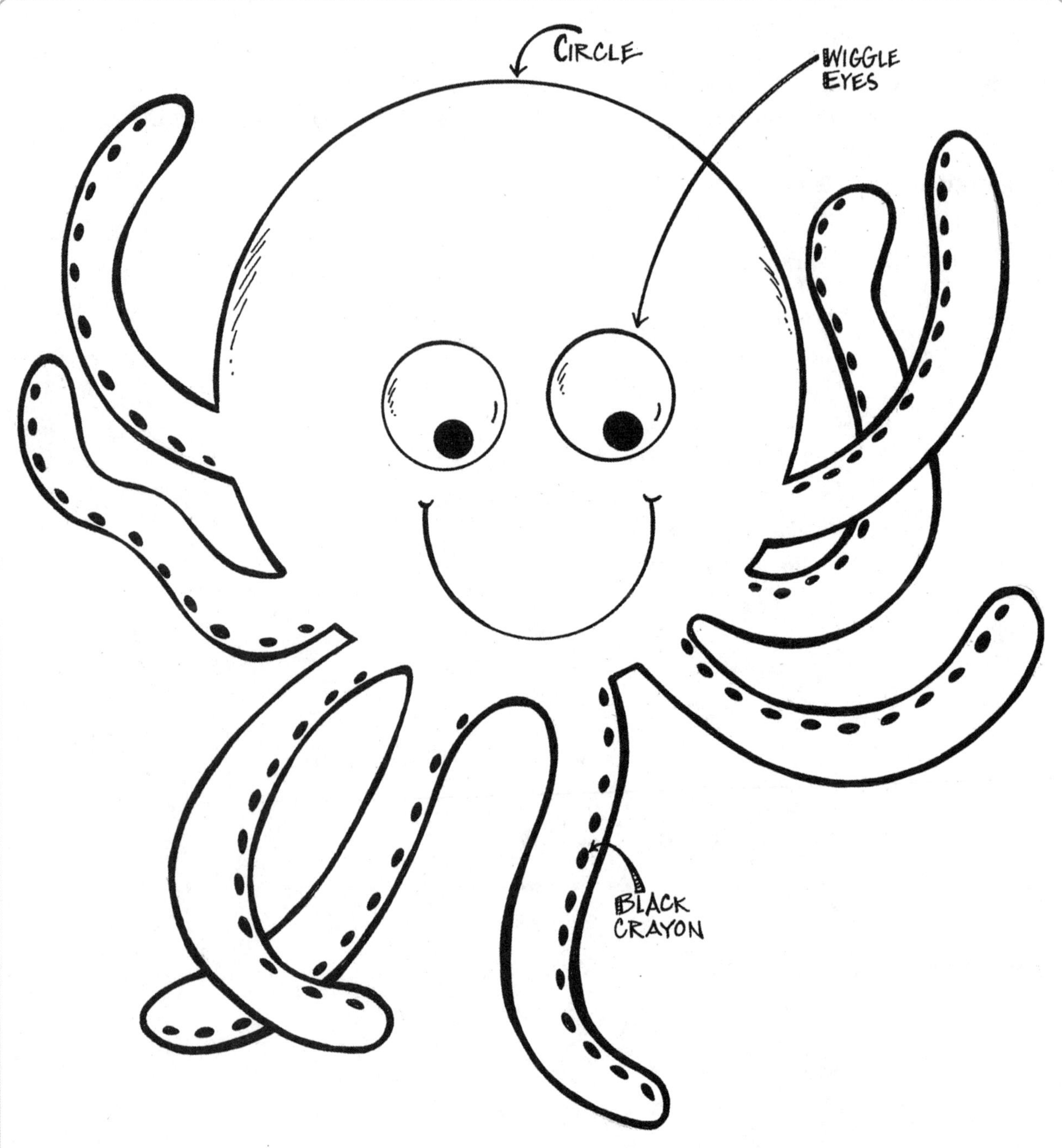

Related book *Octopus's Den* by Deirdre Langeland

Related poem **An Octopus** by Mary Brehm

An octopus has eight long arms,
And very small eyes.
He can be two inches tiny or
Thirty five feet in size.

He can change colors — orange, tan,
Coral, purple, and silver gray, too.
Sometimes he squirts out purple ink
To obscure him from view.

He has suckers on his arms to feel,
And catch something to eat,
Like crab, clam, shellfish, and
Sea urchins that taste sweet.

He can squeeze his body to fit
In a very small space,
And he makes a fence of glass
And shells to mark his place.

Mary Brehm, Aurora, OH

Paper Plate Monkey

Materials

two paper plates
brown and yellow construction paper
scissors
stapler
glue
buttons
crayons or markers

What to do

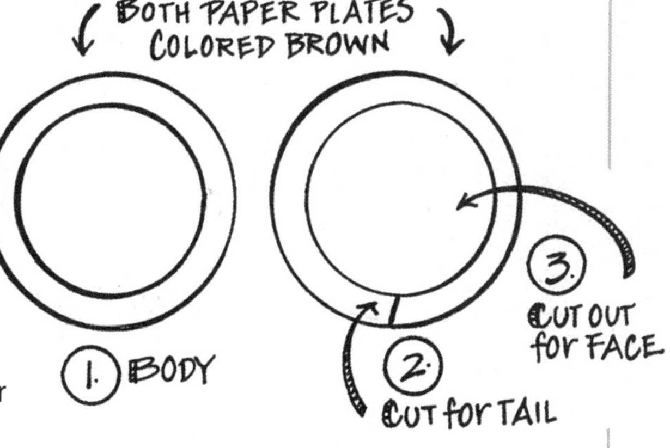

1. Give each child two paper plates. Ask them to color their plates with a brown crayon or marker.
2. Help the children cut out the inside circle (usually clearly marked) from one of the paper plates, leaving just a rippled, outer edge.
3. Help them staple the inside circle on top of the second paper plate to make the monkey's head and body.
4. Ask the children to staple the rippled, outer edge from the cut paper plate to the bottom of the monkey's body to make a tail.
5. Using yellow construction paper, cut out a monkey shape face and give one to each child. Ask them to glue it onto the head.

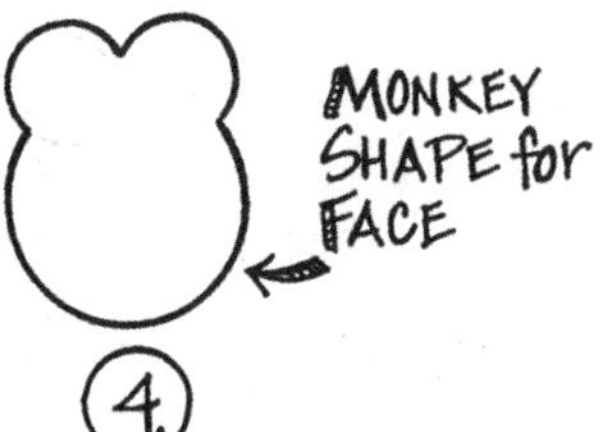

6. Let them glue on buttons for eyes.
7. Using brown construction paper, cut out two ears, a nose, mouth, and four long strips about 1" wide for arms and legs. Children could draw the nose and mouth with a crayon or marker instead of cutting them out.
8. Help the children glue all the body parts to the paper plate head and body.

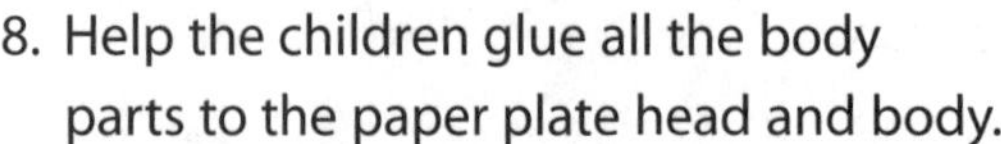

9. It is fun to display these monkeys in the classroom, hanging them by their tails!

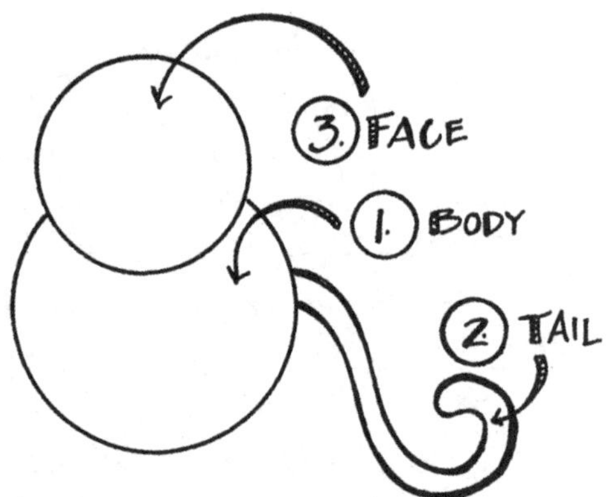

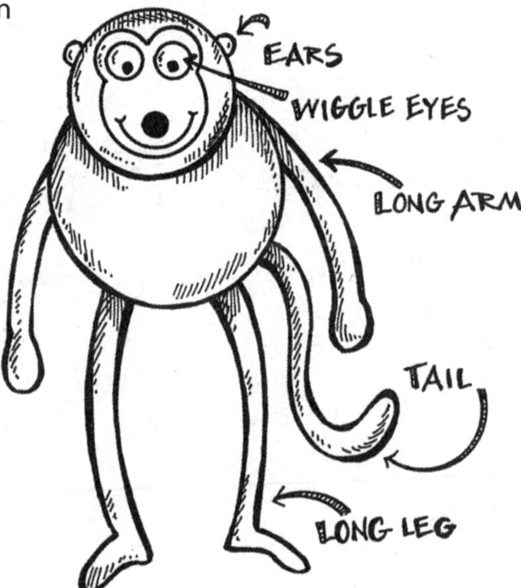

 *Andrea Hungerford, Plainville, CT*

White-Throated Capuchin Monkey Puppet

Materials

oak tag or cardboard
pencils
scissors
tan lunch bags and black craft bags
tan and black construction paper
white cotton or fiberfill
23-mm wiggle eyes
white glue
pink, brown, and black markers

What to do

1. Make copies of the patterns below, enlarge, and trace on oak tag or cardboard. Cut out each piece to make a pattern.

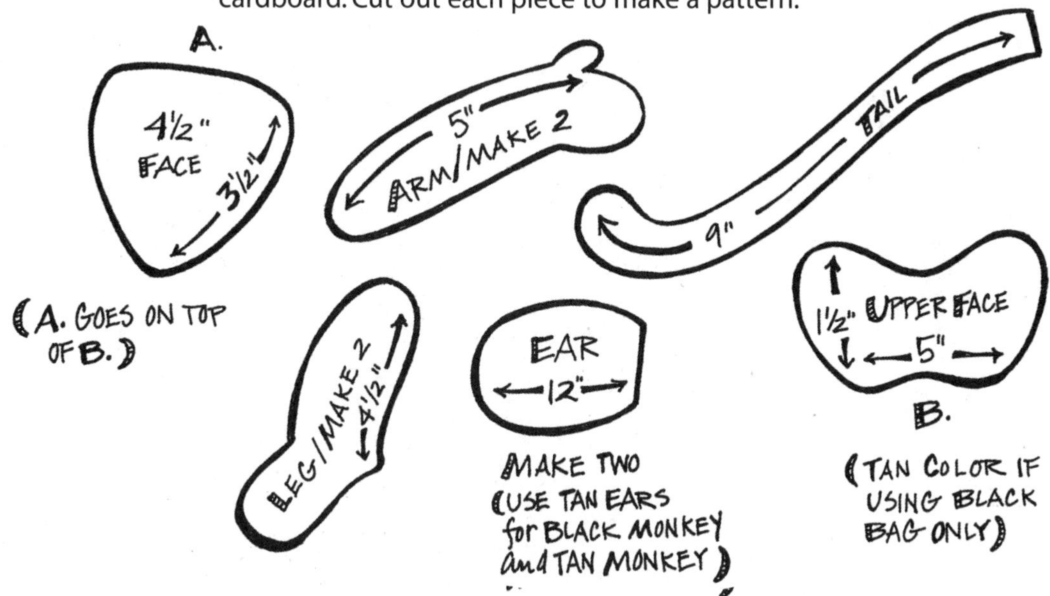

2. Let the children choose whether they want to make a tan or black monkey. Provide tan and black bags for them to choose.
3. Help them trace the patterns onto construction paper. If they are making a tan monkey, ask them to trace the ears, upper face, and lower face on black paper. If they are making a black monkey, they trace the ears and face on tan paper.
4. Each child traces two arms, two legs, and one tail onto black paper (for black monkey) or tan paper (for tan monkey).
5. Let the children cut out all of their patterns. Help them glue the face area on the bottom end of the fold in the bag, ears on the sides of the bag (by face), arms on the inside fold of the bag, and legs near the bottom of the bag.
6. Show the children how to shape cotton or fiberfill to fit around the entire face in a heart-shape, and glue in place.
7. The children use pink markers to color the inside of the ears. They use a brown marker to draw a nose, fingers on both sides of hand, and toes. They use a black marker for the mouth and nostrils.
8. Provide wiggle eyes for them to glue on the face.
9. Help the children glue cotton under the monkey's chin up to fold of bottom end of bag.
10. Ask them to glue the tail on the back of puppet. Help them curl the end of the tail around a thick pencil.

Mary Brehm, Aurora, OH

Children's Book Index

Index

Index

N

O

P

General Index

Index

C

D

G

Index

Index

Index